The GREEN GUIDE
Chicago

Chicago River © Anne Evans/Chicago Architecture Foundation

| **General Manager** | Cynthia Clayton Ochterbeck |

THEGREENGUIDE **CHICAGO**

Editorial Manager	Jonathan P. Gilbert
Contributing Writers	Kelly Aiglon, Linda Lee
Production Manager	Natasha G. George
Cartography	Peter Wrenn
Photo Editor	Yoshimi Kanazawa
Proofreader	Jane Donovan, Elena Fysentzou
Interior Design	Chris Bell
Cover Design	Chris Bell, Christelle Le Déan
Layout	Michelin Apa Publications Ltd., Alison Rayner
Cover Layout	Michelin Apa Publications Ltd.

Contact Us

The Green Guide
Michelin Maps and Guides
One Parkway South
Greenville, SC 29615, USA
www.michelintravel.com

Michelin Maps and Guides
Hannay House
39 Clarendon Road
Watford, Herts WD17 1JA, UK
✆01923 205240
www.ViaMichelin.com
travelpubsales@uk.michelin.com

Special Sales

For information regarding bulk sales,
customized editions and premium sales,
please contact our Customer Service
Departments:
USA   1-800-432-6277
UK   01923 205240
Canada 1-800-361-8236

HOW TO USE THIS GUIDE

PLANNING YOUR TRIP

The blue-tabbed PLANNING YOUR TRIP section gives you **ideas for your trip** and **practical information** to help you organize it. You'll find tours, practical information, a host of outdoor activities, a calendar of events, information on shopping, sightseeing, kids' activities and more.

INTRODUCTION

The orange-tabbed INTRODUCTION section explores the city today, **Nature** and geology. The **History** section spans from Fort Dearbon to Contemporary Chicago. The **Art and Culture** section covers architecture, art, literature and music, while **The City Today** delves into modern Chicago.

DISCOVERING

The green-tabbed DISCOVERING section features Principal Sights by region, featuring the most interesting local **Sights**, **Walking Tours**, nearby **Excursions**, and detailed **Driving Tours**. Admission prices shown are normally for a single adult.

ADDRESSES

We've selected the best hotels, restaurants, cafes, shops, nightlife and entertainment to fit all budgets. See the Legend on the cover flap for an explanation of the price categories. See the back of the guide for an index of hotels and restaurants.

Sidebars

Throughout the guide you will find blue, orange and green-colored text boxes with lively anecdotes, detailed history and background information.

🙂 A Bit of Advice 🙂

Green advice boxes found in this guide contain practical tips and handy information relevant to your visit or to a sight in the Discovering section.

STAR RATINGS★★★

Michelin has given star ratings for more than 100 years. If you're pressed for time, we recommend you visit the ★★★ or ★★ sights first:

★★★	**Highly recommended**
★★	**Recommended**
★	**Interesting**

MAPS

- 🗺 Principal Sights map.
- 🗺 Rapid Transit map.
- 🗺 Area maps.
- 🗺 Driving tour maps.
- 🗺 Local tour maps.
- 🗺 Floorplans.

All maps in this guide are oriented north, unless otherwise indicated by a directional arrow. The term "Local Map" refers to a map within the chapter or Tourism Region. A complete list of the maps found in the guide appears at the back of this book.

© Ralf-Finn Hestoft/Corbis

© David Dunai/Apa Publications

PLANNING YOUR TRIP

INTRODUCTION TO CHICAGO

CONTENTS

© City of Chicago/GRC

DISCOVERING CHICAGO

YOUR STAY IN CHICAGO

Welcome to Chicago

Over the years Chicago has managed to capture and preserve the essence of myriad ethnic groups in its diverse neighborhoods. Other areas have developed distinct characteristics as artists' meccas or shopping havens. Together, the districts combine to form a colorful "city of neighborhoods."

DOWNTOWN (pp72–156)

Center of the city, the **Loop** offers a lesson in American urban architecture—bar none. Lined with stores, State Street is the city's original shopping thoroughfare. Since the 1960s, the **Magnificent Mile**, a boulevard of glitzy shops of international renown, has eclipsed it. Trendy and upscale **River North** has garnered a reputation for its art galleries and charming bistros and boutiques. In the **South Loop**, recently rehabilitated Printer's Row caters to a young crowd with its coffee shops and bookstores.

NORTH SIDE (pp157–188)

The affluent **Gold Coast**, most of it preserved as a landmark historic district, provides a restful retreat from bustling Michigan Avenue. One of the city's oldest neighborhoods, **Old Town** includes an offbeat assortment of comedy clubs, shops and restaurants. Just west of Lincoln Park, gentrified **Lincoln Park/DePaul** encompasses an array of theaters and jazz and blues clubs, as well as a wide range of eateries.
Considered the artistic area of Chicago, **Wicker Park** and **Bucktown**, both found along Milwaukee Avenue, present comfortable coffeehouses, alternative performance venues and unique bookshops. Just south of Milwaukee Avenue, **Ukrainian Village** forms the core of a small but lively Ukrainian community, distinguished by quaint ethnic shops and cozy eateries. A large number of Chicagoans of Polish origin reside north of **Logan Square**. Located in the North Clark Street area, the hip community of **Andersonville** offers bistros, bars and restaurants. Center of the city's gay population, **Lakeview/ Wrigleyville** is a diverse area boasting funky nightclubs, vintage-clothing stores and inexpensive restaurants. **Argyle Street**, just north of Uptown, is home to a large community of recent Asian immigrants, who have set up Vietnamese and Korean shops and restaurants. Farther north lies **Devon Avenue**, lined with a variety of ethnic restaurants reflecting the different waves of settlement in the area: Pakistani, Indian, Jewish and Thai.

WEST SIDE (pp189–195)

Located on the Near West Side, **Little Italy** offers a choice concentration of Italian restaurants and markets; just north, the delicious aromas of Greek fare pervade the streets of **Greektown**. Heart of the Hispanic community, **Little Village** and **Pilsen** on the Lower West Side feature stores selling imported goods as well as a variety of Mexican restaurants. Also on the Lower West Side is **Heart of Italy**, one of Chicago's original Italian neighborhoods. Along Western Avenue and 47th Street, the **Brighton Park** neighborhood is home to a large number of Lithuanian immigrants, while domed Orthodox churches stand out in **Ukrainian Village**.

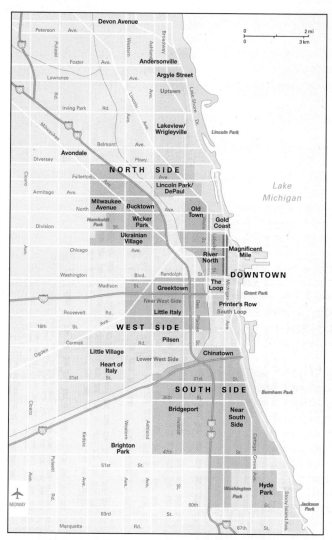

Devon Avenue

Andersonville

Argyle Street

Uptown

Lakeview/
Wrigleyville

Lincoln Park

Avondale

NORTH SIDE

Lincoln Park/
DePaul

Milwaukee
Avenue
Bucktown

Old
Town

Gold
Coast

Wicker
Park

Ukrainian
Village

Magnificent
Mile

River
North

DOWNTOWN

Greektown

The
Loop

Grant Park

Near West Side

Printer's Row

Little Italy

South Loop

WEST SIDE

Pilsen

Little Village

Chinatown

Heart of
Italy

Lower West Side

Brighton
Park

SOUTH SIDE

Bridgeport

Near
South
Side

Burnham Park

Washington
Park

Hyde
Park

Jackson
Park

MIDWAY

Lake
Michigan

SOUTH SIDE (pp196–227)

Central Station on the **Near South Side** is rapidly becoming the neighborhood of choice for young professionals and empty nesters moving to the city. **Bronzeville**, Chicago's historic African-American community, features renowned blues and jazz clubs and some of the city's oldest religious edifices. Visit **Chinatown** for its numerous restaurants that offer authentic regional Chinese cuisine, and Chinatown Square for imported souvenirs and Chinese-language books. **Bridgeport** is famous for its Irish mayors, including Richard J. Daley, who served six terms (1955–76), and presided over Chicago politics for years. A liberal and eclectic area surrounding the University of Chicago campus, **Hyde Park** is best known for its well-stocked bookshops and student hangouts.

Wrigley Building and a tour boat on the Chicago River
© Ralf-Finn Hestoft/Corbis

When to Go

CHICAGO'S SEASONS

Chicago's temperatures can drop as low as -20°F (-29°C) during the winter and soar up to 100°F (38°C) in the summer months. The city averages 33in (84cm) of rain and 40in (102cm) of snow each year. Lake Michigan has a noticeable effect on the city's weather: temperatures near the lake are markedly cooler in summer and warmer in winter. Most tourists visit Chicago in the summer, between Memorial Day and Labor Day.

SPRING

A brief and generally unpredictable season, spring begins in late March and lasts through the end of May. Daytime highs usually reach the 50s (10–15°C) and nighttime lows rarely dip below 35°F (2°C). Snow remains a possibility well into April.

SUMMER

From Memorial Day to Labor Day, Chicagoans flock to parks and beaches to take their fill of sun. Daytime temperatures are hot, averaging in the 80s (26–31°C). The relative humidity can be uncomfortably high, and a haze often settles over the city. In the evenings temperatures are normally in the 60s (15–20°C); bring a light jacket or sweater to stroll along the lakefront.

AUTUMN

Lasting from mid-September through October, autumn may be the most pleasant time to visit Chicago. Crisp, clear days with temperatures in the 50s and 60s (10–20°C) give way to cool nights, usually dropping into the 40s (4–8°C). Deciduous trees turn color in the fall, putting on a brilliant show; and tourist attractions are noticeably less crowded than in the summer. Hints of the impending winter may appear, with an occasional frost and freeze warning.

WINTER

This is Chicago's longest season and is a part of the city's culture. It can extend from mid-October through April. Brutal winds sweep between towering buildings and windchills have been known to fall to a dangerous 60° below zero (-51°C). Daytime temperatures average between 20–40°F (-7°C to 4°C); nights drop to 15–20°F (-9°C to -7°C). Lake-effect snow occurs throughout the season. These small storm systems often reach several miles inland and bring with them large amounts of snow (12–24in/30–60cm) in short periods. Protective clothing (coats, boots, gloves, hats) is essential when venturing outside. Note that the abundantly used road salt will leave a white residue on shoes and boots.

Lurie Garden in Grant Park, summer

© Anne Evans/Chicago Architecture Foundation

TEMPERATURE CHART

Month	Average high	Average low	Precipitation
January	29°F (-2°C)	14°F (-10°C)	1.6in (4.1cm)
April	59°F (15°C)	39°F (4°C)	3.7in (9.5cm)
July	83°F (28°C)	63°F (17°C)	3.6in (9.3cm)
October	64°F (18°C)	43°F (6°C)	2.3in (5.8cm)

HIT THE HIGHLIGHTS

To explore Chicago in-depth requires weeks, but if your time is limited, we offer several itineraries below to make sure you don't miss the must-sees.

FIRST DAY IN CHICAGO

Morning – Get a bird's-eye view of the city from the observation deck atop the **Willis Tower**★★★ (formerly Sears Tower) or the **John Hancock Tower**★★★. Once you have your bearings, spend some time exercising your credit cards in the many high-end stores along North Michigan Avenue, a.k.a. the **Magnificent Mile**★★★.

Afternoon – Visit the **Art Institute of Chicago**★★★ to ogle their stellar collection of Impressionist art and much, much more. Be sure to check out the new **Modern Wing**, and if time permits, linger over lunch at Terzo Piano restaurant.

Evening – Treat yourself to a stellar multicourse meal—perhaps cooked by a celebrity chef—at one of the many fine dining establishments downtown (see Where to Eat).

SECOND DAY IN CHICAGO

Morning – Whether or not you have children, make a beeline for the Museum Campus to visit the **John G. Shedd Aquarium**★★★, and while you're there, be sure to see the new multimedia dolphin presentation.

Afternoon – Head next door to the **Field Museum of Natural History**★★★, where you will find the famous T-Rex, **Sue**★★ and a host of other denizens of the natural world.

Evening – Take in dinner and a show in **Chicago's Theater District** in the **Loop**★★★.

THIRD DAY IN CHICAGO

Morning – Have breakfast at **Lou Mitchell's** in the Loop (565 W. Jackson Blvd.); then see stars at the **Adler Planetarium**★★. If time permits, take in the lakefront from **Millennium Park**★★★.

Afternoon – Ride the Ferris wheel on **Navy Pier**★★, then hop aboard one of the lake cruises that departs from the Pier.

Evening – Sample the city's famous deep-dish pizza for dinner; laugh off the calories afterwards at **Second City**.

THEMED ITINERARIES
CHICAGO FOR SPORTS FANS

Both spectator sports fans and those who like to get out there themselves will find plenty to keep them occupied year-round in the Windy City.

In spring, be sure to catch a **Cubs** game at Wrigley Field, or see the **White Sox** play at U.S. Cellular Field—depending on whether you're a National or an American League fan. Baseball lovers will want to eat at one of **Harry Caray's** two locations (33 W. Kinzie Ave., and on Navy Pier), filled with baseball memorabilia related to the late Cubs' announcer.

Summer sees folks **running** and **biking** along the lakefront, and brings a host of recreational activities in the city's many public parks—including playing a pick-up game of **volleyball** on Oak Street Beach. You can even rent a **sailboat** and navigate the lake for yourself.

Cheer for "da Bears" at Soldier Field or attend a **Bulls** game at United Center in the fall. **Ice-skating** and **cross-country skiing** are just a couple of favorite winter activities.

CHICAGO FOR FOODIES

Long synonymous with beef, this former meat-packing center now ranks as a destination for foodies. Start with the classics: a Midwestern prime steak at the original **Morton's** *(1050 N. State St.)*; a Chicago hot dog (never served with ketchup!); and a deep-dish pizza. Then indulge in a magnificent meal prepared by one of the city's many star chefs—think Charlie Trotter, Grant Achatz, Rick Bayless, Jean Joho (*see Must Eat*). On the less expensive end of the spectrum, ethnic food abounds in Chicago's diverse neighborhoods. Enjoy souvlaki in **Greektown**; dig into a heaping bowl of pasta marinara in **Little Italy**; taste the authentic flavors of Mexico in **Pilsen**, or savor shark-fin soup in **Chinatown**.

And don't miss a trip to **Green City Market**, Chicago's only year-round farmer's market *(south end of Lincoln Park, between Clark St. and Stockton Dr.; Wed and Sat 7am–1pm)*.

CHICAGO FOR ARCHITECTURE BUFFS

A mecca for those who appreciate stellar architecture, Chicago harbors a trove of skyscrapers and historic structures in its downtown core. The best way to see the highlights is to take one of the myriad tours offered by the **Chicago Architecture Foundation**. Whether you opt for a river cruise or a walking tour, you will loop the **Loop** and see the most noteworthy skyscrapers on **North Michigan Avenue** (*312-922-3432; http://caf.architecture.org; *see p21*). Then take an excursion to **Oak Park**, the suburban Chicago birthplace of the Prairie School of architecture and home to the highest concentration of houses designed by the school's leader, Frank Lloyd Wright.

DOWNTOWN CHICAGO FOR KIDS

You can keep the kids happily occupied for days without ever leaving downtown. Your first stop should be the **Museum Campus**, home to the **Field Museum of Natural History**, the **Shedd Aquarium**, and the **Adler Planetarium**. You could easily spend a day at each of these institutions, whose exhibits, live-animal presentations, 3-D films and star shows will entertain young and old alike.

Millennium Park is the perfect place to let the kids loose to admire their reflection in the stainless-steel *Cloud Gate* sculpture and splash in Crown Fountain, between a shifting array of 50ft faces projected on video screens. Next on the docket, **Navy Pier** provides tons of family fun. Between the Ferris wheel, the Transporter FX thrill ride, the Children's Museum, fireworks displays *(Wed & Sat nights in summer)* and the countless lake cruises that depart from the Pier, no one will be bored here.

CHICAGO GREETERS

Whether you are new to Chicago, or have lived here for years, you can always discover something new—courtesy of the Chicago Greeter program. Choose to explore one of 25 diverse neighborhoods and customize your experience with your personal areas of interest. No matter what area you choose, a knowledgeable Chicago volunteer will guide you on a two- to four-hour tour via foot and public transportation.

If you are pressed for time, 60-minute **InstaGreeter** tours offers an on-the-spot introduction to downtown *(departs from the Chicago Cultural Center Visitor Information Center, 77 E. Randolph St.)* or Millenium Park *(departs from the Millennium Park Welcome Center, 201 E. Randolph St.)*. All Chicago Greeter tours are free. Longer tours *(daily 10am and 1pm)* require registration 7 to 10 business days in advance. InstaGreeter tours are held on a first-come, first-served basis *(Fri–Sun 10am–4pm; last tour leaves at 3pm)*. For more information, call *312-744-8000 or check online at www.chicagogreeter.com.

Know Before You Go

USEFUL WEBSITES

The following websites will link you to a lot of good information about Chicago:
www.explorechicago.org
www.chicago.metromix.com
www.chicagonews.com
www.chicagolandchamber.org
www.choosechicago.com
www.cityofchicago.org
www.gochicago.com
www.themagnificentmile.com
www.chicagotraveler.com

TOURISM OFFICES

Contact the following agencies before your trip to obtain multilingual maps and information on points of interest, accommodations and seasonal events. These offices can often provide information about travel packages, as well as giving out complimentary copies of the *Chicago Official Visitors Guide,* published by the Chicago Convention and Tourism Bureau. For additional information, access the websites listed above.

♦ **Chicago Office of Tourism** – Chicago Cultural Center, 78 E. Washington St. at Michigan Ave., 4th Floor, Chicago IL 60602, ☎312-744-2400 or 877-CHICAGO. Here you will find a Culinary Concierge, who can suggest restaurants (but not make reservations) and grocery stores around the city.

♦ **Chicago Convention and Tourism Bureau** – 2301 S. Lake Shore Dr., Chicago IL 60616, ☎312-567-8500.

♦ **Millennium Park Welcome Center** – 201 E. Randolph St., at Michigan Ave. ☎312-742-1168.

♦ **Chicago Water Works Visitor Center** – 163 E. Pearson St., at Michigan Ave. ☎312-742-8811.

♦ **Illinois Market Place** – 700 E. Grand Ave. on Navy Pier. ☎800-226-6632.

INTERNATIONAL VISITORS
FOREIGN CONSULATES IN CHICAGO

♦ **Brazil**
401 N. Michigan Ave., Suite 1850. ☎312-464-0244. www.brazilconsulatechicago.org.

♦ **Canada**
Two Prudential Plaza, 80 N. Stetson Ave., Suite 2400. ☎312-616-1860. www. chicago.gc.ca.

♦ **France**
205 N. Michigan Ave., Suite 3700. ☎312-327-5200. www.consulfrance-chicago.org.

♦ **Germany**
676 N. Michigan Ave., Suite 3200. ☎312-202-0480. www.germany.info.

♦ **India**
NBC Tower Bldg., 455 North Cityfront Plaza Dr., Suite 850. ☎312-595-0405. www.chicago.indianconsulate.com.

♦ **Indonesia**
211 W. Wacker Dr., 8th floor. ☎312-920-1880. www.indonesiachicago.org.

♦ **Japan**
737 N. Michigan Ave., Suite 1000. ☎312-280-0428. www.us.emb-japan.go.jp.

♦ **Mexico**
204 S. Ashland Ave. ☎312-738-2383. www.consulmexchicago.com

♦ **Switzerland**
737 N. Michigan Ave., Suite 2301. ☎312-915-0061. www.eda.admin.ch/chicago.

♦ **United Kingdom**
400 N. Michigan Ave., Suite 1300. ☎312-970-3800. www.ukinusa.fco.gov.uk.

ENTRY REQUIREMENTS

Citizens of countries participating in the **Visa Waiver Pilot Program (VWPP)** are not required to obtain a visa to enter the US for visits of fewer than 90 days, provided they have a machine-readable passport. If not, they must have a US visa. Citizens of nonparticipating countries must have a visitor's visa and a valid passport. Upon entry, nonresident foreign visitors must present a valid passport and round-trip transportation ticket. Canadian citizens should present a passport to enter the US. Naturalized Canadian citizens should carry their citizenship papers. Inoculations are generally not required, but check with the US embassy or consulate before departing. Many countries have consular offices in the city. For visa inquiries and applications, contact the nearest US embassy or consulate, or access the US State Department Visa Services Internet site: www.travel.state.gov.

CUSTOMS REGULATIONS

All articles brought into the US must be declared at the time of entry.
Exempt from customs regulations: personal effects; one liter (33.8 fl oz) of alcoholic beverage *(providing visitor is at least 21 years old)*; either 200 cigarettes, 100 cigars (not from Cuba) or 1.36 kilograms (3lbs) of smoking tobacco; and gifts *(to persons in the US)* that do not exceed $100 in value. International visitors may carry in or out of the country up to $10,000 in US or foreign currency.
Prohibited items: plant material; firearms and ammunition *(if not intended for sporting purposes)*; and meat and poultry products (including canned, fresh and dried meats). For further information regarding US Customs, contact the **US Customs Service** *(1300 Pennsylvania Ave. NW, Washington, DC 20229; ☎202-354-1000 or www.customs.gov)*. Contact the customs service in your country of residence to determine re-entry regulations.

HEALTHCARE

The US does not have a national health program. Before departing, visitors from abroad should check with their health care insurance to determine if it covers doctor's visits, medication and hospitalization in the US. Prescription drugs should be properly identified and accompanied by a copy of the prescription.

ACCESSIBILITY

Throughout this guide, wheelchair access is indicated by the ♿ symbol in admission information accompanying the sight description. Most public buildings, attractions, churches, hotels and restaurants provide wheelchair access. On all CTA transportation a designated seating area is available, as are reduced fares, for people with disabilities. Most CTA and Pace lines are wheelchair accessible via either ramps or lifts, and Metra has added lift-equipped cars to all lines. Disabled travelers using Amtrak and Greyhound bus lines should contact these companies prior to their trip to make special arrangements and receive useful brochures. For more information about travel for individuals or groups, contact one of the following organizations:
Mayor's Office for People with Disabilities *(121 N. LaSalle St., Room 1104; ☎312-744-4492 or ☎312-744-4964 TTY; www.cityofchicago.org/disabilities)*.
Society for Accessible Travel & Hospitality *(347 Fifth Ave., Suite 605, New York, NY 10016; ☎212-447-7284. www.sath.org)*.

SENIOR CITIZENS

Most attractions, hotels, restaurants and CTA transportation (trains, subways, buses) in Chicago offer discounts to visitors age 65 and older (proof of age may be required). The **AARP** offers additional discounts to its members *(601 E St. N.W., Washington, DC 20049; ☎202-434-2277 or 888-687-2277; www.aarp.org)*.

Getting There

BY PLANE
O'HARE INTERNATIONAL AIRPORT

☎773-686-2200. www.ohare.com. 14mi northwest of the Loop via I-90 West. Most international flights arrive and depart from O'Hare. **Airport information booths** *(open daily 6am–10pm)* are located on the lower level of the domestic terminals (nos 1–3), as well as the upper and lower levels of the international terminal (no. 5); there is no terminal 4. When departing, allow the maximum amount of time recommended by your airline. You must present valid photo identification at the ticket counter when checking in. **Restaurants** are located in terminal 1, concourses B and C; in terminal 2, concourse F; in the rotunda of terminal 3 and in concourse K; and in terminal 5, on the upper and lower levels of concourse M. Smoking is prohibited in the airport. A **medical clinic** is located in terminal 2, upper level. **Foreign Currency Exchanges** are located on the lower level of terminal 5, Seaway bank in Terminal 2 and by Gate K11 in Terminal 3. An **Airport Transit System** provides free transportation between the terminals and long-term parking lots. **Buses** and **hotel shuttles** depart from the level below baggage-claim. For buses and hotel shuttles, follow the red signs for the bus/shuttle center located across from the airport Hilton hotel.

Taxis

The "starter" taxi system is in effect at O'Hare Airport. Passengers are obligated to wait in line and allow a starter to hail the next available cab. Taxi service to the Loop *($35–$40)* takes approximately 50min in rush hour. All cab companies offering airport service participate in the **Shared-Ride** discount program, wherein individual riders willing to share a cab to downtown pay a flat rate of $22. Inform the starter or driver if you wish to participate; maximum of four passengers (discounted rate applies even if there are no additional riders). The program is designed for individual riders; groups pay regular posted fares.

Shuttles

Airport Express offers transport between O'Hare, downtown hotels and North Shore suburbs year-round. Shuttles run between the airport and downtown hotels daily 6am–11.30pm *(transit time: 45–60min; $27 one-way/$49 round-trip; ☎888-284-3826; www.airportexpress.com).*

Rental Cars

Rental-car service counters are located on the lower level of terminals 1, 2 and 3. Most major rental-car agencies have shuttle buses offering transportation to their lots. Conduct all rental-car business in the terminal before boarding a shuttle.

Trains

CTA Blue Line trains operate between O'Hare and downtown daily 24hrs/day *(transit time 40–45min; $2.25; ☎312-836-7000; www.transitchicago.com).* Trains depart every 5–15min *(daily midnight–11.45pm)* from the O'Hare station, located in terminal 2 under the Hilton Hotel.

CHICAGO MIDWAY AIRPORT

☎773-767-0500. www.chicago-mdw.com. 10mi southwest of the Loop via I-55 South/Cicero Ave. Many travelers find this smaller airport easier to navigate. Flights are limited to domestic carriers. **Airport information booths** *(open daily 10am–6pm)* offering airline and transport information are located in concourses B and C and in between.

Taxis and Shuttles

Taxis are located outside the front of the terminal building *(service to downtown 30min; $25–$28).* Operators participate in the **Shared-Ride** discount program *($16 flat* *rate to downtown).* **Airport Express** offers transport between Midway and downtown hotels. Shuttles are located across from the Southwest Airlines ticket counter and depart daily 6am–10.30pm every 15min *(transit time: 30–45min; $23 one-way, $40 round-trip; 888-284-3826; www.airportexpress.com).*

Rental Cars
Rental-car-agency shuttle buses depart from the area near the taxi stands. Conduct all rental-car business in the terminal before boarding a shuttle to take you to the rental-car lots. While driving in Chicago, bear in mind that parking regulations are strictly enforced. Pay special attention to parking restrictions in the downtown area weekdays during rush hour (*see PARKING*).

Trains
CTA Orange Line trains operate between Midway and downtown *(Mon–Fri 3am–midnight, Sat 4am–midnight Sun and holidays 5am–midnight; transit time 25–30min; $2.25; 312-836-7000; www.transitchicago.com).* Trains depart every 6–10min from the Midway station. The walk is lengthy; follow signs in terminal.

BY TRAIN
The **Amtrak** rail network offers a relaxing alternative if you have time to spare. Advance reservations are recommended to ensure reduced fares and availability of desired accommodations. Choose from first-class, coach, sleeping accommodations and glass-domed cars that allow a panoramic view. First-class fares are comparable to air travel; coach is more economical. Major long-distance routes to Chicago are Lake Shore Limited from Boston and New York along the Great Lakes *(21hrs)*; Capitol Limited from Washington, DC *(18hrs)*; City of New Orleans from New Orleans *(19hrs)*; Texas Eagle from Houston and San Antonio *(30hrs)*; Southwest Chief from Los Angeles along the Santa Fe Trail *(39hrs)*; California Zephyr from San Francisco *(42hrs)*; Empire Builder from Seattle *(43hrs)*; International from Toronto *(12hrs)*. In Canada ask your local travel agents about Amtrak/VIARail connections. **All-Aboard America Fare** allows travel within up to four regions. The **North America Rail Pass** offers travel via both Amtrak and VIARail Canada for up to 30 days. Chicago's **Amtrak station** is located at Union Station, 210 S. Canal St. Schedule and route information: 312-655-2066 or 800-872-7245 *(outside North America, contact your local travel agent)* or check online at www.amtrak.com.

BY CAR
Travelers driving to Chicago will find it easily accessible by major interstate highways. The Dan Ryan Expressway (I-90/I-94), the Chicago Skyway (toll) and I-57 serve the South Side, while the Stevenson Expressway (I-55) offers access to the Southwest Side. The Eisenhower Expressway (I-290), called Congress Parkway within downtown Chicago, provides the quickest route to reach the western suburbs. The Kennedy (I-90) and Edens (I-94) expressways service the Northwest and North Sides respectively. Lake Shore Drive (Route 41) follows the lakefront through the city.

BY BUS / COACH
Greyhound offers access to Chicago at a leisurely pace. Overall, fares are lower than other forms of public transportation. **Ameripass** allows unlimited travel for 7, 14 or 21 days (some travelers may find long-distance bus travel uncomfortable due to the longer amount of time required and the lack of sleeping accommodations). Advance reservations are suggested. The main Greyhound station in Chicago is located at 630 W. Harrison St. Schedule and route information is available at: 312-408-5821 or 800-231-2222 (US only); www.greyhound.com.

Getting Around

LAY OF THE LAND

Bordered on the east by Lake Michigan, Chicago is divided into North, West and South sides by the Y-shape of the Chicago River. The Loop, bounded by the lake, the Main Channel and the South Branch of the river, forms the heart of the metropolis. Chicago's most fashionable neighborhoods lie on the North Side of the city. The South Side is home to the city's large African-American population, while the West Side attracts immigrants to its ethnic neighborhoods.

HOW TO FIND AN ADDRESS

Chicago's street system makes it easy to locate any address based on its north and south coordinates. The intersection of State and Madison streets is the zero-mile point. Running north to south, State Street serves as the east/west baseline, while Madison Street, running east to west, functions as the north/south baseline. Every address north of Madison is preceded by "North," every address east or west of State is designated "East" or "West," and so forth. In addition, address numbers originate from this point, usually in increments of 100 for each block (400 = .5mi).

PUBLIC TRANSPORTATION

The **Chicago Transit Authority** (CTA) runs an extensive network of rapid-transit trains (elevated and underground) and buses that serve the city and numerous adjacent suburbs. Other suburbs are served by the **Pace** bus line *(Pace buses run every 30–60min; CTA transit cards and transfers may be used)* and **Metra** commuter trains. For information on wheelchair accessibility, see *Accessibility*. For route and fare information for all systems in the Metro Chicago area, call *☎312-836-7000 (daily 5am–1am; no area code is needed for this telephone number if you are calling from the 312, 773, 630, 847 or 815 area codes).*

CHICAGO TRANSIT AUTHORITY

In this guide, rapid-transit and bus stops are indicated with the **cta** symbol. System maps are available *(free)* at both airports, all train stations, hotels and visitor information centers throughout the city. Detailed system timetables are available from the CTA headquarters at 567 W. Lake St. (at Wells St.), Chicago IL 60602 *(☐open Mon–Fri 8am–4.30pm; ☎312-913-3110; www.transitchicago.com).*

Rapid Transit System
☍*See map on p294.*
Originally, all routes for the city's rapid-transit and railway trains ran on ground-level tracks. However, the advent of the automobile caused the city to pass an ordinance that required the tracks to be elevated. Today the CTA operates elevated and underground trains; the nickname "L" (short for elevated) designates lines circling the Loop. Train-station entrances are indicated by blue "Rapid Transit" signs. Access stairwells to the above-ground (elevated, or "L," lines) and below-ground trains may look somewhat foreboding, but stations and waiting areas are generally clean and well lit. Many trains are accessible to riders with disabilities and some stations are equipped with elevators. Trains run every 3–12min during weekday rush hours, 6–20min at most other times, and every 30min overnight. The eight different lines are referred to by color (note that route names indicate destination or end points). Paper transfers are not needed for changes within the rapid-transit system.

Buses
CTA buses generally operate daily 6am–midnight; some routes run 24hrs/day. During the weekday rush hour, most buses run about every 5–15min, and about every 8–20min at other times. Stops (clearly marked by blue and white signs) are customarily made at posted locations only, one to

CTA LINES		SERVICE HOURS
■ **RED**	(Howard-Dan Ryan)	24hrs daily
■ **BLUE**	(O'Hare-Forest Park)	24hrs daily
■ **PURPLE**	(Evanston)	Mon–Fri 5am–1am (Linden & Howard); Sat 5.30am–2am; Sun 6am–1.30am; peak period service only between Howard and the Loop
■ **GREEN**	(Lake-Englewood/ Jackson Park)	Mon–Fri 4am–1am; Sat 6am–1am; Sun 6.30am–1am
■ **ORANGE**	(Midway-Downtown)	Mon–Sat 4am–1am; Sun & holidays 5.30am–11.30pm
■ **BROWN**	(Ravenswood)	Mon–Fri 5am–10pm, Sat 5am–8pm; additional late evening, Sun & holiday hours (Kimball & Belmont)
■ **YELLOW**	(Skokie -Howard)	Mon–Fri 5am–11pm; Sat–Sun 6.30am–11pm

Times given are approximate; call the Rapid Transit Authority (*☏312-836-7000; www.transitchicago.com*) for specific information.

two blocks apart, and may be verified with the driver. Many routes are accessible to riders with disabilities.

Fares

Most CTA fares are $2.25 one-way (*exact fare required for buses; $1 bills accepted*). Discounted fares are available for senior citizens and people with disabilities; children under seven ride free. CTA transit cards automatically deduct fares and transfers and can be used on trains and buses. (*Train turnstiles do not accept cash.*) Transit cards are available at CTA train stations, banks, currency-exchange offices, and select Jewel and Dominick's grocery stores. Transfers cost 25¢.

Passes, allowing unlimited travel on buses and trains on consecutive days, are available for one day (*$5.75*), three days (*$14*) and seven days (*$28*). Purchase passes at both airports, at Union Station and at visitor centers, or online at www.transitchicago.com.

COMMUTER TRAINS

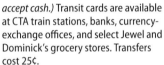

☝See map on p294.

Pullman Historic District, Oak Park, Brookfield Zoo and other outlying sights can be reached by commuter train. In downtown Chicago, Metra operates commuter trains from four downtown terminals: LaSalle Street Station, Millennium Park Station (Randolph Street), Union Station (Amtrak) and Ogilvie Transportation Center (North Western Station). In all, 12 lines service some 220 suburban stations including O'Hare International Airport and outlying cities in Illinois and neighboring states. During rush hour, trains run frequently; at other times, departures are every one to three hours. One-way fares range from $2.25 to $8.50, depending on the distance traveled. Metra's $7 weekend

Water Taxis

Another way to get around in Chicago is via the system of water taxis that operates on a closed loop on the Chicago River between Madison Street on the south branch of the river, La Salle Street and Michigan Avenue on the main branch, and River East on the main branch at Ogden Slip. Boats run daily every 15min, generally during commuting hours. Schedules vary according to destination, $2 one-way. For detailed schedules and other information, call ☏312-337-1446 or access www.chicago watertaxi.com.

pass offers unlimited rides on all Metra lines. Children up to 11 years old ride free with Family Fares. *For schedules and fare information, call* 312-322-6777 *or go to www.metrarail.com.*

TAXIS

Chicago taxis are metered. All Chicago cab companies share the same rate schedule: $2.25 for the first 1/9 mile, 20¢ for each additional 1/9 mile, and $1 for the first additional passenger, 50¢ for others. There are no extra fees for baggage handling or assistance for passengers with physical disabilities. Cabs are easily hailed in the downtown area. Taxi stands are located at most hotels and major attractions *(in other areas, telephone for service)*. The main cab companies in Chicago are **Checker Taxi Co.** (312-243-2537) and **Yellow Cab Co.** (312-829-4222; www.yellowcabchicago.com). To report lost property, call 312-225-7456; be sure to give taxi identification number.

DRIVING IN CHICAGO

For information about Chicago road conditions, call the Illinois Department of Transportation Information Line: 217-782-7820. www.dot.state.il.us. Given the efficiency of the public transportation system, and the ease with which many sights can be reached on foot, a car is not necessary to visit downtown Chicago. However, a car is recommended for visiting other areas. Keep in mind that roads are often congested, street parking can be difficult to find and public parking lots are expensive. **Rush hour**, the peak transit time for business commuters, is weekdays between 7.30am–9.30am and 4pm–7pm. Expect roadways to be clogged and traveling to be slow during these times.

ROAD REGULATIONS

The maximum **speed limit** on major expressways is 55mph (90km/h). Speed limits within the city range from 25mph (40km/h) in residential areas to 35mph (56km/h) on major

streets. The use of **seat belts** is mandatory for all passengers in a vehicle. Child-safety or booster seats are required for children up to age eight years. Illinois law requires motorists to bring vehicles to a full stop when the warning signals on a **school bus** are flashing. Drivers must always yield the **right of way to pedestrians**. Unless otherwise posted, drivers may turn right on a red traffic light in Chicago after coming to a complete stop.

PARKING

Metered street parking is available on some downtown and arterial streets; note that vehicles will be towed if left overnight. Many streets are designated Snow Routes (indicated by red, white and blue signs); parking is not allowed on either side of these streets overnight during winter or when there are two or more inches of snow on the ground. No parking is allowed on many streets during rush hour and during specific street-cleaning days; note signs. Major parking facilities are indicated on maps in this guide with the 🅿 symbol. Parking in some residential areas is by permit only (restricted to area residents). Parking spaces identified by the ♿ symbol are reserved for people with disabilities; anyone parking in these spaces without proper identification is subject to towing and a heavy fine.

RENTAL COMPANY	RESERVATION
Alamo	800-327-9633
Avis	800-331-1212
Budget	800-527-0700
Enterprise	800-325-8007
Hertz	800-654-3131
National	800-227-7368
Thrifty	800-847-4389
(Toll-free numbers may not be accessible outside North America.)	

RENTAL CARS

Most major car-rental companies have offices downtown and at both O'Hare and Midway airports. Rental cars are available for people at least 25 years old, but some rental-car agencies will rent to drivers under 25 for a daily surcharge. The agency has the right to check the renter's driving record for violations before approving the rental. A major credit card and a valid driver's license are required for rental (some agencies also require proof of insurance). The average daily rate for a compact car, when renting for 5–7 days, ranges from $30–$65. Note that rental cars are taxed at the rate of 18 percent.

Note that children under the age of eight are required to be in a child-safety seat; these seats are available from the rental agency.

Where to Stay and Eat

WHERE TO STAY

For price ranges, see the Legend on the front cover flap.

The Chicago area offers a wide range of accommodations from elegant downtown hotels *($200–$350 and up)* located in the Loop and around North Michigan Avenue to more moderately priced motels *($90–$150)* found throughout the city.

Rates tend to be lower in suburban areas (including O'Hare Airport) and on weekends. Amenities can include television, restaurant, swimming pool and smoking/nonsmoking rooms. The more expensive hotels also offer room-service dining and valet service. Most downtown hotels charge a fee for parking. Some hotels located near Lake Shore Drive may be within walking distance of a public beach; inquire when making reservations. All rates quoted are average prices per day for a double room. For information about specific hotels in the city, see *Your Stay in Chicago* at the back of this guide.

BED AND BREAKFAST INNS

Most of the B&Bs in Chicago are located downtown and in the Gold Coast, Old Town and Lincoln Park areas. Many B&Bs are privately owned historic homes *($95–$300)*. Continental breakfast is customarily included. Private baths are not always available. Smoking indoors is usually not allowed. *For a listing of B&Bs, visit Chicago Bed and Breakfast Association at www.chicago-bed-breakfast.com. Furnished apartment rentals ($155 and up) are available through At Home Inn Chicago 800-375-7084 or 312-640-1050; www.athomeinnchicago.com.*

HOSTELS

A no-frills, economical alternative to pricey hotels, **hostels** average $20–$45/day. Amenities include community living room, showers, laundry facilities, full-service kitchen and dining room, dormitory-style and private rooms (guests must bring their own towels). The **Chicago International Hostel** is located at 6318 North Winthrop Ave., Chicago, IL 60660; 773-262-1011.

Hostelling International operates a facility at 24 E. Congress Parkway at Wabash Avenue *($29–$35; reservations recommended; 312-360-0300; www.hichicago.org)* that features 24hr access, self-service kitchen, dining room, on-site cafe, laundry, parking, and complimentary breakfast and WiFi.

WHERE TO EAT

Eateries of all kinds, from Latin American to Polish, Chinese to classic American steakhouses, may be found in Chicago. Fine dining and quick bites alike may be found in the spots we've selected for their "Chicago feel," listed in address books throughout this guide and in *Your Stay in Chicago* at the back of the guide.

What to See and Do

SIGHTSEEING

See inside cover maps.
Chicago offers a large variety of guided tours. Below are some of the principal tours.

TOURS OF THE CITY
TROLLEY TOURS

Offered daily by **Chicago Trolley Co.** *(mid-Mar–end Oct 9am–6.30pm, Nov–mid-Mar 5pm; closed Thanksgiving, Dec 24–25, Jan 9, and for inclement weather; $29; ℘773-648-5000; www.chicagotrolley.com).*
Visitors can hop on and off every 15–20min at any of the 18 stops located at major city attractions.

CARRIAGE TOURS

In general, horse-drawn carriages hold four to six passengers and tour routes depend on passenger preference. Both companies below depart from the corner of Michigan Avenue and Pearson Street.

♦ **Chicago Horse & Carriage Ltd.** *(Mon–Fri 4–6pm; 30min/$40; ℘941-747-7902; www.chicago carriage.com).*
♦ **The Noble Horse** *(10am–4.30pm, 6pm–midnight; 30min: $35; ℘312-266-7878; www.noblehorsechicago.com/ carriages.html).*

GANGSTER TOURS

Untouchable Tours offers a lighthearted and often silly look at Prohibition-era Chicago and the gangsters that ruled this city. *Tours ($25) run daily and schedules vary by season. Call or check online for schedules: ℘773-881-1195 or www.gangstertour.com).*

ARCHITECTURAL TOURS
CHICAGO ARCHITECTURE FOUNDATION (CAF)

Founded in 1966, the Chicago Architecture Foundation is dedicated to preserving and increasing public appreciation of Chicago's architecture. Today the organization conducts more than 80 tours of Chicago's neighborhoods by foot, bus, boat, bicycle and elevated train. Tickets are available at the **CAF Shop and Tour Center** *(224 S. Michigan Ave.; open year-round Mon–Sat 9am–7pm, Sun 9.30am–6pm; ℘312-922-3432).* Cost of tours is discounted for CAF members. Advance ticket purchase is strongly recommended *(to charge tickets by phone, call Ticketmaster at 312-902-1500 or online at www.ticketmaster. com/venue/270350/).*
A sampling of CAF tours is cited below; for a complete listing, visit their website: *http://caf.architecture.org.*

♦ **Architecture River Cruise** – This excellent cruise provides an in-depth study of the Loop's architecture as seen from the Chicago River *(departs from southeast corner of the Michigan Avenue Bridge and Wacker Drive; times and charges vary; 1hr 30min; $32; ✕♿ ℘312-922-3432.*
♦ **Historic Downtown: Rise of the Skyscraper** – This walking tour of the South Loop examines the beginnings of the Chicago school of architecture through study of structures built between 1870 and 1935 *(departs from 224 S. Michigan Ave.; daily Nov–Apr 10am, May–Oct 10am & 3pm; no 3pm tour Wed,*

River cruise with Chicago Architecture Foundation

© Anne Evans/Chicago Architecture Foundation

Thanksgiving, Dec 25, Jan 1; 2hrs.; $16; ☏*312-922-3432.*

◆ **Magnificent Mile** – Stroll along Michigan Avenue to learn how this boulevard became a world-class shopping destination. Along the way, admire Art Deco architecture and some of the city's tallest buildings *(departs from Pioneer Court, 401 N. Michigan Ave.; Apr–Dec Tue & Sat 10am; call for specific dates; 2hrs.; $15;* ☏*312-922-3432.*

◆ **Bike the Lakefront** – Hop on a bike (rent one or bring your own) for a new perspective of the Chicago lakefront *(departs from McDonald's Cycle Center in Millennium Park; one Sunday a month, Apr–Oct; call or check online for specific dates; 3hrs; $15;* ☏*312-922-3432).*

RIVER AND LAKE CRUISES

Commercial tours of the Chicago River and Lake Michigan offer terrific panoramic views of the city's skyline and feature both architectural and historical points of interest.

◆ **Chicago Line Cruises** depart from North Pier Docks at River East Art Center promenade *(Apr–Oct daily; 1hr 30min; reservations suggested; $37;* ✕♿🅿 ☏*312-527-1977).*

◆ **Mercury Cruise Lines**' Urban Adventure tours depart from Riverside Gardens at Michigan Ave. and Wacker Dr. *(mid-May–Sept daily 10am, 11.30am, 1.30pm, 4pm, 5.30pm, 7.30pm, plus 8.30pm on Wed; 1hr 30min.; $24;* ☏*312-332-1368; www.mercuryskylinecruiseline.com).* Arrive 1hr early to buy tickets.

◆ All **Wendella** cruises depart from the northwest corner of the Michigan Avenue Bridge *(daily Apr–Nov.; tour times and charges vary;* ☏*312-337-1446; www.wendellaboats.com).* Arrive 1hr early to purchase tickets.

◆ **Shoreline** cruises of Lake Michigan depart from Navy Pier's Ogden Slip *(daily Apr–mid-Oct; 10am–6pm; 30min; $24).* They also run water taxis between Navy Pier West Dock and the Museum Campus *(mid-Jun–mid-Aug Sun–Thu 10am–9pm, Fri–Sat 10am–10pm; late May–mid-June & mid-Aug–early Sept 10am–7pm; 15min; $7). For info:* ☏*312-222-9328; www.shorelinesightseeing.*

ACTIVITIES FOR KIDS 👥

Sights in this guide of particular interest to children are indicated with 👥 symbol. Many of these attractions offer special children's programs. The Chicago Children's Museum on Navy Pier has interactive exhibits designed for children under age 12. *(☞ See pp108-109 for a listing.)*

Many attractions in Chicago feature discounted admission to visitors under 16 years of age. In addition, many hotels offer special family discount packages and numerous restaurants provide a children's menu.

Two annual events, the **Taste of Lincoln Avenue Kid's Karnival** *(Altgeld St. from Lincoln Ave. to Halsted St.; last weekend in July;* ☏*773-298-6800; www.wrightwoodneighbors.org)* and the **57th Street Children's Book Fair** *(late Sept; 57th St. between Kimbark & Kenwood Aves.;* ☏*773-684-1300; www.57cbf.org)* are conceived especially for children. In summer, the **Family Fun Festival** at Millennium Park features daily programs for youngsters from June until early September. A complete list of kid-friendly attractions and happenings throughout the city—as well as a host of coupons and discounts—is available online at www.chicagokids.com.

Chicago Parent, a free monthly news magazine available at major attractions and libraries throughout the area, includes articles of interest to parents as well as an extensive calendar of family-oriented activities. To obtain copies by mail, write to: *Chicago Parent, 141 S. Oak Park Ave., Oak Park, IL 60302;* ☏*708-386-5555.* You can also access the magazine online at www.chicagoparent.com.

Calendar of Events

Listed below is a selection of Chicago's most popular annual events; some dates may vary each year. For more information about events in Chicago, consult local newspapers or contact the **Chicago Office of Tourism** (*312 -744-2400; www.explorechicago.org*) or the **Mayor's Office of Special Events** (*312-744-3315; www.cityofchicago. org/specialevents*).

SPRING AND SUMMER

St. Patrick's Day Parade – Sat before Mar 17. S. Columbus Dr. from E. Balbo to E. Monroe. www.chicagostpatsparade.com.

Chicago Park District Spring Flower Show – Lincoln Park Conservatory, Apr– mid-May, 2391 N. Stockton Dr. *312-742-7736.* Garfield Conservatory, Apr–mid- May, 300 N. Central Park Ave. *312-746-5100.* www.garfield- conservatory.org.

Art Chicago – Last weekend in Apr. Merchandise Mart. www.art chicago.com.

Annual Mayor Daley's Kids and Kites Festival – 1st Sat in May. Montrose Harbor, LincolnPark. *312-744-3315.* www.chicagokids andkites.us.

Celtic Fest Chicago – 1st weekend in May. Millenium Park. *312-744- 3315.* www.celticfestchicago.us.

Cinco de Mayo – 1st weekend in May Douglas Park. *773-843-9738.* www.el5demayo.org.

57th Street Art Fair – 1st weekend in Jun. *773-493-3247.* www.57thstreetartfair.org.

Chicago Blues Festival – 1st weekend in Jun. Grant Park. . *312-744-3315.* www.chicagobluesfestival.org.

Chicago Gospel Music Festival – 1st weekend in Jun. Millennium Park. *312-744-3315.* www.chicagogospelfestival.com.

East Side Millennium Arts Festival 1st weekend in Jun. Lake St. at Michigan Ave. *846-926-4300.* www.amdurproductions.com.

Park West Antique & Flower Fair – 1st weekend in Jun. 568 W. Arlington Pl. *773-506-4460.* www.parkwestcommunity.com/ antiques.html.

Old Town Art Fair – 2nd weekend in Jun. Lincoln Ave. and Wisconsin St. *312-337-1938.* www.oldtown triangle.com/artfair.html.

Wells St. Art Festival – 2nd weekend in Jun. North Wells St., between North Ave. & Division St. *773-868-3010.*

Grant Park Music Festival – mid- Jun–mid-Aug. Millennium Park. *312-742-7638.* www.grantpark musicfestival.com.

Chicago Blues Festival

23

Calumet/Giles/Prairie Historical Festival – mid-Jun. 3100 S. Calumet Ave. ✆312-225-2257.

Ravinia Music Festival – Jun–mid Sep. Highland Park. ✆847-266-5100. www.ravinia.org.

Taste of Chicago – Grant Park. late Jun–1st week Jul. ✆312-744-3315. www.tasteofchicago.us.

Chicago Country Music Festival – 1st weekend in Jul. Millennium Park. ✆312-744-3315. www.chicagocountryfestival.com.

Independence Day Concert and Fireworks – Jul 3. Grant Park. ✆312-744-3315. www.cityof chicago.org.

Chinatown Summer Fair – mid-Jul. Wentworth from Cermak Rd. to 24th Pl. ✆312-326-5320. www.chicagochinatown.org.

Rock Around the Block – mid-Jul. Lincoln Ave. between Addison & Roscoe Sts. ✆773-665-4682.

Chicago Outdoor Film Festival – mid-Jul–mid-Aug. Grant Park, , ✆312-744-3315.

Magnificent Mile Art Festival – 2nd weekend in Jul. Pioneer Court at the Chicago Tribune Tower. ✆312-409-5560. www.the magnificentmile.com.

Chicago to Mackinac Island Yacht Race – 3rd weekend in Jul. Starts at Monroe Harbor. ✆800-454-5227. www.cyrace tomackinac.com.

Venetian Night – Late Jul. 500 E Jackson Ave. ✆312-744-3370. www.cityofchicago.org.

Bud Billiken Parade and Picnic – 2nd Sat in Aug. 39th St. & Martin Luther King, Jr. Dr. to 51st St. ✆773-536-3710. www.budbillikenparade.com.

Northalsted Market Days – 1st weekend in Aug. Halstead from Belmont to Addison. ✆773-883-0500. www.northalsted.com/ daze.htm.

Chicago Air and Water Show – Mid-Aug. North Avenue Beach. ✆312-744-3315. www.explore chicago.org.

Gold Coast Art Fair – 3rd weekend in Aug. Grant Park. ✆847-926-4300. www.amdurproductions.com.

Viva Chicago Latin Music Festival – 3rd weekend in Aug. Millenium Park. ✆312-744-3370.

Bucktown Arts Fest – Last weekend in Aug. Senior Citizens Memorial Park. 2238 N. Oakley Ave. ✆312-409-8305. www.bucktownarts fest.com.

African Festival of the Arts – Labor Day. Washington Park. ✆773-955-2787. www.aihusa.org.

FALL AND WINTER

Chicago Jazz Festival – 1st weekend in Sept. Grant Park ✆312-742-1168. ww.chicagojazzfestival.org.

Taste of Polonia – 1st weekend in Sept. Lawrence Ave. between Milwaukee Ave. & the Kennedy Expressway. ✆773-777-8898. www.copernicusfdn.org/ tasteofpolonia.html.

Renegade Craft Fair – 2nd weekend in Sept. Division St. between Damen Ave. & Paulina St. ✆773-227-2707. www.renegadecraft. com/chicago.

Ukranian Village Fest – 2nd weekend in Sept. Saints Volodymyr and Olha Ukrainian Catholic Church, 2245 W. Superior St. ✆312-829-5209.

Chicago Marathon – 2nd Sun in Oct. Starts at Grant Park. ✆312-904-9800. www.chicagomarathon.com.

Chicago International Film Festival – 1st two weeks in Oct. Various theaters. ✆312-683-0121. www.chicagofilmfestival.org.

Day of the Dead Celebration – Early Nov. National Museum of Mexican Art. ✆312-738-1503. www.nationalmuseumofmexican art.org.

Magnificent Mile Festival of Lights – mid-Nov. ✆312-642-3570. www.themagnificentmile.com.

City of Chicago Tree-Lighting Ceremony – Day after Thanksgiving. Daley Center. ✆312-409-5560. www.cityofchicago.org/ specialevents.

Caroling to the Animals – 1st Sun in Dec. Lincoln Park Zoo. ☎312-742-2000. www.lpzoo.org.

Kwanzaa Celebration – Mid-Dec. DuSable Museum of African-American History, South Side. ☎773-947-0600. www.dusable museum.com.

New Year's Eve Celebration – Dec 31. Navy Pier. ☎312-595-7437. www.navypier.com.

Chinese New Year Parade – Late-Jan–mid-Feb. Wentworth Ave. from Cermak Rd. to 24th St. ☎312-326-5320. www.chicago chinatown.org.

Chicago Auto Show – 2nd week in Feb. McCormick Place. ☎630-495-2282. www.chicagoautoshow.com.

Basic Information

BUSINESS HOURS

Most businesses operate Monday to Saturday 9am–6pm. Banks are usually open Monday to Friday 9am–5.30pm although some may have later hours. Shopping centers operate Monday to Saturday 10am–7pm or 9pm, Sunday noon–6pm, and offer extended hours between Thanksgiving Day and Christmas Day.

COMMUNICATIONS

A local call from a pay phone generally costs 35¢—or more, depending on the telephone number being called (any combination of nickels, dimes or quarters is accepted).

DRIVING IN THE US

Visitors bearing valid driver's licenses issued by their country of residence are not required to obtain an International Driver's License to drive in the US. Drivers must carry vehicle registration and/or rental contract and proof of automobile insurance at all times. Rental cars in the US are usually equipped with automatic transmission and rental rates tend to be less expensive than overseas. Gasoline is sold by the gallon (1 gallon = 3.8 liters) and is cheaper than in other countries. Most self-service gas stations do not offer car repair, although many sell standard maintenance items. Road regulations in the US require that vehicles be driven on the right side of the road. Distances are posted in miles (1 mile = 1.6 kilometers).

ELECTRICITY

Voltage in the US is 110 volts AC, 60 Hz. Foreign-made appliances may need AC adapters (available at specialty travel and electronics stores) and North American flat-blade plugs.

EMERGENCIES

In all major US cities you can telephone the police, ambulance or fire service by dialing **911**. Another way to report an emergency is to dial 0 for the operator.

LIQUOR LAW

The legal age for purchase and consumption of alcoholic beverages is 21. Proof of age is normally required.

IMPORTANT NUMBERS	
Emergency/ Police/Ambulance/ Fire (24hrs)	☎**911**
Police (non-emergency, 24hrs)	☎311
Medical Society Referrals (Mon–Fri 8.30am–4.30pm)	☎312-670-2550
Dental Society Referrals (Mon–Fri 9am–5pm)	☎312-836-7300
24-hour pharmacy Walgreens	☎800-925-4733
Weather	☎312-976-1212

Most bars and taverns are open until 2am and some have extended weekend hours until 4am or 5am. Almost all package-goods stores sell beer, wine and liquor.

MAJOR HOLIDAYS

Most banks and government offices in the Chicago area are closed on the following legal holidays (many retail stores and restaurants remain open on days indicated by an asterisk*):

January 1	New Year's Day
3rd Monday in January	Martin Luther King, Jr.'s Birthday*
3rd Monday in February	Presidents' Day*
1st Monday in March	Pulaski Day*
Last Monday in May or May 30	Memorial Day*
July 4	Independence Day*
1st Monday in September	Labor Day*
2nd Monday in October	Columbus Day*
November 11	Veterans Day*
4th Thursday in November	Thanksgiving Day
December 25	Christmas Day

MAIL/POST

The lobby of Chicago's main post office (433 W. Harrison St.; 312-983-8130; www.usps.com) is open daily 7.30am–midnight. The post office at the Federal Center (540 N. Dearborn St.; 312-644-3919) in the Loop is open Monday to Friday 8am–6.30pm, Saturday 7.30am–3pm, and Sunday 9am–2pm. For information and hours for other branches, check online at www.usps.com.

First-class rates within the US: letter 44¢ (1oz), postcard 28¢. Overseas: first-class rates for letters and postcards start at 75¢ (1oz) and depend on the country to which it is being sent.

Letters can be mailed from most hotels. Stamps and packing material may be purchased at post offices, grocery stores and businesses offering postal and express shipping services located throughout the city (see the Yellow Pages phone directory under "Mailing Services").

MONEY
CREDIT CARDS AND TRAVELER'S CHECKS

Rental-car agencies and many hotels require credit cards. Most banks will cash brand-name traveler's checks and give cash advances on major credit cards (American Express, Visa, MasterCard/Eurocard) with proper identification. Traveler's checks are accepted, with photo identification, in banks, most stores, restaurants and hotels.

CURRENCY EXCHANGE

Many banks located in the Loop offer foreign currency exchange, including the **Northern Trust Bank** (50 S. LaSalle St.; 312-630-6000; www.northerntrust.com). Banks charge a small fee for this service. Private companies generally charge higher fees: **Thomas Cook** (19 S LaSalle St. 312-807-4940; www.thomascook.com) and **World Money Exchange** (203 N. LaSalle St., Suite M10; 312-641-2151; www.wmeinc.com). **O'Hare International Airport Currency Exchange** offices are located on the lower level of Terminal 5, Seaway bank in Terminal 2 and by Gate K11 in Terminal 3.

Most banks are members of the network of Automated Teller Machines (ATMs), allowing visitors from around the world to withdraw cash using bank cards and major credit cards. ATMs can usually be found in banks, airports, grocery stores and shopping malls. Networks (Cirrus, Plus) serviced by the ATM are indicated on the machine. To inquire about ATM service, locations and transaction fees, contact your local bank, Cirrus (☎800-424-7787) or Plus (☎800-843-7587).

American Express Company Travel Service office is located at 605 N. Michigan Ave., Suite 105. ☎312-943-7840. www.americanexpress.com. To report a lost or stolen credit card, call: American Express, ☎800-528-4800, www.americanexpresstravel resources.com; Diners Club, ☎800-234-6377, www.dinersclub.com; MasterCard, ☎800-622-7747, www.mastercard.com; Visa, ☎800-847-2911, www.visa.com; or the issuing bank.

NEWSPAPERS

Chicago's two main daily newspapers, the *Chicago Tribune (www.chicago tribune.com)* and the *Chicago Sun-Times (www.suntimes.com),* are distributed in the morning. The arts and entertainment sections appear in the *Tribune* on Friday and Sunday, and in the *Sun-Times* on Friday. Learn local news through the *Daily Herald (www. dailyherald.com),* which reports on the Chicago suburbs. And keep your finger on the pulse of the city's business world with *Crain's Chicago Business (www.chicagobusiness.com).* The *Chicago Defender (www.chicago defender.com),* another popular newspaper, caters to the African-American population, while the *Chicago Free Press (www. chicagofreepress.com)* caters to the city's gay and lesbian community. Weekly alternative publications available at bookstores and restaurants around town include *Newcity* and the *Chicago Reader,* a comprehensive entertainment guide.

TAXES AND TIPS

In Chicago, the sales tax is 10.25 percent, one of the highest in the country. Tax on food items in grocery stores is 2 percent; magazine and newspapers are exempt. The tax rate for rental cars is 18 percent. The hotel occupancy tax within the

city of Chicago is 15.4 percent; tax percentages vary in outlying suburbs. When booking hotel and rental-car reservations, note that the rates quoted do not reflect the taxes. In restaurants it is customary to tip the server 15–20 percent of the bill. At hotels, porters should be given $1 per suitcase and hotel maids $2 per day of occupancy. Taxi drivers are usually tipped 15 percent of the fare.

TIME ZONE

Chicago is located in the Central Standard Time (CST) zone, which is one hour behind Eastern Standard Time (EST) and six hours behind Greenwich Mean Time (GMT). Daylight Saving Time is observed from the second Sunday in March (clocks are advanced one hour) to the first Sunday in November.

☺ Safety Tips ☺

Chicago is a relatively safe city. Visitors should remember these common-sense tips to ensure a safe and enjoyable visit:

◆ Avoid carrying large sums of money and don't let strangers see how much money you are carrying.
◆ Keep a firm hold on purses and knapsacks, carry your wallet in your front pocket and avoid wearing expensive jewelry.
◆ Stay awake when riding public transportation and keep any packages close by. CTA buses and trains are equipped with devices that enable riders to notify personnel of emergencies.
◆ Always park your car in a well-lit area. Close windows, lock doors and place valuables in the trunk. Exercise caution when visiting areas on the South and West Sides of Chicago.

Stained-glass window, Frank Lloyd Wright Home and Studio, Oak Park
© David Dunai/Apa Publications

The City Today

The greater "Chicagoland" area today sprawls over eight Illinois counties, northward into Wisconsin and southeast into Indiana. Suburbs, exurbs, and collar counties encircle the city like growth rings on a tree. In all, some 9 million people live in the 7,214 square miles covered by this metropolitan area. Chicago proper prides itself on its neighborhoods, some 175 in all. While a few are the stuff of developers' dreams, many trace their outlines around the historic ethnic enclaves from which the city was built.

POPULATION

Outranked in population size only by New York and Los Angeles, Chicago remains the bold and brash metropolis that Norman Mailer dubbed "perhaps the last of the great American cities." In this polyglot city of nearly 3 million, the neighborhood is the common measure of all, a source of identity and pride and a lingering reflection of Chicago's incredible immigrant heritage. A patchwork of neighborhoods unfurls westward from the lakefront, from tiny Old Town Triangle on the North Side to the anchor communities of Rogers Park and Englewood.

The creators of this patchwork have been an eclectic lot since **Jean Baptiste Point du Sable**, a fur trader of French, Caribbean and African descent, built the earliest permanent dwelling on the banks of the river in 1779. At first a blended society of French, English and Indian settlers, the town developed a growing reputation for opportunities and accessibility, luring refugees from Europe by the 1830s. Fleeing famine, persecution and revolution, great waves of immigrants poured in between 1840 and 1924. By 1890 the foreign-born (largely German, Irish and Scandinavian) and their children accounted for 79 percent of a population of about 1.2 million. They transplanted their shtetls, villages and parishes to the shores of Lake Michigan, establishing neighborhoods that offered the familiarity of home. In a pattern that would repeat again and again, newcomers settled near downtown and then dispersed outward—ultimately to the suburbs—as the next groups arrived.

This migratory ebb and flow has yielded a city that today is 37 percent African American, 26 percent Hispanic and over 4 percent Asian. Some 80 ethnic strains enrich the mix, from American Indians to Croats, and Pacific Islanders to Assyrians.

POPULATION: 1837 TO 2005

1837 — **4,066** Chicago incorporates as a city.

1848 — **20,243** Chicago and Galena Union Railroad, the city's first, begins operation.

1860 — **112,172** Chicago has become the center of the world's largest railroad network. The building of the railroads attracts workers from the US and abroad.

1871 — **335,000** The Chicago Fire in October flattens much of the city, but the immediate push to rebuild sustains it through the financial panic of 1873.

1889 — **1,098,576** Chicago annexes 120 surrounding square miles by popular referendum, thereby boosting the population over the 1 million mark. The federal census of 1890 marks Chicago's official status as "Second City," its population having surpassed that of Philadelphia.

1893 — **1,315,000** World's Columbian Exposition is held in Chicago.

1900 — **1,698,575** Chicago's population now includes more Poles, Swedes, Czechs, Dutch, Danes, Norwegians, Croatians, Slovaks, Lithuanians and Greeks than any other American city.

1914 — **2,437,526 Immigration** from Europe slows with World War I. The migration of southern blacks, drawn in part by war-industry jobs, begins.

1920 — **2,701,705** African-American population reaches 109,000 and will continue to grow to a quarter million by 1929.

1924 — **2,939,605** The Johnson-Reed Act essentially ends foreign immigration through quotas.

1932 — **3,236,913** Chicago is hard hit by the Great Depression; more than 750,000 are unemployed. Between 1930 and 1940, Chicago grows by only 20,000.

1950 — **3,620,962** A strong postwar economy along with the baby boom and the annexation of 41 additional square miles boosts Chicago's population to its peak.

1956 — **3,552,300** O'Hare Airport opens and soon becomes the world's busiest, maintaining Chicago's position as transportation hub. The urban population has started to fall, however, and the flight to the suburbs begins.

1990 — **2,783,903** The population of the city proper falls below 3 million for the first time in 70 years. Los Angeles replaces Chicago as the official "Second City."

2000 — **2,896,016** Chicago still ranks as the nation's third-largest city.

2007 — **2,836,658** (city estimate) Chicago's urban area tops 9,725,000; the city retains its place as the third-largest US city.

Irish

First to arrive in large numbers, the Irish came to build the Illinois & Michigan Canal in 1836 and later to flee the Potato Famine of the 1840s. Many settled along the South Branch of the Chicago River in an area now called **Bridgeport,** which in the 20C would produce five Chicago mayors of Irish descent, including **Richard J. Daley** and his son **Richard M. Daley.** From humble beginnings as laborers, teamsters and domestic servants, Chicago's Irish rose to prominence in politics, the police department and the Catholic Church.

Germans

The failed revolution of 1848 drove Germans from their homeland by the thousands, and by 1860 they outnumbered other groups in Chicago. They moved north from Chicago Avenue, through **Old Town** and Lakeview, and up along Lincoln Avenue, where **Lincoln Square** remains a center of Teutonic society. Germans were as active in the labor movement as in the development of Chicago's culture, organizing trade unions and fraternal groups, singing and sporting clubs. In the shadow of anti-German sentiment during two world wars, German solidarity faded in favor of greater assimilation.

Scandinavians

Swedes, Norwegians and Danes streamed steadily into Chicago over the years, some to stay, others to seek out the rich farmland of the northern Midwest. Settling in shantytowns near the central city, they prospered in the construction trades, small businesses and later in the professions, eventually migrating north and northwest. **Humboldt Park** was once a center of Norwegian and Danish life, and in Andersonville on the Far North Side of the city, the Swedish influence lingers in shops and restaurants.

Jews

Jewish immigrants arrived in two great migrations. First came the generally affluent and secular German speakers from Central Europe, and beginning in the 1880s, mostly Orthodox refugees fleeing pogroms in Eastern Europe flocked to the city's crowded **Near West Side**. The urbane Germans assimilated easily, building retail and dry-goods businesses and adopting something of a paternalistic attitude toward their impoverished Russian and Polish counterparts abiding in the ghetto around Maxwell Street. Out of that ghetto, however, came a profusion of actors and writers, jurists and businessmen. Many Jews now live on the city's Far North Side and in the northern suburbs.

Poles

Chicago is home to more than 1 million residents of Polish ancestry. They arrived in droves between 1870 and 1930, bringing a devotion to Catholicism that manifested itself in the building of elegant churches at the center of their communities. Over the years, the Poles moved northwest along **Milwaukee Avenue**, which remains in places a Polish commercial corridor. Today many Poles live in the Avondale neighborhood. Another wave of immigration followed the Solidarity movement in Poland in 1980.

Italians

Beginning in the 1880s, Italians flocked to Chicago. Hailing mostly from southern Italy, they sometimes transplanted entire villages to the New World. Newcomers were often at the mercy of unscrupulous padrones—labor agents—for railroad and construction work. As they settled in, however, many Italians opened small businesses, took up public service and went into stonecutting and masonry. **Little Italy**, on Chicago's Near West Side, celebrated its heyday in the 1920s; though disrupted by urban renewal, it remains a center of Italian culture today.

Greeks

Latecomers to Chicago, the Greeks arrived after the turn of the century to settle in the Delta on the **Near West Side**. Almost half of them were single men who came alone to earn

a living and return to Greece. Still, by the late 1970s, Chicago had the largest Hellenic population outside Greece. As restaurateurs, the Greeks have been extremely successful; by 1919 they already owned one out of three Chicago eating establishments.

African Americans

Blacks had lived in Chicago since its first settler, and their numbers grew with the city's reputation for abolitionism. Not until the 1910s, however, did they arrive en masse during the Great Migration, seeking jobs in an exodus from the increasing hardships of the rural South. The most populous "black belt" developed along the **Near South Side**. At its heart, Bronzeville—"the Harlem of Chicago"—pulsed with life, its lively restaurants, cabarets and theaters were the incubators of the new Chicago-style blues. Gradually, competition with whites for work and housing created conflict; at the same time, prejudice and racism stunted the progress of blacks attempting to escape the ghetto. The advent of public housing in the 1940s relieved the worst of the slums, but institutionalized overcrowding in African-American neighborhoods. In 2000 the Chicago Housing Authority enacted a plan to transform the city's dangerous high-rise public housing enclaves into scattered site and mixed income developments. At the same time, a growing middle class, inheritors of the considerable legacy of Chicago's early African-American professionals and entrepreneurs, is dispersing throughout the metropolitan area, somewhat relieving the city's reputation for segregation.

Hispanics

Under the broad rubric "Hispanic" exists a tremendous divergence of experience. Mexican immigration began in earnest around 1916, as the railroads and steel mills recruited workers to make up for slackening European immigration in the face of World War I. Combined, the **Pilsen** and Little Village neighborhoods are today home to the largest Mexican-American population in the

Chicago SummerDance

© City of Chicago/GRC

region. Young Puerto Ricans, seeking a chance at prosperity on the mainland, are among the poorest Chicagoans, while Cubans, who first came in 1959 as political rather than economic refugees, have met with greater success. Central and South Americans are now increasing the numbers—and diversity—of Chicago's Hispanic community.

Asians

Located south of the Loop, **Chinatown** is the city's oldest extant Asian neighborhood, established in 1912 by Chinese businessmen when the existing downtown enclave became overcrowded. By the 1920s Filipinos and Japanese had also settled in the city. The greatest influx of Asian immigrants began in the 1960s and 70s, largely Southeast Asian refugees who established New Chinatown along **Argyle Street** on the North Side. Farther north, along **Devon Avenue**, Asian Indians and Pakistanis have developed a bustling commercial corridor and many of the city's Koreans have settled in Albany Park.

ECONOMY

Chicago's economy has been shaped by its location at the nexus of the great inland waterways and at the heart of the nation's rich agricultural midsection. Throughout the 19C, as the central marketplace and entrepôt for the bounty of Midwestern farms and fields,

Chicago achieved its legendary status as "wheat stacker, hog butcher, and freight handler to the world," in the words of American writer Carl Sandburg. Still the most important railroad-freight hub in North America, the international center of futures trading and a major producer of food products, the Chicago metropolitan area cultivates roots in its economic past, while a transforming service economy propels the city into the global economy of the 21C.

FROM GRAIN TO BRAIN

The features that made Chicago a funnel for the foodstuffs of the Midwest —location and accessibility—also led to its growth as an industrial center of the Western world. The earliest industries were closely related to agriculture and husbandry: milling, tanning, woodworking and food processing. After the Civil War, the city began to expand its industrial base, as big steel, heavy manufacturing and meat-packing came to dominate its economy.

European immigrants flocked in by the thousands hoping for employment with giant United States Steel, International Harvester or the Union Stock Yards, or any of the hundreds of factories that lined the river and encircled the central business district. By 1960 manufacturing accounted for more than one-third of local jobs, but the stockyards closed forever in 1971, and the steel industry

33

Made in Chicago

At the 1893 World's Columbian Exposition, Mayor Carter Harrison observed that Chicago "knows nothing that it fears to attempt, and thus far has found nothing that it cannot accomplish." Indeed the city's unofficial slogan—"I Will" —conveys the sense of purpose that built the following list of innovations.

Ferris wheel: George W. G. Ferris created a 264ft "bridge on an axle" for the Columbian Exposition. A modern rendition now dominates Navy Pier.

Skyscraper: William Le Baron Jenney designed the Home Insurance Building on LaSalle and Adams Streets around an iron-and-steel frame in 1884, thereby instituting the lineage of Chicago's 20C pride and joy, the Sears Tower.

Juvenile Court system: Established in 1899, this division of the Circuit Court of Cook County was the brainchild of Julia Lathrop, an associate of pioneering social worker Jane Addams.

Lie detector: Leonarde Keeler, an employee of the Scientific Crime Detection Laboratory (the nation's first) at Northwestern University, devised the Keeler Polygraph. His invention earned him a part in the 1948 film *Call Northside 777*.

Successful heart surgery: Dr. Daniel Hale Williams, the first African-American member of the American College of Surgeons, saved James Cornish's life by tying off a severed artery and suturing the heart sac after a barroom brawl in 1893.

Blood bank and trauma center: Cook County Hospital opened the nation's first blood bank in 1937 and the first trauma center in 1966.

Drugstore lunch counter: Faced with a cold winter and falling ice-cream sales, Myrtle Walgreen, wife of the drugstore's founder, began serving hot meals at their soda-fountain counter around 1909.

Ice-cream sundae: Around 1900, ice-cream-parlor owner Deacon Garwood circumvented temperance laws that forbade ice-cream sodas on Sundays by dishing up a concoction of ice cream and syrup he called a sundae.

Ovaltine, Twinkies, Cracker Jacks, Dove Bars: These popular sweets all originated in Chicago between 1893 and 1952.

Zipper: Called the "hookless fastener" when exhibited at the 1893 Columbian Exposition, the device would be dubbed "zipper" by the B. F. Goodrich Company, who used it on overshoes.

Roller skates: Levant M. Richardson made possible the modern roller skate when he invented the ball-bearing wheel in 1884.

Pinball: The automatic-game rage began in Chicago in 1930 with the ten-balls-for-a-nickel Whoopee Game.

fell victim to recession. In recent years, as companies downsize and the manufacturing base dwindles further, the city has come to rely more and more on a service economy—from the largest high-tech industries and accounting firms to the smallest shoeshine parlors —for its livelihood. Today the service sector— government, retail, transportation, hospitality, education, legal and medical— claims nearly 80 percent of the local work force. In the last decade, Chicago has aggressively sought to lure international corporate headquarters to the city, succeeding notably in 2001 with the Boeing Company.

City vs. Suburb
Another factor complicates regional economics: the relationship between the city proper, suburban Cook County and the collar counties, a symbiosis impossible to ignore. Many local employers have fled downtown for less expensive,

Elevated train over the Chicago River
© City of Chicago/GRC

more hospitable locations outside the city limits, creating thriving economic corridors in surrounding communities like Schaumburg and those of Du Page County. As a result, of the more than 4 million people at work in the metropolitan area, less than half are employed in the city. In the 2000s, as the downtown's residential population grows, retailers and other employers are considering city locations in a brighter light.

Commercial Crossroads

As the freight hub of North America, Chicago supports a complex network of railroad, trucking, waterborne shipping and air-freight services. The nation's major inland port, Chicago is connected to the Atlantic Ocean via the St. Lawrence Seaway—which opened in 1959—and to the Gulf of Mexico via the Sanitary & Ship Canal and the Mississippi River. Even with the decline of the steel industry, iron ore remains the largest volume commodity to enter the port aboard deep-draft carriers, and grain is still exported by water around the world. Two commercial airports serve the city: **Midway**, the city's original air terminal on the southwest side; and **O'Hare International**, the country's second-busiest airport (surpassed only by Hartsfield-Jackson Atlanta International Airport), which served nearly 44 million passengers in 2008. As the national hub of passenger rail travel, downtown's

Union Station serves some 6,000 Amtrak riders each day. On a local scale, the buses, subways and elevated trains of the largely urban Chicago Transit Authority traverse 2,500mi of road and track. A consortium of suburban rail lines known as Metra operates over 500mi of track in Illinois, as far north as Kenosha, Wisconsin, and southeast to South Bend, Indiana. Altogether, this integrated system of rail, elevated, subway and bus lines ferries nearly 2 million commuters to work and back each day, along with thousands of occasional riders.

Future Games

The **Chicago Board of Trade (CBOT)**, founded in 1848 and today the world's oldest and largest futures exchange, is a testament to Chicago's agrarian origins. Established to trade grain futures —bulk commodities bought and sold at a predetermined future time—in the days when 60 million bushels passed through the city each year, the CBOT now handles an array of commodities and financial futures. The **Chicago Mercantile Exchange (CME)**, historically the world's busiest market for perishable commodities such as pork bellies, now trades futures and options on agricultural commodities, interest rates, stock market indexes, energy, and foreign currency futures. In 1992 the exchange launched an electronic after-hours trading system to open up a truly global market. In 2006 CME traded 1.4 billion contracts, compared to 231 million just six years before. The following year, the CME merged with CBOT, creating the world's largest derivatives exchange (derivatives are contracts whose value is derived from the movement of other financial instruments, such as stocks and bonds). Now known collectively as the CME Group, this institution makes Chicago a world leader in futures trading.

The **Chicago Stock Exchange**, which opened in 1882, is the third most active stock exchange by volume in the US and the largest (also by volume) outside New York City.

Corporate Superlatives

A survey of the highest income-earning public corporations in Chicago reveals the area's diversified economic base. Included among the 57 Fortune 500 companies located in Chicago are retailer Sears Roebuck and Co., Sara Lee Corp., Motorola, Inc., Boeing, and United Airlines.

The national drugstore chain Walgreen Co. and McDonald's Corp., the nation's largest seller of burgers, maintain headquarters outside Chicago. Chicago has also ranked second to New York as a publishing center since the turn of the century, specializing largely in encyclopedias and educational materials.

Conventions and Tourism

The City of Big Shoulders ranks as the convention capital of the US. From the mammoth National Restaurant Show to such smaller, specialized events as the conference for the Royal Order of Jesters, this $8-billion-a-year industry brings more than 3 million visitors annually to the city. The centerpiece of Chicago's convention business is **McCormick Place**, the country's largest exhibition facility, which hosted 50 trade shows and 44 meetings in 2009. After a $987-million expansion completed in 1997 and another in 2008, which added more than 700,000sq ft to its capacity, the four-building complex today offers 2.6 million sq ft of exhibit space. In addition to business travelers, Chicago welcomed nearly 34 million domestic and international visitors in 2008.

Ivory Towers

Among Chicago's 86 colleges and universities, the city boasts the top graduate fine-arts program in the nation at the School of the Art Institute of Chicago; the University of Chicago's renowned law, medical, MBA, music and graduate programs; and the well-respected Medill School of Journalism at Northwestern. The University of Illinois at Chicago has the largest enrollment with some 26,000 students, followed by Northwestern (its main campus is located in suburban Evanston) with an enrollment of 16,300.

Northwestern University, Evanston

Chicago's North Shore CVB

History

A young city in the scheme of American history, Chicago nonetheless catapulted to critical importance in only a few decades. From the edge of the wilderness to the heart of the nation, it capitalized on its strategic location to become the country's trail and rail hub. After Chicago's remarkable recovery from the devastating fire in 1871, the city went on to host a glorious world's fair only 20 years later. Indeed, this city of the "I Will" spirit has always loved a challenge—from reversing the flow of the river to building the world's tallest skyscraper—and its history proves just that.

TIME LINE
EARLY HISTORY, EXPLORERS

The swampy juncture of the sluggish Chicago River and Lake Michigan was valued by Native Americans and 17C French traders as a link between the Great Lakes and Mississippi River Valley settlements.

After the US gained control of the area in the late 18C, the potential for a canal between Lake Michigan and the Illinois River led to the establishment of Fort Dearborn. It was around this fort that the fledgling settlement of Chicago arose.

c.AD 1000 — Native Americans in Illinois begin to form larger, more permanent settlements and elaborate burial mounds under the influence of the Cahokia civilization near St. Louis.

c.1500 — The prevalence of bison causes Illini tribes to adopt a more mobile lifestyle and traverse the Chicago Portage between Lake Michigan and the Illinois River Valley.

c.1660 — Iroquois tribes begin to raid Illini settlements in northeastern Illinois. By 1800, Potawatomi replace the Illini in the region.

1673 — French explorer **Louis Jolliet** and missionary **Jacques Marquette** encounter the Grand Village of the Illinois near Starved Rock and are directed through the Chicago Portage to Lake Michigan. A year later Marquette winters at Chicago, dying the following spring in Michigan.

1779 — Trader **Jean Baptiste Point du Sable** becomes the first permanent settler of Chicago, building a cabin and trading post on the north side of the Chicago River.

1803 — US soldiers build **Fort Dearborn** on the south side of the Chicago River.

1812 — Frontier tensions spurred by war with England lead to a massacre by Potawatomi natives of 52 settlers fleeing Fort Dearborn.

1816 — The Indian Boundary, securing a canal corridor from Chicago to the Illinois River, is established by treaty. Fort Dearborn is rebuilt after the War of 1812.

1830 — The Illinois & Michigan Canal Commission hires surveyor James Thompson to plat two towns along the canal route, Chicago and Ottawa.

1832 — Native tribes are expelled from Illinois following the suppression of an uprising led by **Chief Black Hawk**.

1833 — About 400 residents incorporate the village of Chicago. The first balloon-frame structure, St. Mary's Church, is built from pre-sawn boards and nails.

INSTANT CITY

Canal construction turns Chicago from a frontier outpost into a boomtown, bringing waves of Yankee migrants,

Irish canal workers and skilled Germans fleeing persecution after the failed 1848 revolutions in Europe. The city grows too fast for its own good, tardily adding sewers, parks and other basic amenities while culture languishes in the pursuit of fast money in real estate, lumber, agriculture, steel and livestock. Innovations like the grain elevator and refrigerated railroad car make Chicago the conduit for the nation's cereal and meat products. The city mushrooms from fewer than 4,000 persons to over 300,000 in less than 35 years.

1836 — Chicago is in the fever grip of land speculation as construction begins on July 4 on the **Illinois & Michigan Canal**.

1837 — 4,000 citizens incorporate the City of Chicago on March 4. A nationwide panic deflates local real-estate speculation and eventually slows canal construction.

1847 — The agricultural boom in the Illinois countryside, where rich prairie soil produces some of the nation's highest yields, leads **Cyrus Hall McCormick** to move his reaper factory from Cincinnati to Chicago. Within two years, he is expanding to fill 1,500 orders per year.

1848 — A boatload of sugar and other goods traverses the newly opened Illinois & Michigan Canal en route from New Orleans to New York. Agricultural goods begin to flow east from Chicago, and the Chicago Board of Trade is created to regulate the grain trade. Chicago's first railroad, the Chicago and Galena Union, inaugurates service on a 10mi route.

1852 — The city allows the Illinois Central Railroad to run tracks along the lakefront in exchange for building a breakwater in order to prevent erosion.

1855 — In the **Lager Beer Riots**, immigrant Germans protest Mayor Levi Boone's temperance edicts, which prohibit the drinking of beer on Sunday, labeling that action "un-American."

1856 — **Chicago Historical Society** is created. US Senator Stephen A. Douglas founds the first University of Chicago in alliance with the Baptist church.

1860 — The new Republican Party nominates **Abraham Lincoln** for president in Chicago's Wigwam Hall, built for the occasion at Lake and Market (now Wacker Dr.) streets. Chicago is the center of the world's largest railroad network, which totals almost 3,000mi of track.

1865 — Civil War ends. **The Union Stock Yards** are organized on Chicago's South Side to consolidate the city's slaughterhouses around a central railroad yard. Marshall Field and Levi Leiter partner in a dry-goods store that will become Marshall Field & Co. (now Macy's).

1867 — Chicago labor leaders begin the struggle for the eight-hour workday, choosing May 1 to celebrate the contributions of labor to the American economy.

1869 — Chicago's Parks and Boulevards System is created—over 1,600 acres of green space ringing the city in a 28mi loop. The three-part system is designed by Frederick Law Olmsted and Calvert Vaux, William Le Baron Jenney, and Swain Nelson. The **Chicago Water Tower** is

Engraving of The Burning of Chicago (c.1883) by R.H. Stoddard

Photo: ©Constance McGuire/iStockphoto.com

constructed to regulate the pressure of water pumped from Lake Michigan into the city.

THE FIRE

The devastation of the Chicago Fire appears catastrophic in the destruction of homes and businesses throughout the central area, but the city's enviable water and rail connections—and the majority of its industries—remain unscorched, and rebuilding commences immediately. Chicago's phenomenal growth continues as the population triples in the decade after the fire. The fire also draws architects from across the country, who eventually develop the Chicago school. By the 1880s up to 10,000 immigrants arrive in the city each week, leading to health problems and overcrowding.

1871 — On October 8, the **Great Chicago Fire** starts in the barn behind Mrs. O'Leary's house on DeKoven Street. For two days, the fire burns north and east, destroying the whole of downtown Chicago and much of the North Side. Some 300 die and a third of the city's population of 335,000 is left without shelter.

1877 — The Great Railroad Strike affects Chicago as 30 workers are killed in the "Battle of the Viaduct" on Halsted Street.

1879 — The Chicago Academy of Design (founded in 1866) is reorganized to include a school and a museum, the **Art Institute of Chicago**. In 1885 the Institute constructs its first edifice (since demolished), designed by Burnham & Root, at Michigan Avenue and Van Buren Street.

1880 — George Pullman hires architect Solon S. Beman to design the town and railroad-car factories of **Pullman** near Lake Calumet.

1884 — The first steel-frame building, the 10-story Home Insurance Building, is erected in the Loop, designed by **William Le Baron Jenney**.

1886 — Striking workers meet to hear the mayor and other speakers on May 4 in Haymarket Square. As the meeting disperses, 170 policemen arrive. Someone throws a bomb, killing seven policemen. Eight anarchist labor leaders are brought to trial in an event that garners worldwide attention, but Chicago civic leaders and newspapers condemn the anarchists. Four are eventually hanged and one commits suicide while three remain in jail. The incident becomes known as the **Haymarket Riot**.

1889 — Social reformers Jane Addams and Ellen Gates Starr found Hull-House on the Near West Side to aid immigrants, who outnumber Chicago's US-born population. The **Auditorium Building** by Adler & Sullivan is completed.

WORLD'S FAIR, WORLD CITY

The city determines to prove that it is not an uncultured hog town by inviting the world to the largest party of the 19C, the World's Columbian Exposition of 1893. The fair's gleaming Neoclassical buildings celebrate the progress of the American Republic in sciences and arts, creating a seemingly perfect "White City." The success of the fair engenders the "City Beautiful" movement nationwide. Chicago continues to feed the East and reap the West as more people keep migrating across the continent.

1891–92 — Theodore Thomas founds the **Chicago Symphony Orchestra**. The **University of Chicago** opens in Hyde Park thanks to the beneficence of oil magnate John D. Rockefeller. Local artists form the **Little Room Salon**.

1893 — The **World's Columbian Exposition** opens in Jackson Park, drawing 27 million visitors to the 650-acre "White City" over the summer. The adjacent Midway features the first Ferris wheel and the racy "hootchie-kootchie" dancing of Little Egypt.

The city's first elevated train brings visitors to the fair from the Loop. Illinois governor **John Peter Altgeld** pardons the three surviving Haymarket defendants, earning the enmity of business and anti-immigrant forces. The Field Columbian Museum, later the **Field Museum of Natural History**, is founded.

1894 — In the midst of an economic depression, the **Pullman Strike** disrupts railroad traffic nationwide as workers suffer layoffs and wage cuts in George Pullman's company town. President Grover Cleveland sends federal troops to break the strike. **Clarence Darrow** defends the strikers in a trial that leads to the end of the company town.

1897 — The **Union Loop Elevated Railroad** is completed, girdling downtown with steel.

1900 — The **Chicago Sanitary and Ship Canal** opens, permanently reversing the flow of the Chicago River. By 1914 it will replace the Illinois & Michigan Canal as the city's primary shipping route. The Union Stock Yards' hundred companies employ 30,000 workers.

1905 — **Robert S. Abbott** founds the Chicago Defender to serve the city's growing African-American community.

1906 — **Upton Sinclair** publishes his novel The Jungle. His descriptions of the meat-packing industry lead to the reforms of the Pure Food and Drug Act.

1909 — **Daniel Burnham** and **Edward Bennett** release their **Plan of Chicago**, which provides a Classical template for the city's future development. Frank Lloyd Wright's quintessential Prairie-style Robie House is completed in Hyde Park.

1912–19 — The **Chicago Literary Renaissance**, a school of social realism in literature, flourishes in Chicago. Margaret Anderson founds the *Little Review*; Edgar Lee Masters' *Spoon River Anthology* and Carl Sandburg's *Chicago Poems* are published. Theodore Dreiser and Sherwood Anderson release their early novels.

1919 — A **race riot** leaves 40 dead and hundreds injured on the city's South Side. The Chicago White Sox lose the World Series, and a year later eight players are banned for conspiring with gamblers to "throw" the series.

PROGRESS AND PROHIBITION

Civic leaders work to transform downtown Chicago into a modern civic center with the creation of Wacker Drive, North Michigan Avenue and the museums of Grant Park. But the Roaring Twenties leave Chicago with a permanent scar, as bootlegging gangs commit hundreds of murders in their attempts to control the illegal liquor business. **Al Capone** becomes Chicago's most notorious figure, heading a large criminal syndicate that survives his imprisonment.

1922 — The *Chicago Tribune* announces a worldwide competition to design its new skyscraper on North Michigan Avenue.

1924 — Approximately 20,000 illegal retail liquor outlets operate in Chicago. Bootlegger Dion O'Banion is killed in his North Side flower shop as Al Capone seeks to expand his empire.

1929 — Al Capone's men gun down seven members of the rival Bugs Moran gang on North Clark Street in the **St. Valentine's Day Massacre**. Capone, now a media celebrity, earns roughly $50 million a year bootlegging.

1931 — Al Capone is sent to prison for tax evasion. He is released eight years later, his body and brain wracked by syphilis.

1933 — An assassin's bullet intended for President-elect Franklin Delano Roosevelt kills Chicago mayor Anton Cermak in Miami. The mayor's office falls to **Ed Kelly**, who with Pat Nash founds the city's Democratic political machine, which dominates for the next 50 years.

1933–34 — Chicago's **Century of Progress International Exposition** draws millions to a new lakefront site inspired by the Burnham Plan. The fair focuses on the innovations of the modern era. The **Museum of Science and Industry** opens in Jackson Park. Federal agents shoot to death Public Enemy Number One John Dillinger outside the Biograph Theater.

1937 — Police kill 10 striking steelworkers and sympathizers on Memorial Day as they march on the Republic Steel plant in South Chicago.

MID- TO LATE-20C

Chicago's population peaks in 1950, and the ensuing decades witness large-scale expressway and urban-renewal projects that mark the triumph of the automobile. Chicago becomes the center of the nation's airline system at Midway and

Al Capone (left) with U.S. Marshall Laubenheimer in the 1930s

© Imagestate/Tips Images

O'Hare airports. The social turbulence of the 1960s peaks at the Democratic National Convention in 1968. In the 1970s Chicago declines as its industrial base bleeds away and an increasing number of white middle-class residents move to the suburbs.

The city's new ethnic mix elects the first African-American mayor in 1983, while Chicago's continuing role as a financial and commercial center spurs new urban redevelopment efforts.

1942 — Enrico Fermi and a team of University of Chicago scientists create the first controlled, self-sustaining **nuclear reaction** underneath the school's abandoned football stands.

1949 — Construction begins on 860–880 N. Lake Shore Drive by **Ludwig Mies van der Rohe**.

1955 — **Richard J. Daley** is elected mayor of Chicago for the first of six times. He will die in office in 1976. O'Hare Airport opens on the northwestern fringe of the city.

1968 — The assassination of **Dr. Martin Luther King, Jr.** leads to widespread rioting on the South and West sides. In August demonstrators converge on the **Democratic National Convention**, provoking a violent response from police and US National Guard forces. Confrontations in Grant and Lincoln parks resound with the chant, "The whole world is watching." The **Chicago Seven** trial the following year holds radicals and astudent leaders responsible for the melees.

1971 — The Union Stock Yards close. McCormick Place Convention Center, the largest in the world, opens on the south lakefront.

1974 — **Sears Tower** is topped off as the tallest building in the world.

1979 — A January blizzard dumps a record amount of snow and freezes the city for over a month. City Hall's unpreparedness and lack of response to the snow lead to the ouster of Mayor Michael Bilandic by **Jane Byrne**, Chicago's first female mayor.

1983 — **Harold Washington** becomes Chicago's first African-American mayor. A city council majority of 29 white aldermen struggles for power during three years of bitter "council wars."

1987 — Mayor Washington dies seven months after his resounding re-election, leading to a traumatic 10-hour city council session that elects **Eugene Sawyer** as mayor.

1988 — Lights for night baseball are installed at **Wrigley Field**.

CONTEMPORARY CHICAGO

A century after it first sought the world's approval, Chicago again seeks recognition as a world-class city. Still the fulcrum of American commerce, the city is redeveloping from within, transforming industrial land into middle-class neighborhoods, solidifying its role as a financial center and convention venue, and building its reputation as a tourist destination and cultural metropolis.

1989 — **Richard M. Daley**, son of Richard J. Daley, is elected mayor.

1991 — **Michael Jordan** and the **Chicago Bulls** win the National Basketball Association championship for the first time, and proceed to triumph again in 1992, 1993, 1996, 1997 and 1998.

1992 — A company driving pilings into the Chicago River pierces a portion of the city's old freight-tunnel system, causing flooding in basements throughout the Loop and the evacuation of the entire downtown in the middle of a business day.

1994 — The first **World Cup** soccer tournament in the US opens in Chicago with a 1-0 victory by Germany over Bolivia.

1995 — A summer heat wave kills more than 700 Chicagoans as the temperature reaches 106°F.

1996 — The Democratic National Convention returns to Chicago. The Petronas

Towers in Kuala Lumpur, Malaysia, surpass the Sears Tower as tallest buildings in the world.

1997 — Field Museum of Natural History purchases a Tyrannosaurus rex skeleton for $8.3 million. *Chicago Tribune* columnist **Mike Royko** (b. 1932) dies.

1998 — Long-time Chicago Cubs broadcaster **Harry Caray**, known for leading home crowds in singing "Take Me Out to the Ball Game," dies at age 77. The Chicago Bulls win their sixth NBA championship in eight years.

1999 — Michael Jordan retires from basketball in January.

2000 — Residents move into historic and modern homes at Fort Sheridan, the decommissioned North Shore military base.

2003 — In an expected overnight action, Mayor Daley closes downtown airport Meigs Field. Its lakefront site had been controversial since its 50-year lease expired in 1996.

Soldier Field, home of the NFL Chicago Bears, completes a $632 million facelift. The new 70,000-seat stadium is built inside the shell of the historic 1926 structure.

2004 — Stunning, $475 million Millennium Park opens in downtown Chicago, the centerpiece of a downtown renaissance for residents, visitors, and businesses alike.

2005 — Chicago White Sox win the World Series for the first time in 88 years in a four-game sweep against the Houston Astros.

2006 — Macy's replaces Marshall Field's, Chicago's 153-year-old department store, taking over its State Street building and all other branches of the beloved franchise.

2007 — Mayor Richard M. Daley wins re-election to tie his father for a record-breaking sixth term.
Located in its landmark Louis Sullivan building on State Street since 1903, Carson Pirie Scott's flagship store closes in March.

2008 — Chicago resident and Illinois senator Barack Obama is elected 44th President of the United States. The President delivers his acceptance speech in Grant Park.

2009 — Illinois governor Rob Blagojevich is ousted from office after being convicted of abusing his powers. He tried to sell the Senate seat vacated by Barack Obama after Obama was elected President.

2010 — The Chicago Blackhawks NHL hockey team take back the Stanley Cup for the first time since 1961.
Two Chicago restaurants win coveted James Beard awards: Koren Grieveson of Avec win the title of Best Chef Great Lakes; while the Outstanding Service Award goes to Alinea, owned by cutting-edge chef Grant Achatz.

A POLITICAL PAST

Chicagoans who travel abroad are used to the reaction that the mention of their home city usually elicits. The city's historic reputation for vice and corruption, epitomized by the machine-gun-toting gangsters of the 1920s, casts a long shadow over those other ingredients that today make it a world-class metropolis. This dual nature defines Chicago in all of its aspects, particularly politics. The city struts its gruff frontier reputation while successfully cultivating the trappings of class and sophistication. In city politics, the simultaneous tension and symbiosis between vice and virtue have created the inextricable tangle of good government and power politics that ultimately gave rise to the country's most enduring political machine: a mighty Democratic Party exerting influence and dispensing favors to keep the city running smoothly. Indeed, the successful among Chicago's 45 mayors have understood that the electorate's primary concern is the efficient delivery of city services—from garbage pickup to safety on the streets. In 1837 Chicago's first mayor, **William Butler Ogden**, used his own wealth to finance city improvements and even bailed out the city on his personal credit when financial panic struck.

POLITICAL PRELUDE

As the city's population soared in two decades to over 93,000, the adolescent boomtown seethed with prostitution, gambling and crime. Subsequent mayors—largely symbolic leaders with little real authority—turned a blind eye to the flourishing netherworld, but 6ft 6in "Long John" Wentworth burst into office in 1857 determined to purge the vice districts, perhaps the first effort at reform in Chicago. In a dramatic move, he and a posse literally pulled down the ramshackle brothels, saloons and gambling dens situated in a seedy patch by the river known as the "Sands." Though demonstrative, his other attempts to eradicate such areas had little effect. Chicago's underworld had already taken sturdy root, and it would be for later mayors to discover the value of compromise.

THE SMOKE CLEARS

As Chicago reinvented itself in the aftermath of the Great Fire of 1871, the breach between wealth and poverty widened, enhancing the city's split personality. Growth continued unabated, dictating a personal kind of politics conducted in the neighborhoods. Vast inner-city immigrant populations represented powerful voting blocs, and ward bosses were quick to exchange jobs and

Coined in Chicago

Along with colorful characters, Chicago's world of politics and crime has spawned some picturesque phraseology as well.

Underworld: Civic leaders of the 1850s elevated Chicago out of the marshland and resurfaced the "mudtropolis" with earth and stone. Crime lord Roger Plant and his gang of roughs took control of the resulting maze of tunnels, underground byways and caves that stretched from Wells Street to the South Branch of the Chicago River, creating the first "underworld" crime empire.

Smoke-filled room: Harry Daugherty, campaign manager for President Warren G. Harding in 1920, predicted that the Republican National Convention in Chicago would be decided by a small group of men sitting "around a table in a smoke-filled room."

"There's a sucker born every minute": Sometimes attributed to P. T. Barnum, local legend claims it was the answer given by Mike McDonald, 1890s crime boss, to his partner who worried about attracting enough business to their many gaming tables.

Public enemies: Eye-catching title of the list—topped by Al Capone—of 28 gangsters given to the press by Col. Henry Barrett Chamberlain, operating director of the Chicago Crime Commission.

Mickey Finn: Owner of the Lone Star Saloon and Palm Garden in the late 1890s, who concocted two knockout drinks to render patrons unconscious so that Mickey and his wife could rob them.

One-way ride: In the 1920s gangster Hymie Weiss recognized that the secrecy and security of late-model cars offered the perfect venue for mobile murders. When hood Steve Wisniewski hijacked a beer truck, Weiss dispatched him on the first one-way ride.

other favors for their support. Nurtured by this ward-by-ward spoils system, the "Machine" began to incubate.

After the fire, the Democratic Party gained momentum, propelled by the votes of the huge foreign-born population. With the election in 1879 of **Carter Harrison I**, a flamboyant Kentuckian with empathy for the working man and a live-and-let-live philosophy, Chicago had a modern mayor who understood his constituents' practical needs. His appeal crossed class and ethnic lines and his belief in personal liberties endeared him to the city's considerable underworld. He served four consecutive terms between 1879 and 1887, only to be assassinated in 1893 by a disgruntled office seeker on the heels of his proudest accomplishment: serving a fifth term as Chicago's "World's Fair Mayor" during the Columbian Exposition.

Despite his tolerance of powerful gambling kingpin **Michael McDonald**, Harrison earned the devotion of the electorate as well as a reputation for honesty, even among his detractors. Meanwhile, "King Mike" presided over a wide-ranging empire—which included much of the county board, the police department, the Democratic Party and the Cook County sheriff, along with bunco artists and con men—from offices in the largest of his gambling emporiums, a lavish downtown establishment known as The Store. In years to come, Mike McDonald's most famous heir would be Al Capone.

FROM SALOON TO CITY HALL

Harrison's tolerant administration—and the five intermittent terms served by his son, Carter Harrison II, between 1897 and 1915—achieved a precarious balance between vice and virtue that later mayors would envy. Still, power resided in the wards and the saloons where the likes of Aldermen **"Bathhouse" John**

Coughlin and **Michael "Hinky Dink" Kenna** held sway. Their rollicking First Ward included the infamous Levee, the city's sprawling underbelly and home of the Everleigh Club, the most elite of 200 brothels in the district. Not satisfied with the take from protection money they earned in the Levee, the two staged annual First Ward balls to line the coffers of the ward organization. To these drunken brawls came prostitutes and politicians, policemen and aldermen, all players in an absurd parody of city government.

By the 1890s aldermen were learning that more profit and long-term reward might be garnered in collusion with businessmen than on the streets of the Levee. Utilities wishing to lay cable and traction magnates seeking rights of way along city streets paid the aldermen thousands of dollars in "boodle" annually for favorable votes in council. In return, Chicago gained a modern transit system with electrified trains, and the burgeoning Machine rose from the saloons to City Hall.

In the meantime, the face of organized crime in Chicago was changing, developing into a vicious and insidious network supervised by the likes of Johnny Torrio, "Big Jim" Colosimo, Al Capone and their rivals. Whereas gambling had been the mainstay of the Victorian warlords, the gangsters of the Prohibition era made bootlegging their stock in trade, and by 1920 the "Outfit" had a lock on the city that would last for decades. **Alphonse Capone** initiated the most infamous six years in Chicago's history when he succeeded Johnny Torrio as head of Chicago's syndicate in 1925. Capone eliminated his rivals in a bloody gang war that culminated in the 1929 St. Valentine's Day Massacre, when hit men rubbed out several of gangster Bugs Moran's associates in a North Side garage. Between 1925 and 1931, 439 gangland slayings rocked Chicago, most of which were never solved. Indeed, bombastic mayor **William Hale "Big Bill" Thompson**, indebted to Capone for political and financial support, coddled the mob, and some Chicagoans even considered the ruthless Capone a folk hero. Although brought down by tenacious federal agent Eliot Ness for income tax evasion in 1931, Capone had established a dynasty that would last well beyond his death from syphilis in 1947.

THE MODERN MACHINE

Throughout the 1920s, "new-breed" Democrats had been working to create an organization with widespread influence over all of city government. Their quest to institutionalize the Machine coalesced under the leadership of **Anton J. Cermak**, who succeeded

Crowd at the Democratic National Convention in Grant Park, 29th August 1968

© Bettmann/Corbis

Jimmy Carter and Richard J. Daley (right) at the Illinois State Democratic Convention in Chicago, 9th September 1976

Thompson in 1931. Cermak built a revolutionary multi-ethnic coalition unified by a powerful party organization. He advocated reform, efficiency and economy, and backed up his promises with the strength of that organization. Even though an assassin's bullet meant for President-elect Franklin Delano Roosevelt cut short his term in 1933, Anton J. Cermak had paved the way for the legendary Richard J. Daley.

In most cities the Great Depression marked the end of urban self-sufficiency. Local organizations could no longer control money, policy and jobs because of the increasing presence of the federal government and unions. But the Chicago Machine gained momentum, expanding its base of support as far as Washington, DC, where leaders recognized the importance of a friendly Chicago mayor. At the same time, organized crime generated considerable income for the Machine through gambling and protection. The party courted and won the support of the city's increasing African-American population, only to stumble later over issues of open housing and desegregation.

The Machine hit its stride under **Richard J. Daley**, "Hizzoner da Mare," between 1955 and his death in 1976. A consummate administrator and career politician, Daley, like Cermak, believed in good government through party politics. He brought the rambunctious city council

under control, consolidated the power of the mayor's office and extended his reach to state and nation. He engaged professionals to streamline the system. His "City that Works" did so because Daley understood how to exchange influence and favors to get things done. The stronger and more centralized his office, the greater his clout.

By the late 1960s, however, chinks had begun to show in the armor. Daley grew more conservative, his organization less able to please and appease the city's increasingly disparate communities split by racial and political strife. Open housing marches, riots following the assassination of Dr. Martin Luther King, Jr., violence surrounding the 1968 Democratic National Convention, and the mayhem of the Days of Rage the following summer pushed the Machine to the limit. Still, Daley prevailed through a tumultuous time when other big-city mayors failed. He cultivated a reassuring civic stability that played well among a largely conservative electorate confused and somewhat threatened by rapidly changing times, and he delivered city services, thereby guaranteeing loyalty. The period following Daley's sudden death in 1976 could not have provided more of a contrast. Disputes over his successor set the tone as African-American politicians and their constituents—led by the **Rev. Jesse Jackson**—clamored for recognition, and Poles, feeling too

Spring in Millennium Park

© Patrick L. Pyszka/City of Chicago/GRC

long estranged from City Hall themselves, put forth their own candidates. Ultimately, mild-mannered **Michael Bilandic**, a Bridgeport alderman, came to office first as acting mayor and then by election in 1977. Although a competent mayor, he lacked Daley's ability to consolidate power, and the factions that had begun to form in the party gained strength.

It was a January blizzard in 1979 that sounded the death knell for the old Machine. Unable to liberate the city from its snowy grip, Mayor Bilandic succumbed to a challenge from the irrepressible, reform-minded **Jane Byrne**, Chicago's first woman mayor. With power leaking from the mayor's office, the next few years passed in a tumultuous free-for-all fueled by strikes and a difficult economy. When **Harold Washington**, the city's first African-American mayor, took office in 1983, the rhetoric turned shrill and racist, leading to a standoff between mayor and council that immobilized the city. Promising peacemaking efforts that marked Washington's second term were cut short by his untimely death in 1987. The furor finally quieted in the 1990s.

In 1989 Illinois Senator **Richard M. Daley** was elected mayor. At first indebted to his father's legacy, Daley has emerged as a no-nonsense mayor of moderation. He presides over a multicultural city council (one alderman for each of 50 wards) whose attentions have shifted from parochial infighting to the staggering concerns of all American cities: revenue generation, a growing underclass and gang violence, a deteriorating infrastructure and economic challenge from the suburbs. And, since the terrorist attacks in New York in 2001, there have been new concerns about urban security.

In 2007, Daley won his sixth term in office, though patronage scandals and spending criticism have come close in recent years to bursting the bubble. He has worked hard to make Chicago a model green city, and he promotes tirelessly the city's public schools, culture, music and beauty—he presided over the construction of Millennium Park—to help attract visitors and enrich the lives of residents. His enthusiastic support won Chicago the honor of vying with other world-class cities to host the 2016 Summer Olympics. Unfortunately, despite Daley's efforts, Chicago lost the Olympic bid to Rio de Janeiro, Brazil. What *Time* magazine called Daley's "imperial" governing style might account in part for the recent plummet of his approval rating to an all-time low of 35 percent. But should Daley remain in office beyond December 2010, he will become the longest-serving mayor in Chicago history (a record currently held by his father, the late Richard J. Daley).

Art and Culture

Chicago's vibrant character imbues every one of the arts as they have evolved here. Modern American architecture, of course, arose from the ashes of the Fire. Swaggering Chicago-style theater, the wail of the blues, the sardonic world of improvisational comedy and even television programs and movies feed on the city's rough-cut persona. Dance, though a slow starter, has truly come into its own since the mid-1990s. The historic tension between the city's origins in industry and commerce and its early aspirations to gentility plays a major role in the city's visual arts and their exhibition. Chicago's literary legacy bears the grit and growl of muckraking journalism. And nowhere is the city's muscle-bound image more apparent than in the fanaticism of its sports fans.

PERFORMING ARTS
THEATER

Some 200 theater companies throughout Chicago present everything from sweeping Broadway musicals like *Oklahoma!* and *Wicked* to the classics of Shakespeare and Tennessee Williams. But Chicago's native theatrical tradition has little to do with such crowd pleasing. The gritty edge of "off-Loop" theater, perhaps best exemplified by the work of local playwright **David Mamet** *(American Buffalo, Glengarry Glen Ross)* and the acting of John Malkovich and William L. Petersen, is in part the legacy of the **Hull-House Players**. Conceived by pioneering social worker Jane Addams as part of her community work at the turn of the century, the Players were reactivated in the revolutionary 1960s, introducing avant-garde theater to Chicago with plays by Edward Albee, Samuel Beckett, Athol Fugard and their contemporaries. Featuring difficult subjects staged and acted with raw intensity, Hull-House productions prepared audiences to appreciate what would evolve into the visceral Chicago style. Small, innovative theaters with elemental names—Body Politic, Organic, and Remains—flourished in the ensuing years, fueled by enthusiastic audiences, generous donors and an energetic crop of young performers, writers and directors. As the Chicago style matures at theaters like Steppenwolf in an atmosphere of more restrained funding, scores of upstart, itinerant companies work to remain inventive and solvent, continuing to experiment with new and often outrageous approaches to stagecraft.

DANCE

Although most of the performing arts have long found expression here, Chicago has been a slow starter when it

Steppenwolf Theatre

© City of Chicago/GRC

49

The Second City

© City of Chicago/GRC

comes to dance. In spite of the efforts of such dance greats as Ruth Page and Maria Tallchief Paschen, traditional ballet companies initially failed to gain a solid toehold in the city. **Hubbard Street Dance Chicago** truly put the city on the terpsichorean map. Founded in 1977 by Lou Conte, the company pioneered a hybrid, thoroughly American style that incorporates the excitement and energy of jazz with the precision of ballet. In 1990 choreographer Twyla Tharp chose Hubbard Street as a repository for her small-scale works. in 1995, artistic director Gerald Arpino moved his **Joffrey Ballet** from New York City to Chicago. The company concluded its 52nd season in 2009 and now has a permanent home at Joffrey Tower in the heart of the Loop. Other notable Chicago dance ensembles include Ballet Chicago, Gus Giordano Jazz Dance Chicago, and the Joel Hall Dancers. Muntu Dance Theatre presents traditional African dance, and in the 2000s flowered a variety of ethnic, folk, liturgical and street style dance troupes.

"Chicago is the archetypal American city …
For visitors who are interested in a city that's really America, this would be the one to visit."

Studs Terkel

COMEDY

The twin muse of Chicago's dark dramatic style is the satirical, incredulous "improv" comedy that has shaped the national sense of humor since the television show *Saturday Night Live* (SNL) took to the air in 1975. Also vestiges of Hull-House, improvisational exercises were employed by recreational counselors there to help immigrants adjust to their new life. Modern progenitor of the style, **The Second City** was founded in Hyde Park in 1955 as the Compass Players and today thrives in Old Town. Scores of comedians started there, including Alan Alda, Elaine May, Ed Asner, Ann Meara, Joan Rivers and a galaxy of SNL stars led by John Belushi, Dan Aykroyd and Gilda Radner. Nightclubs throughout the city and suburbs feature other improv groups and stand-up comics, both known and new.

VISUAL ARTS
A MATTER OF TASTE

The World's Columbian Exposition of 1893 did much to establish an artistic aesthetic that prevailed in the city for 40 years. The Art Institute of Chicago had been organized in 1879, and its president Charles L. Hutchinson strongly believed in the power of great art to uplift the human spirit and counter civic and commercial corruption. He also felt that a respected art museum would elevate Chicago's image.

In the same vein, the hardworking industrial city hoped that the glittering Beaux-Arts World's Fair would appear sophisticated and genteel to the rest of the world, proving conclusively that though their money had been made in railroads and meatpacking, Chicago's elite had also developed considerable taste. More than 10,000 art objects crowded the huge Palace of Fine Arts, most of them European works of conservative appeal. Volume and predictability, it seems, equaled culture.

Perhaps the most representative local artist of the day was sculptor **Lorado Taft**, whose works can be seen today in parks and cemeteries throughout the city. Employing a highly allegorical style, Taft believed in the ennobling power of art. His monumental *Fountain of the Great Lakes* (1914), outside the South Wing of the Art Institute, was the first public sculpture to be underwritten by the Ferguson Fund, established in 1905 by wealthy lumberman Benjamin Franklin Ferguson to decorate Chicago with European-style monuments. Even the School of the Art Institute, the Midwest's preeminent academy of the fine arts, trained students under the French academic plan, emphasizing the naturalistic rendering of the human form and the copying of classical art. Among collectors, the impetus to acquire art was largely inspired by investment value and fashion, and focused on the works of European artists. The lavish collecting style of the Potter Palmers, eventually responsible for much of the Art Institute's famous French Impressionist collection, contrasted sharply with the more curatorial approach of later collectors like Arthur Jerome Eddy and Frederic Clay Bartlett, who championed the Modernist movements of the teens and twenties.

TURNING POINT

In 1913 the controversial **Armory Show** in New York City contested public taste by introducing Modernism into this milieu. The works of, among others, Gauguin, Picasso and Duchamp met with widespread chagrin, moving students at the School of the Art Institute to hang Matisse in effigy. Chicago's art world faced off: nonjuried exhibitions challenged the conservative standards of the Art Institute and a new echelon of collectors promoted the avant-garde. A community of Modernists began to grow, among them painter Rudolph Weisenborn (*Chicago,* 1928*)*, who may be best remembered for organizing several anti-establishment artists' groups. Highly diverse in style, Chicago's young artists shared instead a rejection of formal art training and, like abstract master Wassily Kandinsky, sought the inspiration of inner experience, a common thread in subsequent Chicago art. Finally, by 1933, the Century of Progress

Untitled (1967) by Pablo Picasso, Richard J. Daley Center

© City of Chicago/GRC

Cloud Gate (2004-06) by Anish Kapoor, Millennium Park

© Anne Evans/Chicago Architecture Foundation

Outdoor Sculpture

Chicago is a veritable treasure trove of public art. Below is a sampling of the 100-plus works of sculpture found in and around the Loop.

Sculptor/Work

Ivan Mestrovic
The Bowman and The Spearman
Location Grant Park, Grand Entrance

Alexander Calder
Flamingo
Location Federal Center plaza

Augustus Saint-Gaudens
The Seated Lincoln
Location Grant Park, Court of
Presidents

Lorado Taft
Fountain of the Great Lakes
Location Art Institute of Chicago,
South Wing

Edward Kemeys
Lions
Location Art Institute, main entrance

Marc Chagall
Four Seasons
Location First National Bank Plaza

Louise Nevelson
Dawn Shadows
Location Madison Plaza

Joan Miró
Miró's Chicago
Location Washington Street, next to
Chicago Temple

Pablo Picasso
Untitled
Location Daley Center Plaza

Virginio Ferrari
Being Born
Location Intersection of Ohio,
Ontario and Orleans streets

Jean Dubuffet
Monument with Standing Beast
Location James R. Thompson
Center Plaza

Anish Kapoor
Cloud Gate
Location Millennium Park

Magdalena Abakanowicz
Agora
Location Grant Park

Exposition proudly proclaimed Chicago's embrace of the modern. The Art Institute exhibited 27 galleries of Modern art, signaling a mainstream acceptance of the movement.

SCENES AND IMAGES

Some Chicago artists of the 1920s and 1930s combined elements of Modernism and Realism to depict the urban landscape around them, making the city a center of American scene painting. Inspired by the brief teaching stint of social realist George Bellows at the School of the Art Institute, painters like Emil Armin *(Towers,* 1931*)* and Ramon Shiva *(Chicago MCMXXIV,* 1924) rendered the city with an expressionistic edge and an honesty reminiscent of New York's Ashcan school. African-American painter Archibald Motley, Jr. created lively scenes of life in Chicago's black neighborhoods *(Black Belt,* 1934). Linked to the larger Regionalist movement made popular by Art Institute students Grant Wood, John Steuart Curry and Thomas Hart Benton, the Chicago scene painters shared a sense of place, recognizing Chicago's gritty urban landscape to be as legitimate a subject as the French countryside.

Members of the most recognizable Chicago school came to be known in the 1960s as **Imagists**. Precursors of the movement included **Ivan Albright** *(That Which I Should Have Done I Did Not Do,* 1931–41), whose disturbing canvases express a personal vision rather than an external reality, and artists June Leaf, H. C. Westermann and Leon Golub. Their work, dubbed "monster art" for its totemic, elemental style, drew inspiration from the Art Brut movement of the 1950s popularized by Jean Dubuffet. The Imagists, too, relied heavily on inner experience and personal imagery; their disparate work catalogs a fantastical world of organic abstraction with stronger ties to Surrealism than to the Abstract Expressionism of Jackson Pollock. Among the best known of the Imagists were the **Hairy Who**, a band of artists—including Gladys Nilsson, Art Green, Karl Wirsum, James Falconer and Suellen Rocca—whose group shows in the 1960s set off a flurry of outrageous exhibits that were part theater and part art. From the vibrant and ambiguous portraits of **Ed Paschke** *(Elcina,* 1973*)* to the darkly comic, misshapen figures of **Jim Nutt** *(Is This the Right Way,* 1979), the fantasies of Imagism have influenced a generation of Chicago artists.

THE CONTEMPORARY SCENE

Recently Chicago has seen a burgeoning of interest in art and a commensurate increase in related activities. Since 1967 the Museum of Contemporary Art has made the artists of the avant-

Detail of American Gothic (1930) by Grant Wood

Art Institute of Chicago, Friends of American Art Collection.

garde accessible to a broad and eager audience. That same year came the unveiling of the 50ft Picasso sculpture in Daley Plaza, one of Chicago's first non-commemorative public artworks. Public sculpture has since proliferated, thanks in part to the **Percent for Art Program** enacted by the city in 1978, which mandates that one percent of the cost of every city project with public access be applied toward the purchase of art for the site. The million-dollar collection of art at the Harold Washington Library Center represents the largest project the program has undertaken.

A new generation of artists seeking inspiration beyond Imagism emerged in the late 1980s, fueling a phenomenal boom in the number and popularity of art galleries. Held in the spring at the Merchandise Mart, **Art Chicago** ranks among the world's leading art marketplaces.

THE OTHER ARTS

Chicago occupies an undisputed place in the history of design and photography. European Modernist **Laszlo Moholy-Nagy** brought the principles of the German Bauhaus to the city in 1937, establishing a school that would evolve into the Institute of Design, a part of the Illinois Institute of Technology since 1949. The holistic curriculum reflected a well-integrated variety of disciplines, from industrial and graphic design to architecture. As a center for the teaching of photography as art, the school boasts a fine roster of instructors over the years—Harry Callahan, Arthur Siegel and Aaron Siskind among them—as well as a long list of prominent graduates. Major collections of photography are located at the Art Institute and the Museum of Contemporary Photography.

MUSIC
JAZZ, BLUES, ROCK

Chicago's development as an immigrant city has imbued it over the years with a rich musical heritage. But the most interesting phenomenon has been the power of the city to transform certain styles. The **blues**, for one, would never be the same once they came to Chicago. From the hollows, fields and churches of the rural South, migrants brought their music to the city in the 1910s. As artists such as Big Bill Broonzy and Papa Charlie Jackson began to play together, a hybrid guitar-driven style based on urban themes emerged. In the 1940s musicians experimented with amplification and by 1950, Chicago surfaced as the capital of the hard-driving electric blues, with **Muddy Waters** (McKinley Morganfield) as its king. Other greats like Willie Dixon, Howlin' Wolf and Sunnyland Slim spent their careers in Chicago. Koko Taylor, the preeminent female blues artist, made her name in the city, and veteran Buddy Guy owns a local blues club. Every summer the public flocks by the thousands to the Chicago Blues Festival to hear the world's best sing the blues.

Jazz came up from the South as well after the fall of New Orleans' Storyville vice district and in Chicago became an integrated art. During the 1920s, when jazzmen King Oliver and Louis Armstrong came to play the clubs in the Black Belt, young and restless white musicians like Gene Krupa, Bud Freeman and Jimmy McPartland embraced their style. The resulting hybrid Chicago-style jazz pulsed with a hot tempo, explosive rhythm sections and elaborate instrumental interplay. Much fine jazz, from traditional to contemporary, can be heard in clubs and cabarets around the city to this day, as well as at the **Chicago Jazz Festival** held each summer in Grant Park.

Chicago remains a center of innovation when it comes to contemporary music, particularly **rock**. In the early 1980s cutting-edge Chicago DJs produced a frenetic, fast-paced dance music called "house" that went on to have considerable influence in rap and "industrial" rock trends. The meteoric ascent of the Smashing Pumpkins, Liz Phair, Veruca Salt and Urge Overkill in the early 1990s perpetuated the city's reputation for fertile creative ground. And Chicago's 21st-century rock scene promises no less. From Wilco's alternative blends of country and rock and the punkish

Films starring Chicago

Underworld (1927)	**About Last Night** (1986)
The Front Page (1931)	**The Color of Money** (1986)
Little Caesar (1931)	**Ferris Bueller's Day Off** (1986)
Scarface (1932)	**The Untouchables** (1987)
In Old Chicago (1937)	**Eight Men Out** (1988)
His Girl Friday (1940)	**Music Box** (1989)
Call Northside 777 (1948)	**Backdraft** (1991)
Wabash Avenue (1950)	**The Fugitive** (1993)
Native Son (1950, 1986)	**Blink** (1994)
The Man with the Golden Arm (1956)	**While You Were Sleeping** (1995)
Al Capone (1959)	**Home Alone III** (1996)
Compulsion (1959)	**Blues Brothers 2000** (1997)
A Raisin in the Sun (1961)	**Stir of Echoes** (1998)
Robin and the Seven Hoods (1964)	**Message in a Bottle** (1998)
Gaily, Gaily (1969)	**High Fidelity** (2000)
Medium Cool (1969)	**Return to Me** (2000)
The Sting (1973)	**Road to Perdition** (2002)
Carrie (1976)	**Barbershop** (2002)
The Fury (1978)	**The Weather Man** (2005)
The Blues Brothers (1980)	**The Break-Up** (2006)
My Bodyguard (1980)	**The Lake House** (2006)
Ordinary People (1980)	**Stranger Than Fiction** (2006)
Risky Business (1983)	**The Dark Knight** (2008)
Sixteen Candles (1984)	**Public Enemies** (2009)
	A Nightmare on Elm Street (2010)

pop of Fall Out Boy to the unabashed rap of Kanye West and the power pop music videos of Ok Go, Chicago's deep rock roots have yielded a sturdy crop of diverse and original styles.

CLASSICAL MUSIC

Chicago's considerable classical music heritage harkens back to the early city elite who wished to convey a sophisticated image of Chicago by encouraging the development of "high culture." The first orchestra performed in 1850, and an opera house opened in 1865. Visiting artists and ensembles reinforced a taste for the classical, and by 1891 city boosters realized that a permanent orchestra would enhance Chicago's reputation.

The **Chicago Symphony Orchestra (CSO)** was thus founded under the direction of Theodore Thomas of New York. Over the years the CSO has grown in stature under the batons of such luminaries as Frederick Stock, Fritz Reiner, Sir Georg Solti, Daniel Barenboim and Pierre Boulez.

Opera has always found a willing audience in Chicago, but the grand Italian style is expensive to produce, and at least six major companies have come and gone over the years. Finally in 1954, under the visionary leadership of Carol Fox, the **Lyric Opera** opened its first season with a performance of *Norma*, featuring Maria Callas in her American debut. Currently under the musical direction of Sir Andrew Davies, the Lyric continues to be one of the world's most exciting opera companies. Light opera finds a comfortable home in Chicago as well at Light Opera Works, and the Chicago Opera Theater presents classic and contemporary works in innovative and intimate settings. Small ensembles, choruses and ethnic companies abound in Chicago, and early music is particularly popular, especially when performed by Music of the Baroque.

CINEMA

Between 1897 and 1918, Chicago prospered as the capital of American filmmaking. William Selig built the world's first movie studio on the Near South Side in 1897, followed a decade later by George Spoor and Gilbert "Bronco Billy" Anderson's Essanay Motion Picture Co. Among them they produced thousands of pictures and employed hundreds of local vaudeville and entertainment professionals. Essanay signed a young Charlie Chaplin for $1,250 a week in 1915, and Selig Polyscope made more than 200 cowboy films featuring Tom Mix.

Eventually, California's better weather and new laws regarding motion picture rights ended the city's moviemaking dominion. The lull lasted until 1976 when Chicago began an aggressive campaign to sell itself to location scouts. Since 1980, more than 750 films and TV productions have been made in the metropolitan area, adding $1.3 billion in revenue to the city's coffers—and that doesn't count the myriad television commercials shot here. Their producers are attracted by the city's fresh profile and cooperative atmosphere. Television dramas such as *ER* have discovered that Chicago's working-class, no-nonsense ethos makes a good setting, apart from the well-worn stereotypes of New York and Los Angeles.

ARCHITECTURE

For over a century, Chicago has been the capital of modern architecture. In the years following the Great Fire of 1871, architects came from all over the country to help rebuild the world's fastest-growing city and in the process created the skyscraper, America's great contribution to architecture. Chicago also nurtured the Prairie school architects who followed Frank Lloyd Wright in developing the clean horizontal lines of the modern American residence. The city remains a mecca for an international coterie of architects wishing to leave their mark on the famous skyline.

FROM STICKS TO STEEL

The earliest buildings date to the city's founding in the 1830s and exhibit the design features of the Greek Revival style popular throughout Jacksonian America. In 1833 Chicago wrought its first architectural innovation with the development of the balloon frame, so dubbed because it supposedly made house construction as easy as blowing up a balloon. Balloon framing involved the substitution of thin plates and studs, held together only by nails, for the ancient and expensive system of mortise-and-tenon joints. This method permitted the rapid construction of economical, lightweight buildings and was particularly suited to the Chicago area's relative lack of forests. Unfortunately, the preponderance of structures made of small timbers meant that the city was built of kindling, which aided the Great Fire of 1871 that ended up leveling the budding metropolis. Wood-frame construction was banned after the Fire, but intact rail connections and industry ensured that the city would be rebuilt, and soon architects and engineers migrated en masse to Chicago. At first the city resembled its pre-1871 self, as local architects John Mills Van Osdel and William Boyington rebuilt a downtown of four- and five-story Italianate buildings—often from pre-fire plans. However, the Great Fire proved that even cast-iron facades were vulnerable, and Chicago architects were called upon to develop better fire prevention techniques.

Civil War engineer **William Le Baron Jenney**, trained at the École Polytechnique and École Centrale in Paris, came to Chicago in 1870 to design the West

Parks and Boulevards. Jenney advocated an iconoclastic "Western" style of architecture in contrast to the European models employed on the nation's East Coast, and helped train Chicago school architects **Louis Sullivan**, **William Holabird** and **Martin Roche**. It was Jenney who developed the skeletal steel frame that allowed **skyscrapers** to be built. The steel members were sheathed in brick for fire prevention, and his 1884 Home Insurance Building (demolished 1929) was the first true skyscraper.

In traditional masonry construction, the walls support the weight of the building. Jenney reversed this previously unquestioned principle of architecture. For the first time, the building supported the walls, which could be draped on the frame like a curtain. Since less space was needed for support, larger windows and hence more light and air could be admitted to upper-floor office spaces. This principle, called curtain-wall construction, made possible the development of modern high rises.

Other technical problems needed to be overcome to allow for buildings of more than 8 or 10 stories. First, the refinement of the elevator in the 1870s provided efficient vertical transportation. Secondly, Jenney and other Chicago architects developed a series of bracing techniques to reduce the effects of wind on tall buildings. A more difficult problem was posed by foundations sinking in Chicago's swampy, shifting soil. John Wellborn Root developed a floating foundation for the Montauk Block in 1882 that allowed building loads to spread out and grab hold in the infirm soil. Adler & Sullivan improved on the design with the development of the caisson foundation, still used today.

THE CHICAGO SCHOOL

These innovations, conceived and executed within the decade of the 1880s, gave birth to the Chicago school of architecture, recognized as the first significant new architecture since the Italian High Renaissance and characterized by the work of four prominent firms. William Le Baron Jenney's engineering

Rookery Building
© peterspiro/iStockphoto.com

innovations exceeded his talent for facade design in buildings such as the 1891 Manhattan Building, but he also helped usher in the department store with his Second Leiter Building of the same year. The partnership of **Daniel Burnham & John Wellborn Root** constructed the Montauk Block (demolished) in 1882, and followed with the Rookery in 1888, which used a partial steel frame, floating foundations, and featured an elegant terra-cotta facade and stunning light court. In 1891 the firm also designed the tallest office building utilizing traditional masonry construction, the 16-story Monadnock Building. After Root's untimely death in 1891, Burnham's firm turned to more traditional styles. One notable exception was the Reliance Building of 1895 (now the Hotel Burnham), designed by **Charles B. Atwood**. With its protruding bays, huge windows and narrow bands of white terra-cotta ornament, the building anticipated the glass skyscrapers of the 1980s. **Dankmar Adler & Louis Sullivan** combined the former's engineering and acoustical genius with the latter's unparalleled gift for ornament in the stunning Auditorium Building of 1889. This edifice owed some debt to the work of Bostonian H. H. Richardson, who had begun to

Reliance Building, 1895

MICHELIN

reinterpret Romanesque architecture in a distinctly American vein. The firm's finest office structures were the Chicago Stock Exchange (1894) and the Prudential Building (1894) in Buffalo, New York. Sullivan went on to design the Carson, Pirie, Scott & Co. department store in 1899, where his ornamental designs explode onto the street. The firm of **William Holabird & Martin Roche** combined the Chicago school innovations into a formula that was repeated in over 80 Loop buildings. Their Pontiac Building (1891), Marquette Building (1895) and Chicago Building (1905) stand as excellent examples of Chicago school skyscrapers.

"FORM FOLLOWS FUNCTION"

While many of the new skyscrapers were cloaked in traditional ornament, a significant number abandoned historical precedent, notably the 1891 Monadnock Building, where the only modulation was provided by protruding bay windows and a gentle flaring at the roof and base. Sullivan, more than any other architect, enunciated the new design philosophy with the phrase "form follows function" and encouraged an approach to high-rise construction that expressed the steel frame beneath. The base should be distinct as the entrance of the building, according to Sullivan, who favored a semicircular arched entrance. The top of the building

should be an overhanging cornice that terminates the composition. Between the base and the top, the office floors should be identical and create a vertical effect so that the building would be "every inch a proud and soaring thing." Holabird & Roche effectively utilized the style, which saw the grid of steel girders expressed on the exterior in brick or terra-cotta, while the bulk of the wall plane was filled with Chicago windows, composed of a large fixed pane flanked by smaller sliding sashes.

The World's Columbian Exposition, under the direction of Daniel Burnham, adopted a Neoclassical style to celebrate the new American empire. Louis Sullivan's acclaimed Transportation Building, with its telescoping arched entrance, was the only building at the fair to follow Chicago school precedents. He later lamented that the exposition set American architecture back 50 years.

THE PRAIRIE STYLE

As Sullivan was working on the pivotal Auditorium Building, he hired a young draftsman from Wisconsin, **Frank Lloyd Wright**, who left to form his own practice in 1893. In contrast to the soaring skyscrapers, Wright developed homes inspired by the flat Midwestern prairie, with overhanging eaves, horizontal

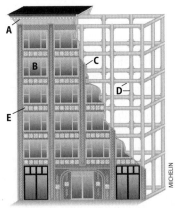

MICHELIN

A Cornice
B Chicago-style window
C Curtain wall
D Steel frame
E Spandel

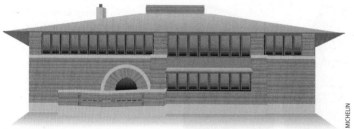

MICHELIN

Arthur Heurtley House, 1902

lines and banded windows of stained glass. Wright also "broke the box" of traditional domestic architecture by allowing rooms to flow into one another, rather than organizing square rooms along long corridors. He eschewed attics and basements as unnecessary, and projected porches and rooflines in an attempt to meld building with landscape. His designs for Unity Temple and Robie House caused a worldwide stir when published in Germany in 1910. Wright's contemporary George Washington Maher developed a more formal and symmetrical take on the horizontal Prairie style in a wealth of residential commissions at the turn of the century, while many other Prairie school architects—among them Walter Burley Griffin, Marion Mahony Griffin, Francis Barry Byrne and John Van Bergen—learned their trade in Wright's Oak Park office. Wright's practice became more eclectic in the 1920s after he left the Chicago area. He designed a "mile-high" skyscraper in his later years, but the horizontal lines of his early Chicago and Oak Park homes still define his role as America's most prominent architectural figure.

REACTION AND REVOLUTION

By the 1910s architectural styles in Chicago and America entered a conservative period, as new skyscrapers were clad in traditional styles—like the Renaissance-inspired People's Gas Building of 1910 and the Wrigley Building of 1921. In 1922 the *Chicago Tribune* held an international competition to design a new high rise for the newspaper, which drew 280 entries from around the world. While the winning

design by Hood & Howells of New York had a Norman Gothic exterior, it was the second-place entry by Eliel Saarinen of Finland that garnered the approval of architectural critics for its modern verticality devoid of historical ornament. Saarinen's design also fitted in with new zoning ordinances that called for stepped setbacks in high-rise construction. By 1928 Chicago boasted several Vertical style, or Art Deco skyscrapers, including 333 North Michigan Avenue and the Palmolive Building by Holabird & Root (the successor firm to Holabird & Roche) and the *Daily News* Building by Graham, Anderson, Probst & White (the successor firm to D. H. Burnham & Co.).

MODERNISM IN CHICAGO

A keystone of Modernism, the International style, which saw buildings as almost purely sculptural objects, originated in many ways with the Bauhaus of Germany in the 1920s and 30s. When the rise of Nazism precluded the modernistic innovations of the Bauhaus, one of its leading lights, **Ludwig Mies van der Rohe**, emigrated to Chicago. As chairman of architecture at the Illinois Institute of Technology, Mies ushered in what came to be called the Second Chicago school. Following World War II, he designed new steel-and-concrete high rises in a completely stripped-down style where attached I-beams provided the only ornament. Deceptively simple, the new architecture depended on a rigid calculation of proportion that allowed little room for error in design. Mies inspired a new generation of architects with designs such as 860–880 North Lake Shore Drive and the Federal Center. Jacques Brownson

Federal Center

© Rich Iwasaki/Tips Images

of C. F. Murphy Assocs. contributed the 1965 Richard J. Daley Center, which is perhaps the best Miesian building not designed by Mies.

Emerging as the premier firm in postwar Chicago, **Skidmore, Owings & Merrill** established an international practice in the design of modern high rises. The Inland Steel Building (1958) first expressed the possibilities of improved construction techniques with its column-free floors and double-glazed walls. Engineer Fazlur Khan helped Skidmore create Chicago's modern landmarks, first with his innovative X-shaped cross bracing on the 1969 John Hancock Center, and finally with the bundled-tube construction of the Sears Tower.

POST-MODERN ERA

The formula of the Skidmore firm held sway throughout the 1970s, as dark steel-and-glass office blocks filled Chicago's Loop. By 1980 the post-Modern movement had arrived, and in Chicago its standard-bearer was German-born **Helmut Jahn**, whose sculptural facades of mirrored glass seemed to echo the streamlined machine aesthetic of the Art Deco period. His Xerox Centre (now 55 West Monroe Building) of 1980 led the way, followed by the daringly different James R. Thompson Center of 1985 and United Airlines Terminal of 1990. Jahn is noted for his soaring interior atrium spaces.

As the 1990s ushered in an era of real estate consolidation, Chicago also witnessed new buildings by architects from Japan, Spain, Italy and New York. Skidmore, Owings & Merrill joined the post-Modern fray with the 1989 NBC Tower by Adrian Smith. Much post-Modern design followed a classical model with modulated concrete surfaces and punched window openings—exemplified by the R. R. Donnelley Building and Park Tower.

A NEW MILLENNIUM

So far, security concerns and a new focus on environmentalism are informing the building trends of the 21st century. The emphasis is on high-tech, secure, self-sustaining buildings and "green architecture." One good example is the ABN AMRO Plaza designed by DeStefano and Partners and completed in 2003. With its garden roof, natural convection of fresh air, and secure, double-level lobby, the building addresses both concerns. The city's green sensibilities became official with policies enacted in 2004 requiring new buildings and renovations to adhere to certain environmental standards, including such features as energy efficiency, roof gardens, coated windows, and recycling of water.

Another strong trend this century is the migration of homeowners into downtown. Scads of residential high-rises and condo conversion flourish in and around the Loop and along the Mag Mile, turning those business and shopping districts into bustling 24hr neighborhoods. Blanketing the rail yards along Michigan Avenue, Millennium Park, with its

MICHELIN

James R. Thompson Center, 1985

exuberant bandshell and snaking bridge by Frank Gehry, opened in 2004, giving Chicago's new downtown residents a stunning front yard. Now, with strongly divided opinions, Chicagoans await the completion of two huge projects: the Trump International Hotel and Tower, projected to open in 2009, and Santiago Calatrava's Chicago Spire, anticipated a year later. The former, designed by Skidmore, Owings & Merrill, will stand 96 floors and just under the Sears Tower in height. The twisted, pointy Spire, however, will trump them both to become North American's tallest structure and the world's tallest residential building with 150 floors.

ARCHITECTURAL GLOSSARY
GREEK REVIVAL (1820–60)

Popular throughout America, this style adopts the pedimented, symmetrical order of Greek temples in a simplified vernacular form suitable for modest houses, grand mansions and larger public buildings. Classical columns in the Doric, Ionic and Corinthian orders ornament the pedimented facade; roofs are often shallow, supported by a heavy cornice, and may include a cupola. The 1836 Clarke House is a rare example in Chicago.

GOTHIC REVIVAL (1830–70)

The picturesque, assymetrical forms of Gothic Revival facades often include towers, battlements and pointed-arch windows with leaded stained glass. Smaller houses have intricately decorated bargeboards at the eaves and steeply pitched roofs. The city's most notable example is the Chicago Water Tower.

ITALIANATE (1840–80)

This style defined much of 19C America through flat-roofed homes and store-fronts with overhanging eaves and brackets. Long, narrow windows with rounded arches often include incised decoration at the lintels and sills. More elaborate homes in the style include rusticated corner quoins and a Classical cupola or tower modeled on Italian villas. The cast-iron front was usually Italianate, as seen in Chicago's Page Brothers Building and Berghoff Restaurant. A good residential example is the Nickerson House.

SECOND EMPIRE (1860–80)

Inspired by Baron Hausmann's redesign of Paris in the 1850s, this grandiose style is characterized by a short, steeply pitched mansard roof pierced by dormer windows. Generally symmetrical facades include quoined corners, projecting bays, windows flanked by pilasters, balustrades and an abundance of Classical decoration. Often mansard roofs were added to Italianate buildings in a close approximation of the style. Examples can be found in the Jackson Boulevard and Wicker Park historic districts of Chicago.

ROMANESQUE REVIVAL (1860–1900)

The round arches, deeply inset windows and door openings and rough stone finishes of the Romanesque style suggest Medieval castles and inspired architects attempting to create permanence amid the rapidly changing landscape of late-19C America. The style was refined by Boston architect H. H. Richardson, who designed the John Jacob Glessner House in 1886. Burnham & Root's St. Gabriel's Church and the Newberry Library by Henry Ives Cobb are fine examples.

QUEEN ANNE (1870–1900)

This style is the one most commonly identified as "Victorian," with its asymmetrical composition, exuberant ornamentation and picturesque design marked by conical towers, projecting bays, elaborately decorated dormers and gables. Adapted to both large residences and city row houses, the style is found throughout Chicago's historic districts, especially Old Town, Pullman and Wicker Park.

CHICAGO SCHOOL (1880–1910)

The design of the world's first sky-scrapers celebrated their engineering and purpose, summed up by Louis Sullivan's phrase "form follows function." The steel-framed buildings express their construction in a gridlike facade of brick or terra-cotta, pierced by large areas of glass. A defined base, or entry level, is surmounted by a series of identical office floors with large "Chicago windows" characterized by a fixed single-pane window in the center flanked by smaller double-hung sliding sash windows. The roofline is capped by a cornice. The first 1880s skyscrapers borrowed elements of Romanesque, Italianate and Queen Anne architecture, but by 1894 most were adopting the new aesthetic of functionalism, eschewing historical ornament to create vertical sculptures made of piers, spandrels and windows. Four firms, **Adler & Sullivan**, **Burnham & Root**, **Holabird & Roche**, and **William Le Baron Jenney**, are the standard-bearers of the Chicago school and are credited with establishing the Modern movement in the US. Chicago's Rookery and Monadnock Building epitomize the early Chicago school, while the Marquette and Chicago buildings demonstrate its maturity. The Reliance Building of 1895 (now the Hotel Burnham) is agreed to be a worldwide landmark, prefiguring the present-day glass-and-steel skyscrapers.

NEOCLASSICAL OR BEAUX-ARTS (1893–1920)

The success of the 1893 World's Columbian Exposition brought a revival of Roman Imperial architecture, symbolizing the rise of the American Republic as a world power. Unlike the simpler Greek Revival, Neoclassical architecture revels in ornamentation: Arched and arcaded windows, balustrades at every level, grand staircases, applied columns, decorative swags, garlands and even statuary embellish the edifices. A good residential example is 1500 North Astor Street on the Gold Coast. Sometimes called Beaux-Arts for its association with Paris' École des Beaux-Arts, the style was well-suited to public and cultural buildings, such as the 1893 Art Institute and 1897 Chicago Cultural Center.

PRAIRIE STYLE (1895–1915)

Largely identified with **Frank Lloyd Wright,** the Prairie style revolutionized traditional residential architecture by creating low, horizontal compositions inspired by the flat Midwestern prairie. Roofs are very shallow in pitch and have long, overhanging eaves. Windows are casements, often arranged in broad bands of stained and leaded glass. Roman brick with raked horizontal joints further emphasizes the horizontal, and entrances, instead of being the organizing principle of the home's facade, are often hidden. Interior rooms flow into each other rather than being organized around corridors. Attics, basements and ancillary spaces are rare. Many of the style's premier examples are in Chicago and Oak Park, including Wright's Robie House, Unity Temple, Heurtley House and Laura Gale House.

ARTS AND CRAFTS (1895–1920)

In response to the proliferation of machines in the industrial age, Englishmen William Morris and John Ruskin called for a return to handcrafted

"Make no little plans; they have no magic to stir men's blood and probably themselves will not be realized. Make big plans; aim high in hope and work, remembering that a noble and logical diagram once recorded will never die, but long after we are gone will be a living thing, asserting itself with growing intensity. Remember that our sons and grandsons are going to do things that would stagger us. Let your watchword be 'order' and your beacon 'beauty.'"

The oft-repeated exhortation of Daniel Burnham

articles of everyday life and reveled in simplicity. Frank Lloyd Wright and others responded to the movement, which in architecture is characterized by overhanging wooden beams, delicately mortised together to form the gable ends and porches of homes.

ART DECO OR MODERNE (1925–40)

Rejecting the revivalist tradition, the Art Deco style first appeared during the 1925 "Exposition Internationale des Arts Décoratifs et Industriels Modernes" in Paris. US zoning laws, which called for skyscrapers to "step back" to provide light and air to the street, helped define the architectural aspects of Art Deco that favored setbacks and piers to emphasize verticality. Often designed in smooth stone or terra-cotta shiny surfaces, edifices featured highly stylized carved ornament in low relief with a pronounced muscularity and abstraction, recessed windows and spandrels. Chicago examples include the Chicago Board of Trade, 333 North Michigan Avenue and the LaSalle Bank building.

INTERNATIONAL STYLE (1930–70)

This Modernist movement abandoned applied ornament for sleek, sculptural lines in buildings, furniture and other designed objects, summarized by Mies' dictum "Less is more." Concrete, glass and steel are celebrated in buildings with boxlike massing and raised lobbies surrounded by arcaded overhangs. Exterior walls of glass and steel minimize both ornament and modulation, deriving their design from proportion and materials alone, allowing the structures to express their function. The Federal Center and 860–880 North Lake Shore Drive by Mies, along with the Richard J. Daley Center by C. F. Murphy Assocs., are some of the best examples in Chicago.

POST-MODERN STYLE (1975–2000)

This style is characterized by cavalier application of historical elements and references to buildings that express modern materials of mirrored glass, concrete and surfaces generally more colorful and modulated than the severe lines of the International style. Helmut Jahn brought the style to Chicago with his 1980 Xerox Centre, now 55 West Monroe Building, and exposed both its ambition and failings in his 1985 James R. Thompson Center and Citicorp Center. In the 1990s, post-Modern architecture followed two tracks. A new classicism offered rectilinear concrete wall surfaces and neatly punched window openings, enlivened by dramatic curving entrances and awnings. This style, seen in the R. R. Donnelley Building (1992, Ricardo Bofill) and 730 North Michigan Avenue (2000, Elkus/Manfredi), occasionally veers into an homage to Art Deco, notably in the NBC Tower (1989, Adrian Smith) and the Park Tower (2000, Lucien LaGrange), both off the Magnificent Mile. Expressionistic post-Modernism continued the deconstructivist style first seen in the 1980s and epitomized by the curving sculptural forms of Frank Gehry's bandshell, which looms over Millennium Park.

CURRENT TRENDS (2000–PRESENT)

Too young, and perhaps too diverse, to be classified, architecture in the 21st century faces a smorgasbord of new challenges. Architects must address issues of security brought into sharp focus after the terrorist attacks of September 11, 2001. Concerns over climate change have stimulated exciting new directions in green building and sustainability. Rapid changes in technology and the digital environment demand consideration, as do cutting-edge materials and systems. In addition, city planners and architects alike are working together to rethink the very nature of the city, reassessing their approaches to public housing, public spaces, athletic venues, public transportation, neighborhood development, building reuse and the streetscape. It remains to be seen whether a definitive architectural style will coalesce out of these evolving millennial influences.

Milestones in Chicago Literary History

1872	1903	1912	1916	1935

1872
E.P. Roe, *Barriers Burned Away*

1880
The Dial founded

1893
Harriet Monroe, *Columbian Ode*

Henry Blake Fuller, *The Cliff Dwellers*

1895
Henry Blake Fuller, *With the Procession*

1900
Theodore Dreiser writes *Sister Carrie*. Frank L. Baum and William Denslow complete *The Wizard of Oz*

1903
Will Payne, *Mr. Salt*

1904
Robert Herrick, *The Common Lot*

Frank Norris, *The Pit: A Story of Chicago*

1906
Upton Sinclair, *The Jungle*

1909
Jane Addams, *Twenty Years at Hull-House*

1911
Harriet Monroe founds *Poetry* magazine

1912
Sister Carrie released

1914
Margaret Anderson founds *The Little Review*. Theodore Dreiser, *The Titan*

1915
Edgar Lee Masters, *Spoon River Anthology*. Willa Cather, *The Song of the Lark*. Sherwood Anderson, *Windy McPherson's Son*

1916
Carl Sandburg, *Chicago Poems*. Ring Lardner, *You Know Me Al*

1919
Sherwood Anderson, *Winesburg, Ohio*

1920
Floyd Dell, *Moon-Calf*

1928
Ben Hecht and Charles MacArthur, *The Front Page*

1929-34
James T. Farrell writes *Studs Lonigan* trilogy

1935
Willa Cather, *Lucy Gayheart*

LITERATURE

The explosive growth that propelled Chicago from frontier outpost to major industrial center far surpassed any development in the arts—including literature—or in other refinements associated with civilization. The city throbbed with power, and when a literary culture did bloom in the late 19C, it was indelibly marked by the earthy, money-grubbing nature of the immigrant metropolis. Its tradition of social realism and street-level literature continued to the end of the 20C with poet Gwendolyn Brooks (1917–2000) and newspaper columnist Mike Royko (1932–97).

In the 21st century, Chicago fiction continues to explore the tensions and triumphs of urban life, with considerable attention still focused on the immigrant experience. For, although the faces and neighborhoods have changed, the stories remain compelling and rich, and often troubling. Dealing with themes of ever-accelerating change, building up and tearing down, politics, drugs and poverty, modern Chicago writers add their voices to the city's long tradition of unblinking and unembellished literature.

LITERATURE OF THE BIG SHOULDERS

The writings emerging in Chicago during the mid-19C were indistinguishable from the mass of other moralistic or romantic works churned out by artists from London to New York to Los Angeles. Only after the 1893 Columbian Exposition focused world attention on this vibrant city did local writers emerge with a style to match the pace of Chicago life. During that frenetic decade, the city began to reduce its cultural shortcomings by erecting a new art institute (1893) and the first permanent library (1897), and by developing its musical and literary tastes. Still, the business of Chicago was business, and writers focused on the race to riches in novels like *The Cliff Dwellers* (1893) and *With the Procession* (1895) by Henry Blake Fuller, and *The Pit: A Story of Chicago* (1904) by Frank Norris.

These early social realists, part of the **Little Room** salon, began exploring the contradictions of a society that, though modeled on democracy, favored the industrial elite over the working classes. This was the first literary school to look at both the front and the back, at the

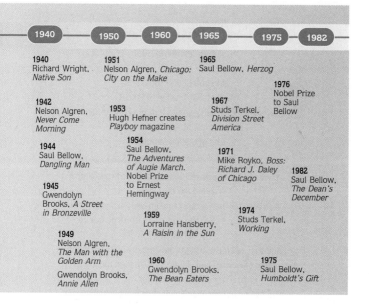

1940	1950	1960	1965	1975	1982

1940
Richard Wright, *Native Son*

1942
Nelson Algren, *Never Come Morning*

1944
Saul Bellow, *Dangling Man*

1945
Gwendolyn Brooks, *A Street in Bronzeville*

1949
Nelson Algren, *The Man with the Golden Arm*

Gwendolyn Brooks, *Annie Allen*

1951
Nelson Algren, *Chicago: City on the Make*

1953
Hugh Hefner creates *Playboy* magazine

1954
Saul Bellow, *The Adventures of Augie March*. Nobel Prize to Ernest Hemingway

1959
Lorraine Hansberry, *A Raisin in the Sun*

1960
Gwendolyn Brooks, *The Bean Eaters*

1965
Saul Bellow, *Herzog*

1967
Studs Terkel, *Division Street America*

1971
Mike Royko, *Boss: Richard J. Daley of Chicago*

1974
Studs Terkel, *Working*

1975
Saul Bellow, *Humboldt's Gift*

1976
Nobel Prize to Saul Bellow

1982
Saul Bellow, *The Dean's December*

public and the private, and in so doing, discovered subject matter so rich that it remains fertile to this day.

Best known of these early novels is **Upton Sinclair**'s *The Jungle* (1906), a stark, heart-wrenching story meant to waken awareness of the plight of immigrant workers; instead, it fomented a reform of food laws following Sinclair's harrowing descriptions of life in the stockyards. Lamented the author: "I aimed at the public's heart, but by accident I hit it in the stomach." Probably the most important novel of the period was **Theodore Dreiser**'s *Sister Carrie*, written in 1900 but suppressed until 1912 due to the risqué nature of the story, which celebrates a heroine who parlays her lost innocence into a successful career. It inspired the next generation of Chicago writers, who peered behind every street lamp and back alley in their search for the raw, rude stories of a fast-paced American city.

Many Chicago writers worked for the newspapers, and added a journalistic and often humorous strain to the Chicago tradition, as seen in Finley Peter Dunne's "Mr. Dooley" series and Ring Lardner's fictionalized sports stories.

Some preferred fantasy to the starkness of urban life: L. Frank Baum and artist William Denslow completed the American classic *The Wizard of Oz* in 1900; and Edgar Rice Burroughs' 1912 Tarzan series was inspired by his visits to the Lincoln Park Zoo.

CHICAGO LITERARY RENAISSANCE

In 1911 Harriet Monroe, whose "Columbian Ode" celebrated the 1893 World's Fair, founded *Poetry* magazine. The publication included the pioneering work of poets Marianne Moore and William Carlos Williams, and created a stir by publishing the modern, free-verse works of T. S. Eliot and Carl Sandburg. Margaret Anderson's *Little Review* was born at the Fine Arts Building in 1914. In it she serialized James Joyce's *Ulysses*, a novel that so scandalized conservative Midwesterners that the US Postal Service refused to handle the magazine; by 1917, Anderson and her path-breaking review had left town for New York. The year 1915 saw the publication of Edgar Lee Masters' *Spoon River Anthology*, a stark portrayal of the underside of small-town life. Sherwood Anderson

Chicago
(Carl Sandburg, 1916)

Hog Butcher for the World,
Tool Maker, Stacker of Wheat,
Player with Railroads and the Nation's Freight Handler;
Stormy, husky, brawling,
City of the Big Shoulders:

They tell me you are wicked and I believe them, for I
have seen your painted women under the gas lamps
luring the farm boys.
And they tell me you are crooked and I answer: Yes, it
is true I have seen the gunman kill and go free to
kill again.
And they tell me you are brutal and my reply is: On the
faces of women and children I have seen the marks
of wanton hunger.
And having answered so I turn once more to those who
sneer at this my city, and I give them back the sneer
and say to them:
Come and show me another city with lifted head singing
so proud to be alive and coarse and strong and cunning.
Flinging magnetic curses amid the toil of piling job on
job, here is a tall bold slugger set vivid against the
little soft cities;

Fierce as a dog with tongue lapping for action, cunning
as a savage pitted against the wilderness,
Bareheaded,
Shoveling,
Wrecking,
Planning,
Building, breaking, rebuilding,
Under the smoke, dust all over his mouth, laughing with
white teeth,
Under the terrible burden of destiny laughing as a young
man laughs,
Laughing even as an ignorant fighter laughs who has
never lost a battle,
Bragging and laughing that under his wrist is the pulse.
and under his ribs the heart of the people,
Laughing!
Laughing the stormy, husky, brawling laughter of
Youth, half-naked, sweating, proud to be Hog
Butcher, Tool Maker, Stacker of Wheat, Player with
Railroads and Freight Handler to the Nation.

continued the tradition of exposing rural America's hidden foibles in *Windy MacPherson's Son* (1916) and *Winesburg, Ohio* (1919), while Dreiser created more novels on the failings of the American Dream with *The Financier* (1912) and *The Titan* (1914). While a reporter for the *Chicago Daily News*, **Carl Sandburg** published his *Chicago Poems* (1916) and later won a Pulitzer Prize for his biography of Abraham Lincoln. Sandburg's poem "Chicago" remains the most frequently quoted description of the "City of the Big Shoulders."

Carl Sandburg

Library of Congress/Wikimedia Commons

DAILY NEWS AND DEPRESSION

The Chicago literary renaissance ebbed in the 1920s, but the gutsy, lusty style of Chicago writing continued at the *Chicago Daily News,* where reporters Ben Hecht and Charles MacArthur penned *The Front Page* (1928), a hilarious send-up of journalistic moxie. Like many Chicago writers, the pair tasted success and soon moved to New York. The *Daily News* was also home to Eugene Field, the "children's poet," who rhymed the classics "Wynken, Blynken and Nod" and "Little Boy Blue."

The Depression set the tone for a return to social realism, and the Federal Writers' Project brought together the next generation of authors, including **James T. Farrell**, **Richard Wright**, **Nelson Algren**, **Gwendolyn Brooks**, **Studs Terkel** and **Saul Bellow**. Farrell recollected his rowdy Washington Park youth in the *Studs Lonigan* trilogy (1935), while Wright's epochal *Native Son* (1940), set on the South Side, launched a career that took him not only out of Chicago but out of the country whose racism he so eloquently exposed. The publication of Algren's first novel *Never Come Morning* (1942) was marred by the political reaction of Chicago's Polish community, who cringed at having their seamy underside exposed. Algren achieved greater success describing a war veteran hooked on morphine and poker in *The Man With the Golden Arm* (1949). Brooks—first African-American female Pulitzer Prize winner (1949)—published her first collection of poems, *A Street in*

Bronzeville, in 1945, and remained in Chicago despite her fame. She succeeded Carl Sandburg as Poet Laureate of the State of Illinois and served until her death in 2000.

THE LAST FEW DECADES

Oak Park native **Ernest Hemingway** was awarded the Nobel Prize for Literature in 1954. A year earlier, Hemingway won a Pulitzer Prize for his magnificent novel, *The Old Man and the Sea*. Lorraine Hansberry completed *A Raisin in the Sun* in 1959 before leaving for New York. Two writers emerged in the 1960s and 70s from the old Federal Writers' Project circle: **Saul Bellow** and **Studs Terkel**. Bellow released a series of novels that culminated in *Humboldt's Gift,* for which he received the 1976 Nobel Prize, while Terkel honed his skills as the nation's best interviewer with his television and radio programs and award-winning oral histories, including *Working* (1972) and *The Good War* (1984). Due out in 2007, Terkel's memoir *Touch and Go* chronicles his 95 years. Newspaper columnist Mike Royko captured Mayor Richard J. Daley in *Boss* (1971) and carried on the tradition of Algren, Sandburg and Dreiser. Current literary figures include Larry Heineman *(Paco's Song)* and Scott Turow *(Presumed Innocent, Burden of Proof)*. Stuart Dybek and Sandra Cisneros are pushing the boundaries of literary realism with forays into feminism, fantasy, memory and ethnic experience.

Nature

Located in Illinois, less than an hour's drive from Indiana to the southeast and Wisconsin to the north, Chicago occupies a strategic position on the southern end of Lake Michigan, at the point where America's heartland abuts the Great Lakes. Residences, commerce and industry crowd the shoreline, all vying for visual and physical access to the vast body of water, the only Great Lake whose borders lie entirely within the US. The lake has played a significant role in the city's epic transformation into the commercial center of the country's agricultural midsection and hub of a national transportation network, funneling the Midwest's goods across the US and around the globe.

AN INAUSPICIOUS SITE

Today's sprawling city lies on a plain flattened by glaciers and their meltwaters some 13,500 years ago. At that time, the site was located 60ft below the surface of glacial Lake Chicago (ancestor of Lake Michigan). The weight of the ice and of the lake compacted a heavy layer of clay over the dolomite-limestone bedrock

(Niagaran formation), which stretches across the Great Lakes area. The poor drainage of the soil above the clay created a swampy, inhospitable site.

Gradually, the glaciers retreated and, in places, the land rose, creating a sub-continental divide between the Great Lakes and the Mississippi River.

The divide was defined by the Valparaiso Moraine—a glacial ridge that circles the southern end of Lake Michigan about 8mi from the present shoreline—which contained the waters of Lake Chicago. The moraine was breached at the **Chicago Portage**, located at the southwestern edge of the modern city, and the lake's outflow carved the Des Plaines and Illinois river valleys as the water drained toward the Mississippi. Originating in wetlands north and southwest of present-day Chicago, the Chicago River formed about 6,000 years ago; through the years, it remained a small, muddy channel that followed a meandering sandbar and emptied into Lake Michigan.

Around 4,000 years ago, the waters receded farther and the earth rebounded, allowing the ridge to rise again and separate the Des Plaines and Illinois rivers, which continued to flow toward the Mississippi from the Chicago River.

Lake Michigan by North Avenue Beach and Lincoln Park

© Patrick L. Pyszka/City of Chicago/GRC

A Feat of Engineering

The earliest designs for the **Illinois & Michigan Canal** called for a channel 8ft deep and 60ft wide. Owing to financial constraints, the original canal bed was dug only 6ft in depth; the proper water level was to be maintained by a pumping station and feeder canals. Although it was deepened to the planned 8ft in 1871, the canal remained too shallow to allow for the river's permanent reversal. Devastating epidemics—blamed on polluted drinking water—decimated the city in the 1880s, and the weary populace clamored for action. A Sanitary District was quickly created with a mission to dig a new, larger and more effective channel. The resulting Sanitary & Ship Canal was 25ft deep, 100ft wide and over 30mi long. Its construction entailed the removal of more earth than that of the Panama Canal, and when completed in 1900, it easily reversed the flow of the sluggish Chicago River. The Sanitary District also built the Calumet Sag Channel and North Shore Channel in the early 20C to maintain water flow in the correct (wrong) direction. However, the combined storm and sewer system continued to back up after heavy rains, and the river would occasionally flow back into the lake. In the 1970s, the Sanitary District (now known as the Metropolitan Water Reclamation District of Greater Chicago) began construction of the Tunnel and Reservoir Project (TARP) consisting of tunnels 30ft in diameter and 300ft deep, plus three surface reservoirs that store storm runoff until it can be treated. The tunnels now run 109mi through the area, but it will be years before the entire system goes online.

UP FROM THE MUD

The Potawatomi Indians populating the region in the 17C named the area around the present-day city *Checaugou*, referring to the garlic growing wild throughout the swamp. Not considered suitable for settlement by Native Americans, the area was nevertheless chosen by trader **Jean Baptiste Point du Sable**, who erected a homestead here in 1779. The Chicago Portage—one of the shortest and lowest points in the divide—provided a crucial link between the Great Lakes and the Mississippi River and would soon become the key to a major travel route through the middle of the continent. Native Americans, traders and settlers portaged their canoes between the Des Plaines River and a low, wide, swampy fork of the Chicago River called "Mud Lake"; when the water was high, the portage even became navigable. Already in 1673 French explorer Louis Jolliet had proposed the construction of a canal to bridge the divide and effectively link the Atlantic Ocean to the Gulf of Mexico. The canal would be realized almost two centuries later, spurring Chicago's growth.

The city's early history was characterized by the muddy soil on which the city rests. The quagmire not only thwarted road and building construction, but also contributed to the spread of disease. In the 1850s the city began installing sewers throughout the settlement. Since laying the lines underground proved nearly impossible, they were placed at street level, and the streets and existing structures raised or jacked up around them. Unfortunately, the sewers dumped both storm overflow and sewage into the Chicago River, which emptied into Lake Michigan, the source of the city's water supply. To keep the drinking water safe, engineers had to devise a way to reverse the flow of the river. A canal would not only provide a link from the Chicago River to the Des Plaines River, but—if deep enough—could also allow the river's waters to be diverted into it. Rather than continuing its natural course toward the lake, the river would empty into the canal. At the same time, locks would be needed to regulate the amount of lakewater now draining into the unused section of the original riverbed and into the canal.

Chicago's skyline at night
© City of Chicago/GRC

Downtown

The Loop★★★

Source and center of Chicago, the Loop forms the heart of a commercial metropolis that invented the skyscraper and the department store. Culture, commerce and politics are focused in an area bordered on the north and west by the Chicago River, on the east by Lake Michigan and on the south by Congress Parkway. Originally a muddy swamp, today this bustling district is an outdoor museum of architecture and sculpture girdled by a loop of steel elevated tracks.

A BIT OF HISTORY
A Prairie Grows Wild

Chicago began as a frontier trading post at the intersection of Lake Michigan and the Chicago River, in the shadow of Fort Dearborn. Set between the watersheds of the Great Lakes and the Mississippi, the site offered the possibility of an inland waterway connecting New York to New Orleans, and canal planners laid out the original Loop grid at the mouth of the river in 1830. The **Illinois & Michigan Canal** opened in 1848, followed immediately by railroads. Soon Chicago became the largest railroad center and fastest-growing city in the world, expanding from barely 4,000 people in 1837 to 30,000 in 1850 and then tenfold to 300,000 by 1870. Chicago's formidable rail and shipping network supplied lumber and steel to the emerging West and grain and meat to the established East. By the 1880s a ring of cable-car tracks linking neighborhoods to the downtown had created the "Loop," a nickname made official by the 1897 construction of the Union Loop Elevated, connecting transit lines running north, west and south.

A City Reborn

On October 8, 1871, a devastating fire destroyed, the entire Loop in two days. While the conflagration was a monumental tragedy, it was also an opportunity. Fortunately, the city's industry

- **Michelin Map:** pp76–77.
- **Info:** Chicago Office of Tourism Visitor Information Center, 77 E. Randolph St. ℘877-244-2246. www.choosechicago.com.
- **Location:** The intersection of State and Madison streets constitutes the heart of the Loop, indeed of the city. State divides addresses east and west; Madison divides them north and south.
- **Parking:** Some metered parking exists. Underground North and South Grant Park garages along Michigan Avenue and Millennium Park Garage just east of the Loop on Columbus between Randolph and Monroe streets offer the best prices for eight hours. If you arrive first thing, many garages offer early-bird discounts.
- **Don't Miss:** The Chicago Architecture Foundation's Architecture River Cruise. ℘312-922-3432. www.architecture.org.
- **Kids:** The Willis Tower Skydeck offers kid-sized exhibits and an awesome view of four states.
- **Timing:** Plan a full day if sightseeing on your own; more time if you wish to take organized Loop tours.
- **Also See:** Magnificent Mile, River North, Art Institute of Chicago, South Loop, Grant Park, Millenniumn Park, Museum Campus.

GETTING AROUND

BY L: CTA Brown, Green, purple, pink or Orange line to **Adams**; Red or Blue line to **Jackson**.

Tiffany favrile dome inside Macy's

© David Dunai/Apa Publications

and continental rail connections had not burned, and its commercial future was never in doubt. Architects Daniel Burnham, John Root, Louis Sullivan, William Holabird and Martin Roche were drawn to Chicago by the prospect of rebuilding a metropolis. Skyrocketing land values encouraged ever-taller buildings that allowed for more rentable space on each parcel of land. The straight lines of the city's grid gave rise to rows of rectangular buildings. Pioneering skyscrapers such as the Rookery, Monadnock, Marquette and Reliance buildings illustrated an aesthetic that celebrated functionalism and helped usher in the modern world. Chicago architects sank foundations into the swampy soil, developed windbracing and fireproofing techniques, and erected ever-higher steel frames. They developed an artistry based on engineering that would be emulated worldwide.

The 1890s witnessed the emergence of many of the city's cultural venues as it sought to dispel its provincial, avaricious image. The Art Institute (founded in 1879), public library and opera provided stylish landmarks in the Loop, while the shopping attractions of State Street's palatial department stores and the ostentatious Palmer House Hotel attracted the newly wealthy. Prior to the Great Fire, real estate investor Potter Palmer determined that State Street should replace Lake Street as the retail thoroughfare, and he lured Field, Leiter & Co. (later Marshall Field & Co., now Macy's) to move its substantial dry-goods business to the street—then lined by various laundries and stables. The new Loop claimed distinct areas—the Water Street Market fronted the river, while LaSalle and Clark streets hosted banks, attorneys and government offices. The construction of the elevated train, or "L," in 1897 dealt Lake Street's retail strength a permanent blow, while State Street grew rapidly, much to Palmer's benefit. Wabash Avenue featured music businesses, and Michigan Avenue evolved into a cultural boulevard stretching from the auspicious Auditorium Building to the grand public library. The South Loop around the various train stations became a red-light district, while theater marquees lined Randolph Street on the north.

Modern Development

The Loop thrived as the economic, political and cultural heart of Chicago for the first half of the 20C. **State Street** became "that Great Street" with eight department stores, some a full block long. LaSalle Street became synonymous with finance, a half-mile canyon of stock exchanges, banks and businesses. Michigan Avenue added Orchestra Hall, new offices and private clubs to its impressive streetscape overlooking Grant Park. The nature of the Loop began to change in the 1920s as the famous 1909 **Plan of Chicago** was implemented. **Grant Park** was redesigned as a Beaux-Arts promenade, the South Water Street Market was relocated, allowing for the creation of two-level Wacker Drive, while the Michigan Avenue Bridge spurred the development of the North Side. High-rise construction continued until the Great Depression, and stunning Art Deco landmarks like the Board of Trade Building dominated the skyline. The end of World War II heralded drastic change: the new automobile culture, with its suburban housing developments and shopping malls, threatened the vitality of an area defined by steel rails. The Loop became the retail center for the urban poor, accelerating the decline of State Street, which North Michigan Avenue was rapidly supplanting as the principal commercial thoroughfare. While business and commerce continued to prod the erection of new skyscrapers after 1955, the Loop lost many of its retail and entertainment functions and became a "daytime" environment. By the early 1970s the city declared the North Loop "slum and blighted" and pushed for its redevelopment. State Street was transformed into a pedestrian mall in 1978, but retail activity remained in a slump. In an effort to revive local commerce, State Street was reopened to vehicular traffic in 1996; its sidewalks were transformed with Victorian-style streetlights, subway entrances and decorative plantings. Architecture continued to flourish. World-famous architects such as Helmut Jahn, Philip Johnson and Cesar Pelli flocked to the "home of the skyscraper" to erect new office towers along Wacker Drive in the 1980s, before the 1990 recession halted construction. In recent years the Loop has come alive as the city's hottest residential neighborhood. Working Chicagoans and retirees are flocking to condos in upscale new buildings and conversions of older office towers. High-rise student housing shared by several downtown colleges has introduced a vibrant youth culture. The renovated venues of the theater district, along with new cafes and restaurants, have revived nightlife in the Loop, while neighboring Millennium Park and a spruced-up riverfront are attracting even more visitors to this historic city center.

WALKING TOURS
1 THE LOOP'S CORE
Distance: 3.3mi.
A walking tour of the Loop combines the vitality of a commercial hub with a wonderful collection of art and architecture, including the Chicago skyscrapers that revolutionized architecture in the late 19C, towers rendered in the Art Deco, International and post-Modern styles, and a panoply of modern sculpture. The Loop bustles with pedestrians from the predawn opening of the stock, commodities and options markets until late into the evening.

Begin at Congress Pkwy. and S. Michigan Ave. Note that sights located in the western section of the Loop, including the Sears Tower, appear after the Walking Tour.

South Michigan Avenue★ forms the eastern facade of the Loop, a mile of attractive historic buildings facing Grant and Millennium parks and presenting an inviting front door to the City on the Lake. As it is almost impossible to admire the detailing that adorns the high rises from the sidewalk, do so from vantage points—including the front steps of the Art Institute and Millennium Park—on the east side of the avenue.

Auditorium Building★★★
430 S. Michigan Ave. Visit by guided tour (1hr) only, Mon 10.30am & noon, Thu 10.30am. Reservations required. $10. 312-431-2389. www.auditoriumtheatre.org.
This building launched the careers of architects **Dankmar Adler** and **Louis Sullivan**. Influenced by **H. H. Richardson**'s Marshall Field Wholesale Store (now demolished), the Auditorium Building ranked as the tallest and heaviest structure in Chicago when it was com-

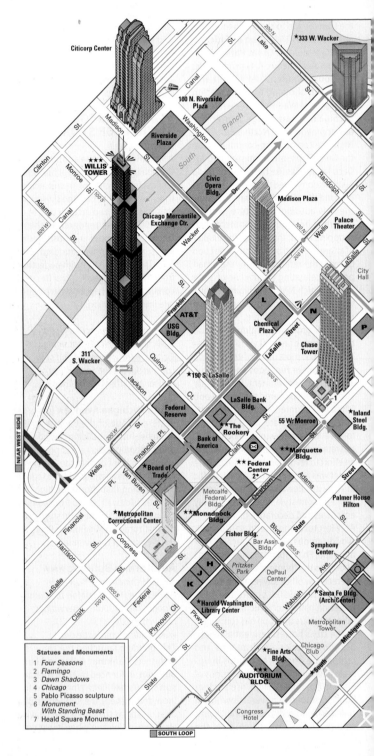

Citicorp Center

★ 333 W. Wacker

100 N. Riverside Plaza

Riverside Plaza

Civic Opera Bldg.

Madison Plaza

Palace Theater

★★★ WILLIS TOWER

Chicago Mercantile Exchange Ctr.

City Hall

AT&T

USG Bldg.

L

Chemical Plaza

N

P

Chase Tower

311 S. Wacker

★ 190 S. LaSalle

LaSalle Bank Bldg.

★ Inland Steel Bldg.

Federal Reserve

★★ The Rookery

55 W. Monroe

Bank of America

★★ Marquette Bldg.

★ Board of Trade

★★ Federal Center 2 ★

Metcalfe Federal Bldg.

Palmer House Hilton

★ Metropolitan Correctional Center

★★ Monadnock Bldg.

Fisher Bldg.

Bar Assn. Bldg.

Symphony Center

H

Pritzker Park

DePaul Center

★ Santa Fe Bldg. (ArchiCenter)

J

K

Metropolitan Tower

★ Harold Washington Library Center

Chicago Club

★ Fine Arts Bldg.

★★★ AUDITORIUM BLDG.

Congress Hotel

NEAR WEST SIDE

Statues and Monuments

1 *Four Seasons*
2 *Flamingo*
3 *Dawn Shadows*
4 *Chicago*
5 Pablo Picasso sculpture
6 *Monument With Standing Beast*
7 Heald Square Monument

SOUTH LOOP

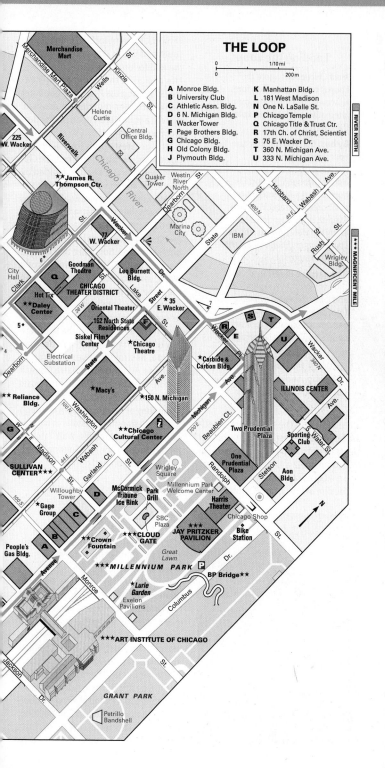

THE LOOP

0 ——— 1/10 mi
0 ——— 200 m

A Monroe Bldg.
B University Club
C Athletic Assn. Bldg.
D 6 N. Michigan Bldg.
E Wacker Tower
F Page Brothers Bldg.
G Chicago Bldg.
H Old Colony Bldg.
J Plymouth Bldg.

K Manhattan Bldg.
L 181 West Madison
N One N. LaSalle St.
P Chicago Temple
Q Chicago Title & Trust Ctr.
R 17th Ch. of Christ, Scientist
S 75 E. Wacker Dr.
T 360 N. Michigan Ave.
U 333 N. Michigan Ave.

RIVER NORTH

★★★ MAGNIFICENT MILE

Merchandise Mart

Merchandise Mart Plaza

Wells

Kinzie ST.

Helene Curtis

Central Office Bldg.

Riverwalk

225 W. Wacker

Chicago River

★★James R. Thompson Ctr.

Quaker Tower

Westin River North

Dearborn

Hubbard

Wabash Ave.

400 N

Marina City

State

IBM

Rush St.

Wrigley Bldg.

City Hall

Clark

Q

Hot Tix

★★Daley Center

6

Goodman Theatre

Leo Burnett Bldg.

77 W. Wacker

Wacker

Lake Street

35 E. Wacker

CHICAGO THEATER DISTRICT

28 W

Oriental Theater

152 North State Residences

Siskel Film Center

F

Chicago Theatre

State

Wacker

7

R E S T

U

5

Electrical Substation

Dearborn

4

★★Reliance Bldg.

100 N

Washington

Macy's

★★150 N. Michigan

★Carbide & Carbon Bldg.

Michigan Ave.

Wacker Dr.

ILLINOIS CENTER

G

W E

Madison St.

44 E

Garland Ct.

Wabash

F

★★Chicago Cultural Center

100 E

Beaubien Ct.

Two Prudential Plaza

Sporting Club

Waters St.

SULLIVAN CENTER ★★★

100 S

Willoughby Tower

Wrigley Square

Randolph

One Prudential Plaza

Aon Bldg.

340 N

★Gage Group

D

McCormick Tribune Ice Rink

Park Grill

Millennium Park Welcome Center

Harris Theater

Stetson

Chicago Shop

C

SBC Plaza

★★★CLOUD GATE

★★★JAY PRITZKER PAVILION

Bike Station

People's Gas Bldg.

A B

★Crown Fountain

Great Lawn

N

Avenue

Monroe

★★★MILLENNIUM PARK

P

BP Bridge★★

★Lurie Garden

Exelon Pavilions

Columbus

★★★ART INSTITUTE OF CHICAGO

Jackson Dr.

GRANT PARK

Petrillo Bandshell

Looping the Loop

Most Chicagoans agree the Loop is best explored on foot. However, the city offers some fun alternative methods of exploring the Loop.

By bus: Chicago Architecture Foundation proposes an overview of the city that includes a drive through the Loop. Or hop aboard a cta no. 151 bus at Wacker Drive and Michigan Avenue, grab a window seat and enjoy the view *(the bus crosses the Loop, stops at Union Station, then returns to State St.).*

By boat: The best way to view the riverfront skyscrapers, river and lake cruises are available from several tour operators and provide a fascinating look at the Loop's architectural diversity.

By "L": Several cta elevated lines circle the Loop, affording an intriguing, if noisy, glimpse of the bustling activity.

pleted in 1889. The pioneering multi-use building, the first constructed under electric lights at night, incorporated a 400-room hotel, a 17-story office tower and a 4,000-seat theater. It influenced the design of the Congress Hotel (1893,

Clinton J. Warren), located immediately south and which was originally called the Auditorium Annex.

The design of the Auditorium Theatre *(50 E. Congress Pkwy.)* by engineer Dankmar Adler remains an acoustic marvel: a young draftsman on the project named Frank Lloyd Wright called it "the greatest room for music and opera in the world—bar none." The Chicago Symphony Orchestra, headed by Theodore Thomas, first played at the Auditorium Theatre, eventually moving to the smaller Orchestra Hall. Abandoned by the Civic Opera in 1929, the Auditorium would have been torn down but for its exceptional size and weight. It served as a USO center during World War II, with bowling alleys installed on the stage. In 1946 Roosevelt University converted the hotel and office areas for its use. The widening of Congress Parkway in the 1950s turned the southern bay of the first floor into a pedestrian arcade, destroying several rooms. In 1967 the Auditorium Theatre Council restored the theater, which now hosts major musical events. The facade is a symphony of design, rising from rough granite to smooth limestone in a series of Romanesque arcades. Walk into the lobby to admire some of Sullivan's intricate organic floriated design.

▷ *Walk north on S. Michigan Ave.*

Fine Arts Building★

410 S. Michigan Ave.
🕐*Open Mon–Sat 7am–10pm (Sat 9pm), Sun 9am–5pm.* ✆*312-566-9800. www.fineartsbuilding.com.*
This 10-story structure (1885, **Solon S. Beman**) symbolizes the 19C transition of South Michigan Avenue from a commercial and residential street to an artistic and cultural boulevard. The "Studebaker" name inscribed above the first floor indicates its original use as a wagon showroom. In 1898 Beman redesigned it as the Fine Arts Building, adding theater and studio spaces and altering the roofline to match the Auditorium Building. The stone and terra-cotta structure, which features Romanesque windows,

Auditorium Building

© Anne Evans/Chicago Architecture Foundation

Fine Arts Building (second from left), South Michigan Avenue

© Benkrut/Dreamstime.com

column capitals and arched entrances, hosted several luminaries: architect Frank Lloyd Wright, William Denslow, who prepared his illustrations for *The Wizard of Oz* in the building, and **Harriet Monroe**, whose *Poetry* magazine began here in 1911. From 1914 to 1917 Margaret Anderson's radical literary journal, *The Little Review*, was published here, introducing a reluctant America to James Joyce's *Ulysses*. Maurice Brown and Ellen Van Volkenburg's influential Little Theater (1912–17) on the fourth floor helped define 20C art theater across the country. The building still houses dance, music and artists' studios. Take the old-fashioned, manually operated elevator to the 10th floor to view eight beautiful murals created by artists of The Little Room—a gathering of resident artists formed in 1892.

The 1929 red Romanesque Revival Chicago Club *(corner of S. Michigan Ave. and Van Buren St.)* mimics the original **Burnham & Root** building that collapsed during renovation in 1929.

▷ *Cross Van Buren St. and continue north.*

At 310 South Michigan Avenue stands **Metropolitan Tower**, originally the S. W. Straus Building, today remodeled as condominiums. At night six 1,000-watt light bulbs enclosed in a blue box illuminate the glass beehive adorning the roof. The imposing structure was erected one year after Chicago's 1923 zoning law, which allowed construction of buildings taller than 260ft, as long as the design included setbacks.

▷ *Cross Jackson Blvd.*

Santa Fe Building★
224 S. Michigan Ave.
Formerly known as the Railway Exchange Building, this 1904 design by D. H. Burnham & Co., finely detailed in pale terra-cotta, combines the structure of the Chicago school with the white Neoclassical ornament popularized by the 1893 World's Columbian Exposition. Burnham was both architect and developer, moving into the building

Interior of Santa Fe Building

© Anne Evans/Chicago Architecture Foundation

and producing his famous 1909 Plan of Chicago here. Step in to see the two-story atrium, reminiscent of **Burnham & Root's Rookery** with its grand staircase, balustraded mezzanine and elaborate metal light standards.

The not-for-profit **Chicago Architecture Foundation Shop and Tour Center** located here offers some of the city's best neighborhood tours, as well as free lectures and exhibits (⊙open Apr–Dec daily 9am–6.30pm (Fri 9am–7pm); ⊙closed Jan 1, Thanksgiving Day, Dec 25; ℘312-922-3432; www.architecture.org).

Orchestra Hall at Symphony Center

220 S. Michigan Ave. ♿✕℘312-294-3000. www.cso.org.

Cornerstone of Symphony Center is the 1904 Orchestra Hall, home of the world-famous Chicago Symphony Orchestra. The Georgian-style hall was planned by orchestra founder Theodore Thomas and completed after his death by D. H. Burnham & Co. In 1997 a $110 million renovation and expansion were completed, which improved the main hall's acoustics and doubled the building's space to 291,000sq ft. The new space includes **Rhapsody**, which serves innovative American cuisine in the elegant dining room or on a landscaped outdoor terrace.

Dominating the Grant Park side of South Michigan Avenue, between Jackson Boulevard and Monroe Street, is the imposing facade of the **Art Institute**. At the corner with Adams Street, look north to view **One Prudential Plaza** (1955, Naess & Murphy), the first high rise built after the Great Depression and the tallest in Chicago when it was completed. It is now dwarfed by **Two Prudential Plaza** (1990, Loebl, Schlossman & Hackl), with its dramatic needle-like spire and chevron roofline. Farther east, the **Aon Center** was designed in 1973 by Edward Durell Stone and Perkins & Will. After a time, its thin marble sheathing began to warp, and the entire building was refaced with thicker North Carolina granite in 1990 at a cost equal to the original construction.

▷ *Cross Adams St. and continue north.*

People's Gas Building (122 S. Michigan Ave.) is a massive Beaux-Arts high rise executed in 1910 by D. H. Burnham & Co. for the city's major natural-gas supplier. Two-story granite Ionic columns, terra-cotta fretwork and stone lion heads almost entirely disguise the steel framework that is characteristic of the Chicago school.

▷ *Continue north to the corner of S. Michigan Ave. and Monroe St.*

The **Monroe Building (A)** (104 S. Michigan Ave.) and **University Club (B)** (76 E. Monroe St.) were designed in 1912 and 1908 respectively by **Holabird & Roche** to cater for the eclectic tastes of the early 20C. The Monroe Building features Mediterranean columns, Gothic terra-cotta ornament and a gabled roof. It was designed to complement the Gothic Revival University Club across the street, which also sports a gabled roof. The exterior of the private club is embellished with leaded-glass windows, protruding bays, and Gothic spires and gargoyles at the crown.

▷ *Cross Monroe St., continue north.*

Gage Group★

18–30 S. Michigan Ave.

Built for the Keith, Gage and Ascher millinery firms in 1899 by Holabird & Roche, this trio exemplifies the typical Chicago school facades that use a brick curtain wall to express the skeletal steel frame. In traditional construction, the walls supported the buildings. The Chicago school reversed architectural tradition by making the building (a steel frame) support the walls, which were draped on the iron skeleton like a curtain. Note the facade by **Louis Sullivan** at no. 18, where his typical flowery ornament enlivens the spandrels and explodes from the piers at the cornice.

Adjacent to the Gage Building, the **Chicago Athletic Association Building (C)** (1893, **Henry Ives Cobb**) draws attention with the interweaving Venetian Gothic

Preston Bradley Hall, Chicago Cultural Center

© City of Chicago/GRC

trefoil arches that adorn its richly varied facade. The 1929 Willoughby Tower *(8 S. Michigan Ave.)* applies Gothic ornament to an Art Deco facade.

▷ *Cross Madison St., continue north.*

6 North Michigan Building (D), executed in 1899 by Richard E. Schmidt, was the site of Montgomery Ward's nationwide mail-order business. Aaron Montgomery Ward performed a great service to Chicago when he sued to keep the lakefront free of buildings.

▷ *Cross Washington St.*

Chicago Cultural Center★★
78 E. Washington St. ⏰*Open year-round Mon–Thu 8am–7pm, Fri 8am–6pm, Sat 9am–6pm, Sun 10am–6pm.* ⏰*Closed major holidays.* ♿✕. ✆*312-744-6630. www.chicago culturalcenter.org.*
This marvelous Neoclassical palazzo served as the city's first permanent library when completed in 1897 after designs by Shepley, Rutan & Coolidge, who also designed the Art Institute. Noteworthy elements include a smooth limestone facade, recessed windows and elaborate Renaissance moldings at the entrance, cornice and balconies.
Step inside to admire the inlaid-marble grand stairway that ascends from the Washington Street entrance to **Pres-**
ton Bradley Hall★, with its Tiffany stained-glass dome. Visit any Wednesday at 12.15pm and Preston Bradley Hall reverberates with the classical sounds of a Dame Myra Hess Memorial Concert. Another magnificent stained-glass dome is located on the north end of the second floor.
A wide array of free public programs is offered here daily, including concerts, film, dance, lectures and art exhibits. This is also the home of the **Chicago Office of Tourism Visitor Information Center** *(77 E. Randolph St., north side of building, 1st floor;* ⏰*open year-round Mon–Thu 8am–7pm, Fri 8am–6pm, Sat 9am–6pm, Sun 10am–6pm;* ⏰*closed major holidays;* ✆*312-744-2400; www. explorechicago.org).* A good place to start a Loop tour, the visitor center features an exhibit on the history of the Loop and a 7min video tour of Chicago's "downtown neighborhood" in eight languages. The Landmark Chicago Gallery *(west side of building)* exhibits photographs of historic buildings throughout the city.
Directly west of the Cultural Center note the Heritage at Millennium Park, erected in 2005. The tallest residential building in the Loop at 57 floors, the Heritage represents the height of the recent downtown condo development trend. At Garland Court and Randolph Street stands Richard Hunt's shimmering steel sculpture *We Will* (2005).

Cross Randolph St. and continue north on N. Michigan Ave.

The unique roofline of **150 North Michigan Avenue**★ (1984, A. Epstein & Sons), beveled and set at a 45-degree angle to the street, marks the end of Michigan Avenue's Millennium Park frontage.

Cross Lake St. and continue north.

Extending over 83 acres along the east side of North Michigan Avenue, **Illinois Center** *(between Michigan Ave., N. Lake Shore Dr., the river and Lake St.)* comprises more than a dozen buildings, grand in conception but muted and sterile in execution. One of the world's largest mixed-use projects was first envisioned in the 1920s for the air rights of the Illinois Central Railroad, which has run along the lakefront since the 1850s.

Built in the 1970s and 1980s, mostly by the successor firms of Mies van der Rohe, the complex includes hotels, offices, shops, apartments. The small Sporting Club (1990, Kisho Kurokawa) is recognizable by its four white, framework towers that pay homage to Louis Sullivan and sport 17ft wind sculptures, called *Children of the Sun* by Osamu Shingu.

Continue to Wacker Pl.

Carbide and Carbon Building★
230 N. Michigan Ave.
Now the Hard Rock Hotel, this Art Deco skyscraper (1929, Burnham Bros.), inspired by Raymond Hood's American Radiator Building in New York, is faced with dark green terra-cotta accented with gold-leaf ornament, especially on the stepped-back tower. A two-story lobby features curvilinear and geometric ornament with incised carving characteristic of the Deco style.

Turn left on Wacker Pl.

Wacker Tower (E) *(68 E. Wacker Pl.)*, designed by Holabird & Root (1928) for the Chicago Motor Club, is a good example of the Art Deco style, defined by setbacks, continuous piers and recessed windows

that emphasize the vertical. Visible just north of the river are the "corncob" towers of the Marina City complex.

Turn left on Wabash Ave., right on Lake St. and continue to State St.

This section of Lake Street is located beneath the elevated Loop railway, first erected in 1897 to connect the various railroad lines serving the central business district. Marking the southeast corner of State and Lake streets, the **Page Brothers Building (F)** (1872, John Mills Van Osdel) features a cast-iron Italianate facade *(Lake St. side)* and is a rare survivor of the building boom that followed the Great Fire of 1871.

Turn left onto State St. and continue south.

One of the city's earliest and largest (4,000 seats) vaudeville movie palaces, the **Chicago Theatre**★ *(175 N. State St.)*, designed by Rapp & Rapp in 1921, is French Renaissance in inspiration. Its terra-cotta facade and multistory **lobby**★ were restored in 1985 after narrowly avoiding demolition.

At the northwest corner of State and Randolph streets, the **Siskel Film Center** and **162 North State Residences** of the Art Institute of Chicago incorporate the facade of the Old Heidelberg restaurant (1934, Graham, Anderson, Probst and White) on Randolph and the 1924 terra-cotta Butler Building on State in a white concrete design (2000, Booth/Hansen Associate of Chicago). The oversized cornice and attic level with porthole windows contains art studios, while the ground level features retail stores and the school's famed Siskel Film Center.

Cross Randolph St.

Macy's★
111 North State St. ⏰*Open Mon–Fri 10am –8pm, Sat 9am–9pm, Sun 11am–6pm.*
✕. ✆*312-781-1000. www.macys.com.*
Occupying an entire city block, this building was constructed in several

stages between 1892 and 1914 by D. H. Burnham & Co. for **Marshall Field**. It combines the firm's structural engineering innovations with the Neo-classicism made popular by the World's Columbian Exposition of 1893. Marshall Field's career in commerce began in the dry-goods business with partners Potter Palmer and Levi Leiter. In the 1860s Palmer left to focus on real estate, and Leiter split off shortly afterwards.

Field became the preeminent department store retailer, succeeding under the dictum "Give the Lady What She Wants." The richly embellished clocks that ornament the corners on State Street are Chicago icons.

The interior contains over 1 million square feet of retail space and features a Tiffany favrile dome *(near State and Washington Sts.)*.

Reliance Building

© Anne Evans/Chicago Architecture Foundation

▷ *Continue south on State St. to Madison St.*

Reliance Building★★

32 N. State St., at corner of Washington St.
Years ahead of its time, this building anticipated the glass and steel skyscrapers of Mies van der Rohe and the Second Chicago school. In 1895, a decade after the invention of the skyscraper, **Charles B. Atwood** of D. H. Burnham & Co. realized the possibilities inherent in skeletal frame construction and designed the Reliance Building.

The facade is almost entirely glass. Extremely narrow piers and spandrels between floors, featuring Gothic ornamentation in creamy white terra-cotta, reduce the solid exterior walls to a minimum. Projecting bays create a play of light across the facade and allow more light into the interior. Initially occupied by dentists and doctors, the structure was neglected for half a century before its 1999 restoration as the 122-room **Hotel Burnham**.

The hotel retains many of the building's original elements, including the ornamental ironwork elevator grills and the marble mosaic floor in the elevator lobby. The renovation included the upscale **Atwood Cafe** (✆312-368-1900; www.atwoodcafe.com) at street level; its generous windows overlook the busy corner.

The heart of the Loop at State and Madison was once acclaimed as the world's busiest intersection. All four corner buildings exhibit the typical "Chicago window." The rusticated, brown **Chicago Building (G)** at 7 West Madison Street (1904, Holabird & Roche) exemplifies an early skyscraper divided into a base, shaft and crown. Of note are the projecting bays of Chicago windows and the fancy cornice. In 1997 the office tower was rehabilitated as a dormitory for the nearby School of the Art Institute of Chicago.

Sullivan Center★★★

One S. State St., at the southeast corner of Madison and State Sts.
Designed by **Louis Sullivan** in 1899, this structure is considered his greatest work. Sullivan decreed that "form follows function," yet he was the consummate 19C ornamentalist, and his gift is nowhere more apparent than here. The upper stories are white terra-cotta, plainly expressing the steel grid underneath, but the first two floors are bedecked with some of the most elaborate and plastic designs ever created by Sullivan. His ability to produce foliate ornament in three dimensions is best seen in the rounded corner, where the

Facade, Sullivan Center

© Anne Evans/Chicago Architecture Foundation

cast iron reaches out to create portholes that hover above the glass, making the massive building seem light and airy. Form does follow function, as the ornament was designed to attract shoppers to the goods in the windows. **Carson Pirie Scott & Co.** acquired the building in 1904, operating its flagship department store there until closing it in 2007.

> ◖ *Cross Monroe St.*

The **Palmer House Hilton** (1927, Holabird & Roche), located at the southeast corner of State and Monroe Streets, is the fourth of this name founded by real estate mogul Potter Palmer. The luxurious interior features a grand Beaux-Arts second-floor **lobby**★ and the Empire Ballroom. In 2007 the hotel launched a comprehensive renovation program.

> ◖ *Turn right on Monroe St. and continue to Dearborn St.*

Inland Steel Building★
30 W. Monroe St.
This elegant high rise (1958, Skidmore, Owings & Merrill) must have been an apparition when it opened, its shining stainless-steel facade surrounded by masonry buildings that were dark with soot. Bruce Graham designed a unique structural cage that supports the building outside of the wall plane, creating

column-free floors. To achieve this, steel pilings were anchored 85ft deep into the bedrock, while the mechanical and elevator systems were placed in a windowless steel tower to the east. In addition to innovative engineering techniques, Inland Steel also pioneered the use of air-conditioning and dual glazing for windows. Richard Lippold's *Radiant I*, a three-dimensional web of steel rods and wires, graces the lobby.

At Dearborn Street, look north to the gracefully rising concave facade of the 60-story **Chase Tower**, designed in 1969 by Perkins & Will. The edifice has extremely wide bays sheltering a large bank on the lower floors and offices above. The popular plaza surrounds the rectangular *Four Seasons* **(1)** mosaic created by artist Marc Chagall in 1974.

> ◖ *Walk south on Dearborn St.*

The **55 West Monroe Building**, formerly the Xerox Centre (1980, C. F. Murphy Assocs.), sports the mirrored wall surfaces and curving facades favored by chief architect **Helmut Jahn**.

Marquette Building★★
140 S. Dearborn St.
Considered one of **Holabird & Roche**'s skyscraper masterpieces, this 1895 Chicago school design expresses the structural frame in the finely detailed

terra-cotta and brick exterior. The piers project forward from the windows, creating a soaring grid best appreciated by looking up from the entrance. The corners are emphasized to suggest solidity. Four bronze panels above the entrance illustrate journal writings of French explorer-missionary Jacques Marquette, one of the first Europeans to visit the Chicago region.

The hexagonal lobby features a stunning Tiffany glass **mosaic**★ by J. A. Holzer illustrating Marquette's journey in the Mississippi River basin, as well as bas-reliefs of early French explorers and Native Americans by Edward Kemeys.

In the office lobby of the JP Morgan Chase Center (2003, Ricardo Bofill) at 131 South Dearborn Street looms a gilded cast of the Louvre's *Winged Victory of Samothrace*.

▷ *Cross Adams St.*

Federal Center★★
On Dearborn St. between Adams St. and Jackson Blvd.

Designed by **Ludwig Mies van der Rohe** in 1964 and completed 10 years later, this three-building complex is an excellent example of International-style architecture and urban space. The one-story post office is as tall as the lobbies of the Dirksen and Kluczynski buildings, set at right angles to each other across Dearborn Street. All three buildings frame the beautiful plaza graced by Alexander Calder's 1973 **Flamingo (2)**, which seems to suggest steel beams that have leapt off the building to dance a bright red ballet. Mies van der Rohe's buildings appear stark and unadorned, but their beauty depends on rigid adherence to laws of proportion, and the edifices are ornamented by attached I-beams that run up the facade like vertical ribs.

Monadnock Building★★
53 W. Jackson Blvd.

Behind the Federal Center rises a long, narrow building that exemplifies the architectural revolution that saw bricks replaced by steel. The northern half of the building (1891, Burnham & Root) is the tallest masonry structure in Chicago. Walls 6ft thick at the base support 16 stories plus an attic of bricks piled on bricks (the thickness of the walls can be seen in the window openings on the ground floor).

Peter and Shepherd Brooks developed the structure, insisting on brick, which they thought was more fireproof than the new steel technology. They also didn't want to pay for ornament. It must have shocked Victorian Chicagoans to see a "naked" building rising in this section of the Loop. Architect **John Wellborn Root** said its design, flared at the base and crown, was based on an Egyptian papyrus or the capital letter "I." Root's skills are apparent in the muscularity of the bays that ripple out of the wall plane along Dearborn Street. The southern half of the building (1893, Holabird & Roche) is partially braced by a steel frame and features more traditional ornament.

▷ *Walk south through the lobby of the Monadnock Building.*

The **interior**★ was painstakingly restored to its original design in the 1980s, including replication of the mosaic floor. The original marble ceiling and restored marble walls are ornamented by cast-aluminum light fixtures and a staircase in foliate forms reminiscent of the Rookery. The large interior shop windows provide a second "street" for retailers and bring light into the corridor from outside.

▷ *Exit the lobby at Van Buren St., turn left and walk east.*

Located at 343 South Dearborn Street, the Gothic-style **Fisher Building** (1896, D. H. Burnham & Co.), inspired by the Reliance Building, is faced with light orange terra-cotta that includes playful references to the owner's name in the form of sculpted fish surrounding the edifice's former entrance in the center of the Van Buren Street facade.

Harold Washington Library Center★

400 S. State St. ⏰Open year-round Mon –Thu 9am–9pm; Fri–Sat 9am–5pm, Sun 1pm–5pm. ⏰Closed major holidays. ♿ ✆312-747-4999. www.chipublib.org.

Hammond, Beeby & Babka won a competition to design Chicago's new library, a grandly scaled 1991 design that announces its public function with classical arcaded facades, ornamental garlands and an overachieving roofline of green metal and glass with looming owls. The building's rusticated base refers to landmarks such as the Auditorium and Marquette buildings. Inside, a mosaic mural on the sterile first floor memorializes the city's first African-American mayor, the building's namesake. Reading rooms fill floors three through eight, and a large skylit "winter garden" tops out the structure. A post-Modern glass wall forms the western facade.

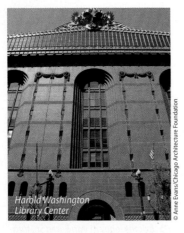

Harold Washington Library Center

© Anne Evans/Chicago Architecture Foundation

▷ *Backtrack on Van Buren St. and cross Dearborn St.*

Look south on Dearborn to admire a trio of late-19C buildings. The **Old Colony Building (H)** (1894, Holabird & Roche), at 407 South Dearborn Street has rounded corners, a hallmark of the Victorian era. Located next door at no. 417, the **Plymouth Building (J)** (1899, Simeon B. Eisendrath) illustrates the use of Gothic ornament to illuminate high-rise towers.

The **Manhattan Building (K)** (1891, **William Le Baron Jenney**), at no. 431, is an experiment in decoration, with polygonal and rounded bays, a granite base and a variety of ornament such as the grotesque faces that stare out from the bottom of each protruding bay.

▷ *Continue west on Van Buren St.*

Metropolitan Correctional Center★

On Van Buren St. between Clark and Federal Sts.

Appearing almost two-dimensional, this unique concrete structure (1975, Harry Weese & Assocs.) resembles an old IBM punch card. The triangular layout affords an easily patrolled plan for the cells holding prisoners awaiting trial in the nearby Federal Center. The cells also dictate the narrow beveled windows, which cannot exceed 5in wide and remain without bars.

▷ *Turn right on Clark St.*

Dominating the lobby of the Metcalfe Federal Building (*77 W. Jackson Blvd.*) is a huge Frank Stella sculpture, *The Town-Ho's Story,* visible from the street.

▷ *Turn left on Jackson Blvd.*

Chicago Board of Trade Building★

141 W. Jackson Blvd.

Considered one of the city's best Art Deco skyscrapers, the 45-story Board of Trade (1930) was designed by Holabird & Root, successor to the Chicago-school firm of Holabird & Roche. Recessed windows and terra-cotta spandrels balance soaring limestone piers that terminate in sculptures. The pyramidal roof is capped by John Storrs' 32ft-tall aluminum sculpture of Ceres, the goddess of the harvest, and Father Time and a Native American cradling grain flank the clock in the center of the main facade. The Board of Trade was founded in 1848 to regulate the trade of grain and commodities from Illinois and the Great Plains through Chicago to the eastern seaboard. In 1980 Helmut Jahn of C. F. Murphy Assocs. designed a rear addition that defers to the older building in scale and form despite its reflective surfaces. In 1997, the Board of Trade underwent a third expansion to the east. This 60,000sq ft annex has four floors (equivalent in height to 12 stories) and is connected to the main building by a bridge spanning a landscaped pedestrian mall.

Since 9/11 the public is allowed only to enter the Visitor Center, where exhibits explain the work and world of the CBOT (⊙ open Mon–Fri 8am–4pm; ℘312-435-3590; www.cmegroup.com).

▷ *Walk north on LaSalle St.*

Chicago Board of Trade Building

© Chicago Architecture Foundation/Anne Evans

The **LaSalle Street** "canyon" stretches from the Board of Trade to the river, its walls formed by banks and brokerage institutions in a unity of architecture that belies the competitive financial world within. **The Bank of America Building** (1924) and **Federal Reserve Bank Building** (1922), both designed by Graham, Anderson, Probst & White, frame the end of LaSalle Street with classical grandeur. Ionic columns and an entrance pediment on the Bank of America are mirrored by a Corinthian portal on the Federal Reserve, the ensemble a fitting anchor for the LaSalle Street canyon. The Bank of America features a restored second-floor banking hall with a coffered ceiling and huge murals by Jules Guerin, illustrator of the 1909 Plan of Chicago. In the small Money Museum in the Federal Reserve you can ogle—but not touch—a million dollars in cash.

▷ *Continue north on LaSalle St. to Adams St.*

As you pass Quincy Court on the left, note the looming Sears Tower.

The Rookery★★

At the southeast corner of LaSalle and Adams Sts. www.therookerybuilding.com
This 1888 structure is one of the earliest designs by **Burnham & Root** and the

Atrium, The Rookery

© Mario Savoia/Bigstockphoto.com

most impressive landmark rehabilitation in the Loop. The building's name comes from a temporary city hall erected here in 1871 that attracted birds. A playful reference to this attraction is found in carved birds (rooks) on either side of the entrance. Noted for the richness of John Wellborn Root's design and detailing, the 12-story facade of red granite, terra-cotta and brick is a combination of Romanesque Revival and Queen Anne elements, the former apparent in the large arched entrance. Two-story columns frame the lower retail floors, while arcades organized around the protruding entrance bay characterize the upper floors.

The square building is organized around a large **light court**★★, an atrium designed to admit natural light to interior offices in the era before gas and electric illumination. Now enclosed by a domed skylight, the light court is considered a work of art in its own right. The interior was remodeled in 1906 by Frank Lloyd Wright, who covered Root's iron columns and staircases with white marble, incised and inlaid with gold leaf. One side of the column to the left as you enter the atrium is exposed to reveal the original Root design. This rare commercial work of Wright features Prairie-style urns framing the central staircase to the east. The west side is dominated by a graceful eight-story spiral staircase. The 1928 elevator lobby by Prairie school architect William Drummond includes whimsical elevator doors by Annette Cremin Byrne, which again play on the building's avian nomenclature. A $103 million restoration in 1992 brought the building back to its full glory.

190 South LaSalle Street★

At the northwest corner of LaSalle and Adams Sts.

Internationally renowned architects come to Chicago to realize their own work and to pay homage to the birthplace of the skyscraper. This 1987 building by Philip Johnson recapitulates Chicago's Masonic Temple (1892, Burnham & Root, demolished in 1939) with its distinctive cross-gabled roof and elaborate iron cresting. Red marble pilasters and and oversized lanterns distinguish the elegant white marble **lobby**, surmounted by a gilded, vaulted ceiling. Art enlivening the lobby includes a 28ft steel sculpture, *Chicago Fugue,* by Anthony Caro.

Located across the street at no. 135, the **LaSalle Bank Building** (1934, Graham, Anderson, Probst & White), erected by the estate of Marshall Field, was the last high rise built during the Great Depression. The edifice stands on the former site of the Home Insurance Building erected by William Le Baron Jenney in 1884. Step inside the huge Art Deco structure to view the lovely two-story lobby featuring chevroned skywalks, fluted chandeliers and an elevator panel in the shape of the building.

▶ *Continue north on LaSalle St., turn left on Monroe St. and walk west.*

Look west to view the 1988 **AT&T Corporate Center** *(227 W. Monroe St.),* linked to the 1992 **USG Building,** both designed by Adrian Smith of Skidmore, Owings & Merrill. The complex reinterprets Art Deco and marks a return to architecture organized around a hierarchy of detail, with ornamented window spandrels and light sconces shaped like the spires atop the structure.

▶ *Turn right on Wells St. and continue to Madison St.*

At the corner of Wells and Madison streets stands **200 West Madison Street** (1982, Skidmore, Owings & Merrill), distinguished by an accordion wall of mirrored glass and steel typical of 1980s architecture. The facade creates numerous corner offices. Inside, the Winter Garden houses Louise Nevelson's sculpture *Dawn Shadows* **(3)**, an intricate group of curving black forms. Marking the southeast corner of that intersection, **181 West Madison Street (L)**, designed by design by Cesar Pelli, features extremely narrow bays and ribbing that dramatize its verticality. Colorful sculptures by Frank Stella, *Loomings* and

Knights and Squires, named for chapters from *Moby Dick,* decorate the barrel-vaulted lobby.

▷ *Walk east on Madison St. to LaSalle St.*

Chemical Plaza *(southwest corner of LaSalle and Madison Sts.)* features the original base of a 1912 building by Holabird & Roche surmounted by a sleek addition (1989) of blue and green aluminum and glass by Moriyama & Teshima. Designed in 1930, **One North LaSalle Street (N)** *(northeast corner of LaSalle and Madison Sts.)* draws the eye to its fifth-floor panels depicting French explorer La Salle, who is thought to have stayed in the area in the late 17C.

▷ *Walk north on LaSalle St. to Washington St. and turn right.*

At the intersection of LaSalle and Washington, look back for an impressive **view** of the canyon culminating with the Board of Trade. The ornate City Hall/County Building *(bounded by Clark, Washington, LaSalle and Randolph Sts.)* was built in two sections, in 1907 and 1911, by Holabird & Roche. Huge, 75ft Corinthian columns (the tallest in the city) span the fifth to ninth stories.

▷ *Continue to the intersection of Washington and Clark Sts.*

Chicago Temple (P)

77 W. Washington St., at the southeast corner of Washington and Clark Sts. Sanctuary. ⚲*Open daily year round 7am–9pm.* ☏*312-236-4548. www.chicagotemple.org.*

When completed in 1923 by Holabird & Roche, this edifice was the city's tallest building and remains the tallest church spire in the world at 568ft. The First United Methodist Church occupies the large, English Gothic-style sanctuary on the first floor, as well as the sky chapel, added to the steeple in the 1950s. Encompassing only 700sq ft, the tiny gem features lovely stained-glass windows and carvings on the oak walls.

A 99-seat theater on the lower level presents productions by the **Silk Road Theatre Project** *(☏312-857-1234; www.srtp.org/temple).*

East of the temple stands Joan Miró's celebrated *Chicago* **(4)** sculpture, resembling an elemental female form. A gift to the city from the artist, the 39ft statue was erected in 1981.

Richard J. Daley Center★★

Bounded by Washington, Randolph, Clark and Dearborn Sts.

In 1965 Jacques Brownson of C. F. Murphy Assocs. designed this fine example of Miesian architecture, bold and muscular as the city it represents. Massive bays, 87ft wide, are joined by huge, cross-shaped beams that narrow as they rise to the top. Only three bays span the main facade of tinted glass and Cor-Ten steel, designed to weather to a bronze patina resembling rust. Rising 648ft, the 31-story structure was named for the late Richard J. Daley. Cor-Ten was also used to fabricate the untitled **Pablo Picasso sculpture**★ **(5)** in the plaza, which stirred controversy when unveiled in 1967 but has since become a beloved symbol of the city. The building houses courtrooms and offices, while numerous cultural events and a farmers' market *(⚲May–Oct every Thu, 7am–3pm)* take place in the plaza.

▷ *Continue north on Clark St. and cross Randolph St.*

The unusual top of the **Chicago Title & Trust Center (Q)** *(161 N. Clark St.),* built in 1992 by Kohn Pedersen Fox, suggests the Chicago River's bascule bridges.

Hot Tix, offering discount and full price theater tickets, is located at 72 E. Randolph Street.

The stately white terra-cotta facades of the landmark Harris and Selwyn theaters (1922, Crane and Franzheim) have been joined to form the new **Goodman Theatre** (2000, Kuwabara Payne McKenna Blumberg) at the northeast corner of Dearborn and Randolph. Established in 1925 as a gift to the Art Institute (in its former location on South Columbus

Chicago Theater

© Patrick L. Pyszka/City of Chicago/GRC

Chicago Theater District

The **North Loop**'s reign as Chicago's entertainment district dates to the late 19C when the Loop was a collection of five-story walk-ups. By 1879 the Central Music Hall stood at State and Randolph; it was joined 12 years later by Adler & Sullivan's skyscraper Schiller Theater (later renamed the Garrick), which rose between Clark and Dearborn. The construction of the Woods Theater in 1917 at Randolph and Dearborn was followed by a troupe of lavishly decorated

Goodman Theatre.

© Jeff Goldberg/ESTO/Goodman Theatre

vaudeville palaces in the Roaring 20s, a period when bright movie marquees lined Chicago's "Great White Way"—Randolph Street— promoting stars of stage and screen.

In the decades following World War II, the rise of television and the flight of city dwellers to suburbia began to bring the curtain down on Randolph Street. In the early 1960s the Garrick Theater was razed and replaced with a parking garage. By the 1970s the North Loop was beset by urban blight. Although preservationists saved the **Chicago Theatre** *(175 N. State St.)* after a struggle in 1986, others such as the Woods (1917–88) and United Artists (1928–89) were demolished. In the late 1990s, local developer Lew Manilow realized his dream of a North Loop theater district with the renovation of the **Oriental Theater** by Ford *(now the Oriental Theater/Ford Center for the Performing Arts; 24 W. Randolph St.)* and the 1999 rescue of the **Palace Theater** by Cadillac *(151 W. Randolph St.).* That same year, the district came full circle as the parking garage that had replaced the Garrick was torn down to create the new **Goodman Theatre** *(170 N. Dearborn St.).* In 2000 the Siskel Film Center of The School of the Art Insititute added cinema to the collection of restored live theater venues. Today theaters in the district offer performances from classic dramas such as Arthur Miller's *Death of a Salesman* to contemporary musicals like *Wicked (for a list of theaters, see p270).*

Drive), the Goodman is considered the oldest residential theater in the US.

James R. Thompson Center★★
Bounded by Clark, LaSalle, Randolph and Lake Sts.
This unusual building, formerly the State of Illinois Center, was named for the Illinois governor who chose the 1985 design by architect Helmut Jahn. Today the center houses state agencies and a large lower-level food court. Note on the plaza Jean Dubuffet's *Monument With Standing Beast* **(6)**, a fiberglass sculpture of curvaceous black and white forms. The building's exterior skin of glass and pastel panels seems ethereal when compared to the stone and steel buildings around it, and its form ignores the street grid to create a sense of dramatic entry. The shape is a post-Modern reference to the Classical domes of government buildings. A visit to the soaring **atrium**★ is a must, since it rises the building's full 17 stories with glass elevators to the beveled "dome within a dome." The effect of light filtering into the space creates a play of shadows that changes constantly. The open office floors and glass skin have caused heating, cooling and noise problems, but few visitors pass up a chance to see this quirky monument.

◯ *Continue north on Clark St. and turn right on Wacker Dr.*

Across the river to the east stand the **Quaker Tower** and Westin River North (formerly Hotel Nikko) development, erected in 1987. Adjacent to the Marina City complex, the IBM Building forces its rectangular form onto its curving riverfront site.

77 West Wacker Drive★
Corner of W. Wacker Dr. and N. Clark St.
Celebrated Barcelona architect Ricardo Bofill designed this 1992 office tower in his "Modern Classical" style with a pedimented top and marble elements that suggest Greek and Roman temples. The firm of DeStefano & Partners supervised construction of the 50-story structure, one of the last skyscrapers to be erected in the Loop in the 20C. The elegant **lobby** in pure white marble from Thásos, Greece, features works by Catalan artists, including a wonderful Bofill's *Twisted Columns,* and the rocklike *Three Lawyers and a Judge* by sculptor Xavier Corbero, set amid live bamboo.

◯ *Cross Dearborn St. and continue east on Wacker Dr.*

At this point, take a moment to absorb the splendid **view**★ east toward the Wrigley Building and Michigan Avenue Bridge. Erected in 1989 by Roche & Dinkeloo and Shaw & Assocs., the **Leo Burnett Building** *(35 W. Wacker Dr.)* resembles a Prairie-school column with its division into a base, shaft and capital. The corners protrude, creating more corner offices. The gray granite facade's square windows are ornamented with chrome. Lobby sculpture includes a semifigurative bronze fountain, *Rite of Spring,* by Bryan Hunt.

◯ *Cross State St. and continue east on Wacker Dr.*

35 East Wacker Drive★
Northwest corner of Wabash St. and Wacker Dr.
Reflecting historical themes popular in the mid-1920s, this buff-colored terracotta high rise (1926, Thielbar & Fugard) is bedecked in a profusion of Beaux-Arts detailing. Originally called the Jewelers Building (note the "JB" initials carved in terra-cotta panels on the facade), until 1940 it featured a car elevator that allowed tenants to drive into the building. The top of the structure is distinguished by four large Neoclassical lanterns at the corners, artfully disguising water tanks, as well as a 17-story central tower capped by a dome housing a presentation room for architect Helmut Jahn. In the late 1920s the 37th through 40th floors were home to Al Capone's Stratosphere, a popular watering hole.
Across Wacker Drive, the **Heald Square Monument (7)** (1941, Lorado Taft and Leonard Crunelle) celebrates Haym Salomon and Robert Morris, financiers

Riverwalk with a boat passing under a jet of water from Centennial Fountain

© Agnieszka Szymczak/iStockphoto.com

Chicago's Riverwalk

The redevelopment of the Chicago River east of Michigan Avenue has inspired the city to create a tree-lined pedestrian path along the south bank from Michigan Avenue to the lake. Beginning underneath Lake Shore Drive where the river meets the lake, the blue-trellised corridor passes the 170ft-long **Riverwalk Gateway** tile mural by Ellen Lanyon, which limns the history of the river in 16 narrative panels and 12 decorative panels. Along the north shore the walk leads to McClurg Court and Centennial Fountain, which emits a jet of water across the river every hour on the hour *(except 3pm and 4pm)*

Relaxing on Riverwalk

© Jason Lindsey/Alamy

in summer. Besides affording fine **views** of Loop skyscrapers across the river, the esplanade passes such noteworthy landmarks as the River East development *(south of McClurg St.)*, the Riverview condominiums (2000, DeStefano & Partners) on E. North Water Street, and Milton Horn's 1954 restored sculpture *Chicago Rising from the Lake (at Columbus Dr.)*, representing the city's leading industries. South of the river, upscale condominium towers are springing up, together forming a new neighborhood called Lakeshore East. When complete, they will add thousands of new residences to Chicago's lakefront.

West of Wabash Street, riverwalk cafes share space with docking facilities for the many tour boats and water taxis that have made the Chicago River the busiest urban river in the nation. Marking LaSalle Gateway Plaza three blocks farther west on the north side of the river is *Crossing,* a 25ft steel sculpture by German artist Hubertus von der Goltz. Its V-shape is topped by a human figure symbolizing the citizen who will, in the artist's words, "contribute to the balancing and blending of the City of Chicago on the brink of the 21st Century."

of the American Revolution. Both figures flank a statue of George Washington. Marking the corner of East Wacker Drive and Wabash Avenue is the round **Seventeenth Church of Christ, Scientist (R)** (1968, Harry Weese & Assocs.). White travertine marble, the prominent site and unusual form give the small building a large presence.

▶ Bear left and continue east on Wacker Dr.

75 East Wacker Drive (S) (1928, H. H. Riddle), built by the descendants of Cotton Mather, is a pencil-thin neo-Gothic skyscraper sheathed in white terra-cotta.

Across the river, Trump International Hotel and Tower rises tall. Completed in 2009, the 92-story behemoth with sky-high condos was briefly the world's highest residence, but has since been eclipsed by other buildings.

▶ Continue east on Wacker Dr. to N. Michigan Ave.

Distinguished by a curving Neoclassical entrance, **360 North Michigan Avenue (T)** (1923, Alfred S. Alschuler) is built on a trapezoidal riverfront site. A Greek lantern caps the building's English Renaissance ornament. Across the street rises **333 North Michigan Avenue (U)** (1928, Holabird & Root), a lovely Art Deco

skyscraper with a dark granite base, stepped-back design and bas-reliefs that relate to the sculpted bridgehouses anchoring the Michigan Avenue Bridge. The building's architecture echoes the design proposed by Eliel Saarinen that won second prize in the 1922 *Chicago Tribune* competition.

▶ If you would like to return to Michigan Ave. and Congress Pkwy., walk south on the Grant Park side of Michigan Ave. for an interesting perspective of the different architectural styles lining the avenue.

② ALONG THE RIVER
1mi.

▶ Begin at the corner of Jackson Blvd. and Franklin St.

Willis Tower★★★
233 S. Wacker Dr. ☎*312-875-0066. www.thesearstower.com.*
The tallest building in the world for over 20 years, this 110-story feat of engineering was formerly known as the Sears Tower. The name was changed in 2009 when London-based insurance broker Willis Group Holdings, Ltd. leased part of the building and obtained the naming rights.
At the time of construction, from 1968 to 1974, the city did not require a zoning variance for the tower, allowing it to rise

Willis Tower

Willis Tower: A Lesson in Size

- **Height:** 1,707ft (including the antennae), as tall as 16 city blocks.

- **Weight:** 222,500 tons, covered by 28 acres of black aluminum.

- The tower has 103 elevators, one of which travels to the top at a speed of 1,600ft/min or 18mph.

- Six automatic window-washing machines clean 16,000 windows eight times a year.

- The tower contains enough phone wire to wrap around the earth 1.75 times and enough electrical wiring to run a power line from Chicago to Los Angeles.

- Even in high wind, the top of the tower never sways more than 6 inches.

- About 25,000 workers and visitors come and go on an average day.

to an unsurpassed height of 1,454ft. Today the tower ranks as the tallest building in the US, and the fifth-tallest freestanding structure in the world. Designed by architect Bruce Graham and chief engineer Fazlur Khan for Skidmore, Owings & Merrill, the tower comprises nine rectangular tubes, resting on more than 100 steel and concrete caissons anchored into the bedrock hundreds of feet below ground. These 75ft-high bundled tubes provide solidity to the tower by maximizing resistance to wind loads: two tubes end at the 50th floor, two at the 66th floor, and three more at the 90th floor. Clad in black aluminum and bronze-tinted glass, the tower's structural skeleton required over 75,000 tons of steel.

Redesigned in 1985, the barrel-vaulted entrance on Wacker Drive is dominated by Alexander Calder's mobile **The Universe**, a collection of brightly colored forms turning and twirling.

Skydeck

Open daily Apr–Sept 10am–10pm, Oct–Mar 10am–8pm. May close occasionally due to high winds. $15.95. 312-875-9447. www.the-skydeck.com.

Your visit to the renovated Skydeck begins with a multimedia elevator ride to the 103rd floor. Once at the top, you'll enjoy spectacular **views**★★★ of the city and the lake from the entirely glassed-in Skydeck. Touch-screen displays explain local landmarks in six different languages and exhibits relate Chicago history. Kids can discover the city through the 4ft-high exhibit, Knee-High Chicago.

▷ *Exit Sears Tower on Franklin St.*

Just south of the Sears Tower stands **311 South Wacker Drive** (1990, Kohn Pedersen Fox), a pale pink concrete skyscraper built on speculation just before the real estate depression of the 1990s. A huge illuminated crown resembling a circular fortress tops the structure.

▷ *Continue north on Franklin St. to Monroe St. Walk west to Wacker Dr.*

On the north side of Monroe, note the oval glass-and-steel facade of the **Hyatt Center** (2005, Pei Cobb Freed & Partners). To the south, **111 South Wacker Drive** (2005, Goettsch Partners) features a unique twist on its interior parking ramp, which corkscrews over the lobby. To the left, the **Chicago Mercantile Exchange** (20 S. Wacker Dr.; www.cmegroup.com) established in 1919 as the Butter and Egg Exchange, has evolved like the Board of Trade from commodities to the fast-paced world of futures and options. The "Merc's" twin towers (1983 and 1988, Fujikawa, Johnson & Assocs.) are linked by a windowless base that encloses two large free-span trading floors. Here traders in the pit still practice open outcry, shouting and using hand signals to buy and sell commodities, though more and more trading is being done electronically as well. A lobby level Visitors Center presents exhibits and interactivities to explain the work of the exchange (○ open year-round Mon–Fri 8am–4.30pm; ○ closed major holidays; ●30min guided tours available; ✕ & ☎312-930-8249).

Farther north, the **Civic Opera Building** (20 N. Wacker Dr.; & ☎312-332-2244; www.lyricopera.org), built by utilities magnate Samuel Insull to house both offices and the opera, combines Art Deco skyscraper design with a block-long Wacker Drive arcade that celebrates the classical origins of opera and theater. The building (1929, Graham, Anderson, Probst & White) was dubbed "Insull's throne" due to its armchair-like appearance from the river.

The former Civic Theater has been incorporated into a complete modernization of the Opera House. Opened in November 1929 with a performance of Verdi's *Aïda*, the theater still presents world-class opera performed by the Lyric Opera of Chicago.

▷ *Turn left on Madison and cross the bridge spanning the Chicago River to view sights to the west of the river.*

Formerly known as the Northwestern Atrium Center, the deep blue and silver **Citicorp Center** (500 W. Madison St.) rises like a giant jukebox, marking the intersection of Madison and Canal streets. Another of Helmut Jahn's soaring atriums unites this combination commuter train station, retail arcade and office tower (1987), which takes its streamlined shape from 1930s "machine age" design.

Just east of Citicorp Center, **Riverside Plaza** (1929, Holabird & Root) was built for the now-defunct *Chicago Daily News*. The stately 26-story Art Deco high rise offers an expansive riverfront plaza, the first developed in Chicago. Built over active railroad tracks, the building incorporated ingenious foundations as well as vents for steam engines, a novelty at the time.

Visible to the north, **100 North Riverside Plaza** (1990, Ralph Johnson, Perkins & Will) is suspended over railroad tracks by means of an exposed rooftop truss reminiscent of the nearby bridges.

▷ *Return to the intersection of Madison St. and Wacker Dr. and walk north on Wacker Dr.*

333 West Wacker Drive★
Bounded by Lake St., Wacker Dr. and Franklin St.

This edifice (1983, Kohn Pedersen Fox) set a new standard for downtown development as it launched the 1980s building boom. The design takes full advantage of the triangular site—a mere parking lot at the time—where the South Branch of the Chicago River diverges from the main channel. The green, mirrored-glass facade both suggests and reflects the river, with horizontal ribs that relieve the sheer height of the structure. When clouds play across it, the facade is stunning. The building's base has more traditional green marble and gray granite accentuated by louvered portholes, while the top folds the curving riverside facade into the flat walls of the Loop.

Notable for its masonry walls and rooftop lanterns, **225 West Wacker Drive** was completed by the same firm in a post-Modern style six years later.

Across the river rises the massive **Merchandise Mart** (300 N. Wells St. ✕ & ℗ ☎800-677-6278; www.merchandisemart.com) commissioned by Marshall

Major Chicago thoroughfares	

Major Chicago thoroughfares

Most are designated with a route number but are commonly referred to by name:

I-55	Stevenson Expressway
I-290	Eisenhower Expressway
US-41	Lake Shore Drive
I-294	Tri-State
I-88	East-West Tollway (toll road)
I-94	Edens Expressway (north of 290)
I-94	Dan Ryan Expressway (south of 290)
I-90	Kennedy Expressway (north of 290)
I-90	Chicago Skyway (south of 290) (toll road)

333 West Wacker Drive

© Gary Blakeley/Fotolia.com

Field & Co. in 1928. With 4.1 million sq ft of space, the Mart is touted as the world's largest commercial building. Architects Graham, Anderson, Probst & White embellished their Art Deco design with simple geometric patterns incised and overlaid on the exterior. In the main lobby (south entrance), murals by artist Jules Guerin depict trading activities around the world. Joseph P. Kennedy purchased the Mart in 1945, and the Kennedy family owned it until 1998. On the first floor, **Luxe-Home** (*open Mon–Fri 9am–5pm, Sat 10am–3pm*) offers the public 100,000 square feet of luxury interior-design boutiques.

▷ *Continue on Wacker Dr. and cross Wells St.*

Located east of the Merchandise Mart, the red stone and green glass Helene Curtis Building was renovated from warehouse space to office building in 1984. Across LaSalle Street stands the Central Office Building (1914), topped by a clock tower.

ADDRESSES

♈/EAT

$$ 17 West at The Berghoff – *17 W. Adams St. ℘312-427-3170. www.theberghoff.com.* Founded as The Berghoff Restaurant in 1898 by brewer Herman Berghoff, this spacious German restaurant changed its image in 2005 from a venerable tavern to a more contemporary scene, offering everything from Wiener Schnitzel to sesame-crusted salmon. For a quick lunch, try a sandwich or a wurst from the Berghoff Café on the lower level.

$$ Russian Tea Time – *77 E. Adams St. ℘312-360-0000. www.russianteatime.com.* Distinguished by red velvet furnishings, this elegant tea room one block west of the Chicago Art Institute buzzes with the polite chatter of art and music lovers. Fine caviar and champagne are de rigueur in the eveningm, as is tea in the afternoon. The restaurant also offers a complete menu highlighting Russian, Uzbek, Ukrainian and Baltic specialties.

$ Heaven on Seven – *111 N. Wabash Ave., 7th floor of Garland Building. ℘ 312-263 -6443. www.heavenonseven.com.* Creole shrimp, crab cakes, and gumbo are just a few of the New Orleans-style dishes served in this small lunchroom (*dinner only on the 3rd Fri of the month*). Most entrées are quite spicy, but connoisseurs of Cajun heat use the bottles of Louisiana hot sauce on the tables to season their food. A slicker version of the original, **Heaven on Seven on Rush** (*$$ 600 N. Michigan Ave., 2nd floor; ℘312-280-7774*) serves lunch and dinner daily.

$ Lou Mitchell's – *565 W. Jackson Blvd., ℘312-939-3111. www.loumitchells restaurant.com. Open Mon–Sat 5.30am– 3pm, Sun 7am–3pm.* The place for breakfast in downtown Chicago since 1923, Lou Mitchell's still serves up hefty portions of fluffy omelets, thick French toast and a heaping stack of pancakes. Pastries are made fresh daily, and the orange juice is fresh-squeezed. Lou's is also open for lunch, but breakfast is served all day.

Magnificent Mile★★★

The Champs Élysées of Chicago, this promenade is the city's most prestigious. Lined with shops, luxury hotels, restaurants and premier residential and office high rises, the "Magnificent Mile" lies along North Michigan Avenue between Chicago's most important waterways, the Chicago River to the south and Lake Michigan to the north. The restaurants, residences and medical facilities of Streeterville occupy the area between here and Lake Shore Drive to the east.

A BIT OF HISTORY
From Mud Plain to Boul Mich

Chicago's first permanent settler, **Jean Baptiste Point du Sable**, built his cabin here in 1779, on an unpromising flat plain on the north bank of the river close to the present site of the Equitable Building. Almost half a century later, when Chicago was incorporated as a city, the area remained a muddy patch of Lake Michigan sediment. By 1860 (the year Abraham Lincoln was nominated as the Republican candidate for president at the Wigwam a few blocks away), various mercantile establishments and ordinary two-story houses bordered the avenue, then called Pine Street. The Great Fire of 1871 leveled all of the buildings on the street except the Water Tower and Pumping Station, still standing proudly at Chicago Avenue.

By the turn of the century numerous businesses, including loft manufacturing establishments, warehouses, sign companies and taverns, transformed the street into a major traffic artery. The 1920 opening of the Michigan Avenue Bridge, which joined the South and North sides of the city, catalyzed an incredible building boom. Most of the landmarks on the avenue, including the Wrigley Building, Tribune Tower, Woman's Athletic Club, Allerton Hotel, Fourth Presbyterian Church, Palmolive Building and the Drake Hotel, were constructed during

- ⛪ **Michelin Map:** pp100–101.
- **Info:** Chicago Water Works Visitor Center, 163 E. Pearson St. ☎877-244-2246. www.themagnificent mile.com.
- ▶ **Location:** Street numbers begin around 400 and increase to 900 as you move north.
- 🅿 **Parking:** On side streets, lots are expensive; some metered parking can be found, but don't count on it.
- 😋 **Don't Miss:** Lunch, brunch, drinks or dinner at the Signature Room atop the John Hancock Center.
- 👪 **Kids:** A day on Navy Pier.
- 🕐 **Timing:** Shop till you drop! But allow at least two days to include Navy Pier.
- ⛪ **Also See:** The Loop, River North, Gold Coast.

GETTING AROUND
BY BUS: CTA Bus no. 151

the decade that followed. A profusion of Art Deco and Neoclassical elements adorned the modestly scaled, limestone edifices, lending the avenue a sophisticated "European boulevard" look that would last until the 1970s. Although the Great Depression and World War II interrupted development, in 1947 Chicago developer Arthur Rubloff dubbed North Michigan Avenue "The Magnificent Mile," forecasting a commercial revival during the 1950s and 60s.

Retail Transformation

Construction of two extraordinary mixed-use complexes contributed to the retail boom of the 1970s that changed the face of Michigan Avenue. Erected in 1969, the landmark **John Hancock Center** ushered in a new era of skyscrapers along the avenue. Completed seven years later, Water Tower Place included one of the first and most successful vertical shopping centers in the US, and began a shift in retail focus from downtown State Street to the more glamorous Michigan Avenue location. The upward spiral continued through the 1980s and 90s as fashionable retailers multiplied each year, creating one of the most affluent shopping districts in the country. Then the avenue's elegant image began to suffer as large-scale developers invaded, often demolishing historic structures to make way for mass-market shops. Long-time residents and architectural purists argue that the stores and their gaudy signage "cheapen" the area, transforming it into a "magnificent mall."

East of the Avenue

Immediately east of the Magnificent Mile lies **Streeterville**, an area originally settled in the 1880s by the infamous **Capt. George Wellington Streeter**. When his ship ran aground on a sand bar near present-day Chicago Avenue, Streeter built a causeway to the mainland and encouraged contractors to dump debris around his grounded craft. The land grew to reach 180 acres, and Streeter declared it the "District of Lake Michigan," separate from the city of Chicago and answerable only to the federal government. He and his wife battled police to a standoff, and his claim for independence wasn't dismissed from the courts until 1918. Most of the buildings east of Michigan Avenue are built on Streeter's landfill.

⚓ WALKING TOUR
.8mi.

▷ *Begin at the corner of N. Michigan Ave. and E. Wacker Dr.*

Michigan Avenue Bridge★

This monumental, double-leaf trunnion bascule, two-level bridge is the gateway to the Magnificent Mile. Like the seesaw for which it is named, the bascule is a kind of drawbridge counterweighted to be raised and lowered easily. Built

to designs by Edward H. Bennett (co-author with Daniel Burnham of the 1909 **Plan of Chicago**), the bridge was completed in 1920. Four corner bridgehouses, each almost 40ft in height, showcase bas-reliefs in Bedford limestone designed by J. E. Fraser and Henry Hering that celebrate important episodes in Chicago history. The Michigan Avenue Bridge affords some of the most spectacular **views**★★ of the gleaming Loop high rises towering over the river.

▷ *Walk north across the bridge on the west side.*

Wrigley Building★★
400–410 N. Michigan Ave.

Set majestically on the north bank of the Chicago River, this sparkling edifice heralded the 20C development of the North Michigan Avenue business district. Designed by Graham, Anderson, Probst & White as the headquarters for William Wrigley, Jr.'s successful chewing-gum company, the structure was built in two stages (the 30-story South section in 1920 and the 21-story North section in 1924); the two towers are connected by an arcaded walkway at street level and on the 3rd and 14th floors. Modeled after Seville Cathedral's Giralda Tower in Spain, the structure represents a fine example of the French Renaissance style. The white terra-cotta cladding dazzles, especially at night when the building is illuminated. Chicagoans use the soaring, four-sided clock atop the South Tower for time checks from several blocks away in every direction. A handsome little plaza sits between the two structures.

▷ *Cross to the east side of Michigan Ave.*

On the northeast bank of the Chicago River rises the **Equitable Building** at no. 401 (1965, Skidmore, Owings & Merrill; Alfred Shaw & Assocs.), a 40-story granite and glazed, bronze solar-glass office tower. Immediately north of the building, the Channel Garden, reminiscent of Rockefeller Center's Channel Gardens in New York City, offers a pleasant rest stop. Pioneer Court, a spacious plaza in front of Equitable's entrance, provides a scenic outlook to the adjacent buildings and those on the avenue beyond. The plaza's sweeping stairway to the south leads down to **Riverwalk**★ (*see LOOP*), an esplanade extending along the north bank of the Chicago River.

Continue east along the promenade.

University of Chicago Graduate School of Business Gleacher Center

450 N. Cityfront Plaza Dr.
Designed by Lohan Assocs. in 1992, this eight-level glass, steel and precast concrete structure features a glassed front facade overlooking the Chicago River and an angled back with cantilevered pods. The university, which did not want the architectural beauty outside to distract its students from their scholarly pursuits, dictated its windowless western wall.

NBC Tower★

455 N. Cityfront Plaza Dr.
Reminiscent of New York's GE Building at Rockefeller Center, this 38-story Art Deco office tower (1989, Skidmore, Owings & Merrill), topped by a 130ft steel spire, rises in a series of setbacks that strengthen its vertical progression. Limestone constitutes most of the building's skin except for the dark green precast concrete spandrels and the green, gray and black granite of its base.

The tower is set on the western edge of **Cityfront Center**, a 60-acre development extending east of Michigan Avenue and north to Grand Avenue that includes office, hotel, entertainment, retail and residential development. The integration of this project with the surrounding city and the river contrasts markedly with the stark monoliths of Illinois Center directly across the Chicago River.

Return to Michigan Ave.

Tribune Tower★★

435 N. Michigan Ave.
Corporate headquarters of the the the Tribune Company, this soaring, crenellated, Gothic-style tower (1925, Hood & Howells) was the first-place winner of the 1922 *Chicago Tribune* international competition to erect "the most beautiful and distinctive office building in the world." Adorned with floodlit flying buttresses, sculpted fleur-de-lis and numerous gargoyles and grotesques, the 36-story, 456ft limestone "cathedral of commerce" echoes the Butter Tower in Rouen, France, and the Tower of Malines in Mechelen, Belgium. Fragments from more than 120 of the world's famous structures—the Parthenon, the Great Wall of China, Westminster Abbey, the Berlin Wall and Notre Dame Cathedral, among others—were collected by *Tribune* correspondents and have been embedded in the exterior walls of the building.

A richly ornamented, three-story arch adorned with a stone screen carved with figures from Aesop's fables marks the entrance to the **lobby**. This harmonious space, restored in 1990 by architect John Vinci, is known to journalists as the Hall of Inscriptions: a series of quotations expressing the ideals and obligations of the press is carved in its travertine marble walls. A papier-mâché map of North America, constructed in 1925 by noted geographic sculptor George Robertson, dominates the East wall.

The Tribune

Tribune Company publishes 11 newspapers, and owns and operates 23 TV stations. Chicago-based WGN radio—World's Greatest Newspaper—broadcasts from a street-level, glass-enclosed studio in the building. In addition, it produces and syndicates information and programming, and also publishes books and information in both print and digital formats.

Cross Illinois St.

Hotel InterContinental Chicago★

505 N. Michigan Ave.

This eclectic 41-story building (1929, Walter W. Ahlschlager) was originally built as the Medinah Athletic Club for members of the Shriners organization. After the club closed in 1934, the building went through a succession of different owners until InterContinental Hotels purchased it in 1988. It opened as the InterContinental Chicago in 1990 following a $130 million restoration by Harry Weese & Assocs. In 1994 the hotel expanded to include its northern neighbor, the Forum Hotel Chicago, and is now contained in two towers connected by a glass lobby. Carved into the Indiana limestone facade, a large Egyptian-style frieze depicts builders parading in front of the pharaoh.

Inside the historic tower, public spaces are adorned with superb inlays of marble, intricately detailed bronze and brass trimming, murals and frescoes. Step through the heavy bronze doors to admire the ornate **entryway**★ whose beamed ceiling is painted with colorful Celtic and Mesopotamian motifs—the lion, fish, eagle and peacock—representing the highest powers of nature. Marble stairways flank the arched greeting Es Salamu Aleikum (Peace Be to You) and are crowned with squat, Moorish-style columns sporting hooded, sleeping knights. The Hall of Lions (2nd floor), King Arthur Foyer and Court (3rd floor), the Spanish Court and the Renaissance Room Foyer (both 5th floor) have all been opulently restored. The 82ft/25m Olympic-size swimming pool on the 14th floor is the last remaining feature of the original Athletic Club (a 23rd-floor miniature golf course no longer exists). An onion-shaped dome and minaret atop the building complete the fantasy (the dome was originally intended as a place for Shriners to dock their dirigibles). Across the street to the west stands the 16-story Art Deco **520 North Michigan Avenue** built in 1929 as the McGraw-Hill Building by

architects Thielbar & Fugard, who had an office there. Clad in limestone on a granite base, the building displays a variety of exterior detail, including sculpted mythological figures and ornamental panels. The limestone facade was completely dismantled and re-erected in 2000 on a new steel structure that houses the **Shops at North Bridge**. North Bridge mall is anchored by the tony department store, **Nordstrom**, which fills a six-story Renaissance Revival building a block to the west. The store's glassy corner entrance at

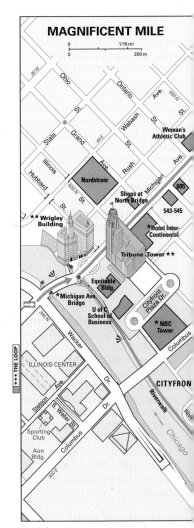

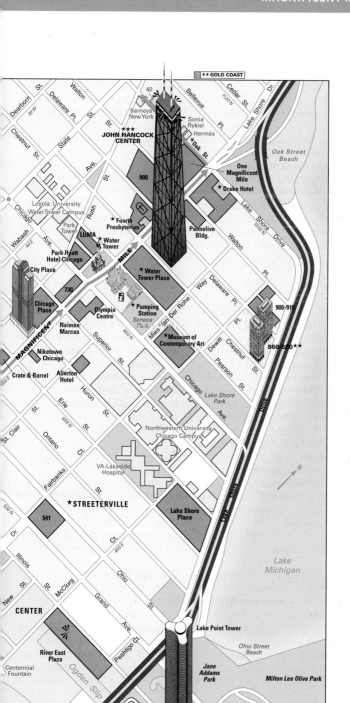

★★ **GOLD COAST**

Dearborn St. · 36 W · Walton · Delaware Pl. · State St. · Bellevue · Cedar St. · Lake Shore Dr. · 1120 N

40

Barneys New York

★★★
JOHN HANCOCK CENTER

Sonia Rykiel · Hermès

Oak St.

Chestnut St.

900

One Magnificent Mile

Oak Street Beach

Loyola University Water Tower Campus

Chicago

Rush St.

★ **Fourth Presbyterian**

★ Drake Hotel

Wabash · 44 E · Ave.

Park Tower

LUMA

★ Water Tower

Palmolive Bldg.

Walton

Lake Shore Drive · 1000 N

Park Hyatt Hotel Chicago

City Place

★ **Water Tower Place**

Way · Delaware Pl.

730

Chicago Place

Olympia Centre

★ **Pumping Station**

Pl.

900-910

MAGNIFICENT · 1000 E

Naiman Marcus

Superior St.

Seneca Park

Mies Van Der Rohe · 860 N

★ **Museum of Contemporary Art**

Dewitt

Chestnut St.

Pearson St.

860-880 ★★

Niketown Chicago

Crate & Barrel

Allerton Hotel

Huron St. · 658 N

Erie St.

Chicago

Lake Shore Park

Lake Shore Ave.

St. Clair St.

Ontario St.

Ct.

Northwestern University Chicago Campus

Fairbanks Ct.

VA-Lakeside Hospital

St.

530 N

★ **STREETERVILLE**

Tivoli

N

541

Dr.

Ct.

Lake Shore Place

400 E

Illinois St.

McClurg Ct.

Ohio St.

Grand Ave.

Lake Michigan

New St.

CENTER

Peshtigo Ct.

Tivoli

Lake Point Tower

River East Plaza

Ohio Street Beach

Centennial Fountain

Jane Addams Park

Milton Lee Olive Park

Ogden Slip

River

Park Dr.

Gateway Park

Wabash and Grand avenues contrasts with the quoined corners and geometric incising of the buff concrete facade on Michigan Avenue.

○ *Cross overpass spanning Grand Ave.*

The intimate scale and decorative architecture of the five-story, Lilliputian gem at **543–545 North Michigan Avenue** (1929, Philip B. Maher) was originally constructed to house the luxurious Jacques dress shop. The sculptured female figures above each doorway, characteristic of the Art Deco style of the building, also served the practical purpose of attracting customers.

○ *Cross Ohio St.*

The four-story Lake Shore Bank at **no. 605** (1922, Marshall & Fox), now Chase, is noteworthy for its temple-like appearance and massive Corinthian columns. Renovation produced a new banking center on the second and third floors, while the first floor was given over to retail shops. On the west side of the street is the former site of 612 and 620 N. Michigan Avenue. After a bitter preservation battle, the historic structures fell victim to the wrecking ball—along with the Arts Club of Chicago, which featured an interior space designed by Mies van der Rohe—to make way for a nine-screen cinema complex and mall.

○ *Continue north.*

On the northwest corner of Ontario and Michigan Avenues at no. 626, the nine-story **Woman's Athletic Club** (1928, Philip B. Maher), one of the oldest private athletic and social facilities for women in the US, provides a stately legacy of the avenue's 1920s understated, low-rise look. The Bedford limestone and pressed brick exterior, mansard roof, second-floor Palladian windows separated by carved ox skulls, and the winged griffins in the seventh-floor niches reflect its French inspiration and the interior's elegance.

Upscale retail shops occupy Michigan Avenue's first floor.
Its neighbor to the north, **Crate & Barrel** (1990, Solomon Cordwell Buenz & Assocs.) at no. 646, makes a contrasting Modernist statement with the stark white aluminum and luminous glass of its exterior and the high-tech trappings of its interior.

○ *Cross to the west side of Michigan Ave. and cross Erie St.*

Across the street to the east at no. 669 is **Niketown Chicago** (👥👤 ☎*312-642-6363; www.nike.com*), a five-level retail theater showcase for Nike's footwear and apparel collections.
Granite **City Place** (1990, Loebl, Schlossman & Hackl) at no. 676 resembles a giant jukebox. Red vertical lines and pink spandrels provide a dramatic contrast to the smoky blue windows whose arrangement demarcates the varied purposes of the building retail streetside with a hotel and offices above. The "bootlike" design with a lower mass at the sidewalk and a tower setback is typical of the skyscrapers built on the avenue in the 1980s and 90s.

○ *Cross Huron St.*

On the corner of Michigan Avenue and Huron Street, the 1924 **Allerton Hotel** was restored to its former Italian Renaissance glory in 1999. The limestone and red tapestry brick "club hotel" is one of the Mag Mile's rare historic landmarks.

Chicago Place
700 N. Michigan Ave.
✕ *www.chicagoplace.com.*
Distinguished by a varicolored two-story base in green and pink granite, this multi-purpose structure (1990, Skidmore, Owings & Merrill; Solomon Cordwell Buenz & Assocs.) also adopts the boot-shaped scheme. A former mall, the eight floors of retail were shuttered in early 2009, with the exception of **Saks Fifth Avenue**, which remains. The empty floors, slated to be converted to office space, are topped by a 43-story

Magnificent Mile lit up during the
Magnificent Mile Festival of Lights

© The Magnificent Mile®

residential tower setback to the west. Its windows are designed in the Chicago style. Step inside the huge **lobby** to view the 23ft x 32ft Thomas Melvin murals depicting Chicago history. Soaring over the atrium is a barrel-vaulted roof whose skylights illuminate the eighth floor. Look north across Michigan Avenue at the **Neiman Marcus store** (no. 737) occupying the low-rise section of **Olympia Centre** (1986, Skidmore, Owings & Merrill), whose 63-story tapering office and residential tower looms over Chicago Avenue to the northeast. On the Sullivanesque arch over Neiman's main entrance, a whimsical glass panel replaces the keystone.

 Cross Superior St.

730 North Michigan Avenue (1997, Elkus/Manfredi Architects, Ltd.) is a classical post-Modern building rendered as four separate facades. Tiffany & Company's refined Art Deco facade in lavender and gray anchors the southern end, followed by the Pottery Barn's Egyptian temple with modernized lotus columns and heavy yellow pylons. Next door, the machined industrial look of Banana Republic's black and buff stone facade is heightened by extruded steel details at the cornice, while Polo/Ralph Lauren's gray Florentine palazzo completes the north end.

Chicago-style Pizza

Chicago undoubtedly ranks as one of the country's greatest spots for pizza. Pizza aficionados rave about the city's deep-dish pizza, sometimes called pizza-in-the-pan, a savory concoction of tomatoes, cheese, sausage and vegetables ladled over a thick, doughy crust. Over 2,000 restaurants serve a variety of this mouthwatering dish, with toppings ranging from the simple to the exotic, from mushrooms to clams and artichokes.

The dough remains an essential ingredient in preparing an old-fashioned deep-dish pizza. A mixture of water, yeast and flour is often embellished by adding sugar, cornmeal, oil and even milk. Once the dough has risen and been kneaded down, it is placed in a pan, pricked with a fork and baked at 475°F for about five minutes. Slices of mozzarella are then layered directly onto the dough, followed by canned tomatoes seasoned with oregano, basil, salt and pepper. Fresh Parmesan is grated over the tomatoes. Next come the various meat and vegetable toppings. Finally, the pie is drizzled with olive oil and baked in a preheated (475°F) oven until the crust is browned, about 30 to 45 minutes.

▷ Cross Chicago Ave.

Visions of another era, the **Chicago Water Tower**★ (1869, **William W. Boyington**) and **Pumping Station**★ (1866) stand like sentinels on the west and east sides of Michigan Avenue, solid reminders that they were the only two buildings in the area to survive the Great Fire. Both are built of Joliet limestone in the castellated Gothic Revival style. The still-operational Pumping Station houses a visitor information center *(163 E. Pearson St.; ⏰open daily 7.30am–7pm; ⏰closed Thanksgiving Day, Dec 25 ✕),* and since 2003 the 270-seat Looking-glass Theatre *(✆312-337-0665; www. lookingglasstheatre.org).* The adaptive reuse of the old structure has earned several awards. Horse-and-carriage rides along the Magnificent Mile and environs, as well as double-decker bus and trolley tours *(⏰see Planning Your Trip),* depart from the charming park adjoining the Water Tower.

The small downtown Water Tower Campus of Loyola University begins at the southwest corner of "little" Michigan Avenue and Pearson Street.

Loyola University Museum of Art (LUMA)★

820 N. Michigan Ave. ⏰Open Tue 10am –8pm, Wed–Sun 10am–5pm. ⏰Closed Mon, major holidays. ⏰$6 (Tue free). ♿✆312-915-7600. www.luc.edu/luma. ☀Guided tours noon, 2pm.

This lovely little gem, opened in 2005, set a big mission "to illuminate the enduring spiritual questions and concerns of all cultures and societies." Its three floors include space for traveling and temporary exhibits of an artistic or historical nature that reflect that mission, such as portraits of the Dalai Lama and an exploration of Pope John Paul II's lifelong connections to the Jewish community. The museum's Martin D'Arcy Collection of Medieval, Renaissance and Baroque art, installed permanently on the third floor in 2007, comprises paintings and sculpture, liturgical pieces, architectural elements, furniture, jewelry and decorative and household art.

▷ Continue north.

Water Tower Place★

835 N. Michigan Ave. ⏰Open year-round Mon–Sat 10am–9pm, Sun 11am–6pm. ⏰Closed Easter, Thanksgiving Day, Dec 25. ▣♿✕✆312-440-3166. www.shopwatertower.com.

Located on the east side of Michigan Avenue, this square-block complex (1976, Loebl, Schlossman & Hackl) salutes its neighbor, the historic Water Tower, in name only. The stark, almost windowless, white-veined marble face it presents to the avenue accommodates a 12-story shopping complex and office space, while a 62-story tower to the east houses the Ritz-Carlton Hotel and luxury condominiums. More than 100 shops, boutiques, services, restaurants and cinemas, anchored by Macy's, moved the center of retail action to this area from State Street downtown. Recognized as one of the most successful mixed-use projects in the US, Water Tower Place is a major tourist attraction. The mall is also the new location of **American Girl Place** *(♟♟ ⏰open Mon–Thu 10am–9pm, Fri–Sat 9am–9pm, Sun 9am–7pm; ⏰closed major holidays; ♿✆312-943-9400; www.americangirl. com)* offers afternoon tea *(reservations required)* in addition to its large variety of popular historically inspired dolls.

▷ Cross Chestnut St.

Fourth Presbyterian Church★

N. Michigan Ave. at Delaware Pl. ⏰Open year-round daily 9am–5pm except during services. ♿✆312-787-4570. www.fourthchurch.org.

Dedicated in 1914, this sanctuary is an elegant reminder of Michigan Avenue's character before the shopping malls and myriad tour buses. It was designed by Ralph Adams Cram, in association with Howard Van Doren Shaw, in the Gothic Revival style (Cram also designed the Cathedral of St. John the Divine in New York City). The church and parish house were fully restored and renovated in 1994. Although originally built for a wealthy and large congregation (the church seats 1,500), the interior is subdued and somber. Stained-glass windows set high on the West and East walls provide color and drama and were designed by Charles J. Connick of Boston, while the intricately painted ceiling is the work of native Chicagoan Frederic Clay Bartlett. At the base of the ceiling arches, 14 sculptured, life-size angels depicting musicians gaze down upon the worshippers. The church is known throughout the city for its Aeolian Skinner organ, and concerts are popular (*year-round Fri 12.10pm–12.45pm*). Outside, the charming cloister and fountain that lie between the church and its ivy-covered parish house provide a serene oasis.

▶ *Cross to the east side of Michigan Ave.*

John Hancock Center

©Henryk Sadura/Dreamstime.com

John Hancock Center★★★

875 N. Michigan Ave.

Nothing represents Carl Sandburg's epithet for Chicago—"the city of big shoulders"—more than this 1,127ft skyscraper (1969, Skidmore, Owings & Merrill). It is the third-tallest building in Chicago, the fourth-tallest in the US and, because of its huge cross-bracing steel members, one of the most recognizable in the city. Its 100 stories of black anodized aluminum and tinted glass are divided between office and residential space.

The tower was constructed at half the cost of a building of comparable height, thanks to engineer Fazlur Khan's efficient design. Applying the braced tube concept to his structure, Khan developed an obelisk-shaped structural framework that functions as a large-scale truss. Comprising some 46,000 tons of steel, the cross braces, columns and beams efficiently carry gravity and wind loads. The tapering tower rises from a 265ft by 165ft base to a top floor measuring 100ft by 160ft, offering an interior space of 2.8 million square feet. For a must-not-miss treat, enjoy city panoramas with drinks or a meal atop the tower at the **Signature Room at the 95th**. Wide steps descending into a large sunken **plaza** frame colorful planters

and a wall waterfall. The plaza affords interesting views of the Magnificent Mile skyscrapers that are looming to the north and south.

⚲ The Hancock Observatory

Open year-round daily 9am–11pm.
$15. 🅿️ ♿ 312-751-3681.
www.hancockobservatory.com.
During the 39 seconds that the elevators take to ascend to the 94th-floor observatory, you almost feel airborne.

Once at the top, you'll enjoy glorious **views**★★★ of the city in every direction, one more spectacular than the next. Step onto the open-air Skywalk, poised 1,000ft above the Mag Mile, or learn about the sites you are seeing through one of the Soundscope talking telescopes.

▶ *Cross Delaware St.*

Rising 871ft on the west side of Michigan Avenue, the 66-story **900 North Michigan Avenue** high rise (1989, Kohn Pedersen Fox) is best known for its anchor tenant Bloomingdale's, the Four Seasons Hotel and the four illuminated lanterns atop the building. The spacious six-story atrium ringed by six levels of shops offers a retreat from the bustling streetscape.

The 37-story, 468ft **Palmolive Building** *(no. 919, 1929)* ascends gracefully in a series of symmetrical setbacks topped by the now-dimmed 150ft Lindbergh Beacon, whose two-billion-candlepower beam could be seen 500mi away by airplane pilots. Sheathed in Bedford limestone above the first two retail floors, which are clad in ornamental cast iron and metal, the edifice was initially called the Palmolive Building for the company that commissioned Holabird & Root to design it as its headquarters. From 1967 to 1989 it was known as the Playboy Building when the magazine's headquarters were located here. Then it became simply 919 North Michigan Avenue. In the early 2000s, the building was converted to fine residences and the original name was restored.

▷ *Cross Walton St.*

The Drake Hotel★
140 E. Walton St.
Listed on the National Register of Historic Places, this 530-room luxury hotel (1920, Marshall & Fox) built on landfill at the edge of Lake Michigan provides an elegant transition to the **East Lake Shore Drive Historic District**, which begins at its back door and marks the northeastern border of the Magnificent Mile. Covered in limestone, its plain exterior is unadorned except for a majestic colonnade on its northern face that looks out over Lincoln Park, Oak Street Beach and the lake. Its simplicity bespeaks the elegance of a grand hotel. Set on a rectangular base, the structure changes to an H-shape at the third floor to suit hotel room layouts. Step up into the dignified lobby and public rooms to admire the plush red velvet wall coverings, the wooden caisson ceiling and the elegant Palm Court. The Drake is now run by Hilton.

▷ *Cross to the west side of Michigan Ave.*

The northwestern border of this area is marked by **One Magnificent Mile** at nos. 940–980 (1983, Skidmore, Owings &

Merrill), a 58-story mixed-use building comprising three hexagonal concrete tubes clad in rose-colored granite, which rise 57, 49 and 21 stories respectively. The three structures are joined together as a bundled tube to resist wind loads, a design originally conceived by engineer Fazlur Kahn and architect Bruce Graham for the Sears Tower.

▷ *Turn left onto Oak St.*

Oak Street★
Between N. Michigan Ave. and Rush St. www.oakstreetchicago.com.
In a single turn one is transported from high-rise shopping flurry to a tree-lined streetscape reminiscent of New York's Upper Madison Avenue—sophisticated, but understated. This is a wonderful block for browsing or buying, and each doorway heralds another upscale boutique: Hermès *(no. 110)*, Jil Sander *(no. 48)*, Prada *(no. 30)* and others reflect the Gold Coast neighborhood's wealth just to the north. At no. 40, a vintage 20-story apartment building erected in 1929 by Drake Hotel architect Ben Marshall conjures up images of a pampered past. Barneys New York *(no. 25)* anchors the western edge of this pleasant area.

STREETERVILLE★
Bordered by Lake Michigan, the Magnificent Mile and the Chicago River, Streeterville exudes a cosmopolitan atmosphere despite its inauspicious beginnings. Enhanced by luxurious residential high rises, fine-dining restaurants, and attractions such as the Museum of Contemporary Art and the ever-popular Navy Pier, the neighborhood is dominated by **Northwestern University**'s Chicago campus—including its medical, dental and law schools, as well as several hospitals of the university's McGaw Medical Center.

Museum of Contemporary Art★
220 E. Chicago Ave. ◷*Open year-round Tue 10am–8pm, Wed–Sun 10am–5pm.* ◷*Closed Jan 1, Thanksgiving Day, Dec 25.* ⊙*$12 (free Tue).* ♿🅿✕ ☏*312-280-2660. www.mcachicago.org.*

Founded in 1967, the museum presents a wide range of contemporary visual and performance arts by both well-established artists and those on the leading edge. In July 1996 the museum moved from limited quarters on Ontario Street to a two-acre site located between the historic Water Tower and Lake Michigan. (In 1969, the museum's former location was the first building in the US to be wrapped by environmental artist Christo.) The present structure, the first in the US designed by Berlin architect Josef Paul Kleihues, features a 16ft-high staircase leading to a grand entrance framed by glass and aluminum panels. The building rises four stories, housing permanent-collection galleries, temporary exhibit space, a book and gift store, and a ground-floor education center with a 300-seat auditorium. On the main floor (level 2) facing Lake Michigan, **Pucks at the MCA** (☎312-397-4034)—a collaborative effort with famed Spago chef Wolfgang Puck—overlooks the one-acre sculpture garden.

The whimsical installation at the museum's front steps called *Short Cut* (Elmgreen and Dragset, 2003) should make even the most skeptical visitor smile. Nevertheless, the task of presenting the avant garde can be daunting, but the MCA attends particularly well to interpretation, attempting to make the works and movements of contemporary art accessible to everyone through thoughtful label writing, audio programming and educational events. Exhibits, mounted on a rotating basis from the museum's 5,000-piece permanent collection, include works since 1945 by the likes of Marcel Duchamp, Max Ernst, René Magritte, Joan Miró, Jean Dubuffet and Andy Warhol. The collection is richly laden as well with pieces by Chicago and Illinois artists such as Ed Paschke, June Leaf, Leon Golub and Jim Nutt. The main floor is devoted to traveling exhibits. In the third-floor video gallery you'll find works by film, video and multimedia artists, while the permanent collection is displayed in the barrel-vaulted galleries on the fourth floor.

541 North Fairbanks Court

Harry Weese & Assocs. (1968) combined the traditions of the Chicago school—the exposed metal curtain wall, regular bay spacing and horizontal window emphasis—with the austere simplicity of the Miesian idiom into the former Time-Life Building. Two environmentally correct and functional designs were incorporated into its 28 stories. Bronze-tinted exterior glass has been used to reflect the sun and reduce the need for air conditioning. The interior elevator cabs were double-decked so that they could service two floors simultaneously during morning and evening rush hours (an arrangement since discontinued).

River East Plaza★

435 E. Illinois St.

Built originally as the Pugh Terminal Warehouse in 1905, this river's edge building was artfully rehabilitated in 1990 by Booth/Hansen & Assocs. as North Pier Terminal to house office space on the upper floors and a retail and entertainment center on the lower. Under new ownership, the 500,000sq ft complex is now called River East Plaza. It houses an upscale market and the **River East Art Center** (🕐*gallery hours vary; call for info;* ✕☎*312-321-1001; www.rivereastartcenter.com*). Observe striking **views**★ of the city from the southern glass galleries or the dockside promenade. On the lower level you can buy tickets for architectural and historical boat tours of the city (🕐*open Apr–Oct daily; 1hr 30min;* ⊜*$37;* ☎*312-527-1977; www.chicagoline.com*).

Lake Shore Drive★

This thoroughfare bordering the lake is lined with an array of high rises, several of which were designed by renowned German-born architect **Ludwig Mies van der Rohe** (1886–1969).

860–880 North Lake Shore Drive★★

The completion of these apartment towers in 1951 by Mies van der Rohe established his reputation as a master of Modernism and prefigured the design of steel-and-glass skyscrapers throughout the 1960s and 70s. Their prominent location, substantial scale and elegance of proportion were the first realization of steel-and-glass curtain wall designs that Mies had been developing for over 30 years. Here he used steel piers encased in concrete and created a strong vertical dynamic by attaching I-beams to the exterior between the window frames. A transparent lobby space produces an elegant effect. The two buildings are angled toward each other and the street, providing many lake views for the apartments. The success of these towers led to another commission two years later at **900–910 North Lake Shore Drive**. Distinguished by dark glass and window frames, these structures represent a more monochromatic design.

Visible from many places in the area is the blue pyramidal roof of **Lake Shore Place** (no. 680), an office and residential complex formerly known as the American Furniture Mart (1926). The 30-story tower and its four corner tourelles are embellished with Victorian Gothic designs, including three-story arches and an ornamental lantern at the top.

At no. 505 **Lake Point Tower** stands alone east of the drive. This unusual high rise was built in 1968 by Schipporeit-Heinrich, students of Mies van der Rohe, who adapted an unexecuted 1920 design by the master. All of the exterior surfaces of the Y-shaped tower are rounded, creating a flowing surface studded with vertical steel piers.

⚌ NAVY PIER★★

600 E. Grand Ave. at Lake Michigan.
🕐*Open Memorial Day–Labor Day Sun–Thu 10am–10pm, Fri–Sat 10am–midnight; Apr–May & Sept–Oct Sun–Thu 10am–8pm, Fri –Sat 10am–10pm; Nov–Mar Mon–Thu 10am–8pm, Fri–Sat 10am–10pm, Sun 10am–7pm.* 🕐*Closed Thanksgiving Day & Dec 25.* ♿♨✕.
✆*312-595-7437. www.navypier.com.*
Designed by Charles S. Frost in 1916, the 3,000ft-long pier was the largest in the world at the time. With an upper level for passengers and streetcar tracks and a lower level for freight, it was an important terminal for several decades. Long freight sheds (since demolished) connected the Head House (now known as the Family Pavilion) to an auditorium building situated at the far end. The pier was used for naval training during World War II and then by the University of Illinois until 1965, at which time it was affectionately known as "Harvard on the Rocks." Renovated in 1959 for the opening of the St. Lawrence Seaway and again in 1976, the pier fell into disrepair until 1991, when the city proposed a

Navy Pier and Chicago skyline at night

© City of Chicago/GRC

Cruising Off Navy Pier

From the south side of Navy Pier you can catch a variety of dinner cruises, charters (*Anita Dee I & II; &312-379-3191; www.anitadee.com*), speed boats, shuttles and the Pier's own four-masted schooner, *Windy (docked across from Riva Restaurant; &312-731-9689; www.tallshipwindy.com*). Here are more options:

Odyssey – This 700-passenger luxury liner offers brunch, lunch, dinner and moonlight cruises (*&866-391-8439; www.premieryachtsinc.com*).

The Spirit of Chicago – Board this 600-passenger ship for brunch, lunch and dinner cruises featuring live entertainment and dancing (*&866-391-8439; www.spiritcitycruises.com*).

Seadog I, II, III & IV – Sleek, bright yellow speedboats, Seadogs provide 30min lakefront rides or 75min architectural river tours for up to 149 passengers (*&866-391-8439; www.premieryachtsinc.com*).

Shoreline Sightseeing – Operates daily lakefront and river tours from the southwest corner of Navy Pier (*&312-222-9328; www.shorelinesightseeing.com*). Shoreline also offers water-taxi service between Navy Pier and the Willis Tower (*southwest corner of Gateway Park & Adams St.*) and between the Pier and the Museum Campus (*check online for schedule; two-day sampler unlimited rides $32*).

$190 million redevelopment plan, which foresaw the pier as an extension of **McCormick Place Convention Center**. Today encompassing more than 50 acres of shops, eateries, gardens and attractions, the pier has regained its fame as one of the largest entertainment piers in the country. A bustling and festive place that draws throngs of fun-seekers, the pier features an IMAX theater, two museums, boutiques and restaurants in its Family Pavilion. The pier is also home to the **Chicago Shakespeare Theater** (*&312-595-5600; www.chicagoshakes.com*), which offers performances year-round in a 525-seat courtyard-style theater and a flexible 180-seat theater. Adjoining the Family Pavilion to the east, the Crystal Gardens house an indoor tropical park, embellished with Arizona palm trees. At the center of the pier is Navy Pier Park, which showcases a 150ft-high **Ferris Wheel**, a musical merry-go-round and a 1,500-seat outdoor amphitheater called Skyline Stage. With its taut, sail-like roof, the popular venue rises above a one-story retail level. **Festival Hall,** a series of three-story structures designed for conventions, trade shows and meetings, connects the central area to the Terminals Building, with its splendidly restored ballroom. A seasonal beer garden welcomes weary strollers, who enjoy some of the city's best views of the lake and the famed skyline. For fine seafood and great skyline views, try **Riva** (*&312-644-7482; www.rivanavypier.com*). A recent addition to the Pier, **Harry Caray's Tavern** displays museum-quality sports memorabilia (*&312-527-9700; www.harrycaraystavern.com*).

♣♣ Chicago Children's Museum★(M)

At the entrance to Navy Pier. ⏱*Open daily 10am–5pm (Thu 10am–8pm).* 🎟*$10.* ♿🅿 *&312-527-1000. www.chichildrensmuseum.org.*
Founded in 1982 as the Express-Ways Children's Museum, this three-story, hands-on facility is designed to activate the intellectual and creative potential of children from toddlers to pre-teens. Interactive exhibits invite youngsters to build bridges, appreciate grandparents, climb aboard a replica 1850 schooner, and create news broadcasts, all in colorful monitored environment.
In **WaterWays** kids direct the world's most abundant resource through a system of rivers, locks and bridges. For little ones, Treehouse Trails is a pretend landscape to explore. In the Inventing

WaterWays, Chicago Children's Museum

© 2010 Chicago Children's Museum

Lab youngsters create their own flying machine; and Dinosaur Expedition invites them to dig up a real dinosaur.

Smith Museum of Stained-Glass Windows★

Same hours as Navy Pier. Closed Thanksgiving Day, Dec 25. ⟨⟩ P 312-595-7435. www.navypier.com.
Occupying an 800ft-long series of galleries along the lower level of Festival Hall, this museum showcases 150 stained-glass windows. Most were installed in Chicago between 1870 and the present. Both religious and secular windows are arranged by artistic style (Victorian, Prairie, Modern and Contemporary). Their designers include Louis Comfort Tiffany and John LaFarge, as well as Chicago artists Ed Paschke and Roger Brown.

ADDRESSES

⏚/EAT

$$ Bistro 110 – *110 E. Pearson St.* 312-266-3110. www.bistro110restaurant.com. The roasted garlic bulb that accompanies your crunchy baguette at this bright, bustling French bistro sets the tone for wood-oven-roasted salmon or steak au poivre—all redolent with garlic. Be sure to save room for the signature silky crème brûlée, made with Tahitian vanilla beans.

$$ Foodlife – *In Water Tower Place, mezzanine level.* P 312-335-3663. www.foodlifechicago.com.
Create an eclectic meal from the Chinese, Mexican or Middle Eastern sandwich, burger and pizza stands housed in this hip food court. At the entry, pick up a coded card, then select your entrées. After you visit a stand, staffers add the cost of your food to the electronic tally on your card; you pay the grand total when you leave. Prefer full service? Try comfort food at the **Mity Nice Grill ($$** 312-335-4745).

$ Billy Goat Tavern – *430 N. Michigan Ave. (lower level).* 312-222-1525. www.billygoattavern.com. The gruff grill chefs at the Goat inspired John Belushi's famous "cheezborger, cheezborger, cheep, cheep, no fries, cheeps" skit on *Saturday Night Live*. Framed newspaper clips and photos on the walls provide interesting slices of obscure Chicago history.

$ Garrett Popcorn Shop – *625 N. Michigan Ave.* 312-944-2630. www.garrettpopcorn.com. The line that routinely winds out onto Michigan Avenue on weekends leads to Garrett's, a local favorite since 1949. With six downtown locations, it retains a loyal clientele who swear that the caramel, cheddar-cheese or old-fashioned butter popcorn is the best around.

☕ TIME FOR TEA

Palm Court – *140 E. Walton Pl., in the Drake Hotel.* ✆*312-787-2200. www.the drakehotel.com.* Decorated with potted palms, the lobby of the Drake Hotel is a perfect spot to take a break after a shopping spree along Mag Mile or Oak Street. An elegant British-style high tea is served in the lobby every afternoon *(seatings every half-hour daily 1pm–5pm, last seating at 3.30pm; $30; reservations recommended).*

The Peninsula Chicago – *108 E. Superior St.* ✆*312-337-2888. www.chicago.peninsula.com.* Sipping afternoon tea in the opulent fifth-floor lobby at The Pen is a Chicago tradition.

Nosh on a gemlike variety of tiny pastries and tea sandwiches while you take in the view of Michigan Avenue through the floor-to-ceiling windows *(Mon–Fri 3pm–5pm, Sat 2.30pm–4.30pm, Sun 4pm–6pm; $38; reservations recommended).*

Seasons Lounge – *120 E. Delaware Pl., in the Four Seasons Hotel.* ✆ *312-280-8800. www.fourseasons.com/chicagofs.* Warm wood paneling—and a crackling fire in winter—in the lobby lounge area make cozy digs in which to take the chill off with a cup of comforting tea and all the accompaniments in the afternoon *(Mon–Sat 3pm–5pm; $32; reservations recommended).*

River North★

Nestled in the crook between the Chicago River and its north branch, bounded by Rush Street on the east and Oak Street on the north, River North is an eclectic neighborhood of historic buildings, modern skyscrapers and churches that punctuate endless blocks of ordinary city. Site of Chicago's earliest industries, River North is today most famous for its art galleries, trendy restaurants, bars and clubs.

A BIT OF HISTORY
From Factories to Flophouses
River North encompasses one of Chicago's oldest areas: Wolf Point, a small promontory around which the river turns north. Here in the 1830s early settlers, French-Canadian fur traders and Potawatomi Indians mingled at trading posts and taverns while small industries sprang up nearby. By mid-century, factories crowded the water's edge. Grain elevators, lumber mills, brickyards, tanneries and breweries bustled and spewed. Between the north and the main branches of the river, insalubrious shantytowns spread, housing laborers and their families. Waves of immigrants—Irish, Norwegians, Danes,

- 🚻 **Michelin Map:** p116.
- ▶ **Location:** The art galleries are located several blocks west of the walking tour suggested here.
- 🅿 **Parking:** It is possible to find street parking, but don't count on it.
- 👥 **Kids:** ESPN Zone can be fun and games for sports-minded kids, and the restaurant is family friendly.
- 🕐 **Timing:** You might plan a day to see the neighborhood and a day for the art galleries.
- 👁 **Also See:** The Loop, Magnificent Mile, Gold Coast.

GETTING AROUND
BY L: 🚇 Brown or Orange line to State; Red line to Grand.

Swedes and later Italians—settled south of Division Street, while in the blocks around Washington Square Park and just west of Michigan Avenue, Chicago's elite established an early North Side enclave. In 1871 the **Chicago Fire** devastated shanties and mansions alike as it leapt the river and raged northward. Rebuilding began immediately, and the area re-emerged as a corridor of elegant homes flanking the eastern edge of a working-class neighborhood. By 1900 the blighted and lawless northwestern corner was known as Little Hell. As industry burgeoned, the population continued to increase. Around World War I, the newest immigrants—African Americans moving up from the South during the Great Migration—took their place in the melting pot that characterized this neighborhood.

In 1920 the completion of the Michigan Avenue Bridge ensured the destiny of that boulevard as the fashionable Magnificent Mile. Desirable neighborhoods along the avenue attracted wealthy residents from the blocks between Wabash Avenue and LaSalle Street to the west, leaving the old homes there to be subdivided into apartments and rooming houses. Washington Square Park, nicknamed "Bughouse Square," became the center of Chicago's bohemia, an open forum for soapbox orators, hobo poets and a parade of characters expounding on everything from Nietzsche to free love. Clark Street north of the river became the magnificent mile of the demimonde, lined with flophouses, bars and dance halls.

In the former Little Hell, massive urban-renewal efforts throughout the 1940s and 50s produced the controversial Cabrini-Green housing projects, which eventually deteriorated—a sad reminder of good intentions gone awry.

In 1995, a new era in public housing began with a wholesale teardown of the projects. Mid-rise condos and rowhouses, which must include a certain percentage of low-income housing, took their place.

All remnants of Cabrini-Green are scheduled to be gone by 2010.

A New Start with Art

In the 1970s art dealers frustrated by rising costs on Michigan Avenue sought less expensive gallery spaces. The deserted warehouses in the old industrial district south of Superior Street and west of Wells Street offered a perfect alternative, and they were soon full with artists, buyers and lookers. After a decade of prosperity, tragedy struck in 1989 when fire destroyed the entire block between Orleans and Sedgwick streets south of Superior Street, consuming nine galleries. On its heels the economic downturn of the early 1990s caused several more to close or leave, some for the West Loop, today the home of Chicago's edgier galleries. Around 50 remain, however—the greatest concentration in the city—sustaining River North's reputation as Chicago's center of contemporary art.

WALKING TOURS

River North covers a large area that can be roughly divided into six sections. Of most interest are the first three areas: the eastern corridor, stretching from the river to Pearson Street; the Washington Square neighborhood, primarily along Dearborn Street; and the gallery district concentrated around Wells, Orleans, Superior and Huron Streets. In addition, River North contains the Mart District, including the behemoth Merchandise Mart, the Ohio-Ontario corridor of trendy restaurants and the cathedral district, centering upon Holy Name Cathedral.

EASTERN CORRIDOR★

1.5mi.

Located across the river from the Loop's bustling business district, this area offers a varied blend of architecture and purpose, including modern office buildings, 19C residences and religious edifices, that can be best appreciated on foot.

▷ *Begin at the intersection of N. State St. and Wacker Dr.*

Marina City★

300 N. State St.

From the river's edge rise the twin "corn-cob" towers of Bertrand Goldberg's prototype urban community. Revolutionary when conceived in 1959, the columnar apartment buildings were an attempt to encourage young professionals to resist the lure of the suburbs by providing not only living space but entertainment and services as well. Above the 18-story parking garages, pie-shaped units radiate from each tower's central core, where most of their load is borne. The cast-concrete construction and undulating surfaces of the towers contrast dramatically with the Miesian "glass boxes" so popular at the time.

Across State Street, for example, stands **330 North Wabash**★ (1971; formerly the IBM Building), the last American work of Ludwig Mies van der Rohe. Although still on the drawing board when the architect died in 1969, the edifice is quintessential Mies in its purity of form and function. Wrapped in a bronze-tinted curtain wall, its rectangular mass ascends from a spacious plaza.

Marina City

© Anne Evans/Chicago Architecture Foundation

▷ *Turn right on Hubbard St.*

▷ *Walk west along the river, then cross it via Dearborn St. bridge and continue to Westin River North; turn left and walk west along the riverfront promenade to Clark St.*

An unlikely duo—the building at **321 North Clark Street** and **Westin Chicago River North** (*320 N. Dearborn St.*), formerly the Hotel Nikko Chicago—are connected by a riverbank promenade called Riverfront Park. Architects Skidmore, Owings & Merrill invoked the spirit of their own Lever House (built 30 years earlier in New York) in the 35-story rectangular office tower (1987), now the headquarters of the American Bar Association. The lines of the much smaller hotel (1987, Hellmuth, Obata & Kassabaum) next door seem soft by comparison. The serenity of the Westin's lobby is enhanced by the lovely riverside garden that it overlooks.

▷ *Descend the stairs from the plaza to Clark St. and walk north.*

The elegant office tower of articulated glass and steel at 353 North Clark Street was designed by Chicago architect Dirk Lohan of Lohan Anderson and is scheduled for completion in 2009.

Courthouse Place (Cook County Criminal Courts Building)
54 W. Hubbard St.

Identifiable by its stern Romanesque Revival facade, this quiet professional building (1892) was for years the center of much judicial and journalistic hubbub. Celebrated defense attorney **Clarence Darrow** defended Chicago murderers Nathan Leopold and Richard Loeb here in 1924—saving them from the death penalty—and journalists Ben Hecht and Charles MacArthur were inspired enough by the press room to write *The Front Page* in 1928. The courts moved out in 1929, leaving the building to the more mundane city agencies that occupied it until its renovation in the mid-1980s.

▷ *Walk east on Hubbard St. and turn left on State St.*

The slab-like building at **515 North State Street**★ is Japanese architect Kenzo Tange's only office tower in the United States (1990). The razor-sharp, 45-degree angle that bisects the building on the west and the four-story cutout near the top lend the 30-story headquarters of the American Medical Association a most unusual profile.

113

River North Gallery District

This bustling district in River North *(bounded by Chicago, Wells, Huron and Orleans Sts.)* features the greatest concentration of art galleries in Chicago. Offerings include contemporary and ethnic art; 19C and 20C American works; ceramics and furniture; Chicago artists; photography; and a sampling of European paintings, sculpture and prints. Openings of new exhibits usually take place on Friday evenings, when the artists may be present. The first Thursday of each month, many galleries extend their hours and host free receptions *(5pm–7pm)*. *Most galleries are open Tue–Sat 10am–5.30pm (call to confirm). For schedules, call ☎312-649-0064 or visit www.artline.com/associations.*

The following is a sampling of River North Galleries:

Robert Henry Adams Fine Art
715 N. Franklin St. ☎312-642-8700. www.adamsfineart.com. Modern American art from 1910 to 1970.

Andrew Bae Gallery
300 W. Superior St. ☎312-335-8601. www.andrewbaegallery.com. Contemporary works by Asian artists.

Carl Hammer Gallery
740 N. Wells St. ☎312-266-8512. www.hammergallery.com. Focuses on "outsider" and self-taught artists.

Ken Saunders Gallery, Ltd.
230 W. Superior St. ☎312-573-1400. www.marxsaunders.com. Contemporary studio glass and sculpture.

Perimeter Gallery, Inc.
210 W. Superior St. ☎312-266-9473. www.perimetergallery.com. Contemporary painting, sculpture, works on paper and masterworks in ceramic and fiber arts.

Maya Polsky Gallery
215 W. Superior St. ☎312-440-0055. www.mayapolskygallery.com. International contemporary art, with a special interest in Russian artists.

Printworks Gallery
311 W. Superior St. ☎312-664-9407. www.printworkschicago.com. Contemporary prints, drawings, photographs and artists' books.

Roy Boyd Gallery
739 N. Wells St. ☎312-642-1606. www.royboydgallery.com. Abstract paintings, works on paper and sculpture.

Zolla/Lieberman Gallery
325 W. Huron St. ☎312-944-1990. www.zollaliebermangallery.com. The first gallery to come to River North, in 1975, showcases contemporary works by emerging and established artists.

For more on Chicago's art galleries, visit www.chicagogallerynews.com.

▷ *Continue walking north on State St. to the intersection with Ohio St.*

Built in three stages between 1894 and 1913, **Tree Studios** *(601–623 N. State St.)* were the inspiration of Judge Lambert Tree, who, as a prominent patron of the arts, wished to persuade artists to settle and work in Chicago by providing them an inexpensive place to live. The building was remodeled in 2004 for commercial use.

▷ *Walk east on Ohio St. to Wabash Ave.*

Bloomingdale's Home Store occupies the curious mosque-like edifice at 600 North Wabash Avenue. The former Medinah Temple was built for the Shriners in 1913 for fraternal meetings and ceremonials. It once accommodated the annual Shriners Circus, as well as a variety of civic events. The interior was remodeled in 2003 for Bloomingdale's, but the exterior retains its exotic Arabian look. Note the textured brickwork, the interlocking designs around the entrance, the stained-glass windows, and the onion domes.

▷ *Walk north on Wabash Ave. to Erie St.*

At the corner of Wabash Avenue and Erie Street stand two remnants of the gracious living that once characterized the eastern corridor of River North: the **Ransom R. Cable House**★ (1886, Cobb & Frost) at 25 East Erie Street and the **Samuel M. Nickerson House**★ (1883, Burling & Whitehouse), diagonally across the street. The two imposing residences display the Victorian tendency toward extravagance, stylistic eclecticism and mass. The Cable House, built by the president of the Chicago, Rock Island & Pacific Railway Co., exhibits the hallmarks of the Richardsonian Romanesque style, fusing a variety of architectural elements and design motifs into a uniform whole. Of particular interest are the turret, dormers, recessed windows, arches, surface decoration and steeply sloping slate roof.

The rectangular symmetry of the Nickerson House is more traditionally Italianate. But the dark, brooding exterior belied the Baroque luxuriance of its renowned interior, often referred to as the "marble palace." Samuel Nickerson, president of the First National Bank when he commissioned the home, spared no expense.

A dazzling mélange of woods, marbles, tile and glass decorates each room on the mansion's three floors. After 10 years housing the R. H. Love Gallery, the mansion underwent a thorough exterior cleaning and rehab in 2007 as a home for the art collection of investment banker Richard H. Driehaus. Next door at 50 East Erie Street, the incongruous facade of the **John B. Murphy Memorial Auditorium** (1926) looms over the sidewalk. Named after a prominent physician, the structure houses an auditorium once used by the American College of Surgeons and now available for rental.

▷ *North on Wabash Ave. to Huron St.*

Episcopal Cathedral of St. James★

65 E. Huron St. ○*Open Mon–Fri 10am –5pm.* ●*Free guided tour first Sun of the month after the 10.30am service. Art exhibit and concert event times vary.* &℘*312-787-7360. www.saintjames cathedral.org.*

From the outside, this Victorian-style cathedral (1857, Edward J. Burling; 1875, Burling & Adler; restored 1985, Holabird & Root) seems typical of the Chicago churches built of local limestone around the time of the Great Fire. The original structure of 1857 was destroyed in the blaze; only the 1867 bell tower remains standing, still bearing telltale char marks.

The Civil War memorial in the narthex also survived the fire and served as a temporary altar until the church could be rebuilt in 1875. The **interior**★ of the church is truly breathtaking; its meticulously restored stencilwork, originally applied in 1888, draws heavily on the naturalistic designs and colors of the Arts and Crafts movement.

▷ *Continue north on Wabash Ave. to Superior St. and turn left.*

At the corner of Superior and State Streets, **Holy Name Cathedral** *(735 N. State St.)*, an impressive structure dating back to 1875, serves as the Cathedral of the Catholic Archdiocese of Chicago. The Gothic Revival edifice was renovated in 1914 and 1968. Pope John Paul II celebrated mass here during his 1979 visit to the city.

▷ *Return to Wabash Ave. and continue north to Chicago Ave.*

At Chicago and Wabash Avenues, note the **Hotel St. Benedict Flats** (1882). These apartments were designed to attract upper-middle-class residents—an unprecedented concept since apartment living was then considered déclassé.

To dispel that image, architect James J. Egan devised the facade to resemble attached row houses.

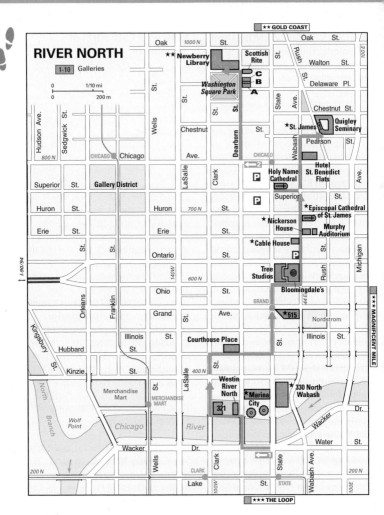

RIVER NORTH

1-10 Galleries

0   1/10 mi

0   200 m

Oak   1000 N   St.

★★ Newberry Library

Scottish Rite

Washington Square Park

Chestnut   Ave.

CHICAGO   Chicago

Gallery District

Superior   St.

Huron   St.   Huron   700 N   St.

Erie   St.   Erie   St.

Ontario   140W

Ohio   600 N   St.

Grand   Ave.

Illinois   St.

Hubbard

Kinzie   St.

Merchandise Mart

MERCHANDISE MART

Wolf Point

Chicago

Wacker

200 N

★ St. James

Quigley Seminary

Pearson

Holy Name Cathedral

Hotel St. Benedict Flats

Superior   St.

★ Episcopal Cathedral of St. James

★ Nickerson House

Murphy Auditorium

★ Cable House

Tree Studios

Bloomingdale's

GRAND

★515

Nordstrom

Illinois   St.

Courthouse Place

400 N

Westin River North

321

★ Marina City

★ 330 North Wabash

River

Wacker

Water   St.

200 N

Lake

CLARK   Clark   100W

STATE

Wabash Ave.

100 E

Continue north on Wabash Ave., turn right on Pearson St. and continue to Rush St.

At 831 North Rush Street, the Gothic-style **Archbishop Quigley Preparatory Seminary** (1919, now closed), named for the archbishop dedicated to building Chicago's Catholic schools, bears testament to the heyday of Catholic architecture in the city. On the second floor in the southwest corner, the **Chapel of St. James**★, modeled after Sainte-Chapelle in Paris, is noteworthy for its stunning windows (open year-round Tue & Thu–Sat noon–2pm; free tours Sat 9am–11am; closed Jan 1, Easter weekend & Dec 23–25; 312-782-3532; www.windows.org). Each window comprises 45,000 pieces of antique English glass that is truly "stained" (the glass, while molten, is mixed with pigment) and not merely painted. The building was converted to house the archdiocese's pastoral center in 2007.

Walk north on Rush St., turn left on Delaware Pl. and continue to Dearborn St.

Washington Square

Bounded by Dearborn St., Walton St., Clark St. and Washington Pl. **Washington Square Park** is Chicago's oldest surviving park, donated to the city by developer Orsamus Bushnell in 1842, who hoped it would attract wealthy home builders to his subdivision. Today the mansions along Dearborn Street give a sense of the area as it must have looked in the late 19C Perhaps more famous as "Bughouse Square," a gathering place for poets and protesters, soapbox orators and bohemian philosophers since the early 20C, the park is still occasionally the site of speeches and debates during the summer.

Directly east of the park along **North Dearborn Street** stand three reminders of the neighborhood's residential heyday. At no. 915, the **John Howland Thompson House (A)**, designed by Henry Ives Cobb and Charles S. Frost in 1888, features a lively roofline balancing the massive quality of its rusticated sandstone surface. The 1895 **George H. Taylor House** (no. 919, **B**) is purely Georgian in style, while the adjacent **George B. Carpenter House** (no. 925, **C**) combines massive stone with elegant, rounded bays. The **Scottish Rite Cathedral** (no. 929) began life in 1867 as Unity Church. The Great Fire destroyed all but the church's Gothic limestone walls, and it was rebuilt in 1873 by the architectural firm of Burling & Adler. Dankmar Adler, who established his reputation for superior acoustics with this commission, would go on to become Louis Sullivan's partner and an expert in theater and auditorium design.

The church was eventually sold to the Oriental Consistory (Scottish Rite Bodies, a Masonic lodge), which renovated the inside to meet its needs. In the early 2000s, the cathedral, indeed the block, passed into the hands of developers who plan to build condominum towers and commercial space while preserving the historic buildings.

Newberry Library★★

60 W. Walton St. Reading rooms.
🕐*Open Tue–Fri 9am–5pm, Sat 9am–1pm.* 👣*Guided tours Thu 3pm, Sat 10.30am.* 🕐*Closed major holidays.* ♿
✆*312-943-9090. www.newberry.org.*

Established in 1887 with a bequest from merchant, banker and land speculator Walter L. Newberry (1804–68), this venerable institution ranks among the top independent research libraries in the country for scholars in the humanities. Its collections are impressive both in quality and quantity: 1.5 million volumes and 5 million manuscript pages include materials as diverse as a 1481 edition of Dante's **Divine Comedy** and a 17C Mexican manuscript on tree bark. Its map, music, American-Indian and Midwestern literature holdings are unparalleled. Researchers come from around the country to use its genealogical resources. Architect **Henry Ives Cobb** designed the Spanish Romanesque edifice in 1893. A 10-story stack and storage wing by Harry Weese & Assocs. was added in 1982. For the casual visitor, a look around the lobby, with its tall ceilings, grand staircase, terrazzo floors and lovely reproduction light fixtures, imparts a sense of the building's grandeur. Rotating exhibits in the galleries located just off the lobby draw heavily on the collections, offering the non-researching public an opportunity to sample the library's treasures.

ADDRESSES

🍽/EAT

ONTARIO STREET
Between **Dearborn and Wells Streets**, this neon-lit artery forms the hub of River North nightlife, drawing hordes of tourists to such popular chain restaurants as the **$ Hard Rock Cafe** *(63 W. Ontario St.; ✆312-943-2252. www.hardrockcafe.com)*, the **$ Flagship McDonald's** *(600 N. Clark St.; ✆312-867-0455)* and **$ Ed Debevic's** *(640 N. Wells St.; ✆312-664-1707. www.edebevics.com)*, a Chicago institution known for its sassy staff, who often dress as characters from 1950s movies and TV shows. **Ontario at Wells Street** is also the new location of **$ Gino's East** *(633 N. Wells St.; ✆312-943-1124. www.ginoseast.com)*, Chicago's favorite deep-dish pizzeria, renowned for its two-inch-thick pies and graffitti-splattered wooden

Deep-dish pizza from Gino's East

Gino's East

booths. Call ahead and order your pizza, or be prepared to wait at least 30min for it to cook.

OTHER CHICAGO CLASSICS

$ Pizzeria Uno and **$ Pizzeria Due** – *Uno: 29 E. Ohio St.; 312-321-1000. Due: 619 N. Wabash Ave.; 312-943-2400. www.unos.com.* These sister restaurants, located in converted Victorian mansions, always rank at the top of local "best deep-dish" polls. Both restaurants are very popular on weekends, and the staff will take your pizza order before you sit down to help reduce the wait (which can run up to an hour). At lunchtime, Uno and Due offer an express service, delivering an individual-size deep-dish pie to your table in 20 minutes.

$ Mr. Beef – *666 N. Orleans St. 312-337-8500. Tonight Show* host Jay Leno put this place on the map. He discovered it as a struggling stand-up comic working the nightclub circuit and has been recommending it to his Hollywood pals for years. But don't go to Mr. Beef just to catch a glimpse of a visiting celebrity; go for the Italian beef sandwich—a soft Italian roll piled high with thinly-sliced marinated beef garnished with *giardinère* (pickled peppers, celery and spices). Variations on the basic sandwich include "hot" (topped with chili peppers), "sweet" (with roasted red and green peppers) and "wet" (dipped in the beef's juices).

OUT AND ABOUT

Jazz Record Mart – *27 E. Illinois St. 312-222-1467. www.jazzmart.com.* Impresario Bob Koester has been a fixture on the local scene for decades, and his commitment to and enthusiasm for jazz and blues make his record store one of the most popular in town. While the Mart's comprehensive selection of albums, CDs and cassettes includes everything from Bix Biederbeck and Thelonious Monk to Kenny G., serious jazz aficionados flock to the shop in search of vintage vinyl, imports and other rare recordings Koester and his staff are renowned for tracking down.

Pizzeria Uno

Pizzeria Uno Corporation

Art Institute of Chicago★★★

One of the great museums of the world and the preeminent arts institution of the Midwest, the Art Institute of Chicago is a comprehensive center for art collections, conservations and exhibitions. Its permanent collection includes more than 260,000 objects across 10 curatorial departments and spans 5,000 years of visual expression. The museum's reputation is built on its collection of Impressionist and Post-Impressionist paintings, one of the largest and most important outside France. The eagerly awaited 264,000 sq ft Modern Wing, designed by Renzo Piano, opened in 2009. Since then, it has attracted attention in its own right for its display of 20C and 21C art and design.

◔ **Michelin Map:** pp76–77 and plans p120, p128 and p134.

▶ **Location:** 111 S. Michigan Ave. at E. Adams St. cta Bus no. 151.

◔ **Opening Times:** Open year-round Mon–Wed 10.30am–5pm, Thu–Fri 10.30am–8pm, Sat–Sun 10am–5pm. ◔ Closed Thanksgiving Day, Dec 25 Day and Jan 1. $18 (children under 14 free). Audio guides available $7. ✕⚬ ℘312-443-3600. www.artic.edu.

◔ **A Bit of Advice:** Certain galleries may be closed (ask at information desk or check the website) and specific works of art may be off view or exhibited in locations other than those indicated here.

A BIT OF HISTORY
The Building

Founded in 1866 as the Chicago Academy of Design, the Art Institute was one of the first art schools in the US. Reorganized to incorporate a school and a museum in 1879, the institution occupied its own building two blocks south of its current location by 1887. The Institute's board of directors, determined to create a world-class center for art education and exhibition, used the occasion of the World's Columbian Exposition of 1893 to construct a new facility. Architecturally intended to embody the cultural attainments of Chicago, the Neoclassical edifice countered the city's tough, working-class reputation.

The core structure, planned with its future as an art museum in mind, would be utilized by the World Congresses during the Fair and then turned over to the Art Institute. It was the only World's Fair pavilion located off the fairgrounds in Jackson Park. Created by Shepley, Rutan & Coolidge, the building had initially been designed by architect John W. Root, who died before the construction began.

From the original 50,000sq ft of the Allerton Building, the Institute has now expanded to over 1 million square feet. Coolidge & Hodgdon designed McKinlock Court (1924), the open-air garden to the east, today attached to the museum's Garden Cafe and used for alfresco dining.

Subsequent additions included the Goodman Theatre (1926, now demolished) by Howard Van Doren Shaw; the Ferguson Building (1958) by Holabird & Root & Burgee, to the north of the Allerton Building; the Morton Building (1962) by Shaw, Metz & Assocs.; the Rubloff Building (1976) by Skidmore, Owings & Merrill; and the Rice Building (1988), designed by Hammond, Beeby & Babka. Also of note is the reconstruction of Louis Sullivan's Trading Room from the Chicago Stock Exchange (1893).

The most ambitious of the Institute's additions is the 264,000sq ft **Modern**

FIRST FLOOR

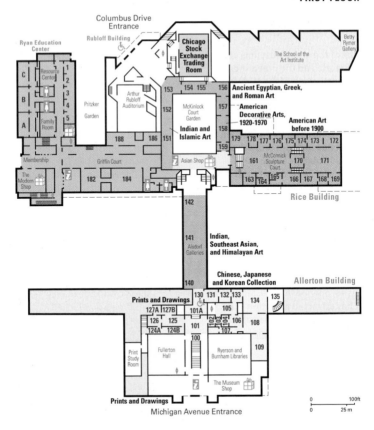

Columbus Drive Entrance

Ryan Education Center

Rubloff Building

Chicago Stock Exchange Trading Room

Betty Rymer Gallery

The School of the Art Institute

Resource Center

Family Room

Pritzker Garden

Arthur Rubloff Auditorium

McKinlock Court Garden

Indian and Islamic Art

Ancient Egyptian, Greek, and Roman Art

American Decorative Arts, 1920–1970

American Art before 1900

Membership

Griffin Court

Asian Shop

McCormick Sculpture Court

The Modern Shop

Rice Building

Indian, Southeast Asian, and Himalayan Art

Aladorf Galleries

Chinese, Japanese and Korean Collection

Allerton Building

Prints and Drawings

Print Study Room

Fullerton Hall

Ryerson and Burnham Libraries

The Museum Shop

Prints and Drawings

Michigan Avenue Entrance

0   100ft
0   25 m

Wing (2009), a three-story glass and limestone structure designed by **Renzo Piano**. Located on the museum's northeast corner, the wing houses the modern and contemporary art collections, and features a dramatic "flying carpet" roof and a bridge connecting it to Millennium Park across Monroe Street. The new construction adds 65,000sq ft of gallery space, an increase of more than 33 percent. The museum also houses many facilities for arts appreciation and conservation, including study rooms for prints and drawings, textiles, architectural drawings and photographs. The **Ryan Education Center** in the Modern

Dining Out

A favorite for outdoor summer dining, the **Garden Cafe** (open daily 11am–4pm) is a casual spot for sandwiches, salads, pizza and burgers.

For a more upscale experience, **Terzo Piano** in the Modern Wing (open daily 11am–3pm and Thu 5pm–9pm), run by acclaimed chef Tony Mantuano, turns out artfully plated (and markedly pricier than the cafe) seasonal specialities (see Must Eat). Its cheese cave keeps a bounty of American artisanal cheeses at the perfect temperature and humidity. During warm months, diners swarm the restaurant's patio that overlooks Millennium Park and the stunning Chicago skyline. Reservations are highly recommended.

SECOND FLOOR

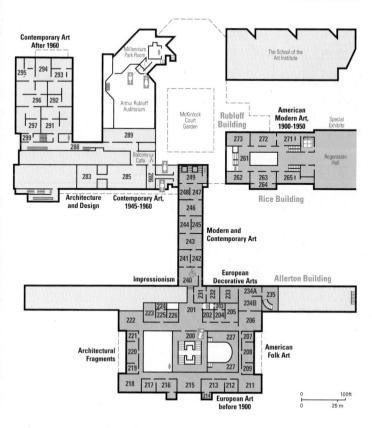

Wing attracts kids, teens and families to its studios and classrooms to further enhance their visits. The Ryerson and Burnham libraries were founded by **Martin Ryerson**, an art collector who donated his books on the fine and decorative arts, and by architect Daniel Burnham, whose architectural journals, drawings and letters formed the nucleus of the library collections. Today the Art Institute's monumental Indiana limestone facade on Michigan Avenue reveals its relationship with the other Beaux-Arts buildings of the World Fair's "White City."

The broad staircase, a popular people-watching and meeting place, makes a suitably grand entrance. Inside, another sweeping staircase leads to the galleries on the second level. Skylights restored as part of an extensive rehabilitation of the museum in 1987 heighten the drama of the space with a warm, natural light.

The Collections

The museum's seminal holdings flourished, thanks to the enthusiasm of civic leaders whose wealth—derived from railroads, manufacturing, real estate and lumber—enabled them to amass personal collections. Their financial and material donations established the museum's reputation for large-scale, high-quality acquisitions. Among the earliest material donations to the Art Institute was the Henry Field Collection of 41 Barbizon school paintings. The museum made its first large purchase in 1894, acquiring the Demidoff Collection of 14 Dutch and Flemish masterpieces. Chicago's early art collectors reveled in their independence; they built their col-

121

THIRD LEVEL

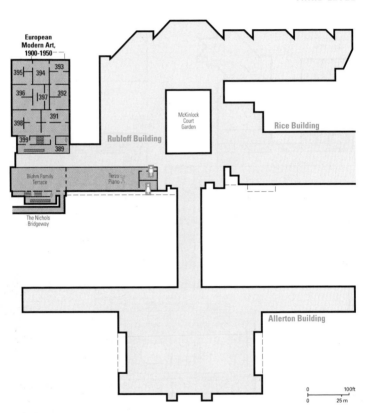

European Modern Art, 1900-1950

395	394	393
396	397	392
398	391
399	389

Rubloff Building

Bluhm Family Terrace

Terzo Piano

The Nichols Bridgeway

McKinlock Court Garden

Rice Building

Allerton Building

0   100ft
0   25 m

lections based on personal taste, in spite of criticism for ignoring expert advice. Because of this radical independence, by 1890 more collectors of French **Impressionist** and **Post-Impressionist** paintings lived in Chicago than in Paris. Succeeding generations of Chicago collectors continued to challenge prevailing tastes and many of the museum's finest collections, including those of Asian, African and 20C art, have their roots in this determined acquisition style. The Art Institute's prominent donors include Bertha Honoré Palmer, socialite wife of Potter Palmer, one of Chicago's most successful real-estate developers. Palmer established her role as collector and advocate of the Impressionists through her friendship with artist Mary Cassatt. Her bequest of the Potter Palmer Collection of 52 Impressionist paintings in 1922 helped

secure the Art Institute's reputation in this field. Lumber baron Martin Ryerson bequeathed an amazing 227 American and European paintings, as well as drawings and Asian and European decorative arts, to the museum. The donations of Clarence Buckingham and his sister, Kate Sturges Buckingham, form the foundation of the department of Asian art. A 1997 gift of 400 Indian, Himalayan and Southeast Asian pieces from the collection of James and Marilynn Alsdorf has made the Art Institute's Asian holdings among the finest in the US and now sits in a new Renzo Piano-designed gallery. The collection of avant-garde post-Impressionist paintings donated by Frederic Clay Bartlett in memory of his wife, Helen Birch Bartlett, includes many of the treasures of the museum, in particular George Seurat's *A Sunday on La Grande Jatte – 1884* (1884–86).

Short On Time?

If you have only two hours to visit the Art Institute, spend them seeing the following masterpieces (listed in order of visit):

- **Thorne Miniature Rooms** (*Allerton, lower level, gallery 11*)
- **Rubloff Paperweight Collection** (*Allerton, lower level, gallery 15*)
- **Tripod Food Container** (*Allerton, lower level, gallery 11*)
- **Seated Buddha** (*Allerton, 1st floor, gallery 141*)
- **The Assumption of the Virgin**, El Greco (*Allerton, 2nd floor, gallery 211*)
- **Old Man with a Gold Chain**, Rembrandt van Rijn (*Allerton, 2nd floor, gallery 213*)
- **Paris Street; Rainy Day**, Gustave Caillebotte (*Allerton, 2nd floor, gallery 201*)
- **A Sunday on La Grande Jatte – 1884**, Georges Seurat (*Allerton, 2nd floor, gallery 240*)
- **Six Versions of Stacks of Wheat**, Claude Monet (*Allerton, 2nd floor, gallery 206*)
- **Tiffany Lamp** (*Rice, lower level, gallery 177*)
- **The Child's Bath**, Mary Cassatt (*Rice, 2nd floor, gallery 273*)
- **Nighthawks**, Edward Hopper (*Rice, 2nd floor, gallery 262*)
- **American Gothic**, Grant Wood (*Rice, 2nd floor, gallery 263*)
- **Alaya Altarpiece** (*Rubiloff, 1st floor, gallery 157*)
- **The Old Guitarist**, Pablo Picasso (*Modern Wing, 3rd floor, gallery 391*)
- **Bathers by the River**, Henri Matisse (*Modern Wing, 3rd floor, gallery 391*)
- **Golden Bird**, Constantin Brancusi (*Modern Wing, 3rd floor, gallery 395*)
- **Joseph Cornell Boxes** (*Modern Wing, 3rd floor, gallery 397*)
- **White Curve**, Ellsworth Kelly (*Modern Wing, Pritzker Garden,1st floor*)
- **Nichols Bridgeway** and **Bluhm Sculpture Terrace** (*Modern Wing, 3rd floor*)

The Edwin and Lindy Bergman Collection, donated in 1987 and 1991, brought the museum 78 significant paintings, collages, constructions and works on paper by noted American and European Dada and Surrealist artists.

The Donna and Howard Stone Collection of contemporary art, gifted to the Art Institute in 2010, includes 59 pieces ranging from Gerhard Richter and Sol Lewitt, to Rosemarie Trockel and Lawrence Weiner.

VISIT

The main entrance is located on Michigan Avenue, across from Adams Street. The Modern Wing has its own entrance on Monroe Street; visitors can access both the original building and the Modern Wing either there or at the Michigan Avenue entrance.

Inside the main entrance, you will enter a foyer housing an information desk and a ticket booth, a coatroom and the main gift shop, well stocked with books, post-

ers, decorative arts and a wide selection of beautifully crafted jewelry. The collections are displayed in the Allerton Building to the west, the Morton Building to the south, the Alsdorf Galleries (formerly Gunsaulus Hall) that connects the west and east buildings, the Rubloff and Rice buildings to the east, and the Modern Wing to the north. All major buildings are connected on the first floor; however visitors may also access the Modern Wing through an entrance in gallery 249 on the second floor.

Begin your visit at the foyer information desk, where you'll find schedules of temporary exhibits, special events, lectures and guided tours. Visitor guides are available in English and Spanish. Just beyond the foyer is the Woman's Board Grand Staircase, the point of departure for the general introduction tours, available every day of the week. Four recorded MP3 tours are available for rent, including a gallery highlights tour, a director's tour, an American art tour and the **Lion's Trail** 🧑‍🧒 for children aged 5 to 10 years old.

The Art Institute's regularly changing temporary exhibits draw from other sources as well as from the museum's own collections; supplemental lectures and demonstrations provide an in-depth experience of the work on view. In addition to special exhibits, the Art Institute offers gallery tours for all ages.

EUROPEAN ART BEFORE 1900★★

Galleries 201–248, Allerton Building, 2nd floor.

This portion of the European painting and sculpture collection features work by masters from all of the major centers of artistic activity from the 15C to the 1800s. The art in these galleries takes religion, historic events, portraits, ancient myths, still life and landscape as its subjects, demonstrating the evolution of media and style from the early Renaissance through the Age of Reason. Small paintings, works on paper, and objects are installed in the connecting hallways.

Renaissance

As the Middle Ages came to an end after 1300, European arts and sciences flourished. The styles, subjects and media of Renaissance art vividly reflect the quickening quest for knowledge and an expanding curiosity about the

---

Renaissance – works of art

Dieric Bouts
Mater Dolorosa, c.1475 *(gallery 202)*

Giovanni di Paolo
Six Scenes from the Life of St. John the Baptist, c.1460 *(gallery 204)*

Sandro Botticelli
Virgin and Child with an Angel, c.1485 *(gallery 205)*

Correggio
Virgin and Child with the Young St. John the Baptist, c.1515 *(gallery 205)*

El Greco
The Assumption of the Virgin, 1577 *(gallery 211)*

---

world. Artists came to understand perspective, and flat landscapes of the Medieval era gave way to works with depth and dimension. Human faces took on an expressiveness, and subjects grew increasingly secular. Flanders, in present-day Belgium, and Florence, Italy, burgeoned as artistic centers, developing distinctly different styles but trading influences.

The Flemish discovered that oil, as a painting medium, imparted to their work a translucent warmth missing in the bright and distinct colors of egg tempera, which remained popular in Italy for some time. Oil paint made possible the rendering of nuance, and the northerners—**Dieric Bouts** and **Hans Memling** *(gallery 202)* among them— became masters of depth and detail. In Florence, painters experimented with perspective and studied anatomy and Classical sculpture, while in Siena **Giovanni di Paolo** and others continued to work in the flattened spatial field of their predecessors. In northern Italy, painters rendered lush canvases; even their Biblical subjects assumed an increased sensuality, as in the works of **Sandro Botticelli**.

Some artists of the High Renaissance like **Correggio** adopted Leonardo da Vinci's pyramidal composition and blending of light and shade, experimenting with new ways to unify their works by softening the rules of perspective and composition. Others, having mastered the human form, began to twist and manipulate it, working from intellectual preconception rather than observable reality. Called Mannerists, they took many cues from Michelangelo—whose influence can be seen in the works of both **Tintoretto** and **Titian**—often producing large, dramatically-lit works filled with complicated juxtapositions of humanity. With typical Mannerist zeal, **El Greco's** animated and elongated figures capture the essence of religious ecstasy, contrasting with the severe Sevillian styles of **Bartolomé Murillo** and **Francisco de Zurbarán** *(gallery 211)*.

Baroque

Baroque painting would eventually encompass a variety of styles, but by 1600, the new realism that distinguished it from Mannerism was emerging. The often tortured forms of the 16C resolved themselves in the sharply illuminated, realistic tableaux of **Caravaggio** and the gentle luxuriance of **Peter Paul Rubens**. In contrast, **Nicolas Poussin** cultivated a heroic Neoclassicism based on the principles of geometry and a vision of the ideal landscape. Baroque style took another turn in Holland, culminating in the work of **Rembrandt**, whose masterful use of light, after Caravaggio, imbued his portraits with poignant realism.

As the 17C waned, a stylistic ostentation inspired by the opulence and ceremony of the pre-Revolutionary court was becoming fashionable in France. Largely popular for their applications in interior design, ornate Rococo forms found expression in the fanciful portrayals of a pastoral world painted by **François Boucher**, **Jean Antoine Watteau** and **Jean Honoré Fragonard** *(gallery 216)*. The murals of **Giovanni Batista Tiepolo** *(gallery 215)* exuberantly epitomize both the decorative and artistic flamboyance of the Rococo. In the revolutionary atmosphere of the late 18C, however, artists rejected the Baroque and Rococo traditions as they had come to represent the hated exorbitance of the nobility.

Neoclassicism, Romanticism and Realism

Out of the humanitarian ideals of the Enlightenment grew two major schools of artistic thought: Neoclassicism and Romanticism. In very different languages, both sought to express the idealism and nationalism of the new world order. Inspired by archaeological discoveries at Pompeii and Herculaneum in the mid-18C, the Neoclassicists—preeminently **Jacques Louis David**—viewed the quiet grandeur, heroic subjects and precise proportions of antiquity as fitting counterpoints to the petty dalliances of their Rococo predecessors. Superb draftsmanship and crisp, classical lines made **J.A.D. Ingres** the finest portrait painter of the era. Rejecting such precision, the painters of the Romantic movement reveled in a freer attitude toward brushstroke and color, relying on historic events and settings for their exoticism, drama and allegory. In a portent of Impressionism, **Eugène Delacroix**, a classic Romantic, declared, "I do not paint a sword but its sparkle." The treatment of atmosphere and light by Englishmen **John Constable** and **Joseph Mallord William Turner** is similarly prophetic. Toward the middle of the 19C, a new movement grounded in reality began to emerge in France. Forsaking the classical ideals and exaggerated emotionalism of the Romantics, the Realists strived to observe and record the world around them. Inspired by **Camille Corot** *(gallery 221 and 224)*, their palette tended to be dark, and, like **Gustave Courbet** and **Jean-François Millet**, their subjects were ordinary people.

IMPRESSIONISM AND POST-IMPRESSIONISM★★★

Galleries 225–226, 201, 240–243, Allerton Building, 2nd floor.

The Art Institute's collection of Impressionist and Post-Impressionist paintings constitute one of the largest, most comprehensive and highest in quality outside France. Chicago collectors, in particular the Palmers, the Ryersons and the Bartletts, began acquiring works by Monet, Renoir, Degas and Cézanne as early as the 1880s, and their gifts to the museum form the core of its holdings. The **Helen Birch Bartlett Memorial**

Collection★★ of Post-Impressionist and early 20C masters on exhibit in gallery 240 comprises an imposing assemblage of painterly genius.

Impressionism

The segue from Realism to Impressionism took place at the hand of **Edouard Manet**, who employed the dark tones and ordinary subjects of his contemporaries to explore the opposition of light and shadow. Indeed, as it evolved, Impressionism sought to define its subjects in terms of their color and reflected light, thereby dissolving the hard outlines that traditionally delineated the painted form and, in the extreme, recasting subjects as an arrangement of colors and light. **The Impressionists** understood the ephemeral nature of their quest and painted rapidly to record moments in time with quick brushstrokes that would give a spontaneous "impression" of a scene.

They often worked outdoors attempting to capture the fleeting effects of sunlight, and the movement acquired its name, coined derogatorily by an unimpressed critic, from **Claude Monet**'s 1872 painting *Impression, Sunrise*. So radical did these works seem in subject, palette and technique that they were roundly rejected by the art establishment and refused admission to the

The Art Institute of Chicago, Mr. and Mrs. Lewis Larned Coburn Memorial Collection

Two Sisters (On the Terrace) (1881) by Pierre Auguste Renoir

Impressionism – works of art

Edouard Manet
Jesus Mocked by Soldiers, 1865
(gallery 222)

Claude Monet
Six versions of Stacks of Wheat, 1890–91 *(gallery 243)*

Gustave Caillebotte
Paris Street; Rainy Day, 1876–77
(gallery 201)

Pierre Auguste Renoir
Two Sisters (On the Terrace), 1881
(gallery 201)

Edgar Degas
The Millinery Shop, 1879–84
(gallery 226)

annual exhibitions of the prestigious Paris Salon. Undaunted, the Impressionists mounted eight of their own exhibitions between 1874 and 1886, eventually gaining critical acclaim. From the smoky railway stations and wintery grainstacks of Monet to the soft, summery aura of **Pierre Auguste Renoir**, the world as interpreted by the Impressionists was truly colorful and luminous.

Post-Impressionism

Because of its very nature and the diversity of its practitioners, the Impressionist phenomenon, though short-lived, opened the floodgates of artistic interpretation. Arising both out of and in opposition to its precepts, the artists of Post-Impressionism pushed the formal aspects of painting in new emotional, compositional, coloristic, symbolic and scientific directions. At the heart of the activity were several artists who had practiced as Impressionists, including **Paul Cézanne**, **Paul Gauguin** and **Georges Seurat**. In general, they shared a desire to turn from the spontaneity of Impressionism to explore more enduring forms of expression. Individually, each came to represent a different artistic vision. In rejecting the atmospheric realism of the Impressionists, these artists freed themselves to explore new perspectives on color, symbolism, composition and form. Cézanne's interest, for instance, in structure and composition set him apart from the Impressionists and strongly influenced Matisse, Picasso and the Cubist works of the next generation, earning him the epithet "father of modern painting." Tahitian symbolism lends the work of Paul Gauguin a certain spirituality, and his bold planes of color bespeak permanence rather than impression. Seurat, in perhaps the ultimate departure, reduced his images to a near molecular level, only to build them up again using dot patterns of color. This technique, known as **Pointillism**, had its basis in the idea that points of color mixed more brilliantly in the observer's eye than did paint on the artist's palette. Other Post-Impressionist directions

A Sunday on La Grande Jatte – 1884 (1884–86) by Georges Seurat

The Art Institute of Chicago, Helen Birch Bartlett Memorial Collection

can be seen in the work of **Vincent van Gogh**, **Henri de Toulouse-Lautrec** and **Alfred Sisley**.

AMERICAN ART★★
Galleries 161–179, Rice Building, 1st floor; galleries 158–159, Rubloff Building, 1st floor; gallery 227, Allerton Building, 2nd floor; galleries 261–265, 271–273, 2nd floor.
American galleries at the Art Institute exhibit furniture and decorative arts from the 17C, and painting and sculpture to 1900. Beginning with the simple household objects of Puritan New England, the collection chronicles the development of American taste.

Colonial America
Pilgrim-style furniture in gallery 165 shows the influence of Medieval forms and somber Renaissance design. Makers favored carving, turning, and painting for decoration, although little of the painting has survived. Decoration on a chest made in Connecticut gracefully blends the stylized design elements popular at this time. Furnishings in galleries 165–169 reflect an increasing refinement of form and finish that began with the William and Mary, or early Baroque style, around 1690. Pieces grew tall and elegant; high chests came into vogue. By around 1725, the curvaceous and sturdy cabriole leg distinguished the Queen Anne style, to which the Rococo Chippendale designers added claw-and-ball feet. American cabinetmakers introduced undulating fronts to desks and bureaus. Note the bombe-style Bostonian **chest of drawers** and the block front of the **desk** *(both in gallery 167)* made in Norwich, Connecticut. Colonial **silverwares** include arcane receptacles and containers: caudle cups, porringers and patch boxes for storing false beauty marks fashionable in the early 18C. Look for works by several fine Boston and New York artisans—Jeremiah Dummer and Edward Winslow among them. Cornelius Kierstade's **two-handled cup** in gallery 165 is a lovely example of early American Baroque design.

New Republic – works of art

Lorado Taft
Solitude of the Soul, date unknown *(gallery 161)*
John Singleton Copley
Mrs. Daniel Hubbard, 1764 *(gallery 167)*
Raphaelle Peale
Strawberries, Nuts, etc., 1822 *(gallery 169)*
Thomas Cole
Distant View of Niagara Falls, 1830 *(gallery 171)*
William Sidney Mount
Bar-room Scene, 1835 *(gallery 171)*
Frederic Edwin Church
View of Cotopaxi, 1857 *(gallery 171)*
Winslow Homer
The Herring Net, 1885 *(gallery 171)*

The New Republic
Post-Revolutionary Americans adopted English Neoclassicism, sometimes called Federal style in honor of the new republic. Examples of this slender style furnish gallery 168. Popularized in England by George Hepplewhite and Thomas Sheraton, the style tends toward fine proportions, clear lines and Classical motifs. Another Neoclassical movement known as Empire *(galleries 169 and 172)* came by way of Napoleonic France, its massive forms and heavy antique flourishes replacing the delicate shapes of Federalism.

American painting matured with the new nation. Colonial portraitist **John Singleton Copley** painted with volume and luminescence in contrast to the flat, primitive works of his predecessors. **Raphaelle Peale**, son of Charles Willson Peale *(gallery 169)*, became the country's first virtuoso still-life painter, while **William Sidney Mount** rendered his genre scenes of American life with a classical rigor. Soon the drama of light and a heroic sense of landscape captured the imaginations of American artists. Awed by the vastness of the continent, painters of the Hudson River school, such as **Thomas Cole** and others, including **Frederic Edwin Church, Albert Bier-**

stadt and **George Inness** *(gallery 170)*, exulted in the wonder of nature. For **Winslow Homer**, heroism came with human endeavor. And, with a different sense of grandeur, American sculptors of the 19C **Hiram Powers**, **Daniel Chester French** and **Lorado Taft** *(gallery 161, McCormick Memorial Court)* used Neoclassical allegory to describe the ennobling power of art and the glory of the young republic.

Victorian Era

Furniture styles between 1840 and 1920 proliferated in a series of concurrent revivals, including Gothic, Rococo and Renaissance. Victorians delighted in their eccentric shapes, decorations and blends of materials. The rosewood **étagère** in gallery 173 represents in form, fabric and function the spirit of the Rococo Revival, and the excesses of the Victorian era. Silver of the period erupted with florid surface patterns. In gallery 171, Tiffany's magnificent Greek Revival candelabra and **punch bowl** shimmer with the opulence of the age. Pieces in galleries 175 and 176 signal a shift away from the historicism and exorbitance of the Victorian era and a return to handcrafting. The strong Japanese influence on such "art furniture" can be seen in the lovely **side chair** and Tiffany **pitcher** in galleries 158 and 159.

Born of the same ideals, works of the Arts and Crafts movement are exhibited in gallery 177 and upstairs in gallery 158. American painting of the late 19C took many forms, informed by currents in

Europe where several influential American artists studied, lived and worked. **James Abbott McNeill Whistler**, an expatriate since 1855, renounced realism to experiment with light and color, an effort even his titles reflect. The flattering high society portraits of **John Singer Sargent** contrast with the penetrating realism of **Thomas Eakins**. A protégée of Edgar Degas in France, **Mary Cassatt** bathed her intimate views of women and children in the light and color of Impressionism.

20C American Decorative Art

American furniture and decorative arts of the 20C continue a half-flight up in galleries 158 and 159. Prairie school furniture inherited the aesthetic ethos of the British Arts and Crafts movement. Called by innovator **Frank Lloyd Wright** his "architectural sculpture," pieces like the **armchair** of c.1908 echo in miniature the geometry of Prairie school buildings. In contrast, the 1920s heavily influenced by the advent of Modernism, embraced the smooth streamlining of Art Deco. Inventive forms, industrial materials and minimal decoration characterize the post-1940 International style, which had its roots in the German Bauhaus. The molded chairs of **Charles Eames** *(gallery 158)* have become icons of this eclectic modern movement.

American Trends

Although Modernism evolved mainly in Europe, painters like **Georgia O'Keeffe** and **Joseph Stella** helped to Americanize it. But the representational impulse was strong, and much early-20C American art developed along realistic lines, delighting in the American landscape, both urban and rural. Around 1907 the new Realists began to look to city streets for inspiration, but the art establishment, disturbed by their graphic realism, derisively dubbed them the Ashcan school. The lonely urban vistas of **Edward Hopper** *(gallery 262)* owe a strong debt to the Ashcan school. In the 1930s, American painters looked again at the landscape, this time celebrating the countryside in an overt rejection of

---

Victorian Era – works of art

John Singer Sargent
Mrs. George Swinton, 1897 *(gallery 273)*

Thomas Eakins
Mary Adeline Williams, 1899 *(gallery 176)*

Mary Cassatt
The Child's Bath, 1893 *(gallery 273)*

James Abbott McNeill Whistler
An Arrangement in Flesh Color and Brown (Arthur Jerome Eddy), 1894 *(gallery 273)*

Detail of Nighthawks (1942) by Edward Hopper

Art Institute of Chicago, Friends of American Art Collection

American Trends – works of art

Grant Wood
American Gothic, 1930 (gallery 263)

Georgia O'Keeffe
Sky Above Clouds, 1965 (gallery 249)

Joseph Cornell
Series of boxed constructions,
1935–69 (gallery 397)

Willem de Kooning
Excavation, 1950 (gallery 289B)

Modernism. The uncomplicated, figurative styles of **Grant Wood** (gallery 263) appealed to Americans beset by the Great Depression.

American Folk Art

The Grainger Folk Art Gallery (gallery 227)—on top of the Woman's Board Grand Staircase in the Allerton Building —opened in 2009, presenting art objects first noticed by artists and collectors at the end of the 19C. Expect portraits by self-taught artists, weathervanes, quilts, ceramic jugs and even a cigar-store Indian. Folk art enthusiasts valued these works by untrained, indigenous artists because they seemed to relay the American experience, referencing patriotism with subjects that included flags, eagles, American Indians and log cabins. This gallery also provides views into the Ryerson & Burnham libraries, the acclaimed facilities that house the art and architecture academic research collection.

ASIAN ART★★

Galleries 101–109, 130–135, 140–142, 151–153, Allerton Building, 1st floor.
The Art Institute's Asian collection covers nearly 5,000 years, from the Neolithic Age to the 20C, including works in stone, bronze, jade, paint and print, pottery and porcelain. It is particularly strong in Chinese ceramics, Japanese woodblock prints, and Indian, Himalayan, and Southeast Asian artifacts.

China

The **Sonnenschein Collection of Archaic Chinese Jades**★, mounted in a wall case that spans the length of galleries 131A–132, illustrates the beauty of Chinese jade craft. Although difficult to work, jade was believed to possess life-preserving properties, making it the ideal material for the manufacture of grave goods.

Artifacts in galleries 131B and 132 date back to the Bronze Age, which began in China around 2,000 BC. A stunning array of bronze vessels made to contain ritual offerings of wine and food traces the beginnings of Chinese surface decoration, from the tightly wound spirals of the Shang dynasty to the robust relief work of the Zhou. In gallery 131B, compare the 12C tripod **wine vessel**, or *jia*, with a pair of 9C **wine jars**, called

Highlights of the Chinese Dynasties

The Art Institute of Chicago, Gift of Russell Tyson, 1943.1136

Neolithic Period
(5th millennium BC to 18C BC):
An era of emerging regional
cultures with distinct craft
traditions in clay, stone, bone,
basketry and textiles.

Shang dynasty (1766–1111 BC):
Transition to the Bronze Age
accompanied by the rise of cities
and rival clans. Invention of
remarkable piece-mold technique
for casting shapely bronze vessels,
whose artistry is unmatched in
other contemporary cultures.

*Horse shaped tomb figure, Tang Dynasty,
first half of the 8C, buff earthenware
with three-color (sancai) lead glazes and
molded decoration*

Zhou dynasty (1111–221 BC):
An unsettled period of statemaking, but increasing prosperity creates a market
for objects of extreme technical refinement and splendor. Decorative patterns
on stone and bronze become lavish and complex.

Qin dynasty (221–206 BC): Established by the first emperor, this dynasty
represents the beginnings of imperial China. The Great Wall is begun.

Han dynasty (206 B–AD 221): A major dynasty, marked by expansion and the
coming of Buddhism. The decorative dragon becomes prominent, along with
layered and inlaid bronzework.

AD 221–264: Three kingdoms split the empire.

Western Jin dynasty (AD 265–317): A nominal reunion in a time of rebellion
and rivalry, this short-lived dynasty produced an early celadon-glazed
stoneware.

Six Dynasties (AD 317–580): The celadon technique is refined.

Sui dynasty (AD 581–618): The empire is reunited and potters improve glazing
techniques.

Tang dynasty (AD 618–906): A time of power and international prestige with
a taste for splendor. Aristocratic burial rites become increasingly elaborate and
tomb furnishings proliferate in quality and quantity.

Five Dynasties (AD 907–960): Breakdown of the empire into individual states.

Song dynasty (AD 960–1279): Humanistic age of extreme aesthetic richness
renowned for fine and varied ceramics.

Yuan dynasty (AD 1279–1368): This Mongol dynasty favored blue and white
porcelains to trade with Islamic nations.

Ming dynasty (AD 1368–1644): Marked by a return to native rule, this
classic age of blue and white wares featured a proliferation of glazing and
decorating techniques.

Qing dynasty (AD 1644-1911): Foreign rule under the Manchus introduced
delicate ceramics of brilliant color and eggshell translucency.

hu. These variously shaped containers signified the social status of their owners and mark the height of Chinese bronze-working skill. Gallery 133 introduces works from early imperial China. As a growing middle class demanded less costly tomb furnishings of clay and wood, items like ceramic burial models—to make the deceased feel at home in the afterworld—became popular. Note the Han dynasty **pigsty and latrines**. *Mingqi*, or spirit objects representing mortals and animals to attend the departed, also illustrate this increasingly wordly view of the afterlife. A particularly evocative ensemble of carved wooden **tomb figures** dates to the 4–3C BC burials in the Kingdom of Chu. **Earthenware vessels** of the 3C foreshadow the virtuosity of later Chinese ceramics.

The extensive collection of **ceramics**★ in gallery 134 demonstrates the incredible profusion of styles, colors and techniques characterizing Chinese pottery through 1,800 years, from the Han to the Ming dynasties. Kilns proliferated during the cultural flowering of the Song dynasty, and various wares came to be known by their places of manufacture. Note the celadon-glazed stoneware of Longquan, precious because it resembled jade, and the creamy white Ding ware, bound with metal to cover its unglazed edge. A group of **ceramic pillows**, by contrast, typifies the exuberant decorative style of the 10–11C Cizhou potters, whose work was intended largely for a popular audience. Among the Ming ware, ceramics made for the emperor's use include a striking mid-16C **plate** in brilliant yellow (the imperial color) and blue. Despite their diversity, the pieces share an exquisite integration of form and surface design.

Another highlight of the Chinese collection is the elegant earthenware retinue of Tang dynasty funerary statues in gallery 105; most are decorated with polychrome glazes known as *sancai*, or three-color. Dating from the 8C, they reflect the life and fashion among the aristocracy during this golden age. The **equine statues**, for instance, convey the imperial love of fine horses; note the matronly equestrienne and her elegant mount, particularly unusual because it is unglazed.

Japan

The **Weston Galleries of Japanese Art** *(beginning in gallery 102)*, opened in 2010, contain works from the earliest pre-Buddha eras. In fact, one space is devoted solely to the Jomon (14,000–200 BC) through the Kofun (250–552) periods, marking the first time the museum has displayed a wide array of works from this bygone time. There's also an expansive gallery for religious arts, including Buddhist sculpture and decorative arts, and Shinto sculpture, in addition to a gallery for the arts of the Japanese tea ritual.

Gallery 102 exhibits decorative arts together with paintings from the Edo (1615–1868) to Showa (1926–1989) periods, illustrating the dialogue between arts of all media from the most vigorous of artistic production in Japan. Everything culminates at the **Ando Gallery**, a tucked-away space accessible through two-way push doors that swing into a dim room housing jars, screens and other Japanese art pieces. The whisper-quiet hideaway has low-slung benches against one wall, inspiring contemplation and relaxation.

INDIAN, HIMALAYAN, ISLAMIC AND SOUTHEAST ASIAN ART★★★

Galleries 140–142 and 151–152, 1st floor. Explore two new suites of galleries which are devoted to Asian art: the Alsdorf Galleries of Indian, Southeast Asian, Himalayan and Islamic Art (in the passageway previously known as Gunsaulus Hall); and the Galleries of Indian and Islamic Art (on the north side of McKinlock Court).

Both spaces harbor more than 430 sculptures, artifacts and paintings. And because the Alsdorf Galleries connect the East Asian art collections with the Modern Wing, they get a lot of well-deserved traffic.

Deities are an obvious focus. Of particular interest are the 12C stone Buddha from South India, and a bronze *Shiva Nataraja* from AD 1000 that presents the god as the cosmic dancer who set the universe and the forces of life and death in motion.

The new galleries of Indian and Islamic Art contain later works representative of pre-1947 India and also its Imperial Mughal and royal past. Other galleries rotate exhibitions of works from Burma, Thailand, Cambodia, Vietnam, Indonesia and beyond.

EUROPEAN DECORATIVE ARTS★★

This section occupies galleries 231–234 on the second floor, accessible via the grand staircase. Parts of the collection have been integrated into the European Art Before 1900 galleries (201–248) to illustrate the scope of those time periods. The Paperweight Collection has moved to its own gallery (15) on the lower level.

The Art Institute's European Decorative Arts collection comprises a trove of household, ornamental and religious objects produced since 1100 and made more interesting by the wide variety in their materials and manufacturing techniques. To view the collection chronologically is a journey through the evolution of Western design and tastes. Exhibits are arranged roughly by period and place of origin, and include furniture as well as decorative items. The amusing *Monkey Band* (1765–66) in gallery 233—a Meissen grouping of 15 clad music-making monkeys—reflects a contemporary fascination with simians. Marie Antoinette's **corner cupboard** (1785), which may have graced her two-room shepherdess's cottage on the grounds of Versailles, also stands in gallery 233, and the famous Sèvres porcelain **Londonderry vase** (1813), originally commissioned by Napoleon in 1805, graces gallery 218. Biedermeier-style furniture in gallery 232 includes a clever globe-shaped work table (c.1820) from Vienna. Gallery 234, located at the center of these galleries, features the

The Londonderry Vase (1813) by Charles Percier and Alexandre Théodore Brongniart, hard-paste porcelain, gilding and ormolu mounts

stunning **Augsburg cabinet** produced in Nuremberg around 1640, a masterpiece of craftsmanship in ebony with inlaid ivory and carved wood relief.

Paperweight Collection

Deservedly, the **Rubloff Paperweight Collection★** stands on its own on the lower level *(gallery 15)*. The superb assemblage of 1,000 glass paperweights dates from the 19C and 20C with pieces manufactured by Baccarat, Clichy, St. Louis and others. The exhibit also presents a display on the making of "mushroom" and *millefiori* weights. Italian for "thousand flowers," millefiori involves encasing decorative glass canes in crystal for a kaleidoscopic effect.

👥 THORNE MINIATURE ROOMS★★

Gallery 11, Allerton Building, lower level. Of international renown, the 68 rooms in this unique collection arranged in chronological fashion, display a gamut of interior decorative styles ranging from 13C Europe to 20C America. Some of these rooms re-create historic interiors, while others blend stylistic elements into typical—if imaginary—period arrangements. Naturalistic lighting and an occasional glimpse up a staircase or through an open door add to the realism of each setting, from a pre-Revolutionary Connecticut Valley tavern to a chic French library of the 1930s. Mrs. James Ward (Narcissa Niblack) Thorne's childhood interest in miniature decorative objects began when her uncle, an admiral in the Navy, sent her objects he found in his many ports-of-call. Mrs. Thorne (1882–1966) married the son of a founder of Montgomery Ward and Co. and traveled extensively, adding to the collection. Combining a love of miniatures with studies in the history of architecture and the decorative arts, Mrs. Thorne completed her first rooms in the early 1930s. Between 1937 and 1940, she hired skilled craftsmen to reproduce them in exceptional detail at a scale of 1in to 1ft. She even commissioned artists to paint the diminutive canvases that decorate the walls. Their technical excellence, delicate scale and charming variety lend the rooms a romantic sense of history. In 1941 Mrs. Thorne donated the rooms to the Art Institute, where they went on permanent display in 1954.

CHICAGO STOCK EXCHANGE TRADING ROOM★

Rubloff Building, lower level; balcony access from gallery 153.

In its innovative structural design and ornamental detail, the old Chicago Stock Exchange (1893–94) was one of the most important buildings created by world-renowned architects Dankmar Adler and Louis Sullivan. In spite of intense efforts to save it, the structure fell victim to the wrecker's ball in 1972, but its entrance arch and Trading Room were carefully dismantled and preserved. The colorful Trading Room, reconstructed inside the Rubloff Building in 1977, features Sullivan's organic decorative scheme in painted stencils, plaster ornament and art glass. Photographer Richard Nickel, one of Chicago's earliest and most ardent preservationists, was killed when part of the structure collapsed as he was documenting the building's demolition.

AFRICAN ART AND INDIAN ART OF THE AMERICAS★★

Galleries 136–137, Morton Building, 1st floor.

These galleries display artifacts representing the quintessential artistic traditions of Africa and ancient and native America. Ceremonial and festival objects are a focus, and the masks, headdresses and sculptures in wood, ceramic and metal are arranged by culture and region, with many items from Ghana, the Ivory Coast, Nigeria and the Democratic Republic of Congo.

Note the elaborately crafted works, such as the Veranda Post of Enthroned King and Senior Wife by Yoruba sculptor Olowe of Ise; the sculpture portrays the King seated with his head bowed under his beaded crown. Also of note is the Portrait Vessel depicting a forceful ruler. Such ceramic vessels were placed in graves, along with others that portray aspects of the Moche universe. And don't leave without casting a glance at the fragmentary Ball-Court Panel from the late 8C. The stone panel shows two men dressed in elaborate costumes engaged in a ritual ball game.

ANCIENT EGYPTIAN, GREEK, ETRUSCAN AND ROMAN ART★

Galleries 153–157, Rubloff Building, 1st floor. For an electronic overview of the ancient world, spend a moment with Cleopatra, an interactive touch screen located in gallery 153.

Egyptian ceramic vessels, mummy head covers, carved stone wall fragments and small art objects are exhibited in galleries 154 and 154A. Most were found in tombs dating from 2600 BC through AD 200. Greek artifacts in gallery 155, from the Bronze Age to the Roman conquest, comprise works in stone, ceramic and metal, including jewelry, military helmets and coins. Among the collection of black- and red-figure vessels is a wine jar *(stamnos)* by an anonymous artist referred to as the Chicago Painter, because this is his signature piece. Produced in Periclean Athens, it represents the height of the red-figure technique.

The Theodore W. and Frances S. Robinson Collection of **antique glass** from around the Mediterranean occupies gallery 155A. These delicate bottles and ornaments in blown and core-formed glass are as remarkable for their longevity as for their beauty. Gallery 156A includes the Etruscan collection, which includes an incised bronze mirror (c.470 BC) and several lovely pieces of granulated gold jewelry, all testament to Etruscan metalworking skill. A lifelike terra-cotta **votive head** represents a penchant for realistic funerary portraiture. The Etruscans passed their love of the portrait bust on to the Romans, who applied the Greek figurative style to it to create a dynamic new form of sculptural portraiture, as in the marble **portrait of Hadrian** (AD c.100). A variety of Roman art—stone and bronze sculpture, fresco painting, jewelry, mosaic and glass—fills gallery 156. On pedestals are sculptural fragments in relief and in the round from AD 1C to the 3C, and a fragment of a mosaic floor from the 5C.

The **Ayala altarpiece** (gallery 157) is one of the largest intact Medieval altarpieces in America. It was commissioned in 1396 to house a reliquary in the funerary chapel of scenes from the lives of Christ and the Virgin Mary.

PRINTS AND DRAWINGS

Galleries 124–127, Richard and Mary L. Gray Wing, 1st floor.

This collection includes some 70,000 works on paper from Europe and the Americas dating from the 15C to the present. The Dutch and French Baroque are extensively represented with works by Rembrandt, Lorrain, Watteau, Boucher and Fragonard. The substantial 19C and 20C holdings include drawings by Goya, Turner, Delacroix, Daumier, Picasso, de Kooning, Miró and Johns. Because of their fragility, prints and drawings are exhibited on a rotating basis in these galleries.

THE MODERN WING★★★

Designed by **Renzo Piano** (b.1937), the 264,000sq ft addition holds the museum's renowned collection of modern European painting and sculpture, as well as contemporary art including film, video and new media, architecture and design, and photography. Nearly everything is crowned by the aluminum bladed "flying carpet," an innovative sun-shade system that allows natural light into the galleries. All three floors in its east pavilion allow for striking views of Millennium Park.

Of particular interest is the **Nichols Bridgeway**, stretching nearly an eighth of a mile from the edge of the park's Great Lawn to the third floor of the west pavilion. Because it rises 30 feet above Monroe Street, the views are sweeping. To the east of the Modern Wing lies **Pritzker Garden**, a 12,000sq ft terrace of crushed stone and grass flanked by Ellsworth Kelly's *White Curve*, his largest work to date.

Because of its vast offerings—three floors of galleries, a restaurant, a shop, a coffee bar and the kid-focused Ryan Education Center—this new gem could easily require a full day to visit.

MODERN EUROPEAN PAINTING AND SCULPTURE (1900–50)★★

Galleries 389–399.

Early Modernism

Experimentation and progress into the abstract characterize much of 20C art. Artists turned from rendering what they saw to expressing what they felt and finally to creating "subjectless" works reliant only on themselves for meaning. The accelerating pace and increasing complexity of the industrial age hastened the process, constantly challenging artists to respond anew. The free use of shockingly bright colors earned a small group of painters led by **Henri Matisse** the name *les Fauves* ("the wild beasts") when they exhibited together in 1905. Largely concerned with the decorative qualities of color, the short-lived movement inspired reaction from **Pablo Picasso** *(galleries 391, 394, 398)*, who like them experimented with representing three-dimensional forms on a flat surface. When he and **Georges Braque** *(gallery 391A)* first dissolved the bonds of perspective around 1908, unfolding and flattening their subjects, the results were dubbed Cubism. The concept exerted a powerful influence on the course of modern art. The faceted works of **Juan Gris** *(gallery 391B)* and the curvilinear forms of **Fernand Léger** *(gallery 398C)* demonstrate further developments in the Cubist style. Meanwhile, artists in pre-World War I Germany were thinking along very different lines. As the Cubists searched for new ways to render form, the Expressionists turned inward. From the prismatic, mystical visions of **Franz Marc** *(gallery 392A)*, to the spontaneous compositions of **Wassily Kandinsky** *(gallery 392A)*, the Expressionists charged their work with emotion, capturing spirit, if not form. It is not surprising that Kandinsky was the first painter to create completely abstract canvases.

Surrealism

Contemptuous of these serious currents, a group of young artists in 1915 promoted an irreverent anti-art movement known as Dada (a randomly chosen French word meaning "hobby horse"). Using nonsense words, collages

of "ready-made" objects, **Dadaists** like **Marcel Duchamp, Man Ray** and **Max Ernst** *(galleries 396–397)* jabbed mercilessly at society. Spent by 1922, the remnants of Dada fit well into the growing **Surrealist** movement, which practiced an art governed by the subconscious mind. Unexpected juxtapositions, distortions of time and space, and eerie dreamscapes haunt the works of Surrealist painters such as **Salvador Dalí** *(galleries 396A and 397)*. The Surrealist influence can be seen in the works of **Joan Miró** and **René Magritte**, and even the folk fantasies of **Marc Chagall**. Also of note is the expansive display of Joseph Cornell boxes in gallery 397.

CONTEMPORARY ART 1945–60★★

Galleries 289, 291–299.
The Institute's Department of Contemporary Art is one of the most comprehensive contemporary art collections in any general museum in the world. Comprising nearly 1,000 works, the department encompasses almost every significant art movement from 1950 to the present and includes painting, sculpture, installation art, and new-media work. Some of its most notable holdings are works by Willem de Kooning, Jackson Pollock, Eva Hesse, David Hockney, Jasper Johns, Ellsworth Kelly, Bruce Nauman and Gerhard Richter.

Abstract Expressionism and Beyond Expressionism

This movement combined subjectless abstraction with the emotion of Expressionism. The Action Painting of **Jackson Pollock** *(gallery 289B)* epitomized the concept: the artist dripped and hurled paint onto the canvas hoping to create patterns reflecting pure emotion. **Willem de Kooning** worked his painted surfaces over and over to achieve the right effect, and the massive color fields of **Mark Rothko** vibrate with intensity. Many consider this the first truly influential American movement, its large and energetic canvases reflecting a part of the national psyche.

Contemporary Art 1960–Present★★

From its epicenter in New York City, the sweeping influence of Abstract Expressionism stimulated considerable artistic action and reaction around the world. After 1950 a proliferation of movements pushed the bounds of art in all directions. **Ad Reinhardt** tested the limits of nonreference with his serene and subtle series of black surfaces. Others such as **Gerhard Richter** (gallery 296) turned from pure abstraction to explore the human figure anew. Don't miss Charles Ray's monumental Hinoki (gallery 292), one of the largest works ever installed in the Art Institute.

Contemporary Art – works of art

Gerhard Richter
Woman Descending the Staircase, 1965 (gallery 296A)

Roy Lichtenstein
Mirror in Six Panels, 1971 (gallery 297A)

Jackson Pollack
Greyed Rainbow, 1953 (gallery 289B)

Jasper Johns
Corpse and Mirror II, 1974–75 (gallery 289D)

PHOTOGRAPHY

Spanning the history of the medium from its beginning in 1839 to the present, the Art Institute's photography collection contains representative works by many of the medium's most celebrated practitioners. The collection was not begun until 1949, when Georgia O'Keeffe donated a major portion of the Alfred Stieglitz collection.

The acquisition of the Julien Levy collection, a gift of more than 200 photographs by Edward Weston, and purchases of the work of Paul Strand, Eugene Atget and Andre Kertesz have made the department one of the strongest in the works of the modern masters of the world. The collection now houses some 20,000 works, ranging from photographs by William Henry Fox Talbot and Julia Margaret Cameron to Robert Frank and Joel Meyerowitz, and includes major collections: Alfred Stieglitz, Julien Levy, David and Sarajean Ruttenberg, Julia Margaret Cameron and Irving Penn. Rotating exhibitions are on view in galleries 1–4 in the Allerton Building, and in gallery 199 in the Modern Wing.

ARCHITECTURE AND DESIGN

Chicago's best-known contributions to modern art have come in the field of architecture and galleries 283–286 are testament to that fact. The Department of Architecture and Design focuses on national, international and regional issues related to the built environment, as well as design expressions and manifestations. The collection comprises more than 140,000 architectural models, drawings and garments dating from the 1870s to the present. There are significant holdings of works by David Adler, Daniel Burnham and John Wellborn Root, Bruce Goff, Bertrand Goldberg, Marion Mahony Griffin, Louis Sullivan, Ludwig Mies van der Rohe, and Frank Lloyd Wright. Examples of landscape architecture, structural engineering and industrial design are also represented. With new spaces devoted to this collection in the Modern Wing, the department now has 8,000sq ft of design galleries and surpasses the Museum of Modern Art in New York in exhibition space and breadth of holding. In addition to the Modern Wing amassment, you can see fragments of now-demolished buildings by such classic Chicago architects as William Le Baron Jenney, Daniel Burnham and Louis Sullivan encircling the Woman's Board Grand Staircase. Grouped together, they appear to be pieces of ancient temples.

South Loop

Bordered by Congress Parkway, 16th Street, the lakefront and the South Branch of the Chicago River, this neighborhood was taken over by industry after the Fire of 1871 and remained the grimy underbelly of the Loop's business district until its rebirth in the late 20C as a community of rehabbed loft buildings, new apartments and town houses. Today young urbanites frequent the clubs, cafes and bookshops at home in the historic structures along Michigan Avenue and Printer's Row, creating a lively, vibrant atmosphere. In addition to offering convenient access to Loop shopping, this district lies just steps from the city's best museums and parks and the lakefront stadium, Soldier Field.

- **Michelin Map:** Opposite.
- **Parking:** It is possible to find street parking the farther south you go.
- **Also See:** Near South Side, Museum Campus, Grant Park, The Loop.

GETTING AROUND

BY L/BUS: cta Red line to Harrison or bus no. 29.

A BIT OF HISTORY

In the pedestrian city of the 1850s, Michigan and Wabash avenues south of the Loop were lined with fine town houses and churches catering to the upper middle class. Following the 1871 fire, however, the wealthier classes moved away from the Loop to Prairie Avenue and the Near West Side. When the Dearborn Street railroad station was completed in 1885, the streets south of Van Buren between Wabash and LaSalle quickly turned industrial. Attracted by convenient railroad access, printers moved in, creating an international center for the printing industry. At the same time, hotels expanded along South Michigan Avenue near the Illinois Central Railroad passenger station at Roosevelt Road. The printing industry moved out after World War II, abandoning many buildings. Congress Parkway was widened in the 1920s and again in 1957, creating further separation from the Loop. State Street became a skid row, and even South Michigan Avenue declined.

Two events led to the rebirth of the South Loop in the late 1970s: the construction of the Dearborn Park community on vacant railroad land south of Dearborn Station and the creation of the South Loop **Printing House Row Historic District** north of the station with the subsequent rehabilitation of printers' lofts as apartments and offices. Within 10 years almost every building in the district had been redeveloped and a new neighborhood was born, spreading west to the Chicago River with the 1986 construction of the River City apartments and marina. The 1986 renovation of the Hilton Chicago and the creation of residential buildings on Wabash Avenue and in the Central Station development south of Grant Park have given the South Loop a new urbane character.

SIGHTS

Congress Plaza Hotel

520 S. Michigan Ave.

This hotel was built in 1893 as the Auditorium Annex. The Clinton J. Warren design in limestone mimicked its namesake, the Auditorium Building, with arcaded windows and a third-floor balcony. Polygonal bays rib the facade, which was extended to the south in 1902 and 1907 by Holabird & Roche. Step inside the Congress Parkway lobby to see the lovely mosaic tile arches.

Known for its arts curriculum, especially broadcast media and photography, **Columbia College** occupies several South Loop buildings, including the Harvester Building (600 S. Michigan Ave.). The 1907 structure features a limestone base, red brick facade and oversized brackets at the cornice. Today its ground floor houses the Museum of Contemporary Photography.

Museum of Contemporary Photography(M¹)

600 S. Michigan Ave.
🕐*Open Mon–Fri 10am–5pm, Thu 10am–8pm, Sat 10am–5pm, Sun noon–5pm.* ✆*312-663-5554. www.mocp.org.*

The only Midwestern museum dedicated exclusively to this visual art began in 1976 as the Chicago Center for Contemporary Photography. Since then, the museum has amassed an impressive permanent collection of 8,000 works by 900 imagemakers, focusing on American photography since 1936. Masterpieces by Ansel Adams, Diane Arbus, Aaron Siskind, Dorothea Lange and Irving Penn, as well as new works, are featured in changing exhibits.

Spertus Museum(M²)

610 S. Michigan Ave. 🕐*Open Sun–Wed 10am–5pm (Thu til 6pm), Fri 10am–3pm.* 🕐*Closed Jan 1, Memorial Day, Jul 4, Labor Day & major Jewish holidays.* 👁$7. 👍✗🍴✆*312-322-1700. www.spertus.edu.*

This museum of Jewish culture is located in the striking Spertus Institute of Jewish Studies facility. Completed in the late fall of 2007, the construction nearly doubled the museum's exhibit and programming space over its old home in the 1906 building just to the south. Its stunning faceted glass facade admits maximum light into the narrow 10-story building and offers expanded views from the inside. This flood of light echoes the Institute's motto, *yehi or*, "let there be light."

The museum has the largest collection of objects of Judaica in the Midwest, which it incorporates into permanent and temporary exhibits. The Institute also houses the 90,000-volume **Asher Library** and **Spertus College**, which specializes in graduate programs in Jewish studies.

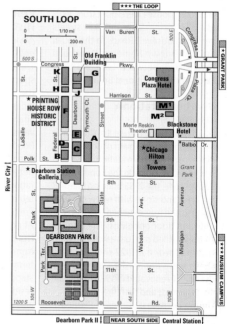

A mansard roof punctuated by dormers and white terra-cotta trim distinguishes the **Blackstone Hotel** (*626 S. Michigan Ave.*), designed in 1908 by Marshall & Fox in the Second Empire style. Marshall & Fox also designed the French-inspired Blackstone Theater (*60 E. Balbo Ave.*) in 1910; the Blackstone is now the Merle Reskin Theatre of DePaul University.

Erected in 1927 by Holabird & Roche, the 25-story **Hilton Chicago**★ (*720 S. Michigan Ave.*) was known when built as the Stevens Hotel, the largest hotel in the world, containing 3,000 rooms, an 18-hole rooftop miniature golf course and a hospital. French in inspiration, the design features a limestone base and cornice framing a red brick facade. The main lobby's ceiling is painted with clouds and angels edged by bands of gold and platinum leaf. Winding staircases on the left lead past a lion-head fountain to the grand ballroom.

The formerly run-down area around State Street and Roosevelt Road has been given new life by the development of modern residential complexes. Set around small parks and courtyards, the **Dearborn Park I** apartments

139

and town houses were built from 1979 to 1987 between State and Clark streets north of Roosevelt Road. To the south the newer town homes of **Dearborn Park II**, built between 1988 and 1997, exhibit more traditional urban design.

Dearborn Station★

47 W. Polk St.

Loop skyscrapers rise to the north beyond the square tower of downtown's oldest surviving train station. Designed by Cyrus L. W. Eidlitz in the Romanesque Revival style, the 1885 building features red brick and stone with nicely detailed cornices and round-arched arcaded window and door openings. The original steeply gabled roof gave way to a third story following a 1922 fire. The train sheds were demolished in 1976 and the edifice renovated in 1986 to contain offices, shops and restaurants.

On the northeast corner of Plymouth Court and Polk Street, the **Lakeside Press Building**★**(A)** *(731 S. Plymouth Ct.)* was designed in 1897 by society architect Howard Van Doren Shaw for the R. R. Donnelley Co., the world's largest commercial printer. Shaw's first nonresidential building sports metallic bays surrounding a richly detailed entrance arch and a top story of semicircular windows alternating with stone medallions. It was redeveloped as apartments in 1986.

Dearborn Station

© David Dunal/Apa Publications

Printing House Row Historic District★

Along Dearborn St., between Polk St. and Congress Pkwy.

This stretch of late-19C and early-20C structures boasts a colorful history. First used by printing and other book-related industries, the buildings were eventually abandoned and some stood empty for years. In the late 1970s, architects Larry Booth and Harry Weese and industrialist Theodore Gaines realized the district's potential and began a massive restoration effort. Today the area is a coveted residential neighborhood dubbed Printer's Row.

At no. 720 stands the **Second Franklin Building**★**(B)** (1912, George C. Nimmons), ornamented with colorful terra-cotta panels depicting the various steps in bookmaking. Redeveloped into residential lofts in 1988, the building also contains shops. The red brick **Rowe Building (C)** (1892) at no. 714, rehabilitated in 1980, features a cast-iron entrance and Luxfer prisms on the stairs, which allow light into the basement.

Across the street, the **Donohue Building (D)** at no. 711 (1883, Julius Speyer) was redeveloped as commercial and residential lofts in the 1970s. A 1913 annex to the south continues the simplified Romanesque Revival style.

Booth/Hansen & Assocs. renovated **Grace Place (E)** *(no. 637)*, a 1915 loft building, in 1985 as a multidenominational worship space. Light streaming in from the circular skylight floods the simple wood interior upstairs.

The restoration of the once-abandoned **Transportation Building (F)** *(no. 600)*, a massive 1911 structure in light-colored brick, was crucial in the area's redevelopment. Today the building contains 294 condos as well as restaurants and shops. Visible to the right, on Plymouth Court, cantilevered balconies jut out from the side of the **Mergenthaler Linotype Building (G)** *(531 S. Plymouth Ct.)*. Built in 1886, the edifice was restored as luxury living spaces in 1980 by Kenneth A. Schroeder & Assocs. Mergenthaler invented the modern Linotype machine in 1884; within 10 years all the daily newspapers were using it.

The **Pontiac Building**★(H) *(no. 542)*, designed in 1891 by Holabird & Roche, is the firm's earliest surviving skyscraper. Brick sheathing covers a skeleton frame, and bays flow rather than project from the surface. At no. 537 the elegant **Terminals Building (J)** (1892, John M. Van Osdel & Co.) features a rusticated limestone base below red brick Romanesque-style bays. The **Hotel Blake (K)** at no. 500 occupies three structures: two late-19C buildings and a modern northern addition designed by Booth/Hansen & Assocs. in 1987. The southernmost building, now the hotel entrance, was built as offices for the Morton Salt Company. It features lion heads above the door and sculpted figures holding up the projecting bay windows. The **Old Franklin Building** at no. 525 (1887, Baumann & Lotz) sports the iron windows and spandrels seen in the Lakeside Press Building *(on S. Plymouth Ct.).*

Central Station

East of Indiana Ave. between Roosevelt Rd. and 21st St.

This ever-expanding residential development south of Grant Park includes a mix of high rises and town houses built on land and air rights over railroad tracks.

River City

800 S. Wells St.

Revolutionary Chicago architect **Bertrand Goldberg** designed this 1985 development—his most famous since the similarly inspired Marina City executed 20 years earlier. Undulating walls ripple along the riverfront marina, while eyelid windows in the facade suggest a futuristic space colony.

McCormick Place Convention Center

2301 S. Lake Shore Dr.

Covering nearly 200 acres at the southern end of Burnham Park, McCormick Place is the largest convention and trade show center in the US. The complex boasts three large buildings, plus McCormick Place West, which opened in 2007 and added nearly 1 million sq ft of exhibition and meeting space.

The campus encompasses convention space and meeting rooms, hotels and restaurants. The facility hosts some 3 million visitors each year.

ADDRESSES

ℙ/EAT

$ Weather Mark Tavern –
1503 S. Michigan Ave. ℘*312-588-0230. www.weathermarktavern.com.* Cruise in for a cocktail and feel like you're just off the race course. With canvas and hardwood decor, some handsome sailing photographs, 40 rums and tasty upscale bar food, this tavern is a sailor's delight. Kids are welcome till 10.30pm.

$ Yolk –
1120 S. Michigan Ave. ℘*312-789-9655. www.yolk-online.com.* This sleek, bright breakfast and lunch joint breaks a lot of eggs to make creative frittatas, pancakes and omelets served all day, along with salads, sandwiches and other lunch fare.

BOOKS AND MUSIC

Buddy Guy's Legends –
754 S. Wabash Ave. ✕ ℘*312-427-1190. www.buddyguys.com.* Owned by blues guitar great Buddy Guy, this is one of the largest and best appreciated blues bars in town. Guy's status as a local legend ensures the performers are top-notch (Eric Clapton has performed here), and that visiting rock stars will sit in for impromptu jams.

Sandmeyer's Bookstore –
714 S. Dearborn St. ⏱*Open Mon–Wed, Fri 11am–6.30pm, Thu 11am-8pm, Sat 11am–5pm, Sun 11am–4pm.* ℘*312-922-2104. www.sandmeyersbookstore.com.* Wooden floors creak comfortably beneath your feet as you browse here. The store stocks a thorough collection of fiction and poetry by local authors and books on Chicago history, but its main section is travel, which features guidebooks as well as creative works about life on the road.

Grant Park★

In Grant Park, Chicago's physical characteristics and urban personality converge. The city's 319-acre "front yard," located between Randolph Street on the north and Soldier Field on the south, marks roughly the midpoint in the swath of parks that trim Chicago's 28mi shoreline. From Lake Michigan on the east to Michigan Avenue on the west, the park segues from lakefront to bustling central city. Despite its checkered history and sometimes haphazard development, the park exudes a sense of the grand urban landscape that early-20C city planners envisioned for Chicago. Today, though bifurcated by busy streets, it offers tranquil corners, peaceful walkways, picnic spots and lovely vistas of the city and lake. In the northwest corner sits the stunning Millennium Park.

⏱ **Michelin Map:** Opposite.

🔳 **Info:** www.chicagopark district.com or www. millenniumpark.org.

🅿 **Parking:** Underground at Millennium Park or Grant Park garage for a fee.

😊 **Don't Miss:** A wander through Millennium Park.

👫 **Especially for Kids:** Splashing around in the Crown Fountain in Millennium Park.

⏱ **Also See:** Museum Campus, The Loop, South Loop.

GETTING THERE

BY L: 🚇 Red or Blue line to **Monroe** or **Jackson**; Brown, Green, Purple or Orange line to **Adams**, **Madison** or **Randolph**.

A BIT OF HISTORY
Public Ground to Public Disgrace

In the 1830s, while selling land to finance construction of the Illinois & Michigan Canal, state commissioners designated a thin strip of shoreline east of Michigan Avenue between Madison and Eleventh streets as "public ground—a common to remain forever open, clear and free of any buildings, or other obstruction whatever." In the ensuing decades, erosion from Lake Michigan, tracks of the Illinois Central RailRoad and city dwellers anxious to build on the prime real estate encroached upon Lake Park. In 1852 railroad tracks went in just off-shore, and the narrow basin created between them and the park was filled in with debris from the 1871 fire, considerably widening the land.

The tracks, stables, an armory, storage sheds, squatters' huts and a city dump crowded park grounds. In 1890, mail-order magnate **A. Montgomery Ward** (1843–1913) began a 20-year battle to clear and keep clear the lakefront park, basing his suits on the commissioners' original declaration. After a long and arduous fight, he prevailed.

A Formal Plan

In 1901 the park's name was changed to honor President Ulysses S. Grant, an Illinoisan. Then, in 1907 the first plans for formal development of the park were published by the **Olmsted Brothers**. Their scheme, based on the gardens of Versailles, called for symmetrical divisions of the space defined by paths and allees of stately trees, promenades, formal gardens, fountains and sculpture. These landscaping principles worked nicely into **Daniel Burnham's 1909 Plan of Chicago**, which envisioned Grant Park as "the formal focal point, the intellectual center of Chicago." The actual execution of the design took another 20 years. The Field Museum was given a home at the south end, and by the 1933–34 Century of Progress International Exposition, the park had assumed much of its modern form.

Since then, Grant Park has both suffered and profited from its central location.

As a result of a 1919 city ordinance, the Illinois Central Railroad agreed to depress its tracks. The rise of the automobile brought the intrusion of major thoroughfares that inelegantly sliced through the park and eliminated much of its open plaza space. An underground parking garage skewed the plan again. In 2004 the park surged to life with the opening of the extravagent **Millennium Park**★★★ in its northwest corner. Today plans are in the works to revamp the three distinct areas of North Grant Park into one cohesive space.

VISIT

Grant Park is divided roughly into large rectangles, each with its own character and purpose. One focal point is **Clarence Buckingham Memorial Fountain**★★ (1927, Edward Bennett). This lakefront jewel aligns on an east-west axis with Congress Parkway. Donated to the city by philanthropist Kate Sturges Buckingham, the fountain was completed in 1927 at a cost of $750,000. A $2.8-million restoration in 1995 returned the fountain to its original splendor. In 2009 the fountain and surrounding landscape underwent another renovation—this one to the tune of $25 million. Modeled on—but twice the size of—the Latona Basin at Versailles, the fountain represents Lake Michigan. In the main pool, four bronze sea horses, each 20ft in length, symbolize the states that border the lake. The fountain pumps and recirculates 1.5 million gallons of water from the lake. As spectacular as its monumental scale are the fountain's summertime **water-and-light shows**. Its 135 jets pump water at a rate of 14,000 gallons a minute, and the central jet shoots water skyward to 150ft. At night, a computer-orchestrated light show plays off the cascading water to create a dazzling effect (May–Oct dusk–11pm; call ☏312-742-7529 to confirm).

143

The park's **Grand Entrance**★ at Congress Parkway and Michigan Avenue retains only vestiges of its original grandeur. When built in 1929, its 100ft-wide staircase, flanked by two heroic equestrian statues—**Indians** (*The Bowman* and *The Spearman*) by Yugoslavian sculptor **Ivan Mestrovic**—welcomed visitors. By 1929 automobile traffic was already determining the shape of such spaces, and the plaza had evolved into a roadway. In 1956 Congress Parkway was extended into the park, at the expense of the grand staircase, to link Lake Shore Drive with the new Eisenhower Expressway. In 1996 the grand staircase and plaza were partly reconstructed.

At Grant Park's southern end stands **Soldier Field**, designed by Holabird & Roche to harmonize with the Field Museum to the north. The formal dedication of the field, named to honor the soldiers of World War I, took place on the occasion of the 29th annual Army-Navy football game, November 27, 1926. Renovated in 2003 by Wood + Zapata, it serves as the home stadium for the Chicago Bears NFL football games (*guided tours (45min) by advance reservation; Mon–Fri 9am–5pm; $15; 312-235-7245; www.soldierfield.net*).

Millennium Park★★★

Map pp76–77. Between Randolph and Monroe Streets, Michigan Ave. and Columbus Dr. Open daily 6am–11pm. For maps, guided tours & audio tours, visit the Welcome Center, 201 E. *Randolph St.; call for hours 312-742-1168. www.millenniumpark.org.*

Despite some grumbling about its cost of $475-million when it opened in 2004, Millennium Park is, all agree, among the city's best assets. Its 24.5 acres offer something to see at every turn.

Above the **Jay Pritzker Pavilion**★★★ hovers the metallic mayhem of architect **Frank Gehry**'s proscenium arch, a seeming scramble of stainless steel. The theater accommodates 4,000 in fixed seats and 7,000 on the lawn. The "waterproof" lawn drains rainwater in 15min, so don't be afraid to bring a picnic dinner on a soggy evening and enjoy one of the many free concerts here throughout the summer *(check online for details)*.

Gehry also designed the **BP Bridge**★★ that meanders across Columbus Drive in 925ft of sultry serpentine curves. Dubbed the Bean, **Cloud Gate**★★★ by sculptor Anish Kapoor will draw you like a moth to a flame. The gleaming, 110-ton, stainless-steel "kidney bean"—66ft long, 33ft high—creates fantastic reflections of the city skyline and the crowds. For the young and young at heart, the **Crown Fountain**★★ provides not only a cool wading pool but a wonderful shifting array of 50ft projected faces. Spanish artist Jaume Plensa created the whimsical work of steel, glass and light. In the **Lurie Garden**★, wooden boardwalks and a watery pool called the Seam bisect the planted spaces.

BP Bridge, Millennium Park

©Steve Geer/iStockphoto.com

Museum Campus★★★

Re-routing the northbound lanes of Lake Shore Drive west of the Field Museum helped create this handsome 10-acre greensward, located just southeast of Grant Park. Known as the Museum Campus, the park unites in spirit and space Chicago's great triumvirate of natural-science museums, devoted to earth, sea and sky: the Field Museum of Natural History, the John G. Shedd Aquarium and the Adler Planetarium & Astronomy Museum. The proximity of these three museums provides them the opportunity to collaborate on outdoor as well as indoor programming, special events and concession sales.

VISIT

The Museum Campus makes a pleasant place to picnic or stroll, through terraced gardens or along walkways bordering Lake Michigan, with great **views**★★ of the Chicago skyline and the boats in Monroe and Burnham Park harbors. The main parking for the museums is at the Planetarium Lot *(east on Solidarity Dr.)* or in the North Garage *(enter off Museum Campus Dr.)*. In summer, alternative methods of transportation to the Museum Campus include a water taxi *(see sidebar, p18)* that ferries passengers back and forth from Navy Pier.

FIELD MUSEUM OF NATURAL HISTORY★★★

1400 S. Lake Shore Dr. *Open year-round daily 9am–5pm. Closed Dec 25. $15 (free 2nd Mon of each month). Additional charge for Underground Adventure and other special exhibits (all-inclusive passes available for $29). 312-922-9410. www.fieldmuseum.org.*

This world-class natural history museum commands a suitably grand presence on the campus. Indeed, there is nothing small about this institution. Nine acres

- **Michelin Map:** p143.
- **Location:** McFetridge Dr. at S. Lake Shore Dr. By car, access the campus and parking from the 18th Street exit, off Lake Shore Drive. Don't plan a visit on Chicago Bears home game days!
- **Parking:** Ample on-site parking serves the campus for $16 a day. If you arrive first thing, find metered parking along Solidarity Dr.
- **Don't Miss:** The skyline view from Café Galileo's at the Planetarium.
- **Kids:** There's something around every corner.
- **Timing:** One day for one museum is a good rule of thumb.
- **Also See:** Grant Park, Art Institute, South Loop.

GETTING THERE

BY BUS: Bus no. 146 (museum bus).

of exhibit halls and over 20 million artifacts inhabit the vast Neoclassical edifice, where collections, exhibits and public programs specialize in anthropology, geology, botany and zoology. Dinosaur bones, ethnographic materials and animal taxidermy are among the museum's traditional strengths, all are today incorporated into spirited interpretive exhibits.

A BIT OF HISTORY
"A Grand Museum"

By the time work was begun on the present-day Field Museum in 1915, the institution already had a long history. Harvard anthropologist Frederick Ward Putnam was determined that the vast ethnographic and zoological collections he had amassed for display at the World's Columbian Exposition in 1893 would have a permanent home after the fair, envisioning for "this great city … a grand museum of natural history." He enlisted the aid of Edward E. Ayer, a collector of Native American artifacts, to persuade department store magnate Marshall Field to contribute the million dollars it would require to establish such an institution. That endowment funded the Field Columbian Museum, which was to be housed in the fair's Palace of Fine Arts in Jackson Park. Never intended as a permanent structure, the palace would not be suitable for long, and the Field soon required another home.

Before his death in 1906, Marshall Field hired architect Daniel Burnham to create a new natural history museum in the august Beaux-Arts style of the World's Columbian Exposition, bequeathing money to pay for and endow it. Burnham's vision of a museum in Grant Park raised a furor with advocates of a lakefront free and clear of building, and it wasn't until the Illinois Central Railroad offered a muddy and desolate parcel of land just south of the park that plans for the Field could be finalized. Begun in 1915, landfilling alone took a year to complete. The museum's doors finally opened in May 1921.

The Building

The monumental scale of the museum is at once awe-inspiring and exhausting. Burnham based the 706ft-long, colonnaded facade on the Ionic order, and even included caryatids modeled by sculptor Henry Hering on those at the Erechtheion on the Acropolis in Greece. Thanks to exterior conservation and an extensive cleaning in 1988, the crisp white Georgia marble cladding once again glows. The Field shares its front yard, a landscaped expanse that sweeps to the water's edge, with the John G. Shedd Aquarium.

The Collections

Equally grand in scale are the museum's collections of more than 20 million artifacts and specimens, only about 4 percent of which are on display in some 25 exhibits. Behind the scenes, millions of artifacts, many from the World's Columbian Exposition and others collected over years of field work or purchased from private collectors, serve as the basis for research projects and publications by scholars from around the world.

The Field's exhibits have undergone considerable updating over the past several years. Lively, colorful and kid-friendly installations include engaging and easy-to-understand labels and interactivities. A hand's-on "Playlab" for little ones opened on the ground level in 2007, and on the upper level, you can watch fossilized bones being prepared for exhibit. The remains of Sue—the world's largest, most complete and best preserved **Tyrannosaurus rex skeleton** and perhaps the museum's most famous artifact—engages visitors in the main lobby.

VISITING THE MUSEUM

Since the museum offers enough to fill several days, you should focus on the subjects of interest to you by consulting the floor plan (available at the admissions desks) and the listing of daily special programs, activities and tours (posted at the admissions desks and on kiosks throughout the museum). Enter the museum through the north or south doors. Take a moment to orient yourself in the 300ft-long, two-story Stanley Field Hall on the main level, location of the 6,000sq ft museum store (southeast corner) and the Corner Bakery (northeast corner). The latter features cafeteria-style service and offers a variety of sandwiches, pizza, salads and pastries. A McDonald's restaurant is located on the ground level.

Main Level

The star of Stanley Field Hall is **Sue**★★ **(A)**, the 42ft-long Tyrannosaurus rex skeleton, which went on view at the museum in May 2000. Named for Sue Hendrickson, the fossil hunter who discovered the skeleton in South Dakota in 1990, Sue stands 13ft tall at the hip (the creature's gender is unknown, but there is evidence to suggest that this T. rex was

Tyrannosaurus rex, "Sue"

© The Field Museum

female). When she roamed the earth, some 65 million years ago, Sue weighed 7 tons. Sue's actual skull, which at 600 pounds is too heavy to be mounted on the structure that holds the skeleton, is displayed on the upper level; the skull in Stanley Hall is a lightweight cast.

In spring 2010, the Field added a new permanent attraction in honor of Sue's 10th anniversary. Enter Sue's prehistoric world in the 3-D film, **Waking the T. Rex: The Story of Sue**, shown in the new **Ernst & Young 3-D Theater** on the upper level.

Other displays in the hall, including a pair of taxidermied bull elephants **(B)**, two Haida totem poles **(C)**, and four 20ft New Guinean ceremonial masks **(D)** reflect the museum's interest in the diversity of life on the planet and the study of human cultures. Behind stately columns on either side of the hall, exhibit spaces unfold into the symmetrical wings. Female statues representing the four purposes of the museum—science, dissemination of knowledge, research and recording—gaze down from each of the four upper corners of the hall.

West Wing

Beginning in the southwest corner of Stanley Field Hall, the **What Is an Animal?** exhibit presents a colorful array of animal life, from head lice to giant squid, arranged so that you can contrast and compare sizes, colors, habitats, skele-

tons, survival techniques and other animal behaviors and characteristics.

Inside Ancient Egypt starts with a tour through the **mastaba tomb**★ of Unis-ankh, son of the last pharaoh of Dynasty V (2428–2407 BC). Part-replica and part-authentic, this is the largest full-size reconstruction of a tomb outside Egypt. In the original chambers, tomb paintings are preserved under glass. A stairway leads to the roof for a good view into the tomb, and from here a spiral staircase winds down to the **ground level** of the museum, where the exhibit continues into the depths of the tomb's burial chamber. The Field's strong collection of Egyptian burial and **mortuary artifacts** fills the following rooms with some 20 mummies, sarcophagi, papyrus scrolls and other funerary objects arranged by dynasty. Admire the tiny **diorama** illustrating the embalmer's art—a two-month process—before exiting through an ancient Egyptian marketplace, c.2450 BC.

The rest of the first floor of the west wing is largely devoted to mammals, birds and their habitats. In the **World of Mammals** and the **World of Birds**, hundreds of creatures are mounted in old-fashioned display cases. To this traditional approach have been added interpretive graphics, sound effects such as bird calls and environmental notes. The galleries in general show off to great advantage the elaborate

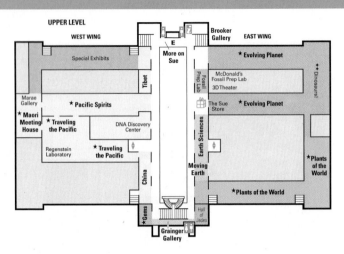

UPPER LEVEL

WEST WING

Brooker Gallery

EAST WING

E

★ Evolving Planet

Special Exhibits

More on Sue

Tibet

McDonald's Fossil Prep Lab

3D Theater

★★ Dinosaurs!

Marae Gallery

Fossil Prep Lab

The Sue Store

★ Evolving Planet

★ Maori Meeting House

★ Pacific Spirits

★ Traveling the Pacific

DNA Discovery Center

Earth Sciences

Regenstein Laboratory

★ Traveling the Pacific

China

Moving Earth

★ Plants of the World

★ Gems

Hall of Jades

★ Plants of the World

Grainger Gallery

North Entrance
(from Grant Park)

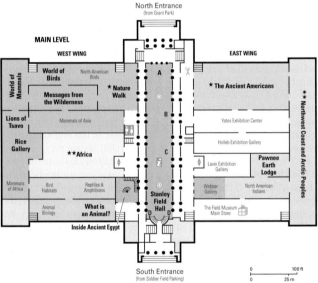

MAIN LEVEL

WEST WING

EAST WING

World of Mammals

World of Birds

North American Birds

A

★ Nature Walk

★ The Ancient Americans

Messages from the Wilderness

B

★★ Northwest Coast and Arctic Peoples

Lions of Tsavo

Mammals of Asia

Yates Exhibition Center

Rice Gallery

Holleb Exhibition Gallery

C

★★ Africa

Lavin Exhibition Gallery

Pawnee Earth Lodge

Mammals of Africa

Bird Habitats

Reptiles & Amphibians

Stanley Field Hall

Webber Gallery

North American Indians

Animal Biology

What is an Animal?

D

The Field Museum Main Store

Inside Ancient Egypt

South Entrance
(from Soldier Field Parking)

0 ___ 100 ft
0 ___ 25 m

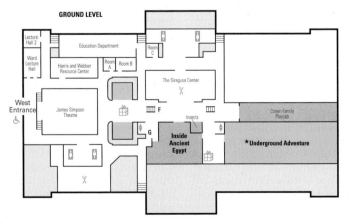

GROUND LEVEL

Lecture Hall 2

Education Department

Room C

Ward Lecture Hall

Harris and Webber Resource Center

Room A

Room B

The Siragusa Center

West Entrance

James Simpson Theatre

F

Crown Family PlayLab

Insects

G

Inside Ancient Egypt

★ Underground Adventure

taxidermy and diorama—largely the legacy of Carl Akeley—for which the Field is famous. Akeley, who worked at the museum between 1896 and 1909, was a sculptor and pioneer in the field of taxidermy and diorama creation, setting the standards for realism and detail that would inform those crafts for 50 years. His most recognizable work is the pair of bull elephants in Stanley Field Hall, but his **Four Seasons**★, on display continuously at the museum since its crafting in 1902, represents the height of his art. The four-part tableau depicts deer in their habitat throughout the year. It can currently be seen in **Nature Walk**★, an exhibit at the north end that takes you on a trek through woods, wetlands and other wild places. To complement Nature Walk, **Messages from the Wilderness** employs diorama to deliver timely messages about environmental issues and extinction.

At the center of the west wing is a kaleidoscopic exhibit entitled **Africa**★★. From the streets of Dakar, Senegal, decked out for the Muslim feast day of Tabaski (which celebrates an Islamic story of Abraham and Isaac), to the sand dunes of the Sahara, where the Tuareg people live and trade, this sweeping presentation investigates African politics, art, environment, wildlife, geography, commerce and family life by focusing on representative regions and peoples. Note especially the **ritual regalia**★ and beautifully crafted tools of the Bamum people of Cameroon in the section on art and society. In conspicuous contrast, a segment on the slave trade compels you to walk through a re-creation of a dimly-lit slave ship's hold and consider such remnants of slavery as shackles and a restraining collar. Blending words, videos and artifacts, this exhibit is designed to appeal to every age group.

East Wing

The galleries to the east of Stanley Field Hall are devoted to the culture groups of North and South America. New in 2007, the stunning **Ancient Americas**★★ exhibit covers 15 millennia of human life in the Western Hemisphere. Empha-

sizing the creative diversity of cultures ranging from the Taino of the Caribbean to the pueblos of the Southwest, the presentation offers a lush eyeful of the rich and sophisticated arts, crafts and lifeways of these ancient people. More than 2,200 artifacts beautifully illustrate the story. The dense **Eskimos and Northwest Coast Indians**★★ exhibit contains a seemingly exhaustive catalog of materials contrasting life on the Northwest Coast and in the Arctic. Especially impressive are a case of Northwest Coast **masks** and a forest of stately carved cedar **totem poles**★ (most collected by anthropologist Franz Boas for the World's Columbian Exposition in 1893), which towers above the display.

Upper Level

At the top of the north staircase is **More About Sue**. Here you'll find the tyrannosaurus's real skull **(E)**—baring a mouthful of frighteningly large, sharp teeth—along with exhibits focusing on theories and speculation about how Sue lived and died.

East Wing

For the complete picture of the evolution of life on earth, including a fabulous **dinosaur hall**★★, visit **Evolving Planet**. In three galleries, the exhibit examines the variety and history of life through fossils, bones and the life-sized re-creation of several key prehistoric ecosystems.

The serene and beautifully crafted exhibit **Plants of the World**★ occupies the southeastern corner of the second floor. Including models of a third of the world's plant species, it is the most complete botanical exhibit in existence. It succeeds in dazzling the visitor with the incredible variety of form, color and function among the world's plants. Made through a process pioneered by Carl Akeley at the turn of the century, each model was meticulously formed of wax or plastic from molds of living plants. A single model may have taken two or three months to complete. Accompanying label text is no less detailed, describing fruits, flowers and leaves for family after family of plants. Interesting facts are highlighted, and you learn, for instance, that as members of the poison ivy family, cashews must be removed from the poisonous juices in their husks before they can be eaten.

West Wing

Reopened in fall 2009 after a sparkling redesign, the **Grainger Hall of Gems**★ presents a shimmering collection of precious and semiprecious stones and jewelry. Careful lighting in a darkened room, just west of the south staircase, brings out the best in the opals, moonstones, rubies and others on display from among the museum's collection of 60,000. Don't miss the 5,899-carat **Chalmers topaz**. More mineralogy can be found in the **Earth Sciences** hall in the southeast section of the upper level.

The remainder of this wing on the second floor is devoted to Asia and the Pacific. Small exhibits on **China** and **Tibet** showcase ritual and secular artifacts from those cultures. Particularly noteworthy are examples of Tibetan ceremonial paraphernalia—prayer wheels, wands, shell trumpets and the like—all forms unfamiliar to the Western eye, each exquisitely tooled and ornamented. Equally fascinating are the Tibetan anatomical and medicinal charts. By way of introduction, a video makes good use of historic footage of monastic life in Tibet.

Two full-scale exhibits focus on separate aspects of the cultures of Oceania: navigating the waters and ceremonial life. To evoke the essence of the islands, **Traveling the Pacific**★ uses "stage settings"—a lava flow, a deserted beach—alongside traditional glass case displays. Hundreds of elaborately decorated artifacts related to canoes, canoe building and canoe ornamentation—including a wonderful assortment of paddles—form the core of the exhibit. Next door, **Pacific Spirits**★ again draws on the museum's vast Oceanic collection to explore the religious beliefs of the peoples of Polynesia, Micronesia, Melanesia and New Guinea. The highlight of this journey around the Pacific is Ruatepupuke, an authentic **Maori meeting house**★ that has been reconstructed here piece by piece. The only such meeting house in the Western Hemisphere, it is a sacred place to New Zealand's Maori people, and curators collaborated with Maori consultants to follow ancient protocols in its installation and reconsecration. The house, which dates from 1881, is 55ft long, 23ft wide and 15ft high, and represents both an ethnographic treasure and a work of art.

Ground Level

In a case under the stairs sits the taxidermed **Man-eater of Mfuwe (F)**, the largest man-eating lion on record. In 1991 this African lion claimed six victims in Zambia. Nearby you'll find **Bushman (G)**, Lincoln Park Zoo's legendary gorilla, now preserved. Bushman captured the hearts of Chicagoans upon his arrival as a two-year-old orphan from the French Cameroons in 1930. He died in 1951 and has resided at the Field ever since.

A favorite with the younger set, **Underground Adventure**★ simulates the creepy, crawly world beneath our feet. Before entering this subterranean scene, you first pass through a "shrinking chamber" where sound effects and mirrors create the impression that you have shrunk 100 times smaller than your normal size. Once the shrinking is complete, walk through the dark, narrow passages, the walls laced with roots plunging down from plants above ground and embedded with numerous creatures. Explore different zones to learn about the diversity of life underground, and watch out for moving critters, like the colossal crayfish and the giant grubeating wolf spider. At exhibit's end, interactive displays focus on managing our soil in the future.

JOHN G. SHEDD AQUARIUM★★★

1200 S. Lake Shore Dr. ◷*Open Memorial Day–Labor Day daily 9am–6pm; rest of the year Mon–Fri 9am–5pm, Sat–Sun 9am–6pm.* ◷*Closed Dec 25.* ⊜ *$26.95*

Oceanarium, John G. Shedd Aquarium

© Shedd Aquarium/Brenna Hernandez

(additional fee for Fantasea and 4-D Experience). ☏312-939-2438. www.sheddaquarium.org.

Located at the very edge of Lake Michigan, the Shedd is the world's largest indoor aquarium. Housing some 8,000 aquatic animals comprising 650 species—from tiny, jewel-like spiny lobsters to 1,500-pound beluga whales—the Shedd's exhibits and programs emphasize conservation and the environment. Seeing its remarkable animals brings this message vividly to life.

A BIT OF HISTORY
Ocean by the Lake

When John Graves Shedd, who rose from stock boy to chairman of Marshall Field & Co. between 1872 and 1926, donated $3 million for the construction of an aquarium in Chicago, he intended the structure to house "the greatest variety of sea life on display under one roof." Architects Graham, Anderson, Probst & White designed a fitting edifice to complement the stately Field Museum nearby. It opened in 1930, one of the last Beaux-Arts buildings in Chicago, and perhaps the final nod to city planner Daniel Burnham's vision of the "City Beautiful," an aesthetic outgrowth of the World's Columbian Exposition of 1893. The octagonal structure, clad in shimmering white Georgia marble, resembles at every turn a monument to Poseidon. Indeed, the sea god's trident

surmounts the building's dome. The aquarium's nautical decor is among its most remarkable features: inside and out, repeating wave and shell patterns decorate doorways, cornices, tiles and pediments; bas-reliefs of elegant sea creatures embellish walls and even lighting fixtures mimic piscine forms. All blend into a delightful aquatic paraphrase of a Classical Doric temple. The building was awarded National Historic Landmark status in 1987.

The aquarium is equally remarkable for its mechanical systems. Original plans called for the latest in materials, piping (75mi of it), water storage (enough for 2 million gallons—four times larger than any of that day) and environmental controls that made life in the aquarium's 200 exhibits possible. Salt water was imported by barge and train from Key West and the Gulf of Mexico until 1973 when the aquarium began mixing its own using water from Lake Michigan.

In 1991 the much-heralded 170,000sq ft oceanarium opened to the southeast of the original building to house marine mammals and an expansive replication of the endangered Pacific Northwest Coast ecosystem. Completed at a cost of $45 million, the addition (Lohan & Assocs.) is covered in marble peeled from the side of the old building now shared by the oceanarium. A broad "curtain of glass," its most distinguishing feature, barely seems to separate the interior from Lake Michigan. Inside, oceanarium planners created a habitat as close to nature as possible—down to the shape of the pools—after considerable study of the needs and behaviors of the animals that would live here.

Waters of the World

A pioneer in the re-creation of aquatic habitats, the Shedd has transformed many of its old-fashioned stacked-rock tank environments into mini-ecosystems supporting not only fish but plants and microscopic life as well. This approach to aquatic exhibition makes habitats as handsome and interesting as their inhabitants. And, in keeping with the Shedd's focus on conservation, these habitats convey the importance of biodiversity and the interrelationships of species with each other and with their surroundings. Of particular interest are endangered and degraded environments; several displays offer you a look at ecosystems that may already no longer exist in the wild.

VISITING THE AQUARIUM

Morning is the best time to visit the Shedd Aquarium, especially in summer when a line is likely to form around the block by 11am. Arrive early for immediate admission to the oceanarium; those who come later must often wait to enter. No matter what time you go, the galleries seem to swim with children and school groups. You'll find the gift shop adjacent to the admissions desk off the main lobby. At lunchtime, **Soundings Restaurant** (*312-692-3277*) in the Oceanarium provides healthy fare and full table service; while the adjacent revamped food court, **The Bubble Net**, offers pizza, burgers and sandwiches to go. **The Phelps Auditorium 4-D Special FX Theater** located in the Oceanarium presents high-definition 3-D movies, complete with "special effects" seats that add a surprising fourth sensory dimension to the experience.

Main Building

Radiating from the central Caribbean Reef situated beneath the rotunda, six 90ft-long rectangular galleries flow one into the other, each focusing on a different type of aquatic system. The darkened spaces contrast with the brightly lit tanks to provide optimum viewing. Centerpiece of the main building, the 90,000-gal **Caribbean Reef**★ habitat displays some 500 tropical fish, from nurse sharks to parrotfish, yellow stingrays, Spanish hogfish and Caribbean spiny lobsters. (Look especially for Nickel, a rescued green sea turtle whose shell was damaged by a boat's propeller.) The exhibit also includes a 3,000-gal reef-within-a-reef built into the original huge tank to facilitate the display of smaller fishes that might otherwise wind up as food for the larger

Fishy Facts

- A large **Caribbean parrot fish** excretes a ton of sand a year. Using two oversized front teeth, it nibbles on seagrass and scrapes algae; another set of teeth in its throat grinds up the coral it ingests.
- The **Amazon River** has more fish species than any other freshwater system on earth; each year the Amazon produces enough fish to fill a freight train more than 5,000 cars long.
- It takes two weeks for a pair of **elegant shrimp** to devour a starfish 100 times their size.
- **Seahorses**, and their relatives pipefishes and sea dragons, share an unusual trait: the males become pregnant and carry their developing young.
- At birth, **Beluga whale calves** weigh between 80 and 150 pounds and measure from 3.5ft to 5ft long.
- **Adult electric eels** 5ft to 7ft long produce enough electricity—600 volts—to stun a horse.

species. Daily feedings (check times at entrance) by scuba-diving animal care-takers are engrossing; the divers narrate their actions underwater as they work. Occupying 10,000sq ft of space in the south wing of the original building, **Amazon Rising: Seasons of the River**★★ allows you to experience a year in the life of an Amazon floodplain forest. The journey begins as you enter a humid tropical "forest," with rain falling behind you and the calls of myriad birds and insects echoing all around. Habitats (river beach, floodplain lake, forest) are stocked with some 250 species of animals, such as lungfish, piranha, bird-eating spiders, an anaconda, poison-arrow frogs and giant bullet ants. Each environment repeats to illustrate the different levels of the river during the year, from low-water season—when the river is only a few feet high—to high-water season, when the Amazon swells to a depth of 30ft and a breadth up to 40mi wide. Displays at the end of the exhibit reinforce the fragile interdependence of the organisms in this ecosystem and stress the global ramifications of human actions.

The balance of the galleries in the old building are devoted to the **Waters of the World**, divided into Oceans, Local Waters, Islands and Lakes, and Rivers. As you enter the Oceans exhibit, don't miss the **seahorses and seadragons**, oddly beautiful creatures that dart and dance. Look carefully for a pregnant male. In the sparkling **anemone tanks**, jewel-like corals, delicate cleaner shrimp, purple sea apples and hypnotic moon jellies live. Another popular denizen in this gallery is the giant Pacific octopus. A solitary nocturnal hunter, the giant octopus can grow to 30ft (from armtip to armtip) and weighs in at 100 pounds. Lively river otters stand out among the inhabitants of local waters resident in the adjacent gallery, Local Waters.

Next door in the Islands and Lakes gallery, beautiful blue iguanas sunbathe. Only 30 remain in their only wild habitat on Grand Cayman Island. And, in the Rivers gallery, don't miss Granddad, an Australian lungfish who arrived at the aquarium in 1933 and is today its oldest inhabitant. Lungfish breathe through both lungs and gills. The curious paddle-fish next door has a long, flat snout covered with sensors to help it navigate and find food in murky waters.

Take the elevator downstairs to the **Wild Reef**★★ and wander among sharks, schooling fishes, rays and coral. The tanks of this Philippine reef habitat have been marvelously installed underfoot, overhead and wall-to-wall. Chock a block with colorful, busy fishes, this exhibit explores all aspects of the coral reef ecosystem, including the threats it faces and the lives of the people who depend on its waters for livelihoods.

Oceanarium★★

One of the world's largest indoor marine mammal pavilions, the airy oceanarium was recently transformed with fresh exhibits and animals. The new **Pacific Northwest** exhibit immerses visitors in the region's coastal habitats, complete with living marine animals and a faithful reproduction in steel and epoxy—down to the last rock and pine needle—of a Northwest coastal ecosystem. Life along this coast lends itself particularly well to exhibit as the ranges of many marine mammals overlap here, and the Sitka spruce forest can be successfully simulated in this setting. Depicting this region also offers an opportunity to demonstrate the dynamics of an entire ecosystem, and an endangered one at that, as the harvesting of North American temperate rain forests proceeds at a devastating pace.

The self-guided stroll "along the coast" follows the edge of the oversized pools where **beluga whales**, Pacific white-sided **dolphins** and **harbor seals** carouse in an expanded habitat. Around each bend loom islands, a tide pool, a fault line and other geological features. The wide expanse of Lake Michigan stretches beyond, a vista barely interrupted by the oceanarium's glass wall. Throughout the day, narrated dives introduce visitors to sea turtles, moraeels, parrotfish and more (check dive times at entrance).

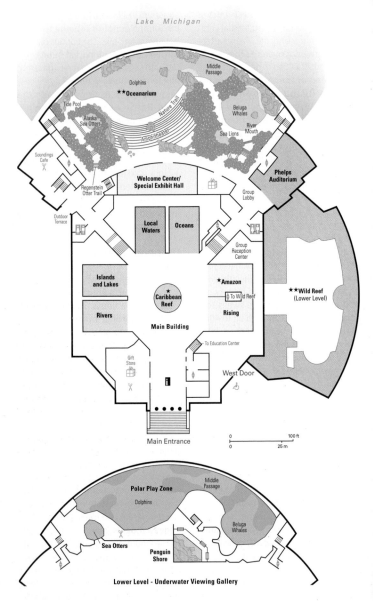

Lower Level - Underwater Viewing Gallery

Don't miss the Shedd's newest show, **Fantasea**. In this high-tech marine mammal spectacle, held in an amphitheater carved into the "rocks" above the pools, dolphins dive, belugas dance and penguins parade to a musical score (check show times at entrance). The animals' performances are not merely tricks, but rather natural behaviors cued by hand signals from a trainer. A "spy-hopping" dolphin in the wild, for instance, stands straight up on its tail for a better view above the water.

One level below the habitat, an **underwater viewing gallery** offers glimpses into the depths of the huge pools. Surrounding it, the new **Polar Play Zone** features interactive experiences for young children. Also here, you'll find colonies of Rockhoppers and Magellanics, two of the world's 17 penguin species. These creatures—found only in the most remote reaches of the Southern Hemisphere—are perfectly suited to their environment, combining the best of bird, marine mammal and fish. Strong "wings" and a streamlined shape allow them to "fly" through the water. Blubber and a complex layering of feathers keep them warm in water 70 degrees colder than their bodies.

The **sea otter** habitat can be viewed from both levels. These smallest of marine mammals lack the bulk and blubber their relatives rely on for keeping warm; instead, their dense fur provides insulation. Clean fur is therefore essential; to an otter an oil spill can be devastating.

A series of interactive exhibits presents topics related to marine mammals such as breathing and diving, locomotion through water, and otters and oil spills. One display explains the workings of the oceanarium, mechanical as well as human, and a video provides a look at the animals "after hours."

One level above the oceanarium is the **Special Exhibits Gallery**, which presents changing exhibits on matters marine and maritime.

ADLER PLANETARIUM & ASTRONOMY MUSEUM★★

1300 S. Lake Shore Dr. ◷*Open mid-Jun –Labor Day daily 9.30am–6pm; rest of year Mon–Fri 10am–4pm, Sat–Sun 10am–4.30pm.* ◷*Closed Thanksgiving Day & Dec 25.* ⊜*$10 exhibits only; additional fee for shows and audio tours. Call for discount days schedule.* ✕&▯ ℘*312-922-7827. www.adler planetarium.org.*

Occupying a beautiful setting, the Adler offers commanding **views**★★ up and down the lakefront. The oldest planetarium in the Western Hemisphere, the Adler is renowned for its fine collection of historic astronomical instruments and splendid sky shows, which appeal to young and old alike.

A BIT OF HISTORY

Intrigued by a German device known as a Zeiss projector for re-creating the night sky on an enclosed dome, philanthropist **Max Adler** (1866–1952) decided in 1928 that Chicago ought to have one "to emphasize that under the great celestial firmament there is order, interdependence and unity." Adler, a retired officer of Sears, Roebuck and Co. (of which his brother-in-law Julius Rosenwald was president), donated $1 million to the city to establish a planetarium and acquired a substantial collection of astronomical instruments for its museum. Architect Ernest A. Grunsfeld, Jr. designed a compact, Art Deco jewel for the dramatic setting at the tip of Northerly Island. When the planetarium opened in 1930, its modern style contrasted with the Beaux-Arts edifices that housed Chicago's other cultural institutions. Bronze bas-reliefs depicting signs of the zodiac punctuate the smooth reddish granite of the original 12-sided, 3-tiered exterior *(now enclosed)*. The whole is crowned by the dome of the original planetarium theater, where the facility's first Zeiss projector operated until 1970 (the theater is currently equipped with a Zeiss Mark VI projector).

In 1977 the **Doane Observatory** opened just east of the planetarium, offering the public a firsthand view of the heavens through its 20-inch cassegrain reflector telescope. The building achieved National Historic Landmark status in 1987. A major renovation, completed in 1999, added a 60,000sq ft wrap-around addition to the old building. The addition contains two floors of exhibit space, with classrooms occupying a middle floor. The glass-enclosed upper level features interactive modules and telescope viewing areas.

VISIT

Gracing the grounds leading to the planetarium are several important sculptures. At the western end of Solidarity Drive (so named in 1980 by Mayor Jane Byrne to honor Lech Walesa and the Polish labor movement) stands the

Adler Planetarium & Astronomy Museum

© City of Chicago/GRC

Tadeusz Kosciuszko Memorial (3), sculpted by Kasimir Chodzinski in 1904. Near the planetarium, a seated **Nicolaus Copernicus (4)** holds an open compass and a model of the solar system. Bertel Thorvaldsen cast the bronze original in Warsaw in 1823.

Henry Moore's 12ft working **Sundial (5)** (1980), which commemorates the golden years of astronomy (1930 to 1980), is installed outside the glass-enclosed Galileo's Café.

Upper Level

The centerpiece here is the **Sky Theater**, where the Zeiss Mark VI star projector re-creates the twinkling night sky on the dome of the historic planetarium. Daily **sky shows**★ *(check schedule at admissions desk)* focus on various aspects of astronomy, such as the fantastic findings of the Hubble Space Telescope. Lively narration accompanies the special effects created by the projector.

In the solarium galleries surrounding the theater, interactive kiosks demystify the solar system and the Milky Way Galaxy. Designed for children aged three to eight, **Planet Explorers** offers hours of interactive fun, from backyard stargazing to hands-on exploration of Planet X. Also on the upper level, **Shoot for the Moon** relates the story of the race to the moon, with a focus on the Gemini 12 mission in 1966. The capsule that carried captain Jim Lovell and pilot Buzz Aldrin has been restored and is on view, along with artifacts pertaining to other Gemini and Apollo flights.

Lower Level

The virtual-reality **Definiti Space Theater**★ *(entrance on lower level)* offers an interactive voyage through the universe using state-of-the-art computer projection technologies. Your simulated interplanetary journey might take you to the edge of the solar system in *IBEX*; or launch you through time and space to unravel celestial mysteries in the Adler's new show, **Journey to the Stars** *(check schedule at admissions desk)*. Also on this level, the **Universe in Your Hands**★ showcases an extensive collection of historic astronomical, navigational, timekeeping, surveying and measuring instruments. The exhibit explains the context and importance of these Intricately decorated metal objects, arcane and curious in appearance and name: orrery, astrolabe, compendium, eclipsometrium. Note the remarkable group of sundials in ivory, brass, wood, silver and stone dating from the 14–18C.

For a glimpse of the sky traditions of cultures around the world, **CyberSpace** presents a real-time look at current sky science, featuring live feeds and NASA broadcasts, interactive stations and parabolic computer screens where you can navigate over the surface of the planets. Adjacent to the Definiti Space Theater, the historic **Atwood Sphere** is Chicago's oldest planetarium, constructed in 1913. Inside this hollow, revolving metal sphere, the constellations are visible via tiny holes in the metal through which light shines.

North Side

Gold Coast★★

This slice of Chicago's lakefront has been home to the city's most prominent and wealthiest citizens for over a century. Nestled between the nightlife district of Oak and Division streets on the south and Lincoln Park on the north is some of the most elegant and expensive residential property in Chicago, encompassing the towering condominium buildings of Lake Shore Drive and the quaint Victorian town houses of Astor Street. To the west LaSalle Street and Sandburg Village mark the transition to the gentrified Old Town Historic District, while the Magnificent Mile lies just a short walk to the south.

A BIT OF HISTORY
Chic Chicago

The young city's moneyed classes first settled in the Prairie Avenue district south of the Loop. By the late-19C, they had relocated to the present-day Gold Coast. Two events contributed to the rise in fame of this patch of land located just south of Lincoln Park. In the 1860s the city's municipal cemetery (established on marshy swampland north of the city limits) was removed to create Lincoln Park, and in 1875 **Lake Shore Drive** opened, improving the area's transportation. Five years later, the Roman

- ♿ **Michelin Map:** p160.
- 🅿 **Parking:** Much of the street parking is by residential permit, though meters might be found along Clark St. As usual, public transportation is best.
- 👪 **Kids:** Oak Street Beach, of course!
- 🕐 **Timing:** The Gold Coast is compact and easy to see in a couple of hours.
- ♿ **Also See:** Magnificent Mile, Old Town, Lincoln Park.

GETTING THERE
BY L/BUS: Ⓒⓣⓐ Red line to **Clark/Division** or bus no. 151.

Catholic Archbishop's lavish residence was built at North Avenue. And in 1882, **Potter** and **Bertha Honoré Palmer**, the city's real-estate king and society queen, erected an ostentatious mansion on Lake Shore Drive. Abandoning Prairie Avenue en masse, the wealthy elite soon followed Palmer, who had wisely purchased much of the land, which quadrupled in value within a decade. Bertha Palmer entertained without pause, exhibiting her collection of French Impressionist works (later donated to the Art

Crowded Oak Street Beach in 1942

© Mansell/Time & Life Pictures/Getty Images

Institute) in the home's famed 75ft-long picture gallery. By 1900 the Archbishop had subdivided and sold his land as well, and the Gold Coast quickly filled with mansions and extravagant stone town houses, detailed in the popular styles of the period: Romanesque, Queen Anne and Beaux-Arts.

Return of an Era

Developers began to erect apartment high rises in the 20C, most featuring full-floor, 18-room units with servants' quarters and all the amenities of a private home. Many Victorian houses were razed in the 1920s, especially on **Lake Shore Drive**, as a rash of luxurious high-rises increased the density of the area without diminishing its prestige. While the Gold Coast was thriving, working-class Irish, German and Swedish immigrants, and soon Italians, settled in the area to the west of LaSalle Street. In 1929 Harvey Zorbaugh documented the contrast in *The Gold Coast and the Slum,* a benchmark in urban sociology. Palmer's Lake Shore Drive "castle" was demolished in 1950 during another spate of high-rise development. More town houses were mowed down and replaced by hundreds of apartments with the most precious of Chicago commodities: a view of the lake. Urban redevelopment in the 1960s targeted the deteriorating area to the west by erecting Carl Sandburg Village along Clark Street from Division Street to North Avenue, initiating the gentrification of the nearby Old Town and Lincoln Park areas. In 1962 Butch McGuire opened the first singles bar on Division Street, turning the southern edge of the Gold Coast into a raucous nightlife district, while a surgeon's stately home became Hugh Hefner's first Playboy Mansion. In 1973 the city designated **Astor Street** a landmark and limited building heights to help stem the high-rise trend and preserve the turn-of-the-century ambience. Four years later the entire Gold Coast, from North Avenue south to Oak Street and Dearborn Street east to Lake Shore Drive, was listed on the National Register of Historic Places, and in 1990 the city

Aerial view of Gold Coast with Oak Street Beach

© PhotoDisc, Inc

designated as landmarks the last seven houses on Lake Shore Drive. In the late 20C and the early 21C many mansions that had been divided into apartments were restored as single-family homes, ushering in a new era of gentility and luxury in this parklike enclave.

WALKING TOUR

2.3mi.

Tucked below the skyscrapers of the Magnificent Mile, the area exudes a sense of elegance and luxury. An early Sunday-morning stroll is probably the best way to enjoy this lovely district, where stately town houses fronted by tiny, manicured lawns bring to mind visions of a bygone era. In the summer, end your walk by heading to the popular **Oak Street Beach**.

▶ *Begin at Bellevue Pl. and Lake Shore Dr. and walk west.*

Bellevue Place

An array of Victorian architectural styles graces this charming, tree-lined street. The handsome, three-story **Bryan Lathrop House** *(120 E. Bellevue Pl.),* designed by McKim, Mead & White (1892) contrasted with the picturesque facades of Queen Anne and Romanesque Revival architecture dominating the Gold Coast in the late-19C. This Chicago landmark brought the comparatively sedate Georgian Revival to the area,

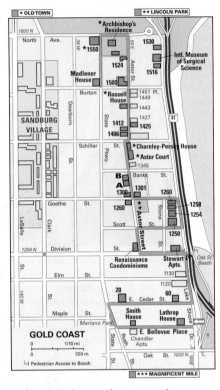

◯ *Turn right on E. Cedar St.*

The 1920s high-rise boom in this smart area led to buildings like the Gothic-style **20 E. Cedar Street** (1924, Fugard & Knapp), which takes the lavish ornament and picturesque rooflines of a Gold Coast town house and stretches them out over 15 stories. The streetscape ranges from well-preserved Romanesque and Georgian Revival town houses to faceless modern high rises. The highlight is the Romanesque Revival **60 E. Cedar Street** (1890, Curd H. Gottig), a confection of turrets, arches and protruding bays in rusticated Georgia marble. Note the lovely stained glass punctuating the facade.

◯ *Turn left on Lake Shore Dr.*

Lake Shore Drive had witnessed $25 million worth of apartment high-rise development by 1928, mostly in the form of elegant structures such as no. 1120 (1926, Robert S. DeGolyer) and no. 1130 (1911, Howard Van Doren Shaw), one of the first cooperatives, featuring full-floor apartments and a Tudor Revival design with Medieval motifs. Marshall & Fox followed in 1913 with the luxurious **Stewart Apartments** *(no. 1200)*, in the Adamesque style with large bay windows. Look south for an impressive **view**★ of the Drake Hotel and East Lake Shore Drive, a row of luxury high rises developed before 1929.

◯ *Turn left on Division St. and continue to Astor St.*

Renaissance Condominiums
1200 N. Astor St.
Originally the McConnell Apartments, this 1897 Holabird & Roche design is one of the area's earliest high rises. Combining Victorian rounded corners with modern brick wall planes and massing,

and by 1900, it became the most popular style. Graceful, rounded bays frame a symmetrical brick facade with an expansive porch and Beaux-Arts detailing. A 1972 restoration by Perkins & Will replicated the original cornice. Built for a real estate magnate who helped found the Chicago Symphony Orchestra, the structure has housed the Fortnightly of Chicago, a women's literary club since 1922. Note the 1887 **Lot P. Smith House** at no. 32, a rare surviving home by **Burnham & Root**, and the four-story, Georgian Revival Chandler Apartments across the street at no. 33, designed in 1911 by Schmidt, Garden & Martin.

◯ *Turn right on Rush St.*

The tiny, pie-shaped Mariano Park contains a 1900 pavilion designed by Birch Burdette Long, a student of Frank Lloyd Wright, and a fountain added by the city in 1998. The bustle of commercial Rush Street contrasts with the quiet residential streets of the Gold Coast.

Houses on Astor Street

© Kim Karpeles / Alamy

the structure is an excellent example of a Chicago school apartment building.

▷ *Turn right on Astor St.*

Early high-rise apartments give way to quaint graystones with delicate wrought-iron railings and miniature front gardens on historic **Astor Street**★★, named for John Jacob Astor, whose American Fur Co. traded in the area before the settlement of Chicago. Note how the attached town houses are staggered along the angled street so that each facade projects forward as you walk north. While other wealthy neighborhoods boasted large lots, many Gold Coast mansions are squeezed into parcels only 25ft wide.

▷ *Turn right on Scott St. and left on Lake Shore Dr.*

Four of the seven houses on **Lake Shore Drive** designated as Chicago landmarks (1990) are located side by side in this block. The Carl C. Heisen House at **no. 1250** (1891, Frank B. Abbott) and Mason B. Starring House at **no. 1254** (1891, L. Gustav Halberg) are heavy Romanesque Revival structures joined in 1990 to create four luxury condos. Holabird & Roche, who designed the flowery Venetian Gothic home at no. 1258 for Arthur Aldis (1898), exhibited Georgian restraint in 1910 at **no. 1260** next door.

▷ *Turn left on Goethe St., right on Astor St.*

Philip B. Maher designed the nearly identical buildings at **1260** and **1301 N. Astor Street** in 1932. The sleek Art Deco towers retain the full-floor luxury of earlier apartment buildings. Potter Palmer II and his wife were the first to occupy three floors in no. 1301. The modern design at **no. 1300** (1963, **Bertrand Goldberg**) contrasts sharply, its slender posts supporting the b0uilding above the automobile-oriented ground level.

James L. Houghteling Houses (A)

1308–1312 N. Astor St.

Designed in 1887 by John Wellborn Root of **Burnham & Root**, these three houses have a beautiful sculptural quality created by variegated massing and polychromatic wall treatments. A rusticated base of red sandstone supports tawny brick walls and metal bay windows, rising to a picturesque roofline of turrets, gables and dormers. Root lived at no. 1310 until his untimely death in 1891 during the planning of the World's Columbian Exposition. His sister-in-law, **Harriet Monroe**, who founded *Poetry* magazine, lived here as well. She was first in the country to publish works by Vachel Lindsay, Carl Sandburg and T. S. Eliot. The Romanesque Revival row houses at **1316–1322 N. Astor Street (B)** were designed in 1889 for real estate mogul **Potter Palmer**. The wall surfaces of the houses gradually progress from heavy rustication to smooth.

▷ *Cross Banks St. and continue north on Astor St.*

More 1960s high rises on the left overwhelm tiny Victorians on the right, such as the multicolored checkerboard at 1345 N. Astor Street (1887, Treat & Foltz). William O. Goodman, who endowed the Goodman Theatre, lived at **Astor Court**★ *(1355 N. Astor St.)*, a stately Georgian mansion (1914, Howard Van Doren Shaw). A small courtyard is visible at the southern entrance behind a gate ornamented with golden door knockers shaped as hands holding apples.

Charnley-Persky House★

1365 N. Astor St. 🚶*Visit by guided tour only: Wed noon (45min; free); Sat (70min) Dec–Mar 10am; Apr–Nov 10am & noon.* ◐*Closed Dec 24–Jan 1.* ⓢ*$15.* ☎*312-573-1365. www.sah.org.*
Frank Lloyd Wright designed this 1892 home while in the employ of Adler & Sullivan. Wright, who immodestly called it the first modern building, managed to create a horizontal composition by employing his trademark Roman bricks and minimizing decoration. Sullivanesque ornament covers the pro-

truding balcony and front door, while the limestone base and broad eaves hint at Wright's future work. The house has only 11 rooms organized around a central skylit stair; a kitchen is located in the narrow basement. The house is the headquarters of the national Society of Architectural Historians, which promotes the study and preservation of the built environment.

▷ *Cross Schiller St. and continue north on Astor St.*

The house at **1406 N. Astor Street** was built for steel scion Joseph T. Ryerson (grandson of philanthropist Martin A. Ryerson) in 1922 by David Adler. In 1931 Adler added the slate mansard roof to enclose a gallery exhibiting local memorabilia (now housed at the Chicago History Museum).
William D. Kerfoot lived at **1425 N. Astor Street**. Kerfoot gained fame in 1871 when his was the first Loop business to reopen the day after the Great Chicago Fire destroyed all of his real-estate holdings. The sign on his wooden shanty—now at the Chicago History Museum—read, "W. D. Kerfoot. Everything gone but wife, children, and energy." By 1895 his energy afforded him this 8,000sq ft graystone Georgian. Skyscraper pioneer William Le Baron Jenney and J. L. Silsbee erected the Romanesque Revival homes at nos. 1427 and 1443 around 1890.

Atrium, Charnley-Persky House

Charnley-Persky House/Donald G. Kalec

Edward P. Russell House★

1444 N. Astor St.

Perhaps the most elegant Art Deco construction in the Gold Coast, the building (1929, Holabird & Root) features a facade of stone from Lens, France, a gently curved three-story metal bay with incised floral decoration and a carved panel depicting graceful peacocks. Delicate oval windows flank a door covered with grillwork.

▷ *Cross Burton St.*

1500 North Astor Street

The huge Renaissance-style palazzo (1893, McKim, Mead & White) at the corner of Astor and Burton streets was built by *Chicago Tribune* publisher and former mayor Joseph Medill as a wedding gift for his daughter, Elinor Patterson. A two-story front porch supported by Doric and Ionic columns is flanked by Roman brick walls with elaborate terra-cotta trim and capped by an elaborate cornice and balustrade. Cyrus Hall McCormick II purchased the home in 1927 and employed David Adler to double its size. The addition is visible at the rear of the structure, which was then divided into eight $1 million condominiums in 1978.

▷ *Continue north on Astor St.*

The rounded corner and brick facade of **1524 N. Astor Street** (1968, I. W. Colburn & Assocs.) harmonizes this modern high rise with the Beaux-Arts and Georgian town houses that first defined the block in the 1910s.

Residence of the Roman Catholic Cardinal of Chicago★

1555 N. State Pkwy.

The oldest Gold Coast home (1880, Alfred F. Pashley), this Queen Anne fantasy in red brick with limestone trim is distinguished by 19 chimneys punctuating the roofline and an uncharacteristic expanse of surrounding land. The mansion was built prior to the rapid rise in real estate values in the 1880s and 90s.

▷ *At the edge of Lincoln Park turn left on North Ave., left on N. State Pkwy.*

1550 North State Parkway★

When it opened in 1912, this Beaux-Arts apartment building set the standard for Gold Coast gentility with 9,000sq ft, 15-room apartments organized around expansive sun parlors. Its architect, **Benjamin Marshall** of Marshall & Fox, grew up rich and expanded his wealth by designing Chicago's most prestigious houses and hotels in the 1910s and 20s, including the nearby Drake Hotel. From its rusticated base to the large urns atop the balustrade, no. 1550 is a tour de force of white terra-cotta ornament and French grillwork. Its balconies overlook Lincoln Park and the cardinal's mansion.

▷ *Walk south on N. State Pkwy. and turn right on Burton Pl.*

Albert F. Madlener House

4 W. Burton Pl. ✎ *Open while there is an exhibit on display, year-round Wed–Sat 11am–5pm (free).* ℘*312-573-1365. www.grahamfoundation.org.*

An epochal 1902 work of Prairie school architect **Hugh Garden**, this mansion was built for a local brewer. The beauty of the **entrance**★, framed by oversized Prairie-style urns and intricate coursing and grillwork, softens the austerity of Roman brick and coursed limestone. The mansion houses the Graham Foundation for Advanced Studies in the Fine Arts, an architectural endowment.

▷ *Return to N. State Pkwy. and continue south.*

Stately town houses continue for several more blocks to the south before giving way to the bustling restaurants and noisy bars of Division and Rush streets.

ADDITIONAL SIGHTS

International Museum of Surgical Science

1524 N. Lake Shore Dr. ⏰*Open Oct–Apr Tue–Sat 10am–4pm; May–Sept Tue–Sun 10am–4pm.* ⏰*Closed major* holidays. ⊛$10 (Tue free). ℘312-642-9516. www.imss.org.

Located on Lake Shore Drive, this landmark mansion (1917, Howard Van Doren Shaw) recalls the Petit Trianon on the grounds of Versailles, France, after which it was modeled. The museum it now houses focuses on the history and development of medicine and surgery. Opened by the International College of Surgeons (1952), the museum was first headquartered next door at no. 1516 and founded in Geneva (1935) by Hungarian-born Chicago surgeon Max Thorek. Exhibits on the four floors cover such topics as spinal surgery, prosthetics, medical imaging, nursing care and pain management. Two top-floor galleries focus on temporary exhibits of medical-themed contemporary artworks.

Highlights of the permanent collection include the Apothecary Shop *(1st floor)* and an iron lung once used by polio patients *(2nd floor)*. Also on the second floor is the wood-paneled library and the Hall of Murals, which features mural panels by Italian painter Gregorio di Bergolo illustrating the development of surgery through the ages. The fourth floor presents a display of primitive alloy tools used by the Incas for *trephination* (brain surgery). A patient's skull is shown beside the tool that was used on it.

Lake Shore Drive Mansions
1516 and 1530 N. Lake Shore Dr.

Built of gray Indiana limestone in the Beaux-Arts style, these two mansions form bookends to the International Museum of Surgical Science. To the south, the **Edward T. Blair House** *(no. 1516)* was designed by New York's McKim, Mead & White in 1914. Designed in 1916 by Benjamin H. Marshall, the **Bernard A. Eckhart House** *(no. 1530)* is now occupied by the Polish Consulate. Howard Van Doren Shaw's creation, now housing the museum, was modeled on Versailles' Petit Trianon at the client's behest.

ADDRESSES

⍭/EAT

$$$ The Pump Room – *In the Ambassador East Hotel. ℘312-266-0360. www.pumproom.com.* During the 1940s, this restaurant was the place to see and be seen for Chicago's smart set and visiting Hollywood stars. They undoubtedly came for the outrageous service: many dishes were delivered on flaming swords, and guests' dogs could dine in the adjacent Pup Room. Now more history than hip, the Pump Room remains an elegant restaurant with an impressive gallery of celebrity photos.

$ The 3rd Coast – *1260 N. Dearborn Pkwy. ℘312-649-0730. www.3rdcoast cafe.com.* Sip cappuccino or claret in this comfortable coffee-house and wine bar *(open daily 7am–midnight)*. Drop by on weekends for the popular brunch or breakfast. Scones are freshly made each morning.

SPLASH

👫Oak Street Beach – Chicago's chic head to the sands at Oak Street and Michigan Avenue. In the summer, the tanned and toned soak up the rays and swim in the shadow of Drake Hotel. To get to the beach (and the bike path that winds along the lakefront), use the underground tunnels at Oak or Division Sts. On the beach, have a meal or a drink at the **Beachstro** *(℘ 312-915-4100. www.oakstreetbeachstro.com)*.

Bike path along Oak Street Beach

Old Town★

Vintage cottages and elegant row houses share tree-lined streets with modern apartments in this upscale residential neighborhood bounded by Division, Halsted and LaSalle streets and Armitage Avenue. Bustling Wells Street, home to the renowned Second City comedy club and a variety of shops, bars and restaurants, cuts a colorful path through the charming Old Town Triangle Historical District north of North Avenue.

A BIT OF HISTORY
German Broadway

In the 1840s and 50s, German immigrants began to settle just north of the city's border at North Avenue. These working-class families built modest homes and started their own businesses or took jobs as semiskilled laborers. Mostly Catholic, they established St. Michael's parish in 1852, and the church at Eugenie Street and Cleveland Avenue soon became the focal point of the German community. In 1871 their wooden cottages burned like kindling during the Great Chicago Fire, but immediately following the conflagration, "relief shanties" began to spring up. In no time, older residents had rebuilt their homes and, as factories crowded the banks of the Chicago River directly west, workers flocked to North Town, later called Old Town. In 1874 the city extended its strict fire ordinance to the community, forcing builders to abandon wood for more fireproof materials. Stone Italianate and Queen Anne row houses, as well as brick cottages and coach houses blended in with the older wooden structures, giving Old Town the variegated architectural look it retains today. By 1900, North Avenue—then known as the German Broadway—was alive with shops, bakeries, taverns and delicatessens. Surviving testaments to Old Town's German heritage include the House of Glunz wine shop at Wells and Division Streets and Germania Place at North Avenue and Clark Street, which

- **Michelin Map:** p167.
- **Location:** You'll see the steeple tower of St. Michael's from blocks around.
- **Parking:** Street parking is limited by permits and meters. Lucky drivers might find a space in Lincoln Park to the east.
- **Kids:** *Sensing Chicago*, the children's gallery at the Chicago History Museum, invites kids to experience the city with all their senses.
- **Timing:** You'll be able to see Old Town in a couple of hours.
- **Also See:** Lincoln Park/ DePaul, Gold Coast, Lincoln Park.

GETTING THERE
BY L: CTA Brown line to **Sedgwick** and **North**.

was built in 1888 as the German Maennerchor singing club's headquarters.

A Century of Progress?

Growth of the community slowed in the early 20C as post-fire buildings began to deteriorate. Impoverished neighborhoods to the west and south teeming with Eastern Europeans, Italians and African Americans pressed in on Old Town while the Germans moved north. By the late 1920s, the dilapidated tenements and boarding houses southwest of Lincoln Park contrasted dramatically with the glittering Gold Coast to the east. Gradually, attempts were made to refurbish the blighted neighborhood. In 1927 a group of artists led by **Sol Kogen** and **Edgar Miller** bought run-down buildings along Carl Street (now Burton Place) and transformed them into fanciful Art Deco-style homes. Wealthy industrialist Marshall Field III tried his hand at urban renewal in 1928 by financing 10 five-story buildings on Sedgwick Street. Few poor families could afford the $35 to $63 monthly rents, however, and the managers let most of the flats remain vacant. In 1934 the Chicago Housing Authority's first effort to clean up the slum in western Old Town failed. When the CHA announced plans to clear 67 acres along Halsted Street, residents protested so vehemently that the city backed down. In another form of urban renewal, the development of Carl Sandburg Village beginning in the 1960s along Clark and LaSalle streets, south of North Avenue, heralded the influx of thousands of young singles and families.

A Community Reborn

By the late 1950s, Asian and Hispanic immigrants had joined the ethnic mix in Old Town, and inexpensive rents attracted artists and musicians. In 1947 a group of neighbors decided to raise funds to spruce up a small park on Eugenie Street. They invited "anyone who painted, sculpted, wove or baked" to display and sell their work. The event evolved into the **Old Town Art Fair**, which today attracts artists from around the world and draws thousands of spectators every second weekend of June. The Old Town School of Folk Music opened in 1957 on North Avenue to preserve America's tuneful traditions and introduce music from around the world. (It has since moved and now has centers on Lincoln and Armitage avenues.) In 1959 comedians Paul Sills and Bernie Sahlins relocated their fledgling theater company from Hyde Park to Wells Street and renamed it "The Second City." The troupe, which performs comedy skits based on improvisation, earned rave reviews for its irreverent fast-and-loose style. Over the years The Second City has trained such great comic actors as Alan Arkin, Joan Rivers, John Belushi, Mike Myers, Steve Carrell and Amy Sedaris. Old Town's "artsy" reputation and affordable housing made it a natural choice for hippies of the late 1960s and early 70s. Politica=l bookstores and psychedelic shops sprouted up all along Wells Street. As part of an urban-renewal project in the early 1970s, the city vacated broad Ogden Avenue from North Avenue to Lincoln Park—only 40 years after it slashed through the neighborhood. Housing developments for low-income families shared the newly vacant land with stunning single-family houses designed by Stanley Tigerman and other prominent Chicago architects. In 1976 the **Old Town Triangle**—bordered roughly by the former Ogden Avenue, North and Lincoln Avenues—was declared a Chicago Landmark District, and in 1984 was listed on the National Register of Historic Places, well-deserved recognition for the revived neighborhood.

◄ WALKING TOUR
1.4mi.
A walk through the Old Town Triangle offers a compact glimpse of Chicago's architectural history and gives a sense of the city's mid- to late-19C residential landscape, down to the narrow streets. Indeed, were it not for the high rises that loom on the perimeter of the neighborhood, it would be easy to lose track of the modern city.

▷ *Begin at St. Michael's Church between Hudson and Cleveland Aves.*

St. Michael's Church★
1633 N. Cleveland Ave. ⏰Open daily 7am–7pm. ♿ 🅿 ✆312-642-2498. www.st-mikes.org.
This is the third church building to serve St. Michael's parish since its formation in 1852. When the Great Fire destroyed all but the east, south and west red-brick walls of the second structure finished in 1869, parishioners rallied to rebuild the interior in just a year's time. The steeple was added in 1888, and in 1913 an 8ft statue of St. Michael was placed in a niche high up on the facade. The church's ornate Bavarian Baroque interior is the result of years of renovation.

▷ *When exiting the church, walk east (right) to Hudson Ave., turn left on Hudson and continue to Willow St.*

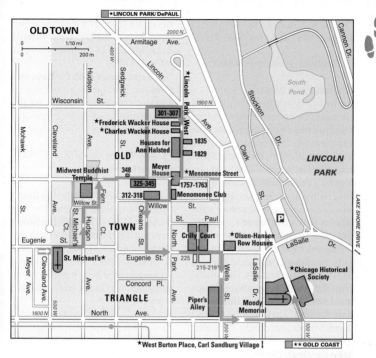

OLD TOWN

1/10 mi

200 m

★LINCOLN PARK/DePAUL

Armitage Ave.

2000 N

400 W

Hudson St.

Sedgwick

Lincoln

Cleveland Ave.

Wisconsin St.

Mohawk

OLD

St.

★Frederick Wacker House
★Charles Wacker House

Houses for
Ann Halsted

301-307

1835

1829

Midwest Buddhist
Temple

348

Meyer
House

★Menomonee Street

325-345

Willow St.

312-318

1757-1763

Menomonee Club

Fern Ct.

St. Michael's Ct.

Hudson Ct.

Willow St.

Orleans St.

TOWN

Eugenie St.

St. Paul St.

North Ave.

Crilly Court

★Olsen-Hansen
Row Houses

Meyer Ave.

Cleveland Ave.

★St. Michael's★

Eugenie St.

Wells St.

LaSalle St.

LaSalle Dr.

225

215-219

★Chicago Historical
Society

Concord Pl.

TRIANGLE

1600 N

North Ave.

Park Ave.

Piper's
Alley

Moody
Memorial

200 N

100 N

Lincoln Park West

1900 N

Clark St.

Stockton Dr.

South
Pond

**LINCOLN
PARK**

P

Cannon Dr.

LAKE SHORE DRIVE /

★West Burton Place, Carl Sandburg Village

★★ GOLD COAST

In temporal, architectural and cultural contrast to St. Michael's stands the **Midwest Buddhist Temple** (435 W. Menomonee St.) built in 1971. Its simple, pagoda-like lines and low profile evoke a Japanese shrine.

▷ *Continue east on Willow St., turn left on Fern Ct., right on Menomonee St. and cross Sedgwick St.*

Menomonee Street★

This quaint street in particular evokes the essence of the historic Old Town. The nine cottages on its south side, **nos. 325–345**, are good examples of the type built in the area during its original settlement, although they were constructed in the years immediately following the fire. These small wooden cottages could be erected in no time using "balloon framing," a Chicago building innovation partially accountable for the rapid growth and combustibility of the city. On the north side of the street, the tiny house at **no. 348** is a rare example of a fire relief shanty, one of 3,000 one-room dwel-

Menomonee Street

© John La Gette/Alamy

lings donated by the Chicago Relief and Aid Society to families left homeless by the fire.

▷ *Proceed north on Orleans St. and turn right on Wisconsin St.*

The brick row houses at **301–307 West Wisconsin Street,** though remodeled, typify the Italianate style popular in late-

167

19C Chicago. Incised sandstone lintels ornament their tall, narrow, bayed fronts.

▷ *Turn right on Lincoln Park West.*

Lincoln Park West★

The well-to-do residents of eastern Old Town built their homes in the open land adjacent to the developing Lincoln Park. Completed in 1874, before the strict fire laws took effect, the ornate **Frederick Wacker House**★ *(no. 1838)* was built by a brewer who embellished its basic form with incised woodwork and other Victorian detail. Next door is the **Charles H. Wacker House**★ *(no. 1836)*, erected by Frederick's son Charles—the city planner for whom Wacker Drive was named—who relocated and remodeled his father's coach house in 1884. To the immediate south, a very different facade spans nos. 1826–1834, the **Houses for Ann Halsted**. These red-brick town houses were designed and built as rental property in 1884 and 1885 by **Louis Sullivan** and **Dankmar Adler** in a simplified Queen Anne style. They represent an early commission for Sullivan, a master of elaborate organic ornamentation, and his hand is especially evident in the terra-cotta stringcourses that top each unit. Across the street, note the handsome and well-preserved Italianate detail on **nos. 1829** and **1835**, both built around the mid-1870s. At the end of the block, the **Henry Meyer House** *(no. 1802)* dates from the same year. Although built as a farmhouse, the abode achieves a sophistication befitting this prosperous neighborhood through the simple decorative touches around its windows.

▷ *Cross Menomonee St. and continue south on North Park Ave.*

Nestled among the town homes and cottages of Old Town are garages and coach houses of the type seen at **1757– 1763 North Park Avenue**. As Chicago's wealthy Gold Coast residents to the east acquired cars in the burgeoning age of the automobile, they built garages and lodgings for chauffeurs on the empty lots in Old Town. This example, which today houses the Old Town Triangle Association, was built for Philip D. Armour in 1915.

The **Menomonee Club for Boys and Girls** *(no. 244)* offers a nondescript wall along North Park Avenue, but the Willow Street facade erupts into an oriel of fanciful woodwork.

▷ *Turn right on Willow St. and continue to Orleans St.*

Built in 1974, a century after Old Town's apost-fire building boom, the row houses at **312–318 West Willow Street** represent the continuing effort to design efficient and comfortable city residences in close quarters. Architect **Harry Weese** modeled these multistory units on London row houses, adding garages at street level.

▷ *Turn left on Orleans St., left again on Eugenie St., and continue to Crilly Ct.*

In 1885 developer Daniel F. Crilly bisected this block with a north-south street and spent the next 10 years erecting residential and commercial space around it. The centerpiece of his **Crilly Court Development** is the line of Queen Anne row houses (1885) along the street's west side. The apartment buildings (1895) across the court bear Crilly's children's names above the entryways. Across Eugenie to the south are four Chicago cottages *(nos. 215–219 and 225)*, all built prior to 1874. Each has the characteristic high basement, steep front staircase and Italianate detail. The wall around no. 225 was added during its renovation.

▷ *Continue east on Eugenie St. to Wells St.*

Across Wells Street, elegant and elaborate Queen Anne row houses flank the north side of Eugenie Street at nos. 164–172. A sharp contrast to the simpler Queen Anne houses in the interior of the Triangle, the **Olsen-Hansen Row Houses**★ (1886) represent the style at its most flamboyant. Irregular rooflines, turrets and a variety of textures, materials and colors adorn the exteriors.

▷ Turn right on Wells St.

Beginning with an existing bakery, architect Stanley Tigerman developed **Piper's Alley** as a multi-use mall between 1974 and 1977. Movie theaters, restaurants, ice-cream shops and gift stores move in and out, but **The Second City** has prevailed at 1616 North Wells Street since 1959. The theater seems to transcend change in this neighborhood where so many other entertainments and diversions have come and gone. Note the terra-cotta heads that ornament the facade; these German philosophers and poets were salvaged from **Adler & Sullivan**'s downtown Schiller Theater when it was demolished in 1961.

▷ Turn left on North Ave. for two blocks, then left again on Clark St.

A wide-open town like mid-19C Chicago attracted its share of evangelists and reformers. Among the revival movement's most powerful voices was that of Dwight Moody, who had come to Chicago in 1856. In 1893 he attracted more than 2 million people to his meetings at the World's Columbian Exposition. **Moody Memorial Church** *(1609 N. LaSalle St.)* testifies to his lasting influence on fundamental Christianity.

Built in 1925, the brick edifice blends elements of Byzantine and Romanesque design, and is said to have been partially inspired by the Hagia Sophia in Istanbul.

▷ Cross Clark St. to the Chicago History Museum to end the walking tour.

Chicago History Museum★

1601 N. Clark St. ◷*Open year-round Mon–Sat 9.30am–4.30pm, Sun noon–5pm.* ⊘*Closed Jan 1, Thanksgiving, Dec 25.* ◈*$14.* ✕&🅿 ☎*312-642-4600. www.chicagohistory.org.*

Sited at the southwestern corner of Lincoln Park, the city's oldest cultural institution presents exhibits and programs that cover the history of Chicago and surroundings. Organized in 1856 by a group of prominent businessmen as the Chicago Historical Society, its collections were damaged in the Great Fire of 1871 and again by fire in 1874. In 1896 the society moved into a Richardsonian Romanesque structure designed by Henry Ives Cobb at Dearborn and Ontario streets. A few decades later, in 1927, the society purchased the vast Gunther Collection of materials relating primarily to the Civil War. To house it, Graham, Anderson, Probst & White designed the institution's Georgian-style east-facing building completed in 1932. A 1971 addition on Clark Street doubled the original space. Aesthetic concerns and the need for yet more room in the 1980s inspired Holabird & Root to create

Chicago History Museum

© City of Chicago/GRC

169

the wraparound facade and the three-story rounded glass-and-steel atrium through which visitors now enter. In 2006, the society unveiled an extensive renovation of its interior exhibit space and announced a name change to the friendlier Chicago History Museum.

A changing exhibit on life in one of Chicago's many neighborhoods greets visitors on the first floor. ▲▲Located around the corner is **Sensing Chicago**, a hands-on, interactive, rough-and-tumble space where kids experience the sights, smells and sounds of the city's history. They can even "become" a Chicago-style hot dog. Also on the first floor, don't miss **Imagining Chicago**, a reinterpretation of the museum's historic dioramas. Originally created by WPA workers in the 1930s, the beautifully crafted scenes depict moments from Chicago's history.

The museum's centerpiece 16,000sq ft exhibit interprets themes in Chicago history, from the days before its settlement to the present. **Chicago: Crossroads of America** displays a colorful array of artifacts from among the 22 million in the collections. Climb aboard the ▲▲**Pioneer locomotive** (Chicago's first train), take a seat on "L" Car No. 1 or listen to Chicago jazz.

ADDITIONAL SIGHTS

Several sights along LaSalle Street, south of North Avenue, are worth noting. The 1927 Art Deco renovations of Sol Kogen and Edgar Miller crowd the cul-de-sac that is **West Burton Place**★, an unusual collection of apartments.

In a complete change of visual scale, **Carl Sandburg Village** looms across LaSalle Street. This expansive agglomeration of high rises, town houses and apartment buildings extending from North Avenue to Division Street was developed between 1960 and 1975. A series of restored houses in the 1300 and 1400 blocks of LaSalle conjures up the elegant late-19C profile of this boulevard. A block farther south, at **no. 1211**, stands a 1929 hotel that was renovated in 1981 as an apartment building. On its eastern and southern walls, Richard

Haas has painted a trompe l'oeil entitled *Homage to the Chicago School of Architecture*. The work's primary elements include, at the top of the southern wall, a depiction of a Louis Sullivan window and, at the bottom, his Golden Doorway from the Transportation Building at the 1893 World's Columbian Exposition. Between the two, Haas painted an imaginary reflection of the Chicago Board of Trade Building, visible two miles south down LaSalle in the financial district.

ADDRESSES

�𝅏/EAT

$ North & Clark Café – *In the Chicago History Museum.* ☎312-642-4600. Located in a sunny corner of the museum, the cafe is a great place to stop for lunch during a walk around the Old Town, a trek through the park or a visit to the museum. The menu lists a variety of salads, sandwiches, grilled items and all-day breakfast.

JOKES & SMOKES

The Second City – *1616 N. Wells St.* ☎312-337-3992. *www.secondcity.com.* Scan the list of Second City "alumni" in the theater's lobby and you will find many famous names. Since the 1950s, comic actors have come to The Second City to learn the art of improvisational comedy. Today the company's best students perform revues featuring skits created from improv games. Scenarios in each show are the same, but the actors vary their performances based on audience feedback.

Up-Down Tobacco Shop – *1550 N. Wells St.* ☎312-337-8025. *www.updown cigar.com.* Since the 1960s, this shop has featured fine smokes from tobacconists around the world. Hand-carved pipes, unique lighters, chic cigarette cases and other smoking paraphernalia are available.

Zanies – *1548 N. Wells St.* ☎312-337-4027. *www.chicago.zanies.com.* The oldest comedy club in the city, this well-worn venue has outlasted a dozen glitzier competitors. Name a stand-up comedian, and chances are he or she has performed at Zanies.

Lincoln Park★★

Unlike many urban areas whose waterfronts have been taken up by industry, Chicago provides unlimited access to the lake via numerous lakefront parks. Among the finest is Lincoln Park. Belying its origins as a soggy cemetery, this sweeping expanse today stretches 6mi and 1,200 acres along the shoreline of Lake Michigan. From Ohio Street north to Ardmore Avenue, Lincoln Park trims the city's watery edge with a pleasant and peaceful greensward. Millions of Chicagoans flock here year-round to enjoy the zoo, conservatory, picnic groves, beaches and playing fields. At North Avenue, the park forms the northern edge of the affluent Gold Coast, and at Clark Street, the eastern boundary of the lively Lincoln Park/DePaul neighborhood, where theaters, restaurants and shops abound.

- ⚑ **Michelin Map:** p173.
- **Info:** Chicago Park District. ☏312-742-7529. www. chicagoparkdistrict.com.
- **Location:** Lake Michigan is always to the east.
- **Parking:** Main parking lots are located north at Fullerton Ave. and Cannon Dr. and south at Stockton Dr. and LaSalle St. Free street parking might be found along Stockton Dr.
- **Kids:** You can't beat a walk in the woods at Lincoln Park Zoo.
- **Timing:** With so much to see, you'll want to plan a day or two.
- **Also See:** Gold Coast, Lincoln Park/DePaul, Old Town, Lakeview/ Wrigleyville.

A BIT OF HISTORY
Back from the Dead

In typical Chicago fashion, Lincoln Park was the product of years of grass-roots activism, a rivalry with New York and copious amounts of landfill. In 1837 the Illinois General Assembly granted the city a large parcel of sand dunes and marshes, between present-day North Avenue and Webster Street, for use as a burial ground. As development crept north toward this remote location, the cemetery's new residential neighbors began to lobby for its closure and conversion into a greensward.

Formation in 1869 of several regional park boards gave the North Side park movement its much-needed impetus. Inspired by Frederick Law Olmsted's Central Park in New York (begun in 1857), the local citizenry, developers and civic leaders banded together and clamored for completion of their lakefront park. Work progressed slowly, since moving the thousands of corpses buried south of Menomonee Street—including Confederate dead from the prisoner-of-war stockade at Camp Douglas on the city's

GETTING THERE
BY L/BUS: ⬛ **Brown** or **Red** line to **Fullerton**, or bus no. 22, 36, 151 or 156.

South Side—proved nearly impossible. Shifting sands, poor records and politics hindered efforts to locate and identify all the graves, and stray bones still turn up today during excavations in the area.

Northward Bound

Named shortly after the assassination of President Abraham Lincoln in 1865, the park grew in stages between 1864 and 1957, at the hands of at least six landscape architects. One of the first sectors to take shape was the old cemetery, today the heart of Lincoln Park. Most corpses had been moved by 1875, and the park's naturalistic style began to emerge: winding pathways, flower beds and ponds, which landscapers **Swain Nelson** and **Olaf Benson** believed would enhance the park's lushness by reflecting the surrounding greenery. Other elements of the modern park appeared: the zoo in 1868, the lagoon in the 1880s. As the adjacent neighborhoods became more populous, landfilling was begun to extend the park northward to Montrose Avenue by 1925, to Foster Avenue by 1936 and to Ardmore Avenue by 1957.

Such extensive landfilling was not undertaken strictly for recreational enjoyment, however. The development of Lake Shore Drive, which today cuts a swath up the lakefront from South to North side, is closely linked with the history of Lincoln Park. The park's promenades and boulevards, designed for quiet strolls and leisurely carriage rides, had been conceived before the automobile. By the 1920s the park's bucolic atmosphere was in jeopardy as daily commuters overburdened its thoroughfares and scenic routes. Lake Shore Drive, today an eight-lane highway, unrolled inexorably up the lakefront, sharing landfill with the park and posing new challenges for planners bent on maintaining a harmonious co-existence between parkland and expressway.

Some balance has been achieved with pedestrian bridges and underpasses, and median landscaping softens the drive itself. The rush of traffic goes unnoticed, however, in this peaceful pleasure ground, where visitors savor lake breezes against a skyline backdrop.

▰▰WALKING TOUR
2.8mi.

▷ *Begin east of the Chicago History Museum (1601 N. Clark St. at North Ave.).*

Augustus Saint-Gaudens' **Standing Lincoln**★ (1887) is a masterpiece and likely the sculptor's finest work. Another of his Lincoln statues resides in Grant Park.

▷ *Take the path heading northwest of the Lincoln statue.*

On a small bluff behind the Chicago History Museum stands the **Couch Mausoleum**. Here rests Ira Couch, pro-

prietor of the Tremont House, Chicago's fashionable mid-19C hotel. The family refused to move his remains when the park was built.

▷ *Continue under LaSalle St. and take the path northeast of the Franklin statue.*

Benjamin Franklin (1896, Richard Henry Park) stands with his back to LaSalle Street.

▷ *Continue up Ridge Dr.*

At the crest of Ridge Drive, a mounted **General Ulysses S. Grant (1)**, the 1891 work of Louis T. Rebisso, surveys the park from atop a massive Romanesque base.

▷ *Continue on Ridge Dr., crossing over South Pond.*

The view★★ south from **South Pond** bridge embodies the city's epithet *Urbs in Horto* ("City in a Garden").

▷ *Continue past Farm-in-the-Zoo, turn right on Stockton Dr. and walk north.*

Café Brauer★
2021 N. Stockton Dr. ◐*Open Memorial Day–Labor Day daily 11am–5pm in good weather.* ⅆ. ℘*312-742-2480.*
Architect Dwight Perkins designed this refectory in 1908 at the behest of restaurateurs Paul and Caspar Brauer. A striking example of the Prairie school style, it hugs South Pond with its main pavilion and two flanking loggias. Arts and Crafts details—chandeliers, tiles, mosaics and windows—lend the interior a suitably rustic charm. A popular gathering place until it closed in the 1940s, the Patio at Café Brauer now offers a sunny spot to relax and enjoy a selection of burgers, kids' meals and wine or beer. In a grove to the northwest sits a bronze **Hans Christian Andersen (2)**, sculpted by John Gelert in 1896.

▷ *Continue north on Stockton Dr. past the Lincoln Park Zoo.*

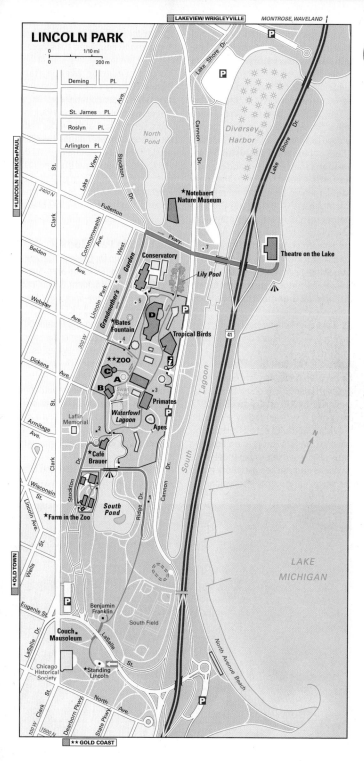

LINCOLN PARK

0   1/10 mi
0   200 m

Deming   Pl.
Ave.
St. James   Pl.
Roslyn   Pl.
Arlington   Pl.

North Pond

Diversey Harbor

Lake Shore Dr.

Cannon Dr.

Stockton Dr.

Lake View St.

2400 N

Clark St.

Fullerton

★ Notebaert Nature Museum

Commonwealth Ave.

West

Lincoln Park

Belden Ave.

Pkwy.   • 7

Conservatory
Lily Pool

Theatre on the Lake

Webster Ave.

Garden
Grandmother's

• 6

★ Bates Fountain

• 5

D

41

Dickens Ave.

300 W

• 4

★★ ZOO

Tropical Birds

C   A

B   Swan Pond

• 3

Primates

South Lagoon

Armitage Ave.

Laflin Memorial

• 2

Waterfowl Lagoon

Apes

Clark St.

Stockton Dr.

★ Café Brauer

Wisconsin St.

Ridge Dr.

Lincoln Ave.

★ Farm in the Zoo

South Pond

Cannon Dr.

LAKE MICHIGAN

Wells St.

Eugenie St.

LaSalle Dr.

Benjamin Franklin

Couch Mausoleum

South Field

LaSalle St.

Chicago Historical Society

★ Standing Lincoln

North Avenue Beach

100 W

Clark St.

1500 N

Dearborn Pkwy.

North

State Pkwy.

Ave.

A broad lawn dominated by a formal garden marks the approach to the **Lincoln Park Conservatory**. South of the garden stands *Johann Christoph Friedrich von Schiller* **(4)**, fashioned in bronze by German sculptor Ernst Bildhauer Rau in 1886. In the center, the **Bates Fountain**★ *(Storks at Play)* presents a joyful tableau *(covered in winter)*. The fountain (1887) is the work of **Augustus Saint-Gaudens.** Since Saint-Gaudens was busy on the *Standing Lincoln*, the credit goes largely to his assistant Frederick MacMonnies. Eli Bates, the Chicago lumber merchant for whom the work was named, left a bequest for both the Lincoln statue and the fountain. Across Stockton Drive, a bronze *William Shakespeare* **(6)** (1894) by William Ordway Partridge rests thoughtfully in the informal **Grandmother's Garden**.

▷ *Continue north on Stockton Dr. to Fullerton Ave. Turn right and walk east.*

Alfred Caldwell Lily Pool

Corner of Fullerton Ave. and Cannon Dr. ⏰*Open daily 7.30am–7.30pm.*
Designed by **Alfred Caldwell** in 1937, this pond is surrounded by a wooded grove, planted with native trees, a tranquil enclave for visitors and migrating birds alike. Low-slung, Japanese-style pavilions and stacked rockwork evoke the site's Prairie school inspiration.

▷ *Exit the Lily Pond, return to Fullerton Ave. and walk east across Lake Shore Dr.*

North of Fullerton Avenue stands **Ellsworth Kelly**'s monolithic stainless steel *I Will* **(7)**, commissioned in 1981, the first new sculpture in Lincoln Park in 30 years. Farther east, at the water's edge, the 384-seat **Theater on the Lake** hosts productions each summer *(𝄋312-742-7995)*. The Prairie school building (1920) first served as the *Chicago Daily News* Fresh Air Sanitarium, located where patients might enjoy the lake's breezes.

SIGHTS
👪 Lincoln Park Zoo★★

2200 N. Cannon Dr. ⏰Memorial Day–Labor Day Mon–Fri 10am–5pm, Sat–Sun & holidays till 6.30pm. Sept–Oct & Apr–May daily 10am–5pm; Nov–Mar daily 10am–4.30pm. ✕♿🅿𝄋312-742-2000. www.lpzoo.org. Parking $17 (30min–3hrs). You can enter the zoo at any of five gates, but we suggest using the entrance off Cannon Dr. on the east or off Stockton Dr. on the west. Both lead to the Main Mall, where you'll find restrooms, stroller rental, concessions and a carousel (⬤$2.75). Pick up a zoo map and information about the day's events at the Gateway Pavilion near the Cannon Drive entrance.
This wonderfully accessible zoo is best enjoyed in an afternoon of wandering.

Lincoln Park Zoo

© Chris McGuire/City of Chicago/GRC

Founded with the gift of a pair of swans from New York's Central Park in 1868, the zoo's collection and agenda today reflect its strong conservation mission, along with aggressive "enrichment" programs, animal activities designed to stimulate natural behaviors. Interpretive labeling focuses sharply on endangered animals and ecological issues.

VISIT

The Main Mall divides the zoo fairly evenly to the north and south. On the south side, beyond the **Kovler Sea Lion Pool (A)** (1889), the 🧒👤 **Pritzker Family Children's Zoo★(B)** takes you on a walk through a 3-acre wood, where regional species dwell—bears, otters, beavers, turtles, snakes and red wolves. Children will find lots of surprising interactivies here, and in the pavilion they can crawl about on the two-story Treetop Climbing Adventure. Nearby, although renovated several times, the **Waterfowl Lagoon** is one of the few remaining elements designed by Swain Nelson in 1865.

The **Regenstein Center for African Apes★★**(Lohan, Caprile, Goettsch Architects, 2004) is a major center of activity. This impressive 29,000sq ft indoor-outdoor habitat houses gorillas in a bamboo forest and chimps who play on 5,000ft of vines, fish for treats in "termite" mounds and scramble around on mud banks. Fun for visitors and apes alike, the center is also part of the zoo's serious commitment to the study and conservation of great apes. In the state-of-the-art Lester E. Fisher Center, the zoo has established a world-class facility for doing just that.

Highlights on the zoo's north side include the **Kovler Penguin and Seabird House★ (C** ,1981) where rockhopper, chinstrap and king penguins rule the 18,000gal pool. **Regenstein African Journey★★(D)** offers a new habitat around every corner, from a dark enclave filled with 10,000 Madagascar hissing cockroaches to a lush, well-populated Tropical Rain Forest. Work continues to transform the South Pond area into **Nature Boardwalk**, a natural ecosystem that will harbor native birds, frogs, mammals and more.

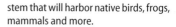

Zoo Facts:
- **Biggest animal:** Binti, an African elephant weighing over 9,350 pounds
- **Smallest animal:** The leaf-cutter ant, less than .5 inch long
- **Total number of lowland gorillas born at the zoo:** 44
- **Number of endangered species at the zoo:** 29
- **Zoo's annual grocery bill:** $285,000

🧒👤 Farm-in-the-Zoo★

1901 N. Stockton Dr. 🕐*Open year-round Mon–Fri 10am–5pm; Sat–Sun & holidays 10am–6.30pm.* ♿ *🕿312-742-2000. www.lpzoo.org.*

This peaceful 5-acre haven, a working farm constructed as part of Lincoln Park Zoo in the 1960s, offers city children a chance to experience rural life. Daily activities include feeding the cows, petting the goats and meeting animals up close *(times are posted)*. Particularly interesting is the **Crown Dairy Barn**, where cows are milked by hand and by machine, yielding fresh milk that feeds the farm's babies. In the **Main Barn** you'll find exhibits on bees, chicks and a John Deere tractor for climbing.

Lincoln Park Conservatory

2391 N. Stockton Dr. 🕐*Open year-round daily 9am–5pm. 🕿312-742-7736. www.chicagoparkdistrict.com.*

Modeled by architect Joseph Lyman Silsbee on London's Crystal Palace, the conservatory (1892) now covers 3 acres. Four main galleries in the glass and copper structure display extensive collections of orchids, palms, ferns and related flora.

🧒👤 Notebaert Nature Museum★

2430 N. Cannon Dr. 🕐*Open year-round Mon–Fri 9am–4.30pm, Sat–Sun 10am–5pm.* 🕐*Closed Jan 1, Thanks-*

giving, Dec 25.✕&⚅$9 (free Thu). ℰ773
-755-5100. www.naturemuseum.org.
This "cluster of wedge-shaped blocks"
was designed by Ralph Johnson of Perkins & Will in 1999 as "an abstraction of
the dunes that used to cover the site."
The museum houses six permanent
exhibits on two levels; outside, the
Greening Project includes a 17,000 sq
ft rooftop garden, a three-story cliff garden, and native flora. Indoors on the first
level, the **Extreme Green House** (con-

tinues upstairs), a life-sized, but offbeat
bungalow, models the green lifestyle
with a house full of fun. **Mysteries of
the Marsh** reveals the secrets of midwestern wetlands.
On level two, the **Judy Istock Butterfly
Haven**★ flutters with some 75 species of
butterflies and moths, and eight types
of bright birds. Next door, **Wilderness
Walk** re-creates a Chicago prairie,
savanna and dune of 200 years ago.

ADDRESSES

ⵟ/EAT

$$$ North Pond Restaurant – 2610 N.
Cannon Dr. ℰ773-477-5845. www.north
pondrestaurant.com. ⏱Closed Mon & Tue
Jan–Apr. Approach by car on Lakeview
Ave.; valet 🅿 available at Deming. Tucked
into Lincoln Park, this little warming hut
has been beautifully converted into a
cozy Arts and Crafts-style jewel with
oak, copper and art-glass accents.
Tall windows look out over the pond,
park and sparkling city skyline. In
winter, reserve a table in the front
room by the roaring fire; or drop by
for lunch on the patio in summer.
Tempting contemporary cuisine fills
the sophisticated market-based menu.

$ Café at Wild Things – At Lincoln
Park Zoo. 312-742-2000. www.lpzoo.org.
The zoo's newest eatery, this seasonal
cafe above the Wild Things gift shop
goes green with sustainable serving
ware and compostable flatware. The

menu follows suit with wraps, salads
and smoothies made from organic and
locally produced ingredients.

🚴🏃RECREATION

Public sports venues (primarily in the
South Field, Waveland and Montrose
areas of the park) include baseball
fields, basketball courts, a soccer field
and tennis courts. The Waveland area
also features a nine-hole **golf course**.
A **bicycle/running path** runs along
the lakefront. Miniature golf and a year-
round driving range are located near
Diversey Harbor.

NORTH AVENUE BEACH

*Access via overpass just north of North
Ave. or via tunnel at North Ave.* This
broad stretch of sand is Chicago's
volleyball mecca. In summer, the Park
District and several private clubs set
up dozens of nets. Many courts are
reserved for league play, but pick-up
games are common.

Volleyballing on North Avenue Beach

© City of Chicago/GRC

Lincoln Park/DePaul ★

The eclectic Lincoln Park/DePaul neighborhood is a checkerboard of lovely residential streets crisscrossed by lively commercial boulevards. From Armitage Avenue on the south to Diversey Parkway on the north, and west to Racine Avenue, Lincoln Park/DePaul is well suited to a pleasant day of walking, window-shopping and noshing. Evenings draw crowds to enjoy music, food and theater.

A BIT OF HISTORY
From Celery to City

Green Bay Road (present-day Clark Street) ran northwest through this territory along the marshy lakefront as early as the 1830s. To the west, German farmers established celery and other vegetable farms. By 1853 the city had annexed the land between North and Fullerton avenues from the lake to the river, and the natural sprawl of the growing metropolis began to shape the area's development. Frame houses supplanted celery gardens, a horsecar line linked the area to downtown, and a public park began to unroll up the lakefront. The Great Fire (1871) devastated the incipient neighborhood before burning itself out at Fullerton Avenue, but the area's location outside the city's strict new fire codes invited speedy recovery. As industry marched up the north branch of the river, German, Irish and Polish workers built cottages in the western reaches of the neighborhood. To the east, well-to-do Germans commissioned fine homes along the edge of the increasingly lovely lakefront preserve known as Lincoln Park.

Catholic Cornerstone

The Presbyterian Theological Seminary was located at Fullerton Avenue and Halsted Street in 1863. Surviving the fire, the seminary (later renamed McCormick in honor of its benefactor, Cyrus H. McCormick, inventor of the reaper) attracted settlers to this distant corner of Chicago, spawned the establishment of several churches, and in 1882, even constructed row houses to let for income. Despite the seminary's influence, the lasting effect on the neighborhood would be wrought by the Vincentian order, which founded St. Vincent de Paul parish in 1875. In 1898 the fathers established St. Vincent's College, from which grew DePaul University, today a cornerstone of the Lincoln Park community.

Location, Location

Over the years the neighborhood grew in both area and population. The city annexed the blocks between Fullerton Avenue and Diversey Parkway in 1889. Ethnic diversity increased as working-class Romanians, Greeks, Italians, Poles, Hungarians, Serbs and African Americans discovered the convenience and affordability of the neighborhood. However, new housing didn't keep pace with the swelling population and

Michelin Map: p179.

Location: The major commercial boulevards—particularly Armitage Ave. and Diversey Parkway, Halsted St. and the two diagonals, Lincoln Ave. and Clark St.—are full of bookstores and boutiques, bars and bistros. Lincoln Avenue and Clark St. slice the neighborhood roughly in pie-shaped thirds. To their west, DePaul University serves as a major focus.

Parking: Street parking is hard to find, so plan on doing it once and walking.

GETTING THERE

BY L/BUS: CTA Brown or Red line to **Fullerton**, or bus no. 22 or 36.

Biograph Theater on July 22, 1934, soon after John Dillinger was killed

© Bettmann/Corbis

Markers of a Dubious Past

Two neighborhood addresses figure prominently in Chicago's gangland history: 2122 N. Clark Street, the site of the garage (since demolished) where the St. Valentine's Day Massacre took place in 1929; and 2433 N. Lincoln Avenue— the Biograph Theater—where federal agents gunned down "public enemy number one" John Dillinger on July 22, 1934.

the existing buildings suffered from overuse. Except for the luxury residences east of Clark Street, Lincoln Park grew dilapidated.

The area's intrinsic advantages, however, served it well. Location, accessibility and a basic architectural soundness stimulated interest, and conservation associations formed to encourage renovation efforts. In 1956 the community was designated an urban-renewal area. Rehabilitation, and the companion phenomenon of "gentrification," proceeded so successfully that Lincoln Park is today one of Chicago's most desirable, attractive, high-priced—and congested—neighborhoods. In the late 1990s Lincoln Park saw a resurgence in the construction of palatial residences, the likes of which had not been seen here since the early 20C.

Boutiques and night spots now populate this area; the former on Armitage Avenue west of Halsted, the latter along Lincoln Avenue between Webster and Belden avenues.

DEPAUL UNIVERSITY

2400 W. Sheffield Ave. ⟋ Campus tours depart from the Welcome Center. ⟐ Open Mon–Fri 11am & 3pm, Sat 10.30am & 11.30am.
⟋ 312-363-8000. www.depaul.edu.
Chartered in 1907 as DePaul University from St. Vincent's College, the campus grew outward from the limestone church buildings in the 1000 block of West Webster Avenue, where the Romanesque Revival **St. Vincent de Paul Church** (1897, James J. Egan) towers over the block.

Today the 36-acre Lincoln Park campus is the largest of six DePaul campuses in the Chicago area. It extends between Montana Street and Webster Avenue and Racine Avenue and Halsted Street. Major buildings face a pedestrian mall created in the 2,300 block of Seminary Avenue in 1992.

DePaul acquired the land east of the elevated tracks from the McCormick Theological Seminary when it moved to Hyde Park in 1973. Embedded in the property is **Chalmers Place**★, a verdant block of privately owned town houses that were originally built by the seminary to generate income. An unembellished blend of Queen Anne and Romanesque Revival styling, their facades of smooth brown brick face each other with no-nonsense solidarity on either side of a parklike square. The two freestanding houses at the eastern end of the square *(834 and 835 W. Chalmers Pl.)* were constructed in the 1880s for faculty members.

LINCOLN AVENUE/ CLARK STREET

Between Lincoln Avenue and Clark Street stand some of the area's most interesting private homes, apartment buildings and churches. On **Cleveland Avenue**, note no. 2147, the **Leon Mannheimer House**, which bears the unmistakable decorative hallmarks of Louis Sullivan, whose firm designed it in 1884. At no. 2150, the **Walter Guest House** was remodeled in 1932 by Edgar Miller. Incised chevrons embellish the expansive leaded-glass windows, and a close look at the front door reveals a frolic of Miller's favorite animals.

The **Ann Halsted House** (1883) at 440 West Belden Avenue is another Adler & Sullivan commission, ornamented along its gable with the firm's signature lotus motif. **The Cobden** apartment building (1892, Charles S. Frost) spans 418 to 424

West Belden and bends around the corner along Clark Street. The Belden Avenue facade is interesting for its surface decoration, undulating bays and crowning gable. At 2325 North Clark Street, the whimsical **Reebie Storage and Moving Co.** warehouse was designed in 1923 in an unabashed celebration of the opening of King Tut's tomb in 1922. The two statues of Ramses II are said to represent the Reebie brothers; hieroglyphics below the right one read, "I give protection to your furniture!"

Since the 1880s **Fullerton Parkway**★ between Clark Street and Lincoln Avenue has been a pleasant street of elegant homes, trees and gardens. Two hardy Romanesque-style churches dominate adjacent blocks: the Episcopal **Church of Our Saviour** (1888) at no. 530 and the **Lincoln Park Presbyterian Church** (1888) at no. 600. Two blocks north, at Deming Place and Orchard Street, **St. Clement Roman Catholic Church**★ (1918), constructed of smooth limestone with twin towers and rose window in the French Romanesque style, boasts

spectacular mosaics and murals. The houses along **Deming Place**★ recall an elegant era; the oldest were built in the 1880s and 90s by successful German businessmen.

CLARK STREET/ LAKEVIEW AVENUE

The 30-story glass and steel structure at **2400 North Lakeview Avenue** (1963) is the last residential high rise designed by **Ludwig Mies van der Rohe** in Chicago. At no. 2466 the **Theurer/Wrigley House**★ (1896) dominates the corner of Arlington Place. Italian Renaissance elegance swaddles its sturdy steel and concrete underpinnings, and a glimpse into the **solarium**★ at the southwest corner hints at the decorative detail inside. Chewing-gum magnate William Wrigley, Jr. purchased the home from brewer Joseph Theurer in 1911. The Wrigley family occupied it until the 1930s when, supposedly, threats of kidnapping necessitated the move to a more secure apartment residence.

The fairy-tale quality of the **Francis J. Dewes House**★ (1896) at 503 West Wrightwood Avenue is perhaps exaggerated by the surrounding modern city. Crisp white Bedford limestone contrasts with a dark slate mansard roof and cast-iron railings. The house's zest, however, derives from its extravagant Baroque detailing, particularly the two disproportionate figures that flank the front door and the elaborate variety of window decoration. Dewes was a German brewer who no doubt hired his architects, German **Adolph Cudell** and Hungarian Arthur Hercz, for their familiarity with European decorative traditions.

At 2750 North Lakeview Avenue, an entirely different architectural spectacle commands the corner at Diversey Parkway. The **Elks Veterans Memorial**★ (◷open Apr 15–Nov 15 Mon–Fri 9am–5pm, weekends 10am–5pm; rest of the year Mon–Fri 9am–5pm; ◷closed major holidays; contribution requested; ♿ P ℘773-755-4876; www.elks.org/mem orial) was completed in 1926 to honor Elks brethren who served in World War I, now re-dedicated to veterans of all succeeding American military conflicts. Inside the relatively sedate Neoclassical Indiana limestone exterior, not a square inch of wall, window or ceiling surface remains undecorated. In the rotunda and reception room, 26 varieties of marble and lavishly carved oak paneling dazzle the visitor, along with gilded statuary, elaborate murals and art-glass windows.

ADDRESSES

⊕ENTERTAINMENT

Kingston Mines – 2548 N. Halsted St. ℘773-477-4646. www.kingstonmines. com. Frequented by top-notch musicians and regular folk, this ramshackle blues club features live music until 4am (5am on Saturday). Seven nights a week, two top local bands take turns playing on the club's two stages. The place fills up quickly, and at 2am fans pour in from B.L.U.E.S. across the street, so arrive early to get a good seat.

B.L.U.E.S. – 2519 N. Halsted St. ℘773-528-1012. www.chicagobluesbar.com. You feel like you can reach out and touch the performers in this tiny, smoky club. Quality players from across the city and a friendly, but down-and-dirty, atmosphere make this one of the most popular blues bars in town. Arrive early on weekend nights if you want to score a stool at the long bar. On Sunday night, you can do two clubs for the price of one: pay the cover at B.L.U.E.S. and get into Kingston Mines free.

Steppenwolf Theatre – 1650 N. Halsted St. ♿ ℘312-335-1650. www.steppenwolf.org. John Malkovich, Laurie Metcalf and Gary Sinise are members of this acclaimed local troupe, which is renowned for the intensity of its performers. The company offers productions of classic and contemporary plays in its state-of-the-art 515-seat Downstairs Theatre and in its more intimate 299-seat Upstairs Theatre. Steppenwolf showcases the work of new playwrights in its Garage Theatre, a converted space on the first floor of the parking structure.

Milwaukee Avenue Corridor

A broad, bustling and colorful artery, Milwaukee Avenue was named for an Indian trail that led to Milwaukee, Wisconsin. The avenue has been the spine of a working-class immigrant community on the Northwest Side since its first settlement in the mid-19C. Historically Polish and currently Hispanic, the neighborhood extending from Chicago Avenue to Belmont Avenue remains a melting pot of diverse cultures and rich streetscapes, confirming Chicago's image as a city of neighborhoods and attracting a wide cross-section of residents.

- **Michelin Map:** p181.
- **Location:** Milwaukee runs roughly parallel to I-90/I-94.
- **Parking:** Some street parking is restricted to residents; mind the signs.
- **Don't Miss:** A stroll through the busy greensward called Wicker Park.
- **Timing:** Driving and walking tours can be done in half a day.
- **Also See:** Lakeview/Wrigleyville.

A BIT OF HISTORY

A Growing Enclave

Lured by industries along the North Branch of the Chicago River, immigrant laborers from Germany began to settle the West Town neighborhood along Milwaukee Avenue following the revolutions of 1848, and the street became known as "Dinner Pail Avenue." Polish immigrants arrived in the 1860s and soon created St. Stanislaus Kostka parish near Division Street. While simple laborers' cottages mushroomed along the avenue, the area around Wicker Park, donated to the city by real estate developers **Joel and Charles Wicker** in 1870, became an enclave of grand mansions constructed by German and Scandinavian businessmen. As the number of Poles steadily increased, Germans and Scandinavians left, following the avenue north and west and establishing the migratory pattern for other immigrant groups.

The development of the West Side Parks and Boulevard System—which was designed to ring the city with broad avenues and greenswards—after 1871 attracted many successful Norwegian and Swedish immigrants, who settled around Humboldt Park and **Logan Square** after 1900. More than eight Polish parishes filled the dense corridor, and 5,000 families attended St. Stanislaus alone. Some 250,000 people, including Russian Jews, Ukrainians, Slovaks and Italians in addition to Polish residents, lived within walking distance of the intersection of Milwaukee and Ashland avenues, the "Polish Downtown," home to local groups and every major Polish-American organization in the nation.

Decline and Transformation

By the 1930s the lower portion of the Milwaukee Avenue Corridor had fallen into decline. Chicago author **Nelson Algren** documented the sordid street life around Wicker Park in the 1940s in his novels and short stories. By the 1960s Puerto Ricans flocked into West Town and Humboldt Park, pushing other immigrants to the northwest to follow the pattern of migration established back in the late 19C. "Urban pioneers" began rehabilitating the Victorian mansions—many built by German and Polish beer barons—of Wicker Park and Logan Square in the late 1970s, when both were listed on the National Register of Historic Places. In the following decade, Wicker Park came to the forefront as an artists' mecca, attracting galleries and theaters that had been priced out of Lincoln Park/DePaul and River West. Today the area has gone from bohemian to affluent with trendy shops and restaurants.

ing extensive community protest, the Kennedy Expressway was routed around the edifice, thereby saving the city's oldest Polish church (1877).

Across the street, Pulaski Park is one of a series of green spaces developed in the 1910s to provide recreational facilities for the poor. Its most prominent feature, the 1912 **Pulaski Park Fieldhouse**, was designed by William Carbys Zimmerman and incorporates elements of the Tudor and Prairie styles.

> ⊳ *Return to Division St. and turn right.*

🚗 DRIVING TOUR

5.8mi (including 1mi 🚶walking tour).

The tour covers a variety of ethnic neighborhoods and an eclectic mix of architecture, cultural sights and shops. Although long sections of the avenue resemble most urban streetscapes with nondescript buildings, discount warehouses and fast-food restaurants, you'll discover some hidden gems.

> ⊳ *Begin at the intersection of Milwaukee Ave. and Augusta Blvd.*

Polish Museum of America

984 N. Milwaukee Ave. ⊙*Open year-round Fri–Wed 11am–4pm.* ⊙*Closed major holidays.* ⊗*$7.* ♿🅿 ✆*773-384-3352. www.polishmuseumofamerica.org.* Located on the upper floors of the Polish Roman Catholic Union of America headquarters, one of the oldest and largest ethnic museums in the US encompasses an extensive collection of fine arts and historical artifacts, from Hussar armor to materials related to the life of pianist **Ignacy Jan Paderewski** (1860–1941).

> ⊳ *Drive northwest on Milwaukee Ave. to Division St. Turn right, then left on Noble St.*

At 1255 Noble Street rises **St. Stanislaus Kostka Catholic Church**, a large brick structure covered with stucco. Follow-

The intersection of Milwaukee Avenue and Division Street marks the heart of the former Polish Downtown.

Just west of Wolcott Street, the **Division Street Russian & Turkish Baths** *(no. 1916)* still offer old-world sauna treatments in a 1907 terra-cotta building (❌🅿 ✆*773-384-9671; www.chicago russiansauna.com).*

> ⊳ *Turn left on Leavitt St.*

The neighborhood of simple, red brick two-flats with neatly groomed lawns, located south of Division Street between Damen and Western Avenues, is known as the **Ukrainian Village**. Built and settled by Ukrainian immigrants after 1900, especially by Catholics from the Carpathian Mountains, the neighborhood's quiet streets and gardens still house Ukrainian families. The **Ukrainian National Museum** *(2249 W. Superior St.;* ⊙*open Thu–Sun 11am–4pm, Mon–Wed by appointment;* ♿ ✆*773-421-8020; www.ukrainiannationalmuseum.org)* displays a number of historic artifacts, costumes, ceramics and *pysanky* (decorated Easter eggs).

Holy Trinity Russian Orthodox Cathedral★

1121 N. Leavitt St. ✆*773-486-6064. www.holytrinitycathedral.net. Tours Sat 11am–4pm.*

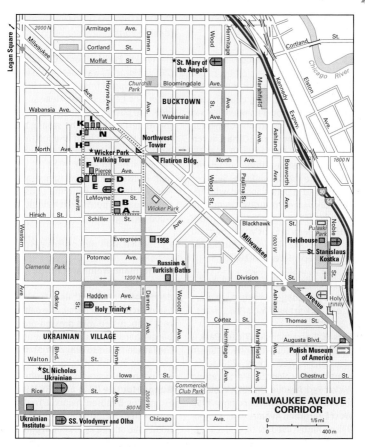

Map labels:

2000 N · Logan Square · Milwaukee · Armitage Ave. · Cortland St. · Moffat St. · Damen · Wood · Hermitage · Cortland St. · Chicago River · Elston · Kennedy Expwy. · ★ St. Mary of the Angels · Churchill Park · Bloomingdale Ave. · Hoyne Ave. · Marshfield · BUCKTOWN · Wabansia Ave. · St. · Ave. · Wabansia Ave. · Ashland · Ave. · Ave. · 1600 N · Bosworth · K L · J M N · H · North Ave. · ★ Wicker Park Walking Tour · Northwest Tower · ← · F · Flatiron Bldg. · North Ave. · Wood St. · Paulina St. · Ave. · 90 · 94 · G · E · D · Leavitt · Pierce · C · Ave. · LeMoyne St. · B · Wicker Park · Hirsch St. · A · Schiller St. · Blackhawk St. · Pulaski Park · Western · Evergreen · 1958 · Milwaukee · 1600 W · Fieldhouse · St. Stanislaus Kostka · Noble St. · Clemente Park · Potomac Ave. · Russian & Turkish Baths · Division St. · 1200 N · ← · Wolcott · Ashland · Holy Trinity · Haddon Ave. · Damen · ★ Holy Trinity ★ · Cortez St. · Thomas St. · Oakley · UKRAINIAN VILLAGE · St. · Hoyne · Ave. · Hermitage · Marshfield · Augusta Blvd. · Walton Blvd. · St. · Iowa St. · Ave. · Ave. · Polish Museum of America · Chestnut St. · ★ St. Nicholas Ukrainian · Rice St. · Ave. · 2000 W · Commercial Club Park · 800 W · MILWAUKEE AVENUE CORRIDOR · Ukrainian Institute · SS. Volodymyr and Olha · Chicago Ave. · Ave. · 0 — 1/5 mi · 0 — 400 m

---

This tiny jewel, designed by Louis Sullivan in 1899, combines his decorative aesthetic with the form of a rural Russian church. The tower topped by an onion dome is trimmed in yellow, while the building's walls are covered in white stucco. The edifice was constructed with a donation of $4,000 from Czar Nicholas II and became a base for Patriarch Tikhon, who was later beatified.

▷ *Turn right on Rice St. and continue to Oakley Ave.*

At Oakley and Rice stands **St. Nicholas Ukrainian Catholic Cathedral**★, the mother church for Ukrainian Catholics in Chicago. The soaring structure features 13 domes symbolizing Christ and his disciples. Built in 1915 by architects Worthmann, Steinbach & Piontek,

St. Nicholas was restored in 1975 and mosaics were added in 1988.

▷ *Continue on Rice St. to Western Ave. Turn left on Western Ave. and left again on Chicago Ave.*

At 2320 West Chicago Avenue stands the **Ukrainian Institute of Modern Art** (🕙open year-round Wed–Sun noon–4pm; 🕙closed major holidays; contribution requested; ♿ 🅿 ✆773-227-5522. www.uima-art.org).
Founded in 1971 and presenting works by artists of Ukrainian descent, the respected museum is located in a one-story building in the heart of Ukrainian Village. Rotating exhibits occupy the large gallery to the left of the entrance, while three connected galleries to the right display the permanent collection

of drawings, paintings, sculpture and multimedia artworks.

▷ Continue east on Chicago Ave.

In the 1960s reforms of Vatican II split the Ukrainian Catholic congregation, and the traditionalists built a new edifice two blocks south of St. Nicholas Cathedral. **Saints Volodymyr and Olha Church** *(739 N. Oakley Ave.)* opened in 1975. Simpler in design, a huge gold dome crowns the massive edifice. Services are still held in Ukrainian, and worshippers follow the Orthodox (Gregorian) calendar. The arched mosaic above the entrance depicts Saint Volodymyr and his mother Olha blessing the Rus people in the Dnieper River in AD 988.

▷ East on Chicago Ave. Turn left on Damen Ave. Continue north to Schiller St. and park to tour Wicker Park on foot.

A small, 3-acre triangle, **Wicker Park** is lined with impressive stone Victorian mansions as well as early-20C apartment buildings along Schiller Street and Wicker Park Avenue. One block south is the red-brick three-flat building at **1958 West Evergreen Avenue** where author Nelson Algren lived for three decades.

▷ Walk west on Schiller St. and turn right on Hoyne Ave.

A city and national landmark, the **Wicker Park**★ neighborhood contains many mansions commissioned by prosperous German and Scandinavian immigrants in the late 19C. Occupying a spacious corner lot at the intersection of Schiller Street and Hoyne Avenue, the **John H. Rapp House**★ *(1407 N. Hoyne Ave.)*, built in 1879 by a wine merchant in the Second Empire style, sports a mansard roof, domed tower, elaborate wood brackets and trim, and a cast-iron porch and fence. Built in the 1880s for a Norwegian furniture maker, **no. 1427 (B)** is an eclectic design reflecting Romanesque as well as Victorian detailing; note the workmanship of the wood and pressed-metal porch.

▷ Cross LeMoyne St. and then continue north.

The **Wicker Park Lutheran Church (C)** *(2112 LeMoyne St.)* was built in 1906 with granite salvaged from a brothel in the notorious Levee on the Near South Side. The pastor reportedly defended the material, saying the stones had "served the devil long enough, now let them serve the Lord." The Second Empire mansion at **no. 1520 (D)** was built in 1886 for Russian lumberman Henry Grusendorf. Note the unusual double-gabled porch, with its intricate wood carvings.

▷ Turn left. Walk west on Pierce Ave.

The **Hermann Weinhardt House**★ **(E)** at no. 2135 (1889, William Ohlhaber) defines ostentation with its unflinching use of architectural detail. The gabled roof is encrusted with pressed-metal bargeboards, and every element of the facade seems to drip with decorative forms in brick, metal or wood. The profusion of balustrades on the **John D. Runge House**★ **(F)** at no. 2138 (1884, Frommann & Jebsen) helped advertise the owner's wood-milling firm. The home later served as the Polish Consulate and hosted a veranda concert by the Polish pianist Ignacy Paderewski in 1930. The Romanesque Revival **Theodore Juergens House (G)** at no. 2141 (1895, Henry T. Kley) features gargoyles and a third-floor ballroom.

▷ Turn right on Leavitt St. and walk north to Concord Pl., one block past North Ave.

The two short blocks of Concord Place and Caton Street were developed by wealthy Scandinavians after 1890. Today their incongruous location behind shops and elevated rail tracks belies their former elegance. Built in 1893, **2156 West Concord Place (H)** features a conical tower and gabled dormer.

▷ Continue north to Caton St. and turn right.

The large mansion at **2159 West Caton Street (J)** was erected two years earlier in the Queen Anne style. Norwegian merchant Ole Thorp developed Caton Street and lived in the large home distinguished by a domed turret at **no. 2156 (K)** (1891, Faber & Pagels). The same architectural firm also designed **no. 2146 (L)**, a red brick Romanesque Revival home with carved column capitals; and the pink sandstone and brick Queen Anne structure at **no. 2142 (N)**.

◗ *Turn right on Milwaukee Ave. and walk south to North Ave.*

The heart of artistic Wicker Park is the intersection of Milwaukee, Damen and North avenues, defined by the 12-story Art Deco **Northwest Tower** (1929, Perkins, Chatten & Hammond), centerpiece of the biannual "Around the Coyote" tour of galleries and artists' lofts. The two-story terra-cotta **Flatiron Building** on the southeast corner of Milwaukee and North Avenues is home to Around the Coyote Gallery, at 2,400sq ft a major center for art and performance.

◗ *Return to car along Damen Ave. Drive north on Damen Ave., right on North Ave., then left on Hermitage Ave.*

Located north of North Avenue between Milwaukee and Ashland avenues, **Bucktown** was a largely Polish working-class community that experienced a real estate boom in the late 1980s as yuppies and artists moved into the quaint brick homes and quiet streets. Stately **St. Mary of the Angels Catholic Church** ★ (1850 N. Hermitage Ave.) dominates the streetscape of Bucktown. The brown brick and white terra-cotta edifice, completed in 1920 by Polish Catholics in a Roman Baroque style and restored in 1992, features a twin-towered facade with an elaborate portico, 9ft-high terra-cotta angels ringing the parapet, and a huge dome and cupola modeled on St. Peter's Basilica in Rome. The interior paintings and elaborate decoration well illustrate the exuberant Baroque style.

ADDRESSES

BOOKSTORES / ♀/ CAFES

The artsy inhabitants of greater Wicker Park have mastered the art of hanging out, and this neighborhood's various haunts deserve a peek inside, if just to people-watch.

Book-lovers should check out **Myopic Books** (1564 N. Milwaukee Ave.; ☎773-862-4882; www.myopicbookstore. com), which has its own cafe and stays open until 1am; **Quimby's Bookstore** (1854 W. North Ave.; ☎773-342-0910; www.quimbys.com) specializing in small press and underground magazines; and the **Occult Book Store** (1164 N. Milwaukee Ave.; ☎773-292-0995; www.occultbookstore.com) for its works on witchcraft, tarot and all things eerie.

Cafe culture in Wicker Park runs the gamut from bohemian/student to staid/banker. **$ Earwax** (1561 N. Milwaukee Ave.; ☎773-772-4019; www.earwax-cafe.com) is the preferred meeting place for vegans, vegetarians and struggling musicians; while many of the neighborhood's denizens frequent the **$ The Northside Bar and Grill** (1635 N. Damen Ave.; ☎773-384-3555; www.northsidechicago.com) for their half-pound Original Big Burger. Daily drink specials and flavorful Mexican food bring the after-work crowd to **$$ Adobo Grill** (200 W. Division St. at Damen Ave.; ☎773-252-9990; www.adobogrill.com).

♫ NIGHTCLUBS

At night, people from across the city flock to the neighborhood's clubs and taverns. Originally a polka lounge, the **Rainbo Club** (1150 N. Damen Ave.; ☎773-489-5999) now specializes in indie rock, as does the **Empty Bottle** (1035 N. Western Ave.; ☎773-276-3600; www.emptybottle.com).

On the fringes of Ukrainian Village, the Bottle books an eclectic mix of experimental jazz, hot local rock acts and bands on the brink. The **Double Door** (1572 N. Milwaukee Ave.; ☎773-489-3160; www.doubledoor.com) rocks with new and promising musicians, along with local favorites.

Lakeview/ Wrigleyville

A dense residential district on Chicago's North Side lakefront, this popular area can be both upbeat and offbeat. Wrigley Field lends its name to the northern blocks, which extend from Diversey Boulevard to Irving Park Road. Graceland Cemetery (established in 1860) offers a unique glimpse into the city's history, art and architecture.

A BIT OF HISTORY

Settled by Germans in the 1830s, Lakeview began as a center of celery farming. Incorporated in 1857 the township was named for the 1854 Lake View House Hotel, a glamorous resort hotel built on the shores of Lake Michigan at present-day Grace Street. The late 19C witnessed the gradual transformation of the quiet lakefront community into a residential neighborhood, spurred by real-estate developers who offered cheap frame houses outside Chicago's fire district.

By the 1960s much of the North Side was in decline. The opening of theaters, clubs and restaurants in the 1970s, however, fueled reinvestment. The neighborhood around historic Wrigley Field, promoted as "Wrigleyville" by apartment redeveloper Seymour Persky, attracted a young crowd in search of affordable digs. Large

- ⚬ **Michelin Map:** p188.
- 🅿 **Parking:** Close to impossible on the street. Take the "L" to Addison.
- ⚬ **Don't Miss:** A Cubs game at Wrigley, if you can get tickets!
- 🕐 **Timing:** Allow a half day.
- ⚬ **Also See:** Lincoln Park/ DePaul and Lincoln Park.

Victorian homes on Hawthorne Place and Hutchinson Street and in the Buena Park area were restored. Gleaming high rises sprouted along the lakefront, which was gradually gentrified north to Irving Park Road. Today Lakeview/ Wrigleyville is best known for its many entertainment options.

SIGHTS

These far-flung sights are best seen by car.

Hawthorne Place District★

Between Broadway and Lake Shore Dr.
Benjamin and John McConnell developed this landmark district of sprawling houses and gardens as Lakeview's showpiece in 1883. Victorian mansions include the **George E. Marshall House (A)** *(no. 574)*, completed in 1886 by Burnham & Root, and the 1884 **Benjamin F. McConnell House (B)** *(no. 568)*, clad in shingles and clapboards. Dating from

Graceland Cemetery

© Steve Geer/iStockphoto.com

the 1890s, the Queen Anne **Herman H. Hettler House (C)** *(no. 567)* owned by the adjacent Chicago City Day School, retains its original corner turret, curving veranda and stone foundation. The **John McConnell House (D)** *(no. 546)*, built in 1885 for the developer and mayor of Lakeview, was extensively renovated in 1993.

Just around the corner, at 3480 North Lake Shore Drive, stands **Temple Sholom**★, a Byzantine-style octagon clad in yellow ashlar limestone that is covered with intricate ornamentation. Designed in 1930 by Loebl, Schlossman & Demuth, this large structure provides an elegant break in the endless wall of lakefront high rises.

Wrigley Field★

1060 W. Addison St. Tours depart from Gate D (call or check online for schedule). Open late-Apr–Oct. $25. 773-404-2827. www.cubs.com.
Built as Weeghman Field for the Chicago Whales of the Federal League before occupied by the Cubs of the National League in 1916, this stadium (1914, Zachary Taylor Davis) is a North Side icon. Many of the adjacent buildings boast rooftop clubs where members watch the game over the outfield walls. The community stonewalled the addition of lights for night baseball until 1988.

Alta Vista Terrace★

3800 block, between Grace and Byron Sts.
Joseph C. Brompton designed the city's first protected landmark district in 1904 as a single work of architecture. Each side of the street contains 20 homes mirrored diagonally on the facing side. The Roman brick homes are 20ft wide and two stories high, except for the four central, three-story limestone structures. Basically Georgian in style, the homes nevertheless exhibit a rich variety of details from the Byzantine, Neoclassical, Gothic and Renaissance styles as well as colorful rooflines.

Graceland Cemetery★★

Map below. 4001 N. Clark St. Open year-round daily 8am–4.30pm (office closed Sun). 773-525-1105. www.gracelandcemetery.org.
One of Chicago's most evocative sites contains notable architecture and sculpture marking the final resting places of many of the city's movers and shakers. The wealthy neighbors of Prairie Avenue and the Gold Coast, including the Palmers, Fields, McCormicks and Pullmans, are once again neighbors here, joined by renowned architects William Le Baron Jenney, Daniel Burnham, John W. Root, Louis Sullivan and Mies van der Rohe. Developed in 1860, Graceland received many reburials from the site of Lincoln Park. Its 119 acres were redesigned after 1883 in a picturesque, naturalistic style by Ossian Cole Simonds.

Lorado Taft sculpted the haunting *Eternal Silence* memorial for hotel owner Dexter Graves in 1909, and the heroic Crusader in 1931 for the grave of *Daily News* founder Victor F. Lawson. Louis Sullivan's masterful **Getty Tomb**★ (1890) was commissioned by lumber merchant Henry Harrison Getty following his wife Carrie Eliza's death. **George Pullman**'s Corinthian column and exedra by **Solon S. Beman** cover a maze of concrete and steel designed to prevent angry workers from disinterring the railroad magnate. Sports legends

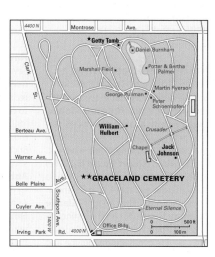

187

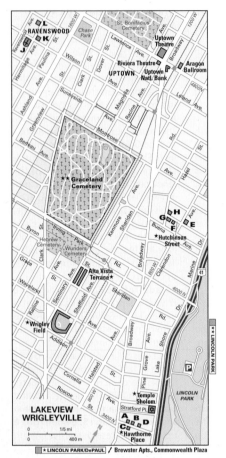

Maher's signature flattened-arch entrance. Maher's 1909 **Grace Brackebush House (G)** *(no. 839)* marks the integration of picturesque period revival elements with the horizontal emphasis of the Prairie school. The 1894 **John C. Scales House (H)** *(no. 840)* resembles a Queen Anne home replete with shingles and round turrets.

ADDITIONAL SIGHTS
Uptown

Known for its great live music venues, this ethnically diverse neighborhood borders the north end of Lakeview. On Broadway, the restored **Uptown National Bank** (4753 N. Broadway; 1924, Marshall & Fox) uses white terra-cotta in a Neoclassical composition, with a curving corner entrance.

The once majestic **Uptown Theatre** (4814 N. Broadway; 1925, Rapp & Rapp) awaits renovation of its 4,400-seat interior. A former hot spot for ballroom dancing, the 1926 Moorish-style **Aragon Ballroom** at 1106 W. Lawrence Avenue now hosts a regular schedule of major rock-and-roll acts, as does the **Riviera Theatre** *(4746 N. Broadway)*, a former movie palace also designed by Rapp & Rapp (1918).

buried here include boxing great **Jack Johnson** and National League founder **William Hulbert**, who lies beneath a large baseball.

Hutchinson Street District★
Between Lake Shore Dr. and Hazel St.
Several designs by Prairie school architect **George Washington Maher**, together with a range of eclectic, single-family houses, provide a welcome diversion from the high-rise lakefront. The **Edwin J. Mosser House (E)** (1902) at no. 750, features oversized urns and a Sullivanesque entrance facing Clarendon Street. At no. 817, the two-story **Claude Seymour House (F)** (1913) is distinguished by banded leaded-glass windows, urns, a wide overhanging roofline and

Ravenswood
Several structures along Hermitage Avenue are worth the trip to Ravenswood, a rediscovered residential area stretching to the west of Uptown. The distinctive 1883 **All Saints Episcopal Church (J)** *(no. 4550)* is a rare Chicago example of Stick-style architecture. Across the intersection, the grand Victorian **Wallace C. Abbott House (K)** *(no. 4605)* was built by the founders of Abbott Laboratories. At no. 4646 stands the **Carl Sandburg House (L)**, a nondescript three-flat where the famous author composed his *Chicago Poems* in 1916.

West Side

Near West Side

Located west and south of the Loop, this neighborhood is bounded by the Chicago River on the east, 16th Street on the south, Ogden Avenue on the west and Kinzie Street on the north. Largely unscathed by the Great Fire of 1871, it has faced other agents of change throughout its history. Encroaching immigrant communities eventually supplanted the "West Side Gold Coast" above Harrison Street, while over the years a number of urban-renewal projects has neutralized the ethnic neighborhoods to the south. However, through the many layers of progress and blight peek the remnants of Chicago's old West Side.

A BIT OF HISTORY
A Study in Contrasts

Most of the Near West Side was included in the incorporation of Chicago in 1837. The Irish arrived in the 1840s and 50s to work in the lumber mills, railroad yards and other riverside industries. Their frame cottages and barns crowded west to Halsted Street and south to Roosevelt Road, establishing the area as a port of entry for immigrants until well into the 20C. Meanwhile, mere blocks to the north and west, the city's merchant class built elegant homes along Washington and Ashland boulevards. Developers widened and paved the streets, installed sewers and planted trees; horsecar lines provided transport to the central city.

In 1871, a fire ignited in the O'Leary barn on DeKoven Street in the heart of the Irish district. The blaze spread rapidly, consuming thousands of wooden shanties along Clinton and Canal streets, but jumped the river and headed northeast without damaging more of the West Side. Spared the flames, the neighborhood provided refuge for thousands of fire victims; the population soared to 200,000 and construction boomed. The wealthy continued to build fine homes along the northern boulevards, and to the south, new waves of immigrants settled in closely-knit enclaves.

- **Michelin Map:** p192.
- **Parking:** Street parking usually possible.
- **Don't Miss:** A meal in Greektown or Little Italy.
- **Also See:** The Loop, Lower West Side.

Land of Opportunity

By the end of the century, congestion, traffic and the spreading industrial city had emptied the exclusive residential sections of the West Side. In addition, violent labor protests frightened many well-to-do homeowners away. The riot at Haymarket Square at Randolph and Desplaines Streets on May 4, 1886 hastened the process. Still the immigrants came, settling up and down Halsted Street in communities anchored by churches, synagogues and other ethnic institutions.

By the 1890s, thousands of Russian and Polish Jews had come to escape the pogroms in Europe. In the vicinity of Maxwell and Halsted Streets, they lived as they had in the Old World *shtetls*, abiding by Orthodox ways. Many worked in the garment district along Jackson Boulevard; many others were peddlers. The legendary **Maxwell Street Market** resembled the open-air bazaars of European villages. Just north, Italians teemed around Halsted and Taylor Streets in the largest Italian community in Chicago. The Delta near Halsted and Harrison Streets became the most populous Greek enclave in the US by 1930.

In the midst of it all, reformer **Jane Addams** established Chicago's first settlement house in 1889 to provide a refuge from the slums, where immigrants could learn American ways, celebrate their own national pride and participate in finding solutions to industrial problems. The renowned Hull House served the community until the 1960s, when the social service programs were relocated to other parts of the city to make way for the University of Illinois' campus.

Chicago Bulls vs.
Sacramento Kings
at United Center

© Icon SMI/Photoshot

United Center

Map of Principal Sights on the inside cover. The Near West Side is home to United Center, a sports venue for Chicago's basketball team, the Bulls, and hockey team, the Blackhawks. Erected at a cost of $175 million, the 1,000,000sq ft structure replaced the 1929 Chicago Stadium, which was torn down in 1994. The old Chicago Stadium gained fame for hosting the first football game to be played indoors in 1932, when a snowstorm forced the players inside. For information on sporting events at United Center, check online at: *www.united-center.com.*

Urban Renewal or Upheaval?

The controversial campus was but one of many redevelopment projects to transform the Near West Side landscape in the 20C. Beginning in 1938, a frenzy of construction resulted in the largest concentration of public housing in the city. In 1941 the state legislature established the Medical Center District just east of Ogden Avenue, incorporating a cluster of facilities that had been operating there since 1884. Despite expressway development, remnants remain. Graystones along Jackson Boulevard echo the street's elegant era. Loft conversions in the garment district preserve the old warehouses. Although disrupted by the university, **Little Italy** prevails, with its trendy trattorias, along Taylor Street. **Greektown** thrives in the restaurants along Halsted Street north of Van Buren Street.

Most recently, African Americans and Mexicans have come to live on the Near West Side, replacing the Jews who moved west. The **Maxwell Street Market** kept bustling—offering everything from hubcaps to hot dogs—until it too was relocated in 1994 to West Roosevelt Road. Today the market takes place every Sunday *(7am–3pm; S. Desplaines St. between Roosevelt Rd. & Harrison St.).*

SIGHTS

The far-flung sights on the Near West Side are best seen by car.

East of the Kennedy Expressway (I-90) stands **Old St. Patrick's Roman Catholic Church** *(140 S. Desplaines St.),* Chicago's oldest extant church building, completed in 1856. The asymmetrical steeples were added in 1885: the onion dome represents the Eastern Church, while the spire symbolizes the Roman Church in the West.

At 558 DeKoven Street, the **Chicago Fire Academy** fittingly occupies the site of the infamous O'Leary barn where the 1871 Chicago Fire started. In front, the tripartite bronze **Pillar of Fire (1)**, sculpted by Egon Weiner in 1961, commemorates the event.

Randolph Street, Museum of Holography ↑

NEAR WEST SIDE

0   1/10 mi
0   200 m

1500 Block of W. Jackson Blvd. ↑

***THE LOOP

Monroe   St.
St. Patrick's
Adams   St.
Jackson   Blvd.
Morgan St.
Sangamon St.
St.
St.
St.
Kennedy Expwy.
St.
St.
Desplaines
Clinton
Aberdeen
Van Buren   St.
400 S
Peoria
Green
Halsted
Van Buren   St.
Mural
Reliable Corp.
Eisenhower Expwy.
I-290
600 S
Education, Communication & Social Work
P
Harrison   St.
Harrison   St.
Behavioral Sciences Bldg.
University Hall
P
Vernon Park   Pl.
800 W
Dan Ryan Expwy.
Polk   St.
Polk
St.
UNIVERSITY OF ILLINOIS AT CHICAGO (EAST CAMPUS)
D
Sheridan Park
Carpenter St.
Miller St.
B
C
★ Hull-House Museum
Desplaines
Jefferson
Clinton
Great Court
Aberdeen
St.
A
P
Taylor   St.
Chicago Fire Academy ■ 1
May
Morgan St.
1000 W
P
St.
St.
Halsted
Union
DeKoven St.
★ Holy Family
★ St. Ignatius Prep
Roosevelt
Rd.
1200 S
Roosevelt   Rd.
Blue Island Ave.
Illinois Regional Library
Newbury Ave.
Ruble St.
13th   St.
Maxwell   St.

■ LOWER WEST SIDE

Jane Addams Hull-House Museum

Jane Addams Hull-House Museum, University of Illinois at Chicago

Holy Family Church and St. Ignatius College Prep★

1076–1080 W. Roosevelt Rd.

This pair of buildings creates an enduring West Side silhouette that transcends the gritty blocks around it.

The church was the cornerstone of the Irish community when the Jesuits built it in 1857.

Next door, the elaborate Second Empire facade of the prep school, built in 1870, has been beautifully renovated.

Across Roosevelt Road stands the **Illinois Regional Library for the Blind and Physically Handicapped** *(1055 W. Roosevelt Rd.)*. The whimsical building, sheathed in boldly colored metal, sports a wavelike window incised along its Blue Island Avenue side. The work of Stanley Tigerman & Assocs., the structure (1975) is designed for easy access.

University of Illinois at Chicago (East Campus)

Halsted, Taylor, Morgan and Harrison Sts. surround the core of the campus. A campus map is posted in the lobby at University Hall, 601 S. Morgan St. ℘312-996-7000. www.uic.edu.

This inner-city campus has generated much controversy since its inception in the mid-1960s. Its location was proposed despite considerable protest by the mostly Italian residents of the densely populated area, and construction began in 1963. Architect Walter A. Netsch, Jr. of Skidmore, Owings & Merrill attempted to create a campus appropriate to its city setting. But what seemed like a fitting, if dramatic, direction for an urban university in the 1960s seems cold today. Inspired by the Brutalist movement, the hulking concrete and brick buildings are pierced by slitlike vertical windows.

From the East Campus, the **Science and Engineering Laboratories (A)** lie to the south, the **University Library (B)** to the west, and the **Chicago Circle Center (C)** (the only original structure not designed by Skidmore, Owings & Merrill) to the east. To the northwest stands the campus' only "skyscraper": 28-story **University Hall**. Due north, the **Architecture and Art Laboratories (D)**

Holy Family Church

© Harvey S. Tillis/Dreamstime.com

represent Netsch's experiment in rotated squares.

Jane Addams' Hull-House Museum★

800 S. Halsted St. ©Open year-round Tue–Fri 10am–4pm, Sun noon–4pm. ©Closed major holidays. ℘312-413-5353. www.hullhousemuseum.org.

Dwarfed by the surrounding campus buildings, the Hull-House Museum offers a glimpse into an important chapter in the history of American social welfare and reform. Founded in 1889 by pioneering social workers **Jane Addams** and **Ellen Gates Starr**, this settlement house became a focal point for citywide and national movements to improve living and working conditions of the nation's poor and disadvantaged.

VISIT

Of the original 13 buildings, just two remain and both are open to visitors. For the first time in 50 years, the museum is undergoing a major renovation. Beginning in fall 2010, the entire second floor of the two-story, brick Italianate **mansion** will be open to the public, including Jane Addams' former bedroom. The rooms on the first floor are furnished with many original pieces, including **Jane Addams' desk**.

Pilsen

What started in the 19C as the largest settlement of Bohemian immigrants in the country today forms the heart of Chicago's Hispanic community.
A working-class community of modest homes and grand churches, it also attracts artists and galleries.

- **Michelin Map:** Above.
- **Location:** Pilsen centers on 18th St. between Ashland Ave. and Morgan St.
- **Parking:** Street parking possible.
- **Don't Miss:** The colorful wall murals everywhere.
- **Also See:** Near West Side.

A BIT OF HISTORY

The industrial district along the South Branch of the Chicago River was settled by immigrant Bohemians after the fire of 1871 and named Pilsen in honor of their homeland's second-largest city. Between long hours of stacking lumber by the river's edge and brewing Pilsener beer, the immigrants erected churches and social halls reminiscent of their native Bohemia. The already crowded district experienced a rapid expansion after the construction in 1854 of Blue Island Avenue. Labor strife rocked the area in 1877 and 1886. The "Battle of the Viaduct," in which 30 workers were killed and 200 injured, took place near 16th and Halsted Streets during the Great Railroad Strike of 1877.

In the 1950s Pilsen became the entrepôt for Mexican immigrants in Chicago. Today, Latinos make up close to 20 percent of the city's population.

GETTING THERE

BY L: Blue line to 18th St.

SIGHTS

This area is best seen by car. Take the 18th St. exit from I-90/I-94 and then continue west.

18th Street

The main thoroughfare in Pilsen, 18th Street (between Morgan Street and Ashland Avenue) is lined with 1870s and 80s Second Empire commercial buildings distinguished by mansard roofs and elaborate window moldings. The limestone St. Procopius Church (1883), at Allport Street, faces the massive, Romanesque-style **Thalia Hall**, named for the Greek muse of comedy and pastoral poetry. One of numerous community centers erected by Bohemians in the late 19C,

Thalia Hall and St. Procopius Church

© Steve Geer/iStockphoto.com

Colorful mural in Pilsen

© David Dunai/Apa Publications

the hall is currently in the process of being renovated as a theater. At the intersection of 18th and Loomis Streets and Blue Island Avenue (southeast corner), the **Rudy Lozano Branch Library** stands out with its lively frieze of decorative tile recalling pre-Columbian monuments in Mitla, Oaxaca.

National Museum of Mexican Art

1852 W. 19th St. ◷*Open year-round Tue–Sun 10am–5pm.* ◷*Closed major holidays.* ♿ ☏*312-738-1503. www. nationalmuseumofmexicanart.org.*
The largest institution of its kind in the US, this respected ethnic center is well known for its Day of the Dead *(Nov 1)* exhibits featuring visiting Mexican artists at work. The museum rotates its 5,500 pieces of folk art, photography, paintings, sculpture, textiles and pre-

1519 artifacts in permanent and temporary exhibits in its 48,000sq ft facility.

ADDRESSES

⑂ EAT

$ De Colores – *1626 S. Halstead St.* ☏*312-226-9886.* Locals love this Pilsen newcomer for the bright flavors in dishes such as pork marinated in pineapple *guajillo*; potato *taquitos* topped with *queso fresco*; and the chunky guacamole, served with warm homemade chips.
$ Nuevo Leon – *1515 W. 18th St.* ☏*312-421-1517.* This tile-decorated restaurant serves some of the best food in Pilsen. The menu ranges from tacos, burritos and nachos to Mexican delicacies like *cesos* (beef brains) and *menudo* (tripe soup). Try one of the dishes prepared with chocolate-spiked mole sauce.

South Side

Near South Side

One of Chicago's oldest areas extends from 16th Street south to 26th Street along the lakefront. It encompasses the grand mansions on Prairie Avenue, an expanding Chinatown and the reviving blocks of Bronzeville. Once scarred by large swaths of urban renewal, the neighborhood remains full of the contradictions and color of a mature urban environment.

A BIT OF HISTORY

In 1835 New York merchant Henry Clarke acquired 20 acres of prairie land on the Near South Side, and the following year he built a lakefront home at Michigan Avenue between 16th and 17th streets. However, the area remained sparsely settled for several decades.

In 1852 politician Stephen A. Douglas developed a 70-acre lakefront tract north of 35th Street, which included the first University of Chicago, opened in 1859 (and closed in 1886). Douglas' famed 1858 debates with Abraham Lincoln led to Douglas' re-election as US senator. During the Civil War, his widow donated land for Camp Douglas, which held Confederate prisoners. Douglas lies buried near his homesite in a massive stone tomb *(636 E. 35th St.)*.

When the 1871 fire destroyed the central city, Chicago's most prominent families moved south to develop a "Millionaire's Row" along Prairie Avenue between 16th and 20th streets. On "the sunny street of the sifted few" lived commercial leader **Marshall Field** and industrial leader **George Pullman**, among others, in mansions designed by architects such as Richard Morris Hunt, Burnham & Root and H. H. Richardson. From 1872 to 1900, Prairie Avenue was the city's most fashionable address. In contrast, State Street between 18th and 22nd streets became part of the notorious **Levee**, an area of saloons and brothels. A small African-American community occupied a thin strip of land on Federal Street south of 22nd Street (later called the Black Belt), while Irish Catholic and

Michelin Map: p201, p202 and p204.

Location: The Near South Side encompasses the Prairie Avenue Historic District, Bronzeville and the Illinois Institute of Technology. The Bronzeville driving tour overreaches neighborhood boundaries and extends into the South Side.

Parking: With all the residential development and Soldier Field nearby, parking is difficult in this neighborhood.

Kids: Catch a White Sox game at U.S. Cellular Field.

German Jewish immigrants developed prosperous middle-class communities along Grand and Drexel boulevards.

Bootleg and Boogie

The establishment of four of Chicago's six major railroad terminals south of the Loop after 1885 benefited the saloons, gaming dens and brothels of the Levee and drove many respectable families away from Prairie Avenue. They gravitated north to the Gold Coast, following **Potter Palmer**'s lead. Finally, the Levee grew too outrageous even for the city, which shut it down in 1915. Throughout the Near South Side, residential uses gave way to warehousing and industry that pushed south from the train stations all the way to 22nd Street.

The 1920s witnessed the rise of bootlegging mobster **Al Capone** (1899–1947), headquartered in the Lexington Hotel, and the rapid expansion of the Black Belt, as the Great Migration of 1914–30 brought thousands of blacks to the area from the American South in search of jobs. By the late 1920s, a "black metropolis" thrived around 35th and State streets, as African-American entrepreneurs built retail and service industries, and black entertainers such as **Louis Armstrong** and **Jelly Roll**

Chinatown

Located at the intersection of 22nd and Wentworth streets, Chicago's Chinatown dates from the 1910s, when Chinese immigrants filled in a tiny neighborhood between the Black Belt on the east, Irish and Italian communities to the south and an industrial area to the north and east along the South Branch of the river. By the 1920s Chinese architectural forms appeared in the district, which has become a popular dining destination for locals and tourists alike.

The entrance arch spanning Wentworth Avenue was erected in the 1970s and features giant ideograms and dragon designs sheltered by red-tile rooftops. Buildings of interest along Wentworth include the **Puitak Center** at no. 2216, with its prominent corner pagodas, balconies and colorful terra-cotta tile decoration. **Woks 'n Things** (no. 2234; *312-842-0701*) sells its namesake pans, along with a wide variety of cookware, as well as a fascinating assemblage of intricate vegetable- and cookie-cutters. The **Emperor's Choice Restaurant** (no. 2238; *312-225-8800*), with its green and white terra-cotta facade enlivened by twisted snake columns, specializes in Cantonese cuisine such as beef with orange peel, and Shanghai noodles. Visit the small **Chinese-American Museum** (238 W. 23rd St.; *312-949-1000; www.ccamuseum.org*).

Morton turned Chicago into a center for jazz and blues. As the Irish and German Jews settled farther south, middle-class blacks moved in and occupied the mansions and row houses of Grand Boulevard, while their poorer brethren filled the Federal Street slums, now torn down.

Rebuilding

If decline hit the South Side first, so did renewal. Arriving in 1937, German refugee **Ludwig Mies van der Rohe** designed a new campus plan for the **Illinois Institute of Technology (IIT)** that eliminated a half-mile stretch of slums along State Street, and Wabash and Michigan avenues south of 30th Street. By the 1940s Michael Reese Hospital and IIT began an urban renewal plan, which would replace acres of derelict housing with modern town houses and high rises. The redevelopment continued into the 1960s as middle-class apartments were erected along the lakefront north of 35th Street, and several public-housing high rises replaced the Federal Street slum. By 1966 industrial growth had caused the demolition of most of Prairie Avenue's once-proud mansions. A public outcry, and the fledgling Chicago Architecture

Foundation saved the Glessner House from the wrecking ball, and a Chicago Landmark District was created in 1979, preserving the remaining mansions. A pocket of homes untouched by urban renewal and known as "The Gap" has been restored by middle-class African Americans, who are also maintaining the mansions along King Drive (former Grand Boulevard) and promoting the Black Metropolis Historic District in an effort to preserve the region's cultural and architectural heritage. Best known today as **Bronzeville**, the area is undergoing considerable restoration as a residential community and enthusiastic promotion for its important place in African-American history.

SIGHTS

It is easiest and safest to tour the area by car.

PRAIRIE AVENUE HISTORIC DISTRICT★

Drive south from the Loop on Michigan Ave., turn left at 18th St. and continue two blocks to Prairie Ave. (no through traffic).

The Prairie Avenue Historic District between 18th and 20th streets preserves a sampling of Chicago's prestigious homes from the late 19C, highlighted by the city's two most historically significant house museums.

Henry B. Clarke House★

1827 S. Indiana Ave. 📷*Visit by guided tour (1hr) only, year-round Wed–Sun noon–2pm.* ⊘*Closed major holidays.* 💲*$10 ($15 for both Glessner & Clarke houses). Wed free. Tours depart from Glessner House.* ♿ 𝒫*312-326-1480. www.clarkehousemuseum.org.*

Built in 1836, this sandstone-colored clapboard home is considered Chicago's oldest surviving structure. The spacious, two-story residence boasts a Doric temple entrance characteristic of the Greek Revival style; grand, 9ft-high triple-sash windows, tiny "frieze windows" and a central hall plan further illustrate the style. In the 1850s an Italianate cupola was added to the cross-gabled roof. The sturdy mortise-and-tenon timber frame construction has allowed the house to be moved twice—in 1872 and 1977.

Inside, period furnishings, artifacts and faithful reproductions of floor, wall and window coverings represent the Clarkes' occupation of the home from 1836 to 1872. Completed in the 1850s, the southern parlors exemplify the Italianate style with brilliant ceiling medallions, pocket doors and a Chickering piano. The upstairs bedrooms feature a marvelous sleigh bed and coal stove along with period toys, china and samplers. The basement contains a reconstructed kitchen and an exhibition gallery displaying photographs, artifacts and models that document the building's history and restoration.

John Jacob Glessner House★★

1800 S. Prairie Ave. 📷*Visit by guided tour (1hr) only year-round Wed–Sun 1pm–3pm.* ⊘*Closed major holidays.* 💲*$10 ($15 for both Glessner & Clarke houses); Wed free.* 𝒫*312-326-1480. www.glessnerhouse.org.*

Designed by **Henry Hobson Richardson** in 1886, the Glessner House revolutionized domestic American architecture with its open floor plan and unadorned Romanesque facades. Richardson, whose work influenced that of both Louis Sullivan and Frank Lloyd Wright, combined Medieval, Renaissance and American Colonial elements in designing the exterior. The fortresslike house turned its back on the street to focus on an inner courtyard, making it the first modern urban home. At the time, its spare exterior shocked many Prairie Avenue inhabitants. The house was commissioned by Glessner, a manufacturer of farm implements who lived on the tony Near West Side until the **Haymarket Riot** occurred there in 1886, spreading fear of labor anarchy and spurring Glessner to move to Prairie Avenue.

The **interior**★ is organized in an L-shape around a sunny southern courtyard. Heavy beamed ceilings (Richardson purposely bowed the beams to create an antique appearance) and a wealth of Arts and Crafts details, including wall and tile patterns by William Morris and furniture by local artist Isaac Scott, exemplify the Medieval motif. Over 80 percent of the items displayed were originally owned by the Glessners, and restoration has been guided by their profuse documentation and period photos of each room. Focal point of the house, the **library** contains a large sampling of the Glessners' extensive book,

Library, Glessner House Museum

Courtesy of Glessner House Museum

print and ceramics collections. In the music room, note the Steinway piano in a Francis Bacon case. The second-floor hall features a walnut Isaac Scott bookcase with Gothic arches and buttresses. The main bedroom has been restored down to the William Morris tiles, draperies, upholstery and carpet.

Across Prairie Avenue stand the **Kimball House** (no. 1801) and **Coleman-Ames House** (no. 1811), both now headquarters of the US Soccer Federation. In 1896 railroad magnate George Pullman, wary of any more "modern" houses on Prairie Avenue, convinced piano and organ manufacturer W. W. Kimball to hire his architect, **Solon S. Beman**. The result is a highly ornate French Châteauesque house with crested turrets and elaborate carvings in limestone. The more restrained Coleman-Ames House was designed in 1886 by Cobb & Frost in the Romanesque Revival style.

South of Glessner House is the spacious **Chicago Women's Park and Gardens**. Along the park's wrought-iron fence, panels depict homes demolished before the Chicago Landmark District was created in 1979. Beyond the park stands the 1870 **Elbridge Keith House** (no. 1900), awaiting restoration. Across the street the **Marshall Field, Jr., House** (no. 1919) retains its imposing mansion-like exterior though it has been divided into six condominiums. Between the Field House and the Coleman-Ames House the avenue is lined with narrow, five-story row houses that appear to date from the late 19C but were built in the early 21C. The architectural firm of Pappageorge/Haymes designed the historic look-alikes.

Farther west on Michigan Avenue, **Second Presbyterian Church** (1874) was designed by James Renwick and features Tiffany stained-glass windows.

🚗 DRIVING TOUR

8.1mi.

Bronzeville

▷ *Drive south from the Loop on Michigan Ave. to 21st St.*

This tour cuts through various South Side neighborhoods important in black history and ends at a museum that pays tribute to African-American culture.

The former **Chess Records Studio** (2120 S. Michigan Ave.) occupied this unassuming building (1911, Horatio Wilson). Here, legends such as Chuck Berry, Howlin' Wolf, Bo Diddley and the Flamingos helped define rhythm and blues. The building was refurbished by Willie Dixon's Blues Heaven Foundation, which the songwriter/bassist established before his death in 1992, as an archive of Chicago Blues music, a revamped studio, and offices for the foundation.

▷ *Continue south on Michigan Ave.*

Known as "Motor Row," this series of early automobile showrooms (1910–30), like much of South Michigan Avenue, is undergoing major renovation as condominiums. The Mediterranean-style **Chicago Defender Building** (southwest corner of Michigan Ave. and 24th St.) originally housed the Illinois Automobile Club.

▷ *Turn right on 24th St.*

Quinn Chapel African Methodist Episcopal Church★

2401 S. Wabash Ave. 📞 312-791-1847. www.quinnchicago.org.

African Americans built this lovely limestone chapel (1892, Henry Starbuck) before they constituted a significant portion of the population. The site, at the time located in a middle-class white neighborhood, was purchased by a fair-skinned member of the congregation who could "pass" for white to avoid community opposition.

▷ *Continue west on 24th St., turn left on State St., and then left on 26th St. Turn right on Martin Luther King, Jr. Dr.*

Extending south to 35th Street, the **Prairie Shores** and **Lake Meadows** developments dominate this boulevard to the east. These tall, white and

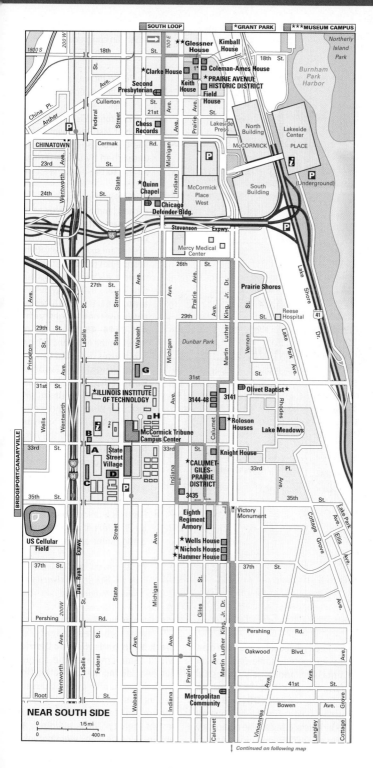

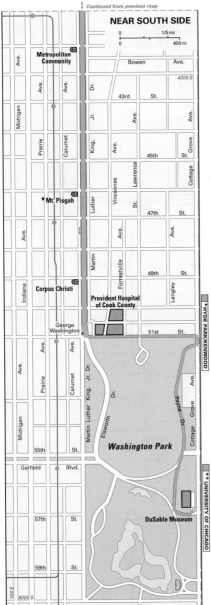

Continued from previous map

NEAR SOUTH SIDE

0 .... 1/5 mi
0 .... 400 m

American congregations, which dates back to 1853.

▷ *Turn right on 31st St. and left immediately on Calumet Ave.*

The cluster of Victorian houses south of 31st Street was named The Gap because it remained untouched by urban renewal efforts to the north, west and east.

In the 1980s the restored homes earned landmark status as the **Calumet-Giles-Prairie District**★. Of note on Calumet Avenue are several lovely Romanesque Revival graystones on the left, a Victorian-style building (1887) by Adler & Sullivan at **no. 3141**, as well as limestone row houses on the right, such as **nos. 3144–48**. South of 32nd Street on the left stand the only row houses designed by Frank Lloyd Wright, the landmark **Robert Roloson Houses**★ *(nos. 3213–19)*, built in 1894 just after Wright left the office of Adler & Sullivan. Sullivan's influence is seen in the large, foliate, terra-cotta panels that enliven the center of the uncharacteristically tall and narrow gabled facades. At no. 3322, the **Clarence Knight House** (1891) is a unique composition by Flanders & Zimmerman in orange stone and Roman brick.

▷ *South on Calumet Ave., turn right on 35th St. and then right again on Indiana Ave.*

Seven buildings located on or near 35th Street comprise the **Black Metropolis Historic District**, which commemorates the cultural flowering during the Great Migration. As the community grew, it developed its own commerce, industry and culture, isolated by racism from the rest of the city. These buildings are unique because many were not inhe-

blue-green pastel buildings were planned as integrated middle-class housing in a massive, and largely successful, urban-renewal effort. To the east at 31st Street, note the **Olivet Baptist Church**★, built as First Baptist Church in 1873 by Wilcox & Miller. The edifice now houses one of Chicago's oldest African-

rited from other ethnic groups, but financed and built by African-American capital. One of the seven buildings is located at **3435 South Indiana Avenue**, a three-story buff brick structure that served as the headquarters of the *Chicago Defender* from 1921 to 1960 and today houses the Second Ward Regular Democratic Organization. Founded in 1905, the influential African-American newspaper is credited with starting the Great Migration; rousing editorials, written by Robert Sengstacke Abbott, extolled Chicago's opportunities, calling for a "New Exodus."

Turn right on 33rd St. and right on Giles St.

Giles Street was named after Lt. George Giles of the "Fighting Eighth," a black regiment formed from the community at the turn of the century. The **Eighth Regiment Armory** (1915) stretches down the left side of Giles Avenue south of 35th Street.
This landmark of the Black Metropolis was restored in 1999 as Chicago Military Academy, a public high school offering military-style education.

Turn left at 35th St. and continue to Martin Luther King, Jr. Dr.

Grand Boulevard was developed in the 19C as part of a 28mi ring of boulevards. Known later as South Parkway, it was renamed in 1968 for the late Dr. Martin Luther King, Jr. The **Victory Monument** (1928, Leonard Crunelle). The first dedicated to African-American soldiers, honors those of the "Fighting Eighth" who fought in World War I.

Turn right on King Dr., staying to the right to drive along the frontage road of the boulevard.

At no. 3624, the **Ida B. Wells House**★ was named a National Historic Landmark in 1973 in honor of the civil rights leader who lived here from 1919 to 1929. Wells, one of the first to document lynching in the US, moved to Chicago in 1893 to con-

tinue a lifelong crusade against racism and sexism. The 1889 Romanesque Revival home features a pressed-metal corner turret. Built in 1886, the **Charles H. Nichols House** *(no. 3630)* is distinguished by rough-faced Romanesque arches enlivened by Queen Anne oriels.
The orange brick and brownstone **D. Harry Hammer House**★ *(no. 3656)* pounds the corner of 37th Street with massive ostentation. Exuberant detailing in terra-cotta, copper and stained glass enlivens this 1885 design by William W. Clay.

Continue south on the main roadway of King Dr.

At the southwest corner of 41st Street stands the **Metropolitan Community Church** (1891, John T. Long), originally 41st Street Presbyterian Church, a Romanesque Revival edifice featuring a large corner tower and gabled facade. 43rd Street bears the honorary name of legendary blues artist Muddy Waters, who lived to the east on Lake Park Avenue.
Just south of 46th Street, the **Mt. Pisgah Missionary Baptist Church**★ occupies the large Sinai Temple designed by Alfred Alschuler in 1910. At 49th Street, note the Renaissance-style towers of **Corpus Christi Church** (1916), noted for its high-quality stained glass by the F. X. Zettler company of Munich.
At 51st Street a large equestrian statue of **George Washington** (1904, Daniel Chester French and Edward Clark Potter) marks the entrance to Washington Park.

Turn left on 51st St. and continue to Cottage Grove Ave.

Provident Hospital of Cook County, to the left, one of the first founded by and for blacks, was established in 1891 by Dr. Daniel Hale Williams, who on July 9, 1893 became the first physician to perform successful open-heart surgery.

Turn right on Cottage Grove Ave. and right again immediately on Payne Dr., which enters Washington Park.

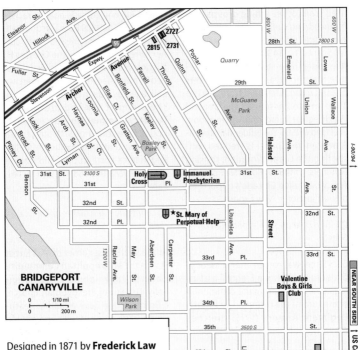

Designed in 1871 by **Frederick Law Olmsted** and **Calvert Vaux**, **Washington Park** is connected to its southern neighbor, Jackson Park, by the Midway Plaisance.

The vast, 100-acre meadow covering the park's northern section was originally mowed by sheep kept in the park for this purpose.

> *Bear to the left at the fork at 55th St. to access the DuSable Museum.*

DuSable Museum of African-American History

740 E. 56th Pl. ○*Open year-round Tue–Sat 10am–5pm, Sun noon–5pm.* ○*Closed major holidays.* ✆*$3 (free Sun).* ♿☐✆*773-947-0600. www.dusablemuseum.org.*

Founded in 1961 by Dr. Margaret Goss Burroughs in her home, the museum now occupies a former park administration building (1910, D. H. Burnham & Co.).

The modern Harold Washington Wing, added to the structure's south side in 1992, houses educational and cultural

programs that supplement permanent and traveling exhibits on African-American life, history and art.

Illinois Institute of Technology (IIT)★

See map p201.

▷ *Drive south from the Loop on State St. to 33rd St., turn left and park in the IIT Visitor Parking Lot.*

Unique in both design and curriculum, IIT fills a campus that largely realizes the plan of master Modernist **Ludwig Mies van der Rohe** (1886–1969), who came to direct the Institute's architecture school in 1937 after fleeing Nazi Germany. The Institute, formed in 1940 by the merger of the Armour and Lewis institutes, has garnered an international reputation for excellence in the fields of engineering, architecture and design. Today the university enrolls more than 7,500 students, who attend classes on the 120-acre campus.

VISIT

Guided tour (1hr 30min) departs daily at 10am from McCormick Tribune Campus Center, 3201 S. State St. $10. Self-guided audio tours also available. 312-567-5014. www.iit.edu.
Located at Federal and 33rd streets, the **Main Building★(A)** (1891, Patton, Fisher & Miller) epitomizes the Romanesque Revival style. Across 33rd Street stands the simpler **Machinery Hall (B)**, erected 10 years later by the same firm. Mies' first construction for the institute, the 1943 **Materials Technology Building (C)**, illustrates the central principle behind his campus design: a "module" of 24ft x 24ft x 12ft "blocks" that compose the buildings and spaces between them. Headquarters of IIT's architecture school, **S. R. Crown Hall★★(D)** is the capital achievement of both the campus and Mies van der Rohe. Calling it a "representational building," Mies abandoned his "module" to create a simple glass-walled pavilion housing a singular space 220ft wide, 120ft deep and 18ft high. The 1956 structure appears to hover above the ground, its flat roof suspended from four huge I-beams that wrap around the building. Entered on floating travertine steps, the building defines space by its structure, stripping away ornament without losing the humanizing effects of proportion and enclosure.
At Wabash Avenue, the **Keating Sports Center (G)** (1966, Skidmore, Owings & Merrill) seems set upon an invisible podium, but its walls are sheer glass, hiding the structural steel beneath. **Carr Memorial Chapel (H)** is the only church designed by Mies. Known as the "God box," this nondenominational chapel features glass facades on the east and west, and brick on the remaining sides. Dutch architect **Rem Koolhaas** designed the **McCormick Tribune Campus Center★**, completed in 2003. Straddling the elevated train, the post-Modern structure challenges Mies van der Rohe's orderly campus design. Don't miss Koolhaas' tribute to Mies at the entrance. Across 33rd Street stands **State Street Village**, architect Helmut Jahn's 2003 student residence hall complex.

ADDRESSES

🎭 ENTERTAINMENT

The Velvet Lounge – *67 E. Cermak Rd.* 312-791-9050. www.velvetlounge.net. This wonderful club offers excellent jazz most nights. Acclaimed saxophonist Fred Anderson owns the place and plays in the legendary Sunday night jam sessions. During the annual Chicago Jazz Festival, players from around the world gather here for impromptu concerts.

U.S. Cellular Field – *333 W. 35th St.* 312-674-1000). Just over the Dan Ryan Expressway from Bronzeville stands the home of the **Chicago White Sox**. The spacious ballpark, known as "the Cell," replaced the oldest ballpark in the country, memorialized in a plaque in the parking lot across the street. Built in 1991 the 40,615-seat stadium retains little of the original Comiskey Park's charm except for the tradition of shooting fireworks from the scoreboard when a Sox batter hits a home run. The pyrotechnics continue after Saturday-night games when the ball club puts on an elaborate fireworks display.

Bridgeport/ Canaryville

This small neighborhood of quiet streets and modest bungalows is flanked to the west and south by large industrial concentrations occupying the site of the former Union Stock Yards district. Settled by Irish canal workers in the 1830s, the community became the focal point of Chicago politics in the 20C.

A BIT OF HISTORY

Irish workers on the I&M Canal settled north of 31st Street and renamed the town for the port area around the Ashland Avenue Bridge. Slaughterhouses along the South Fork were consolidated in 1865 into the Union Stock Yards, which supplied meat to the world for over a century. Canaryville literally stank, drawing the attention of **Upton Sinclair**, whose 1906 book *The Jungle* led to the Pure Food and Drug Act.
In 1933 Bridgeport's Ed Kelly was appointed mayor after the assassination of Anton Cermak. A Bridgeport politician would hold the office until 1979. Mayor for 21 years, **Richard J. Daley** lived his entire life on Lowe Avenue. His son, Richard M. Daley, is the fifth mayor from Bridgeport. The town's power has declined with the dismantling of the city's political Machine. Chinese

GETTING THERE
BY L: 🚇 Red line to 35th St.
🚶 Refer to the local *Michelin map on p204*.

Americans and Mexican Americans now make up a large portion of Bridgeport's population.

SIGHTS

Halsted Street is the commercial heart of the community. **Archer Avenue** holds Italianate storefronts at **nos. 2727** and **2731** and a pre-fire cottage at **no. 2815**. Burnham & Root designed the **Immanuel Presbyterian Church** (*1035 W. 31st St.*) in 1892. The **Monastery of the Holy Cross** (*3109 S. Aberdeen St.*) was built in 1909 for German Catholics. **St. Mary of Perpetual Help**★ (1892, Henry Englebert) sports a copper dome. The Art Moderne **Valentine Boys & Girls Club** (*3400 S. Emerald Ave.*) was designed in 1938 by Childs & Smith. At **3536 South Lowe Avenue** stands the brick home of Mayor Richard J. Daley. Daley's funeral was held in 1976 at the **Nativity of Our Lord Church** (1868). Intriguing **Greifenstein Pharmacy** is a classic drugstore. In Canaryville the **Stock Yards Bank Building** (1924, A. Epstein) and **Union Stock Yards Gate**★ (1879, **Burnham & Root**) are the sole reminders of that industry.

Union Stock Yards (late 19C)

Shsilver/Wikimedia Commons

University of Chicago★★

A famous center of scholarship, the University of Chicago is a world leader in research and education. It is often called "the teacher of teachers" because many of its alumni work in education, and a great number serve as college or university presidents. U of C students live a world apart from the hustle and bustle of Chicago, a division reinforced by a unique physical setting covering about 210 acres of Hyde Park, 8mi south of the Loop.

- **Michelin Map:** p211.
- **Info:** 773-702-1234. www.uchicago.edu. Find maps of the campus in Ida Noyes Hall, 59th St. and Woodlawn Ave., Room 106.
- **Location:** The bulk of the campus lies north of the Midway Plaisance.
- **Parking:** It is possible to find street parking, often along the Midway.
- **Kids:** The children's section at 57th Street Books.
- **Also See:** Hyde Park/ Kenwood, Near South Side.

A BIT OF HISTORY
Rockefeller's Creation

Built on land donated by **Marshall Field**, the University of Chicago was founded in 1890 by the American Baptist Educational Society and oil magnate **John D. Rockefeller**, whose initial $600,000 drew $1 million from Chicago business leaders. Armed with a strong academic vision and Rockefeller's ample purse, President **William Rainey Harper** gathered scholars from leading schools, creating a first-rate faculty that included eight former university presidents. Rockefeller continued to contribute—$35 million over 25 years—and pronounced the university "the best investment I ever made in my life." The University of Chicago opened on October 1, 1892, not with ceremony or celebration, but by starting classes at 8.30am. Within 10 years, it was one of the nation's leading research universities. The architecture is steeped in academic history. Trustees insisted that architect **Henry Ives Cobb**, famous for Romanesque Revival buildings such as the Newberry Library, use a late-English Gothic style, which they considered ennobling. Cobb designed 18 buildings, then passed the baton to the architectural firm of Shepley, Rutan & Coolidge. Gothic remained the style used by U of C architects until 1940. Borrowing from Oxford and Cambridge, Cobb's cloistered quadrangular plan (one of the first used at an American university) guided subsequent development: four city blocks form the main campus, which is divided into six small quads grouped around a seventh central quadrangle.

The Life of the Mind

Despite its conservative roots, the university was quite progressive, admitting women and minorities from the start. It was also rigorous: Harper established a two-year "common core curriculum," mandating that each undergraduate completes course work in physical sciences, social sciences, biology and the humanities, a program still firmly in place. Within two decades of the university's birth, U of C physicists had measured the speed of light and made other important breakthroughs. By the 1920s the university's social scientists had invented modern sociology and developed the first community colleges.

From Football to Physics

In addition to academics, the university also became known for its Big Ten football team coached by **Amos Alonzo Stagg**. The "Monsters of the Midway"

GETTING THERE
BY BUS: Bus no. 6 *(Jeffrey Express)*

Nobels at the U of C

More than 75 Nobel Prize winners have been faculty, students or researchers at the U of C—more than at any other university. The only Nobel never awarded to someone with U of C ties is the Peace Prize.

The first American Nobel laureate in science was the university's Albert A. Michaelson, who received the award in 1907 for measuring the speed of light. Physicists Robert Millikan and Arthur Compton won in 1923 and 1927 for their pioneering work in quantum mechanics. James Dewey Watson, a 1962 winner, co-discovered the structure of DNA. Economist Milton Friedman won in 1976.

University of Chicago may well boast, but its Nobelists would rather study than bask in glory. When physicist James Cronin won the Nobel Prize in 1980, he was asked to hold a 10am press conference. "I can't do it then," he said, "I've got a 10 o'clock class." Impressed by his dedication, the university spokesman asked what class he was teaching. "No, no," Cronin protested, "I'm not teaching a course. I'm taking Chandrasekhar's graduate course on the theory of relativity." Subrahmanyan Chandrasekhar won the Nobel three years later.

dominated in the 1920s and premiered the huddle and the forward pass. The first Heisman Trophy was awarded in 1935 to running back **Jay Berwanger**. Charismatic **Robert Maynard Hutchins** became president in 1929 at age 30 and instituted numerous reforms during his 22-year tenure. He and **Mortimer Adler** created a system of teaching based on the "Great Books" that is still a national model. Hutchins abolished football in 1939 because he felt it detracted from scholarship. In 1942 the unused football stands concealed the Manhattan Project laboratory of physicist **Enrico Fermi**, whose team of physicists achieved the first self-sustaining, controlled nuclear reaction. The top-secret project was the crucial step in the development of the atomic bomb and nuclear energy.

Maintaining Tradition

The university underwent a brief period in the 1930s as a hotbed of radicalism and was engaged in urban-renewal programs in the 1940s and 60s. In 1969 football returned (NCAA Division III) to U of C, and radical students occupied the Administration Building, but none of these events changed the rigorous curriculum. In the 1970s the university began its dominance in economics, while maintaining leadership roles in physics, sociology and Near Eastern studies. The tradition of interdisciplinary

inquiry established by Harper continues today, and the Medical School remains at the forefront of research while developing important medical techniques, especially in cancer and brain research.

WALKING TOUR
2mi.

The tour focuses on the historic buildings and quadrangles, though it also includes examples of the university's impressive modern architecture. While walking through campus, just try to count the number of gargoyles!

▷ *Begin at Ida Noyes Hall, 59th St. and Woodlawn Ave.*

Ida Noyes Hall (A)

Built in 1915 (Shepley, Rutan & Coolidge) as a women's center in a Tudor Revival style, the hall is noteworthy for its finely detailed interior, in particular the beamed ceilings, wood-paneled parlors, original furnishings and a dramatic central staircase with carved monkeys on the handrails. DOC Films, the oldest college film society in the US, shows films daily during the school year in the Max Palevsky Cinema. There's a pub in the basement and offices of the student newspaper, the *Maroon*.

▷ *Cross Woodlawn Ave. to Rockefeller Chapel.*

The mile-long **Midway Plaisance**, designed by **Frederick Law Olmsted** in 1869, connects Washington and Jackson Parks and was the site of commercial side-shows during the 1893 World's Fair.

Rockefeller Memorial Chapel★

5850 S. Woodlawn Ave. ◐Open year-round daily 8am–4pm. ◐Closed during special events, Dec 25–Jan 1. ◐Tours of the carillon Mon–Fri 11.30am & 5.30pm. ℘773-702-2100. www.rockefeller.uchicago.edu.

Completed in 1928, the chapel was designed by **Bertram G. Goodhue Assocs.** and named for its donor in 1937. At 207ft, the structure remains the tallest building on campus. Embodying true Gothic principles, the brick and limestone edifice has little structural steel. The arches carry the weight of the vaulting, while the buttresses help withstand the outward thrust of the walls. Foundations 80ft deep support 32,000 tons of wall, tower and roof.

The 43ft-high nave windows composed of tracery glass in muted tones contrast with the bright cinquefoil window above the altar, added in 1979. Tall proportions draw the eye heavenward to the colored, glazed Guastavino tile ceiling, revealed in a 1988 restoration. The elaborate chancel with its organ pipes, pulpit and carved oak choir seats creates a sense of pomp for the annual graduation ceremonies. Outdoor summer concerts feature the tower's 72-bell carillon *(late Jun–late Aug, Sun 6pm)*, while other productions showcase the 103-stop E. M. Skinner organ.

▷ *Continue north on Woodlawn Ave. to 58th St.*

Argentinian-born **Rafael Vinoly** won an architectural competition to design the **Graduate School of Business** located just south of Robie House. The **Charles M. Harper Center (B)** was completed in 2004.

Robie House★

Northeast corner of Woodlawn Ave. and 58th St. (◐See description at the end of University text, p213.)

▷ *Walk west on 58th St. toward University Ave.*

Chicago Theological Seminary (C)

Dating from 1857, this is the oldest of a cluster of seminaries in Hyde Park. The 1926 edifice (Riddle & Riddle) is composed of two wings connected by a skywalk. Visit the lovely **Hilton Memorial Chapel** *(1st floor; ◐open*

Rockefeller Memorial Chapel

© JasonSmith.com/University of Chicago

209

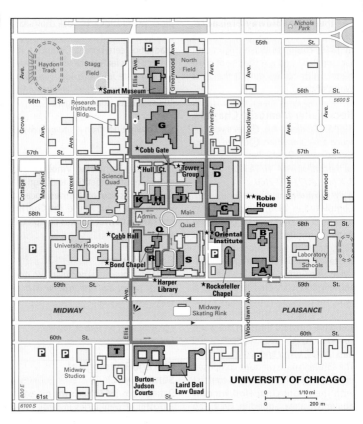

UNIVERSITY OF CHICAGO

| 0 | | 1/10 mi |
| 0 | | 200 m |

year-round Mon–Fri 7am–3pm; ◒*closed major holidays;* ♿ *☏773-752-5757)* and the cloisters beneath the Lawson Tower.

Oriental Institute★★

1155 E. 58th St. ◒*Open year-round Thu–Tue 10am–6pm, Wed 10am– 8.30pm, Sun noon–6pm.* ❦*Suggested donation $7.* ♿. *☏773-702-9520. www.oi.uchicago.edu.*

Dedicated to the study of languages, history and cultures of the Ancient Near East, this research institution is the premier authority in the dating and identification of archaeological artifacts. Its museum contains one of the world's choicest collections of Near Eastern art and antiquities. The majority of the items in the collection have been uncovered by the Institute's own archaeological excavations. Since its inception, the university has been a center for Near Eastern studies. **James**

Henry Breasted, the first American to earn a PhD in Egyptology, led the university's initial field expedition to Iraq in 1904 and began excavating Egyptian and Nubian temples a year later. In 1919 he created the Oriental Institute, funded by John D. Rockefeller, Jr. Archaeologists consulted Breasted in 1922 to positively identify the tomb of Tutankhamen. In 1931 the museum/research institution moved into its permanent home, designed by **Mayers, Murray & Phillip** in the Art Deco style. Researchers from the Institute continue to excavate numerous sites and publish the definitive dictionaries of Assyrian, Demotic (Egyptian) and Hittite languages.

Collections

With more than 75,000 registered artifacts, the institute boasts extensive collections covering Egypt, Assyria, Mesopotamia, Khorasabad, Anatolia,

Israel, Nubia and Persia. Materials are presented in eight attractive galleries. Of particular note are an impressive collection of **tomb servants**, tiny clay dolls intended to serve the deceased in the afterlife in the Egyptian gallery and the huge **human-headed winged bull**, an *lamassu*, dating from the 8C BC in the Khorsabad gallery. Hititte pottery and ivories from the Israeli city of Megiddo evoke a sense of daily life in the ancient Middle East.

After leaving the Oriental Institute, at University Avenue look south to the pointed Gothic spires of Foster, Kelly, Green and Beecher halls, completed as women's dorms in 1893, and now home to the Psychology Department. The 1971 Albert Pick Hall for International Studies suggests Gothic verticality with stone-like facing and lancet windows.

> *Walk north on University Ave.*

The Tower Group★
West side of University Ave.
Located north of Eckhart Hall (1930, Charles Z. Klauder), the Tower Group (1903, Shepley, Rutan & Coolidge) anchors the northeast corner of the main quadrangle. **Leon Mandel Hall**, a theater and assembly hall, imitates the campus chapel with its arched windows and tracery. Mitchell Tower, modeled on Oxford's Magdalen College bell tower, contains the Alice Palmer bells used for the Medieval art of "change ringing." Below the tower is Reynolds Club, a student center inspired by Oxford's St. John's College. Hutchinson Hall's design came from Oxford's Christ Church Hall and is noted for its grand dining hall featuring a hammer-beam ceiling, paneled walls, massive stone fireplaces and portraits.

The distinguished, red brick **Quadrangle Club (D)** *(southeast corner of University Ave. and 57th St.)*, designed in 1922 by Howard Van Doren Shaw, serves the university faculty and their guests.

> *Cross 57th St. and continue north to 56th St.*

Completed in 2002, the surprising dormitories of the Max Palevsky Residential Commons (*1101 E. 56th St.*) extend along 56th St. from University Ave. to Ellis Ave. Architect Ricardo Legorreta infused the three connected buildings with the warmth and color of his native Mexico to create a pool of brightness in the midst of the somber Gothic campus.

> *Turn left on 56th St. and walk west to Greenwood Ave.*

The **Cochrane-Woods Arts Center (F)** (1974) contains the Art History Department and the Smart Museum. The one-story, boxlike museum designed by Edward Larrabee Barnes opens into a courtyard garden.

Smart Museum of Art★
5550 S. Greenwood Ave. ⏰*Open year-round Tue, Wed, Fri 10am– 4 pm, Thu 10am–8pm, Sat & Sun 11am–5pm.* ⏰*Closed major holidays.* ✕ ♿ ✆*773-702-0200. www.smartmuseum. uchicago.edu.*
Opened in 1974 and named for the founders of *Esquire* magazine, this small jewel holds 9,500 pieces spanning 5,000 years. The Smart Museum rotates its permanent collection among the four major galleries surrounding the central Gray Special Exhibition Gallery, where the museum sponsors six to eight traveling exhibits a year. Ranging from Greek kraters and Roman mosaics to contemporary art, the surprisingly diverse collection excels in late-19C and 20C painting, sculpture and decorative art.

> *Continue west on 56th St. to Ellis Ave.*

Across the street to the north is the Gerald Ratner Athletic Center, designed by Cesar Pelli and opened in 2003. Cables attached to masts support the roof, giving the 150,000sq ft facility a dramatic profile.

The three-ton bronze massiveness of **Nuclear Energy (1)**, a 1967 sculpture by Henry Moore, marks the site where Enrico Fermi's team of 41 scientists split the atom on December 2, 1942.

Walk south to 57th St. Turn left.

Snell-Hitchcock Hall *(southeast corner of 57th St. and Ellis Ave.)* was listed on the National Register of Historic Houses for its 1902 "Prairie Gothic" design by Dwight Perkins, who meshed the horizontal Prairie style with the vertical Gothic. Hitchcock and adjacent Snell Hall are the only dormitories remaining on the Main Quadrangle.

Continue east on 57th St.

Joseph Regenstein Library (G)

This massive structure holds most of the university's 5.7 million texts and 7 million other volumes. Two of its seven stories of open book stacks are below ground. The 1970 design by Walter A. Netsch, Jr. (also responsible for the University of Illinois at Chicago) used irregular massing, vertical emphasis and setback to relate to the campus.

Continue east on 57th St. to Cobb Gate, on the right.

A gift to the university from architect Henry Ives Cobb, the ornate **Cobb Gate**★ (1900) leads into the main quadrangles. Tradition holds that the

climbing gargoyles represent students struggling from their first year of college to eventual fourth-year triumph at the apex.

Hull Court★

This courtyard designed in 1897 by Henry Ives Cobb consists of the botany, anatomy, zoology and physiology buildings, joined by pleasant arcades. John C. Olmsted designed the romantic Botany Pond—allegedly the preferred site for marriage proposals—and Hutchinson Court.

Walk south through the quad.

The **Kent Chemical (H)** and **Ryerson Physical Laboratories (J)** (1894, Henry Ives Cobb) exhibit full-blown Gothic ornament, peaked dormers, crocheted finials and crenellated towers.

West of Kent Hall is the **Jones Laboratory (K)** (1929, Coolidge & Hodgdon). A first-floor exhibit documents the weighing of plutonium in Room 405 on September 10, 1942, by Dr. Glenn T. Seaborg. South of the Jones Lab is the Administration Building (1948).

Walk south past the Administration Building to Cobb Hall.

Cobb Hall★

Classes began October 1, 1892, in this building (1892, Henry Ives Cobb) named after Silas Cobb (no relation). Freshmen still take their "common core" courses here. The top floor of the oldest campus building houses the **Renaissance Society** contemporary art gallery *(room 418)*, well regarded for its progressive exhibits *(5811 S. Ellis Ave; ◐open Tue–Fri 10am–5pm, Sat & Sun noon–5pm; ℘773-702-8670; www.renaissancesociety.org).*

Continue east toward the center of the quadrangle.

On the right is **Swift Hall (Q)** (1926, Coolidge & Hodgdon), home to the Divinity School. Its site on campus is intended to represent the centrality of religion to studies.

Cobb Hall

© University of Chicago

Harper Memorial Library

© Chris Strong Photography/University of Chicago

▷ *Walk south toward Harper Memorial Library.*

Harper Memorial Library★
1116 East 59th St. ○*Open year-round Mon–Fri 8am–11pm, Sat 10.30am–5pm, Sun 1pm–11pm.* ○*Closed major holidays.* ♿. ✆*773-834-7943. www. harperlibrarycommons.uchicago.edu.*
Distinguished by two massive, square towers, the library (1912, Shepley, Rutan & Coolidge) anchors the south end of the quadrangle and presents an impressive facade to Midway Plaisance. Bridges connect the library to reading rooms in **Haskell Hall (R)** and **Stuart Hall (S)**.

▷ *Walk through the archway in Haskell Hall and head north.*

Bond Chapel★
1050 E. 59th St. ○*Open year-round Mon–Fri 8am–5pm.* ○*Closed major holidays.* ♿
This delicate gem (1926, Coolidge & Hodgdon), covered with ivy and sculpture, is connected by a covered cloister to Swift Hall. Its intimate interior is noted for its Charles Connick stained glass, elaborate wood carvings and a hammer-beamed ceiling with polychrome angels. The frieze of beatitudes ringing the space conceals heating grates to warm the body as well as the soul.

▷ *Walk south to the Classics Quadrangle, then walk through the arch to 59th St.*

To the west, between 59th and 58th streets the University of Chicago Hospitals occupy 18 buildings covering 14 acres, the largest teaching hospital in the nation. To the south in the Midway opposite the entrance to Harper Library is the peaceful Readers Garden, surrounding a statue of Carl Linnaeus, the Swedish scientist who established the modern system of classifying plants and animals. The garden is a pleasant place to rest, with or without a book.

Robie House★★
5757 S. Woodlawn Ave. ↝*Visit by guided tour (1hr) only, year-round Thu–Mon 11am–2pm (Fri till 3pm).* ○*Closed major holidays.* ☞*$15.* ✆*708-848-1976. www.gowright.org.*
Floating on the corner of 58th Street and Woodlawn Avenue, this quintessential Prairie school home by **Frank Lloyd Wright** made him world famous and helped "break the box" of traditional architecture. Its intersecting rectangular volumes alternately fool the eye, dissolving the borders between interior and exterior and creating fluid spaces. The house was commissioned by **Frederick Robie**, heir to a bicycle and automobile firm. The Robies lived in the house only from 1910 to 1911, when the firm went bust and their marriage dis-

213

Robie House

© University of Chicago

solved. It was sold to the Taylor family, who resided there for 11 months, and then to the Wilber Marshall family. In 1926 the Chicago Theological Seminary occupied it as a dormitory and dining hall, accelerating its deterioration. Saved from demolition in 1957, the house was donated to the university in 1963 and designated a National Historic Landmark that same year. In 1995 the university entered into an agreement with the Frank Lloyd Wright Home and Studio Foundation to renovate Robie House into a house museum.

ADDRESSES

ⵣ EAT

$$ La Petite Folie – *1504 E. 55th St.* *☏773-493-1394. www.lapetitefolie.com. Closed Mon.* A few blocks from campus, this little French place tucked away in Hyde Park Shopping Center is run by Chef Mary Mastricola, a U of C alumna. Her tasty French classics run from Idaho trout Amandine to steak au poivre.

$ Jimmy's Woodlawn Tap – *1172 E. 55th St. at Woodlawn Ave. ☏773-643-5516.* This dimly-lit tavern, named for its late owner, is the off-campus hangout for U of C students. Frazzled graduate students unwind at Jimmy's, talking theory and university politics into the wee hours. Prices are low, the beer selection is good and the bartenders are friendly, so drop by and drink in the relaxed academic atmosphere. .

ⵣ ENTERTAINMENT

Court Theatre – *5535 S. Ellis Ave. ☏773-753-4472. www.courttheatre.org.* Renowned for its excellent productions of Shakespeare's and Molière's works among others, the Court ranks with the Goodman and Steppenwolf as one of the best theaters in the city. Its artistic board corrals Chicago's top caliber actors, production designers and directors for its five or six annual productions *(season runs Sept–Jun)*.

BOOKSHOPS

Seminary Co-op – *5757 S. University Ave., in Chicago Theological Seminary, lower level. ☏773-752-4381. www.sem coop.com.* Founded in 1961, this huge, underground bookstore offers close to 150,000 volumes and caters to more highbrow tastes than its sister shop, 57th Street Books. The staff at this renowned academic bookstore are passionate about books, and will do their best to locate and ship obscure books for you.

57th Street Books – *1301 E. 57th St. ☏773-684-1300. www.semcoop.com.* Wander through this well-stocked bookshop. Though the store is part of the huge Seminary Co-op, 57th Street Books features a selection geared toward general interest rather than academic pursuits. The intelligent, helpful staff encourage browsing, and kids ⵣⵣ can play with toys set out for them in the excellent children's section.

Hyde Park/ Kenwood★

This racially integrated, middle-class community is closely identified with the cerebral University of Chicago and the popular Museum of Science and Industry. Bordered by Lake Michigan on the east, Washington Park on the west, 47th Street on the north and 61st Street on the south, Hyde Park/Kenwood also encompasses renowned architectural landmarks, sweeping greenswards and an array of shops and eateries. The site of the World's Columbian Exposition, Hyde Park/ Kenwood remains a cosmopolitan neighborhood well worth exploring.

A BIT OF HISTORY

Paul Cornell envisioned a quiet residential suburb when he purchased 300 lakefront acres south of Chicago in 1852 and named the area Hyde Park. He lured the Illinois Central commuter train in 1856, barred industry in 1861 and helped create the South Parks Commission in 1869, which hired renowned landscape architect **Frederick Law Olmsted** to design Jackson and Washington parks. To the north, dentist John Kennicott had purchased eight acres near 43rd Street in 1856 and named his suburb Kenwood, subdividing it into large, 50ft-wide lots. By 1874 it was hailed as the "Lake Forest of the South Side" for its large Italianate and Shingle-style mansions. Both communities were conservative and exclusive. They soon established the separate township of Hyde Park and began fighting annexation to the City of Chicago.

As public transportation improved in the 1880s, apartment buildings and commercial strips began to transform Hyde Park into an urban neighborhood. New residents in favor of annexation outvoted their tony neighbors in 1889, and the entire town from 39th Street to 138th Street became part of Chicago. In 1891 Hyde Park was chosen as the site of the **World's Columbian Exposition**,

- ⓑ **Michelin Map:** p217.
- ⓐ **Don't Miss:** View of the Loop from Promontory Point.
- ⓑ **Also See:** Near South Side.

fostering the completion of Jackson and Washington parks and ending the neighborhood's exclusivity. Simultaneously, the University of Chicago was built just north of the Midway Plaisance. The two events forever changed the destiny of the community.

The World's Fair brought an avalanche of real estate development as hotels, apartment buildings and shops sprang up to cater to the 27 million visitors during the summer of 1893. The University of Chicago grew just as quickly, and Hyde Park bustled.

The 1910 arrival of the "L" train increased Kenwood's density, and by the 1920s the crowded Black Belt pushed toward it, setting off racial conflicts that continued for 20 years. While it declined economically, Hyde Park blossomed culturally with jazz and blues clubs, a major artists' colony and a comedy troupe that eventually became The Second City.

Town and Gown

In 1949 neighbors created the Hyde Park/Kenwood Community Conference, and three years later, the University of Chicago organized the South East Chicago Commission to fight urban decline. As the birthplace of modern sociology, the university held a critical role: U of C scholars studied their declining neighborhood and developed guidelines for urban renewal. These studies were formalized into the Federal Housing Act of 1954, and when federal funds were released in 1955, it was no surprise that Hyde Park/Kenwood qualified for the largest urban-renewal project in the nation. More than 900 acres of buildings were demolished over the next decade. Shopping centers replaced mansions on Lake Park Avenue and apartments on 53rd Street. Cottages with porches gave way to town houses oriented around interior courtyards. The radical sur-

The 1893 World's Columbian Exposition

In a spirited battle to host the 1893 World's Columbian Exposition, Chicago earned its enduring nickname "Windy City" because of all the blustery boasting that led to its winning the honor over New York, Washington and St. Louis. Conceived to celebrate the 400th anniversary of Columbus' discovery of America, this world's fair covered over 650 acres along present-day Jackson Park and encompassed some 200 buildings erected by leading architects. From its opening day on May 1, 1893, to its close in October, the exposition awed nearly 27 million visitors with its architecture and attractions, including the world's first Ferris wheel and the infamous "Little Egypt" dancing the hootchie-kootchie. At night, floodlights illuminated the Neoclassical buildings, creating a sparkling white, fairylike atmosphere. But the fair was fleeting as its construction was done entirely of "staff," a temporary material left to crumble away at the event's end.

gery worked: the University of Chicago abandoned thoughts of leaving the city, the neighborhood maintained its integrated middle-class character and the economic decline sweeping the South Side leapfrogged over Hyde Park/Kenwood. Today one of the nation's most successful models for integration, the community remains linked to the university, which helped shape its destiny.

🚗 DRIVING TOUR

9.3mi.

▷ *Begin at the intersection of Drexel Blvd. and 51st St. (Hyde Park Blvd.).*

Drexel Square's restored **Drexel Fountain (A)** is the oldest monument in the boulevard system, dedicated in 1883 by the sons of financier Martin Drexel. To the west lies Washington Park, designed in 1869 by Frederick Law Olmsted.

▷ *Drive north on Drexel Blvd.*

Drexel Boulevard separates Kenwood from Washington Park and was one of Chicago's most fashionable streets from 1880 to 1930. Today large courtyard apartment buildings share the street with mansions from the horse-and-carriage era. On the east side, the Classical Greek temple facade of **Operation PUSH (B)** *(950 E. 50th St.)*, founded by the Rev. Jesse Jackson in 1971, was built in 1923 by the K.A.M. congregation, which later merged with the

Isaiah Israel congregation. The **John H. Nolan House**★ **(C)** *(no. 4941)*, an 1887 work by **John W. Root** of **Burnham & Root**, exemplifies the Romanesque Revival style. Across the street, the **McGill Parc Apartments**★ *(no. 4938)*, created in 1982, occupy the massive, Château-style John McGill mansion (1890, Henry Ives Cobb). At 49th Street note the **Martin A. Ryerson House (D)** *(no. 4851)*, erected in 1887 in the Richardsonian Romanesque style, with its large stone veranda and coach house.

▷ *Turn right on 49th St. and continue east to Ellis Ave.*

To the left at 4848 South Ellis Avenue stands the **Gustavus Swift House (E)** (1898, Flanders & Zimmerman), an exuberant Renaissance palace befitting the meat packer's imperial wealth. Across Ellis Avenue, on the southeast corner, the large, 42-room **Julius Rosenwald House (F)** *(4901 S. Ellis Ave.)* was built for the Sears, Roebuck & Co. chairman in 1903 by Nimmons & Fellows.

▷ *Continue to Greenwood Ave. and turn right.*

On the southwest corner of 49th Street and Greenwood Avenue *(no. 4900)*, note the **Henry Veeder House**★ **(G)** (1907, Howard Van Doren Shaw), a free interpretation of Neoclassical architecture. Respect for the past disappears in the design of the **Ernest J. Magerstadt House**★ **(H)** *(no. 4930)*, an important

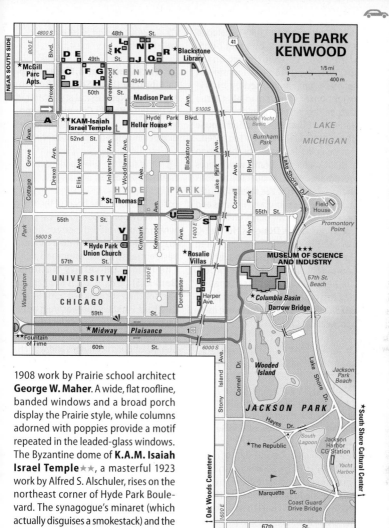

1908 work by Prairie school architect **George W. Maher**. A wide, flat roofline, banded windows and a broad porch display the Prairie style, while columns adorned with poppies provide a motif repeated in the leaded-glass windows. The Byzantine dome of **K.A.M. Isaiah Israel Temple**★★, a masterful 1923 work by Alfred S. Alschuler, rises on the northeast corner of Hyde Park Boulevard. The synagogue's minaret (which actually disguises a smokestack) and the multicolored brick walls are based on a Palestinian precedent from 2C AD. The interior is renowned for its acoustics and features a Guastavino tile dome.

⟫ *Turn left on Hyde Park Blvd., dividing line between Hyde Park and Kenwood, and then right on Woodlawn Ave.*

The **Isidore Heller House**★ (5132 S. Woodlawn Ave.) is an 1897 work by **Frank Lloyd Wright** that illustrates the emergence of his distinctive Prairie style. Wright achieved a horizontal effect on the vertical home by aligning

windows under low-slung eaves and using brick banding and a frieze by sculptor Richard W. Bock. Like all of Wright's Prairie homes, the house has an open interior plan and eschews a front door for a "pathway of discovery."

⟫ *Continue on Woodlawn to 52nd St. and turn right. Turn right on University Ave., right again on Hyde Park Blvd. and left on Woodlawn Ave.*

To the right is **Madison Park**, an exclusive residential area set around a private boulevard, laid out in 1883 by

John Dunham but not fully developed until the apartment-building boom of the 1920s. Past 50th Street, on the left, note the 1916 brick mansion at no. 4944, once inhabited by heavyweight boxer Muhammad Ali. On the northeast corner of 49th and Woodlawn stands the **Elijah Muhammad House (J)** *(no. 4855)*, erected in 1971 in a Mediterranean Modern style for the Nation of Islam leader. The home, which faces four smaller versions built for his sons on the west side of the street, features huge doors, stained-glass windows and a red tiled roof. To the north, on the west side, is the **James Douglas House (K)** *(no. 4830)*, a 1907 Howard Van Doren Shaw design that helped establish the Georgian Revival style in Kenwood. The neighborhood's oldest home is the **Christopher B. Bouton House**★**(L)** (1873), a large, wooden, Italianate mansion located at no. 4812.

◑ *Turn right on 48th St. and right again on Kimbark Ave.*

This block is unique in Chicago for its adoption of the Shingle style, although stone and brick are also used in deference to the climate. The **George Miller House (N)** *(no. 4800)*, an 1888 design copied by George Garnsey from an 1874 H. H. Richardson house in Newport, Rhode Island. Across the street at no. 4801, the **Joseph H. Howard House (P)** (1891, Patton & Fisher) uses pink slate shingles in a picturesque composition of turrets and dormers.

◑ *Turn left on 49th St. and continue to the intersection with Kenwood Ave.*

On the northwest side of the intersection stand two of Frank Lloyd Wright's secret commissions, built in 1892 while he still worked for Adler & Sullivan: the **George W. Blossom House (Q)** *(4858 Kenwood Ave.)* and the **Warren McArthur House (R)** *(4852 Kenwood Ave.)*. Like his Oak Park "bootlegs," these homes are traditional in style, but Wright's restless creativity is visible in windows that sit below wide eaves.

◑ *Continue on 49th St. toward Lake Park Ave.*

The **Blackstone Branch, Chicago Public Library**★ (1902, **Solon S. Beman**) typifies the Neoclassical style inspired by the 1893 **World's Columbian Exposition**, with its dome, acanthus leaves and pedimented temple entrance.

◑ *Drive south on Lake Park Ave. and turn right on 55th St.*

55th Street forms the heart of the Hyde Park/Kenwood Urban Renewal plan, which transformed the street from a jazzy nightlife district into a modern residential strip and shopping mall. The former **University National Bank**★ **(S)** (1929, M. Louis Kroman) on the southwest corner of 55th Street and Lake Park Avenue was built as an automobile showroom, its facade enlivened with playful terra-cotta roadsters, dashboards, engines and wheels. Farther south at 5529 Lake Park Avenue is the **Hyde Park Historical Society (T)**, located in a tiny cable-car station (◷open weekends 2pm–4pm; ✆773-493-1893; www.hydeparkhistory.org). Looming ahead on 55th Street are the twin 10-story towers of I. M. Pei's 1961 **University Apartments (U)**.

◑ *Continue west on 55th St.*

At the northwest corner of 55th Street and Kimbark Avenue, **St. Thomas the Apostle Catholic Church**★ (◷open daily 8am–5pm, check office for admission; ▣ ✆773-324-2626; www.stapostlechurch.com) is a revolutionary 1924 design by Barry Byrne. Byrne was an apprentice of Frank Lloyd Wright and he was the first American to design a European church (the Church of Christ the King in Cork, Ireland).

◑ *Continue west on 55th St. and turn left on Woodlawn Ave.*

Many of the large homes on Woodlawn are owned by the University of Chicago, fraternal associations or theological schools that have clustered in Hyde Park. The massive, Queen Anne **Theodore Rice House**★ **(V)** (1892, Mifflin E. Bell) at the northwest corner of Woodlawn Avenue and 56th Street has colorful pink and gray tiles and a wide porch. Across 56th Street, the Romanesque Revival-style **Hyde Park Union Church**★ (1906, James Gamble Rogers) features orange sandstone and stunning Tiffany and Connick stained glass. South of 57th Street on the west side stands the **Edgar Johnson Goodspeed House (W)** *(5706 Woodlawn Ave.)*, a 1906 Arts and Crafts-style home by **Howard Van Doren Shaw**.

▷ *Turn left on 57th St., right on Dorchester Ave., left on 59th St., then left on Harper Ave. at the Illinois Central Railroad viaduct.*

This quaint street provides insight into Hyde Park's early development, its small lots filled with Queen Anne and Shingle-style homes. The street was originally a planned community called **Rosalie Villas**★, designed in 1883 by Solon S. Beman, who was the architect for nos. 5832–34 and no. 5759. Other architects followed the same vocabulary of wood clapboard siding, shingles and cutout ornament.

▷ *Turn right on 57th St., and right again on Stony Island Ave., heading south to the Midway Plaisance. Follow the Midway west, then double back at the Fountain of Time and follow the Midway east to Cornell Dr.*

The open, grassy expanse of the **Midway Plaisance**★ belies the raucous carnival atmosphere of the 1893 **World's Columbian Exposition**. While the term "midway" is still applied to carnival sideshows, its namesake now serves as the city's broadest boulevard and a foreground for the University of Chicago. Designed in 1869 by **Frederick Law Olmsted** and **Calvert Vaux** as the connecting link between Washington and Jackson parks, the mile-long Midway was intended as a central canal linking the lagoons of the two parks. Although the center of the Midway is depressed below grade level, the water link was never implemented. The **Fountain of Time**★★, a monumental 1922 sculpture by **Lorado Taft**, anchors the western end of the Midway at Washington Park. Inspired by these lines from Austin Dobson, "Time goes, you say? Ah, no!/ Alas, Time stays, we go…," the sculpture took 14 years and a 4,500-piece mold to complete. An **equestrian statue (1)** of St. Wenceslaus by Albin Polasek and dedicated to Czechoslovakian nationalist Tomas Masaryk occupies the opposite end of the Midway. In winter, part of the public park at Midway Plaisance North *(E. 59th St. at Woodlawn Ave.)* becomes an ice-skating rink.

SIGHTS
Jackson Park
E. 56th to 67th Sts., Stony Island Ave. to Lake Michigan.

Located 8mi south of the Loop along Lake Michigan's shoreline, the park's 600 acres of playing fields, lagoons and lush vegetation began as a wasteland of sand dunes and scrub marshes. Renowned landscape architect **Frederick Law Olmsted**'s 1870 plan for the park was only partially implemented when he redesigned and completed it for the World's Columbian Exposition in 1893, creating a series of lagoons and formal ponds as its centerpiece.

A highlight of the park is the gleaming, 24ft-high statue **The Republic**★ by **Daniel Chester French**, cast in 1918 from a scale model of the original 65ft sculpture that stood in the Court of Honor during the 1893 fair. The only sculpture in Jackson Park, it was regilded in 1992 and stands on the site of the fair's administration building.

Olmsted designed **Wooded Island** as a natural area and rookery, known today as the Paul H. Douglas Nature Sanctuary. More than 300 bird species have been spotted on this 16-acre island, located in Jackson Park lagoon. North of Wooded Island is the **Columbia Basin**★, designed by Olmsted as a romantic reflecting pond for the Palace of Fine Arts, now the Museum of Science and Industry. A half-mile south of the park stands the **South Shore Cultural Center**★ (*71st St. and South Shore Dr.;* ○*open Mon–Sat 10am–6pm;* ○*closed major holidays;* ✕⬥🅿 *773-256-0149; www.chicagoparkdistrict.com*), an elegant former country club (1916, Marshall & Fox) that now offers a host of arts and recreational programs as part of the Chicago Park District.

Oak Woods Cemetery

1035 E. 67th Street. Enter off 67th St. at Greenwood Ave. ○*Open daily 9am–4.15pm, office closed Sun.* ●*Guided tours (45min) with one-week advance reservations.* 🅿*. 773-288-3800. www.oakwoodcemetery.net. Pick up a free map in the office.*

Designed in the monumental and picturesque 19C tradition by Adolph Strauch, this 183-acre cemetery hosts occupants ranging from Confederate soldiers to mayors, governors and industrialists. A sculpture of Abraham Lincoln stands at the Grand Army of the Republic Lot. At the **Confederate Mound**★ at the southern end of the cemetery some 6,000 Confederate prisoners of war are buried in concentric trenches under a massive obelisk surmounted by a statue of a defeated rebel. Four cannons guard the corners, while marble tombstones number the nameless Union guards who also died at Chicago's Camp Douglas, where the greatest killers were smallpox and Cholera. More than 4,000 of the deceased are named on the monument erected in May 1895 with elaborate ceremony and 100,000 in attendance.

Distinguished by a red granite marker, the **Jesse Owens monument**, adjacent to the Lake of Memories, is one of the most impressive tombstones; note the stylized Olympic urns flanking the monument. The gray granite **Mayor Harold Washington grave** commemorates the long political career of the city's first black mayor. Among the other notables buried here are Hyde Park founder Paul Cornell, University of Chicago founding president William Rai-

ney Harper, baseball pioneer Cap Anson and nuclear physicist and Nobel prize winner Enrico Fermi.

ADDRESSES

🍴 EAT

$$ Piccolo Mondo – *1642 E. 56th St.* *773-643-1106. www.piccolomondo.us.* The wide, arched windows of this Italian restaurant afford a pleasant view of Jackson Park and the facade of the Museum of Science and Industry. Try the spaghetti and sip Chianti in the candlelit dining room, or grab a sandwich and salad at the gourmet deli counter.

$ Valois – *1518 E. 53rd St.* ⬥. *773-667-0647. www.valoisrestaurant.com.* This cafeteria-style classic has served Hyde Park since 1921, dishing up ample portions of roast beef, baked chicken, greens and casseroles, along with hearty breakfast fare till 4pm. An eclectic crowd gathers here, so the people-watching is good.

🛒 SHOPPING

Artisans 21 Gallery – *1373 E. 53rd St.* *773-288-2450. www.artisans21gallery.com.* One of America's oldest coop-erative art galleries, Artisans 21 is owned and run by a group of artists. Original artwork and one-of-a-kind handcrafted items for sale here include leatherworks, jewelry, ceramics, textiles, paintings and more. Before you leave, take time to chat with some of the artisans who are on-hand to answer questions about their work.

🎭 ENTERTAINMENT

Hyde Park Art Center – *5020 S. Hyde Park Blvd. Open Mon–Thu 9am–8pm, Fri–Sat 9am–5pm, Sun noon–5pm.* 🅿. *773-324-5520. www.hydeparkart.org.* Well worth a peek, this large facility encompasses five galleries and features a round of exhibitions and installations each year by Chicago-area artists. The oldest alternative contemporary art venue in Chicago, the Center also houses artists' studios and offers a full roster of community programs and art classes geared for all ages, from preschoolers to adults. After you have toured the exhibits, take a coffee break at the adjacent **Istria Cafe**, which also serves panini and homemade gelato.

Museum of Science and Industry★★★

Part-amusement park, part-trade show and part-museum, this cacophonous hall of wonders and widgets is one of Chicago's most popular attractions. Located since 1933 in the only building left standing after the World's Columbian Exposition of 1893, the huge museum contains more than 800 exhibits. Dedicated to presenting science, industry and technology in an entertaining way, the museum's hands-on displays invite visitors to push, pull, compute and enjoy.

- ⚅ **Michelin Map:** p217.
- ⓘ **Info:** ☎773-684-1414. www.msichicago.org.
- ◗ **Location:** 57th St. at S. Lake Shore Dr. This large space is difficult to negotiate efficiently. The color-coded stairwells can be a great way to orient yourself.
- 🅿 **Parking:** Ample underground parking for a fee.
- ⊙ **Don't Miss:** The U-505 Submarine exhibit.
- ᠅ **Kids:** Let us count the ways.
- 🕐 **Timing:** To cover everything can easily take two days.
- ⚅ **Also See:** Hyde Park/ Kenwood.

A BIT OF HISTORY
The Building
Perhaps the grandest structure at the World's Fair of 1893, the Palace of Fine Arts represented the essence of that great Beaux-Arts extravaganza. The designer, **Charles B. Atwood** of D. H. Burnham & Co., left no Neoclassical reference unmade by combining elements from the Parthenon and other temples on the Acropolis, along with ancient Roman forms. The sprawling edifice, encircled by 276 columns,

GETTING THERE
BY BUS: ⊞cta bus no. 6 *(Jeffrey Express)* or bus no. 10 *(weekends)*

extends 1,145ft across the front and contains 350,000sq ft of exhibit space. Its two wings, east and west, echo the central pavilion in a rigorous Ionic symmetry. At its rear, the Columbia Basin (North Pond), traversed by gondolas during the 1893 fair, laps at the building's south steps.

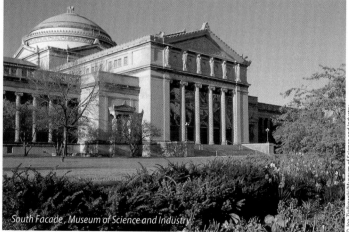

South Facade, Museum of Science and Industry

© Joe Ziolkowski/Museum of Science and Industry

Born Again

Much has happened to the palace since its glory days at the World's Columbian Exposition when it housed works of art from around the world. In its second life as the home of the Field Museum, it slipped into such disrepair as to be dubbed a "scaly, wormy pile." Its condition resulted not from poor maintenance, but rather from the ephemeral materials of its construction, which were never intended to outlive the fair. By 1920, when the Field Museum moved to its new Grant Park facility, the palace's walls, made of brick covered with "staff," a flimsy compound of plaster, cement and hemp, had seriously decayed. It stood forlornly empty in Jackson Park for several years.

Public sentiment to save the building was strong, since it was a remnant of the beloved fair and an unexcelled example of American Neoclassicism. At the same time, philanthropist **Julius Rosenwald**, who had made millions as chairman of Sears, Roebuck and Co., felt Chicago could benefit from a "hands-on" industrial museum like the Deutsches Museum he had seen in Munich, Germany. He would eventually contribute over $7 million to the project.

In 1926 the idea of using the old **Palace of Fine Arts** took root and plans for the complicated renovation got under way. After stripping the moldering plaster skin away from the building's brick and iron skeleton, crews fortified the walls using limestone on the outside and marble on the inside. Fragile skylights were eliminated; 200,000 pounds of copper sheathed the domes. Sturdy stone columns and caryatids replaced their deteriorating predecessors around the facade. Architects gave the interior an Art Moderne look, a most appropriate backdrop for the march of modern technology and science and an acknowledgment of the Century of Progress International Exposition planned to open in 1933 along the lakefront. A portion of the new Museum of Science and Industry (MSI) debuted simultaneously: the revered Palace of Fine Arts would see another World's Fair.

An Invitation to Industry

Times were hard for the museum during the Great Depression. Support was difficult to come by; exhibits remained sparse and restoration incomplete until 1940. The main attraction of those years was the "Coal Mine," its actual bituminous walls so convincing that visitors often wondered where they might place their orders for coal.

The Century of Progress Exposition left the museum with two legacies: many of its exhibits made their way into the collection, and the man who had masterminded the successful two-year pageant, **Major Lenox Lohr**, was hired on as president. In 1940 Lohr, a practiced promoter and showman, left the presidency of the National Broadcasting Company to energize the struggling museum. Injecting life, color and controversy into the serious business of science and technology, Lohr began to shape the modern institution. He invited industries to underwrite, develop and maintain exhibits; he hired architects to enliven the halls; he startled visitors with displays on pregnancy and the human body and he added entertainment to the museum's agenda.

A Continuing Challenge

Lohr remained in charge until his death in 1968. During those years, the museum amassed an amazing array of oddities and wonders, including the U-505 Submarine, Colleen Moore's miniature Fairy Castle, the world's largest model railroad and the world's fastest car. At the same time, the corporate presence grew ever stronger as more and more exhibits carried company logos and transmitted overt and subliminal messages to thousands of daily visitors.

That legacy has bequeathed the museum a continuing challenge: how to weave these disparate parts into a meaningful and evenhanded whole. The master plan introduced in 1990 addressed that concern. The initial effect of the plan was to establish its first admission fee in 1991. Reassessing everything from parking to programs, the plan consolidated the museum's exhibits into six thematic "zones"—human body, transportation, communication, energy and environment, space and defense, and manufacturing. A 1,500-vehicle underground parking facility completed in 1998 is disguised as a six-acre park in the museum's front yard. The subterranean construction houses the **Great Hall**, the entrance to the museum, as well as the renovated 197ft **Pioneer Zephyr train**—featured in a guided tour. Known as the "Silver Streak," the Pioneer Zephyr broke the world's record for speed and non-stop distance in 1934 when it traveled from Denver to Chicago in 13hrs, 5min. A museum store is also located in the Great Hall.

▲▲ VISITING THE MUSEUM

🕐*Open Memorial Day–Labor Day daily 9.30am–5.30pm. Rest of the year Mon–Sat 9.30am–4pm, Sun 11am–4pm.* 🕐*Closed Dec 25.* ⊜*$15(additional fee for Omnimax Theater). Check the website for free days and special exhibit fees.* ✕♿. 🅿($16). ✆773-684-1414. www.msichicago.org.

The museum complex comprises the Henry Crown Space Center, the Great Hall entryway (underground garage) and three floors within central, east and west pavilions. The floors are connected by four color-coded stairwells off the rotunda of the central pavilion; there are also stairs in the east and west pavilions. Elevators and escalators are located near the main entrance and in the red stairwell.

East of the central pavilion, the Crown center is joined to the pavilions by a hallway accessible from the ground floor; the center also can be accessed by a separate outside entrance *(on 57th Dr.)*. Pick up a floor plan as you enter the Great Hall.

Also available here are Omnimax, 3-D Theater and timed tickets for the U-505 Submarine tour *(⊜$5)* and the **Idea Factory**, fun for young children *(up to age 10)*. Waits for these attractions can be long. Flight simulators in Navy: Technology at Sea also attract a crowd.

Amenities

MSI features three restaurants, two on the ground floor along with a vending area. The **Brain Food Court** offers made-to-order sandwiches, stir-fries and salads. A nearby cafe features quick snacks. You'll find **Finnigan's Ice Cream Parlor** at the end of the Yesterday's Main Street exhibit on the main floor.

GROUND FLOOR
Henry Crown Space Center

Located east of the main building, this hall features space-related exhibits. Also here, the **Omnimax Theater** offers a truly sensational experience: its 76ft-high screen nearly engulfs the audience, absorbing them into the film, while the throb of the sound track makes the action nearly palpable. Story lines transport viewers to such spectacular settings as the depths of the ocean and the outer reaches of space (new films are introduced about three times a year). The theater presents two 40min films, shown several times a day. Exhibits on space exploration and travel include the **Apollo 8 command module**★, the first vessel ever to circle the moon in 1968.

U-505 Submarine★★★

Whether or not you choose to tour the sub itself, the surrounding exhibit is a no-miss. Presented in a spectacular setting that explains the history and context of World War II in the North Atlantic Ocean, this German U-boat is the museum's prized artifact. Clever multimedia presentations and compelling films and images rarely seen chronicle the story of its capture off the coast of French West Africa in 1944. The sub was the first enemy warship apprehended by the US Navy since 1815. An "Enigma" code machine and 900lbs of cipher books found aboard enabled American cryptographers to crack a German code used to track ships.

Your timed tour ticket admits you inside the sub, designed to house 56 enlisted men and four officers. An amazingly complicated array of switches, controls, tubes and hardware crowds every inch, punctuated by tiny but efficient living

U-505 Submarine

© Scott Brownell/Museum of Science and Industry

and working quarters. So small are the spaces that sailors could be no taller than 5ft 7in.

MAIN FLOOR
Science Storms★

Opened in spring 2010, this new permanent exhibit puts you in the middle of the action. Unleash an avalanche, create a tidal wave, harness a 40ft tornado, and test the chemistry of combustion in a live fire experiment. Like thunderstorms? Watch as a giant bolt of lightning cracks right above you—thanks to a 20ft Tesla coil suspended overhead; then create your own rainbow. While you're at it, you will unravel the mysteries inside tiny atoms and investigate the physics and chemistry behind some of nature's most powerful forces.

Navy: Technology at Sea★

This exhibit gives you a chance to "tour" three different features of modern US Navy vessels: the aircraft elevator of the carrier USS *George Washington,* the bridge of the fast-attack submarine USS *Chicago* and the control center of the destroyer USS *Arleigh Burke.* For many, the highlight of the galleries is a ride in one of two authentic F-14 Tomcat **flight simulators**★, complete with visuals of a mock bombing run and radio chatter. Taking off, evasive maneuvering, banking and other in-flight drills are so realistic that you are advised to

hold on; landing on the aircraft carrier is a thrilling finale.

The Transportation Gallery

This is an exhibit of juggernauts and superlatives. A steam engine called Buchanan's 999, for instance, broke the record in 1893 by achieving a speed of 112.5mph. A minutely detailed **O-gauge model railroad**★ takes up 3,500sq ft in the middle of the hall.

The layout, including 500 scale buildings and 1,425 feet of track, simulates a rail journey from Seattle to Chicago. Cantilevered from the balcony hangs a United Airlines **Boeing 727**★. It is a thrill to stand beneath its polished underbelly and the impressive starboard wing that stretches 50ft.

Coal Mine★★

Allow 20min for the tour, not including any wait.

This exhibit has thrilled visitors since the museum opened in 1933. From the top of the 60ft "headframe" (which visitors climb to access the mine), an elevator operated by a guide plunges in semidarkness to what seems like a great depth, but which is actually only to the ground floor. (⊙*The experience can be frightening to small children.*) The "mine" itself has walls composed of replica bituminous coal, and the guide demonstrates the grind and groan of the authentic mining equipment on display. In the

Transportation Gallery

© JB Spector/Museum of Science and Industry

"safety room," the guide describes the use of safety lamps to detect methane gas in the mine, creating a contained explosion to illustrate the point. Then a ride in the rattling caged car of a mine train moves the tour along.

Imaging: The Tools of Science★

This fascinating exhibit explores a more modern phenomenon.

"Imaging" refers to the science of gathering, processing and displaying data in visual forms, with the computer as its primary tool. It enables us to picture the far reaches of space, the body's interior, and climatic changes, even on other planets.

Computers invite visitors to manipulate images of their faces, investigate how MRI and CT scans work, and create computer "art" by image enhancement and modeling. Indeed, part of the wonder of this exhibit is the overlap it reveals between science and art.

BALCONY

The second-floor balcony encircles the perimeter of the building and houses a variety of exhibits largely pertaining to chemistry, astronomy, geology, biology, physics and health.

Live demonstrations in the **Grainger Hall of Basic Science** animate fundamental physical theories with discussions and experiments in chemistry and physics.

You! The Experience★

It's all about you at this exhibit in Abbott Hall that explores the connection between the human mind, body and spirit. Centerpiece of the 50 hands-on stations is the 13ft **Giant Heart**. In this 3-D organ, you can watch, both virtually and physically, the blood flow patterns through the heart, and even calibrate its beat to match your own. Elsewhere in the exhibit, you can learn some hip-hop dance moves with the help of a virtual coach; challenge a friend to a game of Mindball, where the most relaxed player wins; exercise in a human-scale hamster wheel; and feel the weighty effect of your favorite snacks.

Take Flight

The eastern portion of the balcony makes a dandy space for the 133ft cutaway Boeing 727 that you marveled at from below. Donated by United Airlines, the aircraft was the seventeenth 727 ever built and remained in service from 1964 to 1991. During its journey to the museum, it became the largest plane ever to land at Meigs Field, Chicago's one-time lakefront commuter airport. Floated by barge to the museum, the huge craft stopped traffic as it was rolled across Lake Shore Drive. Along the balcony, interactive experiments demonstrate how planes fly, and cutaway aircraft parts reveal the complexity of modern flight mechanics.

Pullman Historic District★

> **Location:** 14 miles south of downtown Chicago.

Located in an industrial district on the Far South Side, this fascinating enclave was created by railroad-car magnate George Pullman in 1881 as an experimental company town. After years of neglect, the community was restored and today offers an architectural unity and unique history best sampled by a stroll down the 19C streets.

A BIT OF HISTORY

George Pullman: Entrepreneur

Inventor George Mortimer Pullman (1831–1897) embodied both the American dream and Chicago's "I Will" spirit. He made his first fortune in the 1850s when Chicago raised the street grade to construct sewers in the perennially muddy town. Pullman figured out a way to elevate the buildings by placing hundreds of jackscrews around the foundations and having workers turn them in unison. He bragged that he could raise a hotel "without disturbing a guest or cracking a cup."

For his next venture, George Pullman developed luxurious train coaches—dining cars, club cars, rolling barbershops and his famous sleeping cars—to cater to the tastes of America's wealthy. in 1865, Pullman offered his "Pioneer" sleeping car to transport executives on slain President Abraham Lincoln's funeral train back to Springfield, Illinois. Two years later Pullman incorporated the Pullman Palace Car Co. with a starting capital of $1 million.

A Perfect Town

The 1877 railroad strike shocked the nation. Wishing to isolate his workers from the strike- and strife-prone city, Pullman built a new factory town on 500 acres 13mi south of Chicago at Lake Calumet. In 1880 he hired architect **Solon Spencer Beman** and landscaper **Nathan F. Barrett** to design not only the factories, but also a comprehensive town plan.

Pullman ran his "perfect town" for profit, collecting rents from workers and providing services and necessities. Ever the capitalist, he maintained ownership of all the property in his community; he set rents and refused to let anyone own individual houses. But economic depression in the 1890s brought wage cuts, and to keep the town profitable, Pullman raised rents and food prices. The company's employees rebelled, and strikes and bloody conflict led to the end of Pullman's plan.

In 1971 the town was listed on the National Register of Historic Places. Its restoration continues haltingly today.

VISITING PULLMAN

To access Pullman by car, drive south on I-94 and exit at 111th St. westbound (Exit 66A). The Pullman Historic District is four blocks west of the expressway. To access Pullman by train, take the Metra Electric District Line from the Randolph St. Station; exit at 111th St. (fare and schedule information: 312-836-7000). Begin your visit at the **Historic Pullman Foundation Visitor Center** (11141 S. Cottage Grove Ave.; open year-round *Tue–Sun 11am–3pm;* closed major holidays; 773-785-8901; www. pullmanil.org), which features a video presentation and exhibits. Pick up a self-guided walking-tour brochure or join a **guided walking tour** *(1hr 30min; May–Oct, first Sun of the month; 1.30pm; $7).* A number of historic homes are open for viewing the second weekend in October *(11am–5pm)* for the Annual Pullman House Tour *($20).*

WALKING TOUR

.6mi.

A variety of Victorian homes makes up the 16 blocks of the **South Pullman** residential district. The Queen Anne and Shingle-style homes sport varied and decorative rooflines despite their modest scale. Across 112th Street from the Visitor Center you'll see the **Livery/ Stables Building**★, now an automotive-repair facility. Note the carved horses' heads between the central arches.

▷ *Walk north on Forrestville to the Hotel Florence.*

Hotel Florence★
11111 S. Forrestville Ave.
This grandiose structure (1881), named for Pullman's favorite daughter, exhibits a picturesque roofline with dormers above red brick walls, a wide Eastlake-style veranda and a Joliet limestone foundation. Wooden trim is painted in the color scheme seen throughout Pullman, which combines maroon and two shades of green to offset the red brick and gray roofs.

▷ *Walk south through Arcade Park.*

Arcade Park, restored in 1977, is embellished with 19C gaslight-style lanterns and three formal planting beds.
A series of double houses built for factory foremen flank the park to the east on St. Lawrence Avenue. Most of these structures feature a central shared porch and a roofline punctuated by three dormers, although the compositions are varied and subsequent alterations have created very individual homes.

▷ *Walk east on 112th St. to St. Lawrence Ave.*

At the southeast corner of 112th Street and St. Lawrence Avenue is the **Greenstone Church**★ (Pullman United Methodist Church), a handsome structure dominated by a rich roofline of dormers and a square corner tower. The Romanesque-style walls are faced with serpentine stone from Pennsylvania. The structure was intended to service any denomination and was available for rent. Pullman wanted every element of his community to turn a profit, including the religious edifices.
Designed for skilled craftsmen, the houses to the south on St. Lawrence Avenue included marble fireplaces.

▷ *Continue east on 112th St. to Champlain Ave.*

Market Hall was originally three stories high. The first floor housed a market, which sold the commodities of life to Pullman workers, while the second floor contained an assembly hall and gymnasium; the third floor was devoted to meeting rooms. The building is flanked on all four corners by the two-story curved **Colonnade Apartments and Town Houses**★, creating a unique and attractive streetscape on Market Square. Both the hall and apartments were built in 1892 for the Columbian Exposition.

▷ *Continue east on 112th St. to Langley Ave.*

The modest block houses north of 112th Street on the east side of Langley Street were the meanest in Pullman, designed for unskilled labor.

▷ *Return to Champlain Ave. and walk north to 111th St.*

This block is lined with workers' homes —simple two-story brick row houses. Many have been restored with new porches and trim work painted in the Pullman colors. The homes are small, but the backyards and alleys are ample, rare amenities in the 1880s.
The larger structures at the north end of the block were reserved for company managers. At 111th Street look north to the **Pullman Firehouse**, recognizable by its distinctive Tuscan tower.

▷ *Walk west on 111th St.*

The homes on 111th Street, created for company executives, were once the finest in Pullman.

▷ *Walk north on Cottage Grove Ave.*

Stroll north along Cottage Grove Avenue for a view of the remains of the **Clocktower Building and Erection Shops**, which were burned by an arsonist's fire in 1998.

Excursions

Oak Park★★★

A prosperous integrated suburb bordering Chicago on the west, Oak Park is known worldwide as the birthplace of Prairie-school architecture and the modern American house. Attracting hordes of architecture buffs, as well as lay folk, the town boasts the highest concentration of houses designed by American icon of architecture Frank Lloyd Wright. True to his vision of creating a style of architecture that could embody America's frontier spirit, Wright designed hundreds of unique houses distinguished by horizontal lines, ribbons of stained-glass windows and low, projecting profiles. The adjacent town of River Forest encompasses additional Prairie designs, including six by Wright himself.

- ▶ **Population:** 50,300.
- ⏱ **Michelin Map:** pp232–233.
- ℹ **Info:** Oak Park Area Convention and Visitors Bureau, 1118 Westgate, Oak Park. ℘708-524-7800. www.visitoakpark.com.
- ▷ **Location:** Oak Park lies due west of Chicago.
- 🅿 **Parking:** Municipal lots abound, along with on-street metered parking.
- 👪 **Kids:** Check with the Frank Lloyd Wright Home and Studio for its family-friendly tours.
- ⏰ **Timing:** Plan a day's excursion.
- ⏱ **Also See:** Brookfield Zoo.

A BIT OF HISTORY

Frank Lloyd Wright's best-known works revolutionized residential building design. Born in Wisconsin in 1867, Wright came early under the influence of renowned architect **Louis Sullivan**, apprenticing in Sullivan's studio until striking out on his own at the age of 25. Living and working in Oak Park, he developed his distinctive Prairie style, its strong horizontal lines and overhanging eaves inspired by the flat midwestern land-scape. Inside, Wright flowed rooms one into another, and he designed furniture to complement his organic forms. In a scandal that effectively ended his practice in socially conservative Oak Park, Wright left his wife and six children in 1909 for the wife of a client. He remained in the limelight until his death in 1959 aged 91. His total number of designs exceeds 1,100, with nearly half of them built.

Oak Park: A Suburb Evolves

Prosperous Puritans settled in Oak Park in the years after the fire of 1871 and kept the tiny suburb free from immigrants and alcohol. Oak Park seceded from the township of Cicero and become an independent village in 1902. The population grew rapidly, from 5,000 in 1890 to almost 20,000 by 1910. Novelist **Ernest Hemingway** was born on Oak Park Avenue in 1899. Like Wright, his progressive ideas led him to leave for a world of adventure in 1918. He later derided the conservative suburb for its "wide lawns and narrow minds."

Linked to the city of Chicago by two rapid-transit lines and commuter rail, Oak Park became a suburb of choice for progressive suburbanites in the 20C, swelling its population to 50,000. As racial change swept across Austin in

"The prairie has a beauty of its own. A building on the prairie should recognize the features of its quiet level and accentuate them harmoniously. It should be quiet, broad, inclusive, a welcome associate of trees and flowers, not a nervous, fussy interloper, and should be 'married' to the ground. Hence, broad, sheltering eaves over determined masses, gentle roofs, spreading base and outreaching walls."

Frank Lloyd Wright

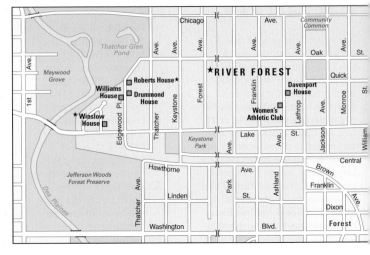

the 1960s and 70s, Oak Park resolved to become an integrated, middle-class community, striving to mix African Americans into its increasingly diverse population, while buttressing its border against the city. In 1973 the Frank Lloyd Wright and Prairie School of Architecture Historic District was listed on the National Register of Historic Places, marking the beginning of restoration efforts. Today Oak Park is known as an economically stable, socially progressive, well-educated community that easily accommodates lifestyles and ideas more radical than those of residents Wright and Hemingway three generations ago.

VISITING OAK PARK

Oak Park lies 10mi west of Chicago's Loop along the Eisenhower Expressway (I-290) between Austin Blvd. and Harlem Ave.

▶ *To access Oak by car, drive west on I-290 and take the Harlem Ave. exit. Turn right onto Harlem and proceed north to Oak Park. By public transportation, take the* cta *Green or Blue line, or take the Metra West commuter rail line from the Metra station at W. Madison and Canal sts. Exit all train lines at Oak Park Ave. or Harlem Ave. stops (for schedules and fares:* ✆ *312-836-7000).*

Stop by the **Oak Park Convention and Visitors Bureau** (*101 Lake St.;* ⏱*open daily 10am–5pm;* ⏱*closed major holidays;*

🅿 ✆*708-524-7800; www.visitoakpark. com*), which offers maps and brochures. An MP3 player and map (⊜*$15*) for **self-guided tours** of the historic district are available at the **Frank Lloyd Wright Home and Studio Museum Shop** (*951 Chicago Ave.;* ⏱ *open year-round daily 10am–5pm;* ⏱*closed major holidays;* ✆ *708-848-1606; www.go wright.org).* 🚶Guided district walking tours (⊜*$15*) begin there on weekends. Privately owned homes and architecturally significant buildings are opened to the public the 3rd Saturday in May for the "Wright Plus" tour (*prices vary*). Advance tickets required (*tickets go on sale Oct 1*).

Oak Park is best experienced by strolling its pleasant tree-lined streets. While feasting your eyes on the architectural marvels, keep in mind that most of the homes are not open to the public, so please respect the owners' privacy. For shopping and dining, head to Lake Street, Chicago Avenue and Oak Park Avenue where you'll find a cluster of shops and restaurants.

SIGHTS
Frank Lloyd Wright Home and Studio★★

951 Chicago Ave. 🚶*Visit by guided tour (1hr) only,* ⏱*daily 11am–4pm.* ⏱*Closed major holidays.* ⊜*$15.* ✆*708-848-1976. www.gowright.org.*

Opened to the public in 1974, this National Historic Landmark helped usher in Oak Park's era as an essential architectural pilgrimage. Wright first built the house in 1889, and continued to remodel and add to it over time; his alterations offer visitors the opportunity to view his architectural growth. The house has been restored to its 1909 appearance, when Wright last lived there and the studio was fully operational.

The tour begins with the 1889 Forest Avenue house that resembles a Shingle-style Victorian but for its horizontal bands of windows and low, earth-hugging profile. The **living room** is centered on the rectilinear hearth and inglenook that would characterize the later Prairie houses. The 1895 **dining room** reveals the emerging Prairie style in elegant, if uncomfortable, high-backed chairs framing the table beneath a false skylight. The tour continues to the modified second floor, where Wright's first office became a bedroom for his growing family. Wall murals in the master bedroom evoke Native-American themes also seen in the 1895 **children's playroom**★, a marvelous barrel-vaulted space with balconies that distort perspective, banded windows and sphere-in-square lanterns. Returning to the main floor, visitors pass a tree that grows through the house (Wright tried to keep natural elements as part of his designs). The two-story **studio**★ addition of 1898 affords a glimpse into the busy, creative world

Frank Lloyd Wright Home and Studio

© Courtesy of Frank Lloyd Wright Preservation Trust/Photo Don Kalec

where Prairie architects apprenticed to the master. The octagonal library and low office entrance include intricate leaded-glass patterns that mimic the environment and intersecting volumes that defy and define interior space. A forest of columns and sculpture by Richard Bock ornament the Chicago Avenue entrance. The basement contains archives, while the museum shop occupies the former garage.

Farther west on Chicago Avenue stand the **Robert P. Parker (A)**, **Thomas H. Gale (B)** and **Walter H. Gale (C)** houses *(nos. 1019, 1027 and 1031)*, "bootleg" homes Wright designed in spite of his exclusive contract with Adler & Sullivan. These 1892–93 Queen Anne structures betray the emerging sensibilities of the 25-year-old Wright with their horizontal clapboards and banded windows.

Nathan G. Moore House★

333 N. Forest Ave.

With its steep roofline, Sullivanesque balustrade fence and Tudor Revival style, the 1895 Moore House presents a dramatic contrast to Wright's later horizontal compositions. The house was a remodeling of an earlier structure that all but disappeared under the busy hand of Wright. The architect rebuilt the home after a 1922 fire, providing Oak Park visitors a rare glimpse of his 1920s experimentation with Japanese themes in encrusted ornament.

Nathan G. Moore House

©Jim Jurica/iStockphoto.com

Arthur Heurtley House★

318 N. Forest Ave.

Wright's admired 1902 design here prefigures many of the elements of his 1909 Robie House, including a raised living space curtained by ornate stained glass, a wide roof that hovers above a band of windows, and horizontally textured brick walls. The front door is hidden by a wall but revealed by a rounded arch, sug-gesting a serene and organic fortress. Wright moved and remodeled the 1883 Stick-style **Hills DeCaro House★** *(313 N. Forest Ave.)* in 1900, adding horizontal shingling and flattening the roof.

Laura Gale House★

6 Elizabeth Ct.

Anticipating Europe's International style of the 1920s, the broad cantilevered planes of this 1909 home also prefigure Wright's 1936 work, Fallingwater. The porches expand the living spaces, "breaking the box" of architecture and shifting it into the landscape.

The Joseph D. Everett House (D) *(228 N. Forest Ave.)*, an 1888 Queen Anne Victorian, represents the dominant residential style in the years that Frank Lloyd Wright wreaked his revolution on the serene side streets of Oak Park.

Frank W. Thomas House★

210 N. Forest Ave.

Considered the first true Prairie-style house by Wright, this 1901 commission abandons all elements and ornaments of Victorian design. The entrance arch below the main floor leads not to a door but to a staircase proceeding to the hidden entry. Flattened roofs and high stucco walls squeeze and shelter bands of art-glass windows.

Unity Temple★★

875 W. Lake St. ◷*Open Mon–Fri 10.30am –4.30pm, Sat 10am–2pm, Sun 1pm–4pm (self-guided tours only).* ⊚*$8.* ✆*708-848-6225. www.unitytemple.org.*

Called "my little jewel" by Wright, Unity Temple (1905) is an intriguing succession of form and space. The small budget ($45,000) dictated the use of unadorned

Pleasant Home

Darris Harris/Visit Oak Park

reinforced concrete for the interlocking rectangular forms of the worship space and social hall. The two are joined with a low lobby shielded from busy Lake Street by a "pathway of discovery" leading from Kenilworth Avenue onto a raised entrance behind a high wall. Entered from behind the lectern, the worship space seems at once massive and intimate. Framed by rectilinear balconies, three levels allow 400 people to sit no more than 45ft from the pulpit. Bathed by a grid of square skylights and clerestory windows, the room is framed with wood trim in a deceptively simple series of borders and inset rectangles with sphere-in-square chandeliers.

ADDITIONAL SIGHTS

On the southwest corner of Oak Park Avenue and Lake Street, **Scoville Square** (1908, E. E. Roberts) exhibits the influence of the Prairie school on commercial architecture with its broad rooflines. Euclid Avenue, near Oak Park, and River Forest High School boasts the **Edward W. McCready House** at no. 231 (1907, Spencer & Powers); note its stately entrance.

Ernest Hemingway Birthplace

339 N. Oak Park Ave. ⏲*Open year-round Sun–Fri 1pm–5pm, Sat 10am–5pm.* ⏲*Closed major holidays.* ⊜*$8.* ℘*708-445-3071. www.ehfop.org.*
This restored Victorian home (1890, Wesley A. Arnold) re-creates the comfortable upbringing of celebrated author Ernest Hemingway (1899–1961), who won the Nobel Prize for literature (1954). Two blocks south, at no. 200, the **Hemingway Museum** (℘*708-524-5383; same hours and website as the* *Hemingway Birthplace)* offers exhibits that explore the author's life.

Pleasant Home★
(John Farson House)

217 Home Ave. Call for tour information. 🅿 ℘*708-383-2654. www.oprf.com/phf.*
This 1897 house was the first of **George Washington Maher** in his modern (Prairie) style, with its broad facade, hipped roof and repeated motifs—the honeysuckle, Roman tray or shield, lion's head and segmented arch—in exterior decoration and interior furnishings.

RIVER FOREST★

The more exclusive town of River Forest encompasses several notable Prairie School Designs. Frank Lloyd Wright's 1893 **William Winslow House**★ *(515 Auvergne Pl.)* was his first significant independent commission. Centered on a square, Sullivanesque arch, the flat and symmetrical facade begins to reach for prairie-like horizontality in its Roman brick, low-pitched roof. On nearby Edgewood Place, an elm tree grows through the parlor of Wright's 1908 split-level **Isabel Roberts House**★ *(no. 603).* The home was restored by Wright in 1955. Next door at no. 559, the **William Drummond House**, designed by its owner in 1910, exemplifies the work of Wright's student with its broad porch and flat roof, while the **Chauncey Williams House** at no. 530 (1895, Frank Lloyd Wright) is a rare, high-roofed Wright design with Japanese influence. Ashland Avenue features Wright's 1901 **Arthur Davenport House** at no. 559, and the elegantly scaled **Women's Athletic Club** at no. 526 (1911, Drummond and Guenzel).

Brookfield Zoo★★

Covering 216 acres in west suburban Brookfield, this expansive zoo in a garden is home to more than 2,000 animals inhabiting carefully re-created rain forests, seascapes, savannas and deserts. For its human denizens, 15mi of footpaths wind through the lovely grounds, and shady stretches of lawn invite picnicking. Formal flower beds complement the patchwork of animal habitats. Nearly two million people each year enjoy this animal haven, leaving with a heightened respect for our fragile environment.

A BIT OF HISTORY

Brookfield Zoo's meticulous attention to habitat continues a long tradition of cageless homes for its animals. The idea was to create a zoo big enough to accommodate natural outdoor habitats, thereby eliminating the use of small, spartan enclosures, and emulating conditions in the wild to provide more realistic study and breeding opportunities. Such was the trend in European zoos, and the Bronx Zoo in New York had incorporated naturalistic settings into its plan when it debuted in 1899. Built on land donated to the Forest Pre-

- **Michelin Map:** Map of principal sights and plan below.
- **Location:** The zoo is laid out roughly in quadrants around Roosevelt Fountain.
- **Parking:** There's lots of parking for a fee.
- **Kids:** Everything—plus the Carousel.
- **Timing:** This is a big zoo with lots to do. Plan a day.

serve District of Cook County by Edith Rockefeller McCormick in 1919, Brookfield opened in 1934 after years of controversy over taxes and public funding. The "barless" Bear Grottos, Goat Mountain and Monkey Island were among the first habitats completed, along with the Small Mammal House, the Reptile House and the Pachyderm House. In the last several decades, the trend toward cageless habitats has moved indoors with the construction of Tropic World: A Primate's Journey (among the world's largest zoo exhibits), The Fragile Kingdom, The Swamp and The Living Coast.

VISITING BROOKFIELD ZOO

The zoo is located 14mi southwest of the Loop in Brookfield. ▶ By car from the Loop, drive west on I-290 to the 1st Ave.

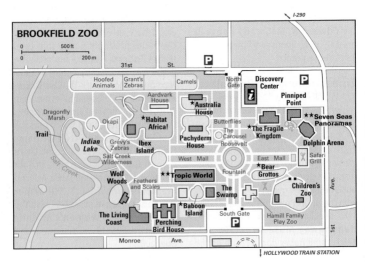

234

Famous Zoo Residents

The Brookfield Zoo's animal collection started with the gift of 143 mammals, 123 birds and 4 reptiles from a private zoo in Holland, Michigan. In the ensuing years, Brookfield has had its share of famous inhabitants, including the first giant pandas in an American zoo: Su-lin arrived in 1937, Mei-mei in 1938 and Mei-lan in 1939. Museka, the first okapi in America, arrived in 1955. Temperamental Asian bull elephant Ziggy (named after his original owner Florenz Ziegfield) lived to the ripe old age of 55; and the zoo's oldest resident, Cookie the cockatoo, turned 75 years old in 2008. The zoos' resident heroine is an ape named Binti Jua who rescued a three-year-old boy who fell into her enclosure and knocked himself unconscious in 1996.

exit, then continue south on 1st Ave. to 31st St. Follow signs to the zoo.
By train, take the Burlington Northern Metra train line from Union Station in the Loop. Get off at the zoo stop at Hollywood Station and walk north four blocks (fare and schedule information: ℘312-836-7000).
Open Memorial Day–Labor Day Mon–Sat 9.30am–6pm; rest of the year, hours vary. Closed major holidays. $13.50 (Jan–Feb & Oct–Dec free admission Tue & Thu). Additional charges for some exhibits and shows. ($9). ℘708-688-8000. www.brookfieldzoo. org. Check at entrances or information kiosks throughout the zoo for schedule of special shows and demonstrations.
Departing just west of the gates, the **Motor Safari** tour offers a narrated overview of the zoo. The tram can also be used to shuttle to the various areas of interest since you can disembark and reboard at any of four tram stops throughout the day *(operates daily spring–late fall, weather permitting; 45min round-trip; commentary; $4;).* During the winter months, you can ride the Snowball Express. Restaurants and snack bars offering varied cuisine are located throughout the zoo.

THE GROUNDS

The park fans out from Roosevelt Fountain, the formally landscaped heart of the grounds approached from four directions by grassy esplanades and pathways. Favorite sights around the zoo include **Regenstein Wolf Woods**, home to a pack of gray wolves, and the new **Great Bear Wilderness**★—the zoo's largest exhibit—where polar and grizzly bears cavort alongside wolves, bald eagles and bison.

The Art Deco **Pachyderm House** and outdoor enclosures are home to black rhinos, Nile hippopotamuses and African elephants. In the **Perching Bird House**, iridescent avian gems reside behind "jewel-box" window enclosures.

Great Bear Wilderness

Chicago Zoological Society/Brookfield Zoo

The Fragile Kingdom★

Northeast of the fountain, a large three-part exhibit explores the complex webs of life and survival in an African desert and an Asian rain forest. In these naturalistic habitats species commingle as they would in the wild, and the experience envelops the visitor as each setting extends to the public areas of the space. **The Fragile Desert** tells a story of survival in a seemingly inhospitable climate and how such animals as meerkats make a home there. Tiny windows reveal a subterranean world of burrowing creatures, including the fascinating naked mole-rats, hairless mammals that live in colonies like bees and feed on underground plant parts. Outside, the big cats are displayed in **Fragile Hunters** in the context of their increasingly difficult struggle to survive as hunters in their vanishing ecosystems. In the **Fragile Rain Forest**, otters play in streams, clouded leopards peer out from the shadows, and bats fly overhead.

Seven Seas★★

Newly renovated in 2010, Seven Seas is perhaps the most popular attraction at the zoo. **Pinniped Point**★ features a series of outdoor pools designed to resemble a Pacific Northwest shoreline environment stocked with pinnipeds—seals and sea lions. An underwater viewing area beneath the pool allows visitors to enjoy the animals at their most graceful. Next door, the revamped **Dolphin Presentation**★ *(several performances daily;* ✆*$4;* ♿*)* is a perpetual favorite. Spectators generally jam the 2,000-seat **Dolphin Arena**—with its new Caribbean theme—to view the antics of Atlantic bottle-nosed dolphins. The performance reinforces the zoo's conservation message, and trainers are careful to explain the significance of dolphin behaviors in the wild.

Tropic World: A Primate's Journey★★

Tropic World offers you a dramatic treetop perspective of rain forest habitats. Realistic trees, foliage, waterfalls, and pools combine in a cavernous environment bustling with activity. Intriguing animals, from the tiny Brazilian golden lion tamarin to the lordly western lowland gorillas reside here.

Nearby, **The Swamp** offers insight into a North American cypress swamp populated by alligators, snakes and a variety of birds, as well as an Illinois wetland alive with otters and alligator-snapping turtles. **Baboon Island**★ houses a colony of rambunctious Guinea baboons.

In **Australia House**★ audio stations guide you through a nocturnal "walkabout" past wombats and into a space alive with free-flying fruit bats. Find kookaburras, echidnas, kangaroos, cassowaries and ostriches outdoors.

Habitat Africa!★

This African exhibit includes **The Savannah**, which covers 5 acres highlighting the continent's diverse wildlife. Giraffes, wild dogs and others populate the dusty plain, while a variety of hoofed animals slake their thirst at the water hole.

The Forest replicates the pristine Ituri rain forest in central Africa's Democratic Republic of Congo. Enter this leafy world, created by combining 545 trees and 775 shrubs with fabricated elements, and discover the diversity of life in the rain forest, from the emperor scorpion to the hoofed okapi. Signs introduce the human residents of the Ituri: the Mbuti people who call the forest home, the Bila villagers who farm the edges of the forest, and the researchers and reserve rangers who study and work there.

The Living Coast★

Glimpse the "underwater" world of the west coast of South America, from the Open Ocean to the Near Shore Waters to the Rocky Shores. In **Open Ocean**, a ceiling-high tank swirls with seaweed, sea turtles and a host of fish; while in **Rocky Shores**, waves crash overhead. Along the way you'll see jellyfish, sea turtles, Inca terns and even vampire bats, while displays relate the surprising connections that exist between the animals, plants and coastal environment.

Morton Arboretum ★

Sprawling over 1,700 acres, this outdoor museum is both a serious scientific laboratory of woody plants from around the world and a very pleasant place to spend the day. Visitors who wander by car and on foot may not realize the contributions to horticulture, botany and ecology that this arboreal microcosm makes possible. Open year-round, the arboretum attracts professional landscapers and gardeners, horticultural hobbyists, bird-watchers and hikers.

A BIT OF HISTORY

Joy Morton, founder of the arboretum in 1922, came by his love of trees naturally. His father, J. Sterling Morton, had been secretary of Agriculture under Grover Cleveland and is well remembered as the creator of Arbor Day. Using his fortune, made at the helm of the Morton Salt Co., which he founded, Morton established the arboretum on 400 acres at Thornhill (his Du Page County estate) and proceeded to carry out the family motto to "Plant Trees." From the beginning, Morton intended the arboretum to be a place to preserve and study trees suitable for growing in Illinois' temperate climate—a veritable "museum of woody plants."

Today the arboretum's far-flung collection is divided into four general categories: botanical groups (plants in the same genus or family, such as the *Quercus*, or oaks), landscape groups (plants with a similar use, such as the ground-cover), geographic groups (plants from the same region, such as the Japan) and special habitat groups (plants that live in "amended" soil or in special sites, such as sand beds).

The grounds also support native landscapes: oak groves, wetlands and prairie. Particularly strong among the arboretum's collections are its Rosaceae (rose family), elms and sugar maples (beautiful in the fall).

- ⚙ **Michelin Map:** Map of principal sights.
- ▷ **Location:** Route 53 separates the Arboretum's east and west sides.
- 🅿 **Parking:** Parking is available throughout the grounds.
- ☻ **Don't Miss:** Be sure to visit at least one or two of the lovely gardens.
- 👪 **Kids:** The Children's Garden is truly special.
- ◷ **Timing:** Take a leisurely day to explore the grounds.

VISITING MORTON ARBORETUM

4100 Illinois Rte. 53.
The arboretum is located on Rte. 53, 25mi west of the city, just north of I-88 and west of I-355. ▷ *By car from the Loop, take I-290 West and then continue west on the I-88 tollway. At Rte. 53, turn north toward the arboretum.*
◷ *Grounds open daily year-round 7am–sunset. ⊜$11 (Wed $7). Tram tours Apr–Oct; call for schedule; ⊜$6/hr or $3/ 30min. ✕ ⚙ ⚲630-968-0074. www.mortonarb.org.*

Begin at the **Visitor Center** (◷ *open daily Mar–Apr and Nov–Dec 9am–5pm; May–Oct 9am–6pm; Jan–Feb 9am–4pm*) on the east side to gather information about the grounds, pick up trail maps and find out what is in bloom. Several gardens can be reached on foot from here, including the ground covers, roses and dwarf shrubs. Excellent open-air **tram tours** ★ depart from the visitor center. Free nature walks are available *(call ⚲630-719-2465 for details)*. Or drive the 11mi one-way route in your car *(a driving map is provided at the entry gate)*. Along the way, 26 parking areas access 14mi of trails that wind through the grounds. You have unlimited access to the woods, glades, gardens and meadows *(a GPS is recommended on the lesser paths as there is little signage)*. Highlights include the **fragrance garden** ★ and 100-acre **Schulenberg Prairie**.

Illinois & Michigan Canal National Heritage Corridor★

The Illinois & Michigan (I&M) Canal, running 96mi from Bridgeport to LaSalle/Peru, first linked the Great Lakes to the Mississippi and helped Chicago build its reputation as an industrial powerhouse. Today a popular recreational area hosting over five million visitors yearly, the National Heritage Corridor encompasses historic canal towns offering a glimpse into bygone days, as well as native prairies and state parks laced with miles of pleasant hiking and biking trails.

Michelin Map: p239 and pp242–243.

Info: Heritage Corridor Convention & Visitors Bureau, 339 W. Jefferson St., Joliet, IL 60435. ℘815-727-2323 or 800-926-2262 (US & Canada only). www.heritagecorridorcvb.com.

Parking: Street and lot parking ample all along the way.

Don't Miss: A hike along the bluffs of the Illinois River at Starved Rock State Park.

Kids: Kids will enjoy the many outdoor activities and living history sites along the corridor.

Timing: Plan two days or more if possible and stay overnight in one of the quaint canal towns, or camp in a state park.

A BIT OF HISTORY

Between 15,000 and 10,000 years ago, meltwaters from retreating glaciers carved a wide valley southwest of Chicago to the Mississippi River. As the glacial lake drained, a low, 12ft-high ridge rose slowly between the Des Plaines and Chicago rivers, separating the watershed of the Mississippi from the Great Lakes. Native Americans traveled by canoe through this corridor, and guided the first Europeans, explorer **Louis Jolliet** and missionary **Jacques Marquette**, to the Chicago Portage between the two rivers in 1673. As the French continued to explore Illinois and establish a lucrative fur trade, they realized that a canal through this low divide would open the continent to commerce.

After the area became part of the US in 1782, a canal was proposed and by the 1820s, a federal commission was established to create the channel connecting Lake Michigan to the Illinois River. Along with the Erie Canal, the I&M Canal would provide an inland link from New York to New Orleans. The towns of Chicago and Ottawa were platted in 1830, and canal construction began at Bridgeport on July 4, 1836. Despite a three-year hiatus caused by Illinois' unstable financial condition, the canal was completed in 1848. Chicago's population boomed from 4,000 to over 20,000 during construction, and other canal towns blossomed as well. As the narrow, 60ft-wide channel brought grains and livestock from Illinois' rich prairie soils to eastern markets, Chicago more than quadrupled its population to over 112,000 by 1860. Stone quarrying, steel production, and coal, zinc and sand mining thrived throughout the corridor in the 19C.

Horses towed passenger boats and mules pulled boats laden with lumber, stone and grains. Although railroads made their appearance in the corridor by 1854, the canal continued to carry freight, reaching its apogee in 1882 when steam-powered boats had replaced the mule teams. Unlike most canals, the I&M paid off its debt by 1871, and was deepened that year from 6ft to 8ft in an attempt to reverse the flow

PRACTICAL INFORMATION

Access – Northern section: Follow itinerary directions in driving tour text. Southern section: Drive south on I-55 for 46mi to Rte. 6 west toward Channahon. For other sights in the Southern section, drive south on I-55 and then west on I-80; exit at Rte. 47 for Morris, Rte. 23 for Ottawa, Rte. 178 for Utica and Starved Rock State Park, and Rte. 351 for LaSalle.

Visitor Information – The I&M Canal is best visited on summer weekends when most activities occur. The route can be difficult to follow as signs bearing the canal logo *(below)* are sometimes hard to locate. For maps and information about accommodations and recreation, contact the **Heritage Corridor Visitors Bureau** (🏛*see Information, previous page).* The **Illinois and Michigan Canal National Heritage Corridor Association** is the official authority in charge of preserving and protecting the historic corridor *(200 W. 8th Street, Lockport, IL 60441; 📞815.588.1100; www.canalcor.org).*

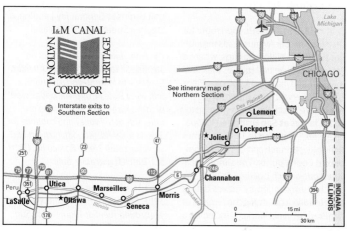

of the Chicago River. The effort was not entirely successful, and after cholera and typhoid epidemics decimated the city in the 1880s, Chicago created a Metropolitan Sanitary District to dig a much larger drainage canal from Chicago to Lockport. Completed in 1900, the canal permanently reversed the Chicago River. By 1914 the northern section of the I&M Canal was replaced as a shipping channel by the new Sanitary & Ship Canal. In 1933 the Illinois River was made navigable, and the obsolete I&M began to be developed for recreational use. The section of the canal in Chicago was filled in for construction of the Stevenson Expressway *(I-55)* in the 1950s. In 1963 the I&M Canal was designated as a National Historic Landmark, and nine years later, the southern section became a state park. Efforts to develop the canal's recreational and historic potential culminated in the designation by Congress of the entire canal route *(120mi)* as a National Heritage Corridor in 1984. Today numerous historic buildings have been preserved and new trails and wayside exhibits promote the region's historic, recreational and economic resources.

🚗 DRIVING TOUR

NORTHERN SECTION — Chicago to Joliet

About 90mi round-trip.

The highly industrialized northern section of the canal borders Chicago and includes several evocative historic sites as well as recreational and natural areas. Note that some sections of the drive are highly commercialized or wind through ordinary suburban landscapes, offering few vistas of the canal. However, quaint canal towns and various museums make this a worthwhile day trip from Chicago. Follow the map and the directions carefully, as this stretch is sometimes difficult to navigate.

▷ *Leave Chicago on I-55 (Stevenson Expwy.) and exit at LaGrange Rd./ Rte. 45 (Exit 279A); bear right and follow the signs to Rte. 171/Archer Ave. South.*

Built in 1836 as a construction route for the canal, Archer Avenue leads through the suburb of Willow Springs, where a 9mi-loop bicycle trail follows the canal towpath, and into the 14,000-acre Palos Forest Preserves. After about 5mi, to the left before Route 83, stands the historic **St. James at Sag Bridge**★ *(10600 S. Archer Rd.)*. Founded in 1833, St. James is the oldest church and cemetery complex in Cook County. The simple local limestone church building (c.1850) sits on a hill surrounded by graves dating back to 1846, containing the remains of hundreds of canal workers, including a large number of Irish immigrants.

▷ *Continue on Rte. 171 as it turns left at Rte. 83.*

The road crosses the Calumet Sag Channel, built in 1911 to link the Sanitary & Ship Canal with Chicago's southern port at Lake Calumet.

▷ *Keep right to follow Rte. 171; turn right after about 3mi at McCarthy Rd., which becomes Stephen St., and drive into Lemont.*

Lemont
Known in the 19C for its dolomite limestone quarries, Lemont is a well-preserved historic canal town set on a bluff in the Des Plaines River Valley. The **Lemont Area Historical Society Museum** *(306 Lemont St.)*, located in an 1861 limestone church, offers exhibits and research facilities; pick up a self-guided brochure to the downtown area here (◷*open year-round Tue & Thu–Fri 10am–2pm, Sat 10am–1pm, Sun 1pm–4pm;* ⬠*$2;* ✆*630-257-2972; www. lemonthistorical.org)*. The downtown shopping area *(Main and Stephen Sts.)* is dominated by 19C Italianate buildings constructed of Lemont stone.

These include the 1870 **Norton Building** *(101 Stephen St.)*, today home to the Illinois State Museum Lockport Gallery; and the highly ornate 1870s **Friedley Building** *(311 Canal St.)*. A 4mi canal trail begins at General Fry Landing, on Stephen Street west of the canal.

▷ *From downtown, backtrack on Stephen St. to Illinois St. and turn right. Continue to State St. and turn right, following State St. over the bridge west of town. Turn left at Bluff Rd. on the other side of the valley and continue for 3mi. At Joliet Rd. (Rte. 53), turn left and continue south 3mi to Romeo Rd. (135th St.). Turn left and drive .5mi.*

👥 Isle a la Cache Museum★
501 E. Romeo Rd., Romeoville. ◷*Open year-round Tue–Sat 10am– 4pm, Sun noon–4pm.* ◷*Closed major holidays.* ♿▣ ✆*815-886-1467. www.reconnectwithnature.org.*

Located on a small island in the Des Plaines River that was named by the French *coureurs de bois* who used the 80-acre haven to hide their trade goods, this museum was newly renovated in 2007. It presents historical exhibits highlighting daily life during the French-Indian fur-trade era. Interactive displays feature maps, Native American dwellings and articles of daily life and the story of the beaver fur trade. Interpreters in Native American and 18C French costume demonstrate how to build a fire, portage a canoe and fire a musket. The modern building imitates a typical French Colonial structure with its steeply pitched roof overhanging a pavilion.

▷ *Return to Rte. 53 (Independence Blvd.) and continue south 2.5mi.*

Just before the intersection with Route 7, on the left at no. 15701, stands the **Fitzpatrick House**. The restored 1850s limestone farmhouse once anchored a 1,000-acre farm.

▷ *Continue south to Rte. 7 and turn left.*

Immediately south of Route 7, on the right, extends the 269-acre **Lockport Prairie Nature Preserve**★, designated in 1983 as the largest presettlement prairie in northern Illinois *(access from Division St., .5mi south of Rte. 7 off Rte. 53; ◷open year-round daily 8am–sunset; ✆815-727-8700; www.reconnectwith nature.org).*

An easy .5mi trail winds through native prairie grass and a profusion of wildflowers. The Route 7 bridge crosses over the meandering Des Plaines River and then the Sanitary & Ship Canal, flanked by large grain elevators, before entering Lockport.

▷ *Turn right on Canal St. before the I&M Canal and continue .5mi to view Lock no. 1. Then turn left at Division St. just past the lock, and left again on State St. (Rte. 171) to enter downtown Lockport. Turn left on 8th St., one block after the intersection with Rte. 7, and park in the Gaylord Building lot.*

Lockport★

Founded in 1836 as the canal headquarters, this picturesque canal town *(www.lockport.org)* features a lovely downtown listed on the National Register of Historic Places. A short drive along the canal leads to **Lock no. 1**, a featured sight on the 2.5mi **Gaylord Donnelley Canal Trail**★ that follows the canal through Lockport and includes several wayside exhibits. This lock was the first of 15 locks used to raise and lower the boats plying the canal.

The **Gaylord Building**★ *(200 W. 8th St.)* was restored in the 1980s to its 1860s appearance. In 1996 the Gaylord became the first industrial building acquired as a historic property by the National Trust for Historic Preservation. The two-story western section of the local limestone building, completed in 1838 as a warehouse for canal construction, now contains the **Public Landing restaurant** *(✆815-838-6500; www.public-landingrestaurant.com).* The three-story 1859 Italianate addition served as the store and offices of the grain companies who occupied the building from 1848 to 1890. Today the structure's first floor houses a permanent exhibit, **Illinois Passage: Connecting the Continent**, limns the history of canal and its impact on the area *(◷open Tue–Sat 11am–5pm, Sun noon–5pm; ✗🅿 ✆815-838-9400; www.gaylordbuilding.org).* The second and third floors display changing exhibits relating to the history of Lockport and the Heritage Corridor. In the Norton Building at 201 West 10th Street, the **Illinois State Museum Lockport Gallery** offers rotating shows of art by Illinois artists, past and present *(◷open year-round Mon–Fri 9am–5pm, Sun noon–5pm; ◷closed major holidays; 🅿 ✆815-838-7400; www.museum.state.il.us/ismsites/lockport).* The massive stone Norton Building was erected in 1850 by the Norton family as part of its complex of mills on the Illinois & Michigan Canal. The exterior has been carefully restored.

South of the Gaylord Building along the canal, **Lincoln Landing** was dedicated in February 2009 to interpret the history of its namesake, Abraham Lincoln, and his support of the construction of the I&M Canal. Centerpiece of the park, which runs from 8th to 9th streets, is a bronze sculpture of Lincoln as a young Illinois legislator.

South of the parking lot on State Street stands the **Will County Historical Society** *(803 S. State St.),* located in the original 1837 headquarters of the I&M Canal Commission. Today the Society building is crammed with artifacts documenting Will County's past *(◷open Tue–Sun noon–4pm; ◷closed major holidays; 🅿 ✆815-838-5080; www.willcountyhistory.org).*

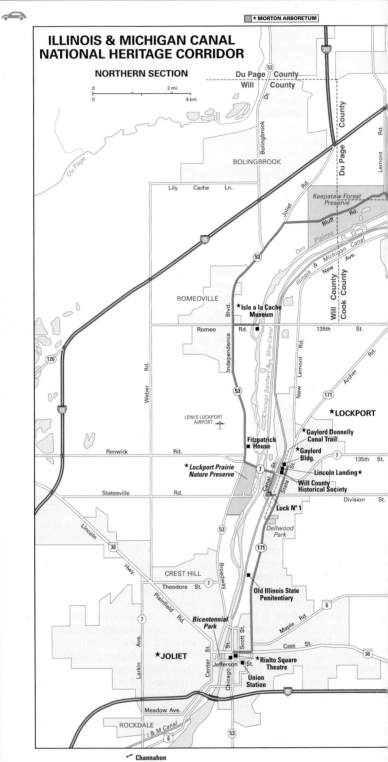

★ MORTON ARBORETUM

ILLINOIS & MICHIGAN CANAL
NATIONAL HERITAGE CORRIDOR

NORTHERN SECTION

0   2 mi
0   4 km

Du Page County
Will County

BOLINGBROOK

Lily   Cache   Ln.

Keepataw Forest
Preserve

ROMEOVILLE

★ Isle a la Cache
  Museum

Romeo   Rd.

135th   St.

LEWIS LOCKPORT
AIRPORT

★ LOCKPORT

Fitzpatrick
House

★ Gaylord Donnelly
  Canal Trail

★ Gaylord
  Bldg.

135th   St.

Renwick   Rd.

★ Lockport Prairie
  Nature Preserve

Lincoln Landing ★

Will County
Historical Society

Statesville   Rd.

Division   St.

Lock N° 1

Dellwood
Park

CREST HILL

Theodore   St.

Old Illinois State
Penitentiary

Bicentennial
Park

★ JOLIET

Rialto Square
Theatre

Union
Station

Meadow Ave.

ROCKDALE

I & M Canal

Channahon

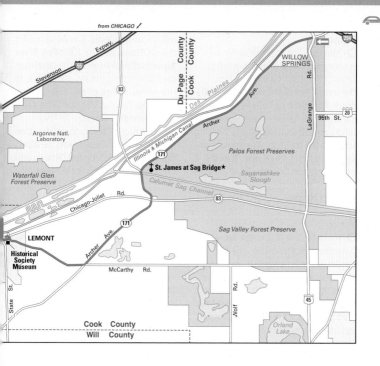

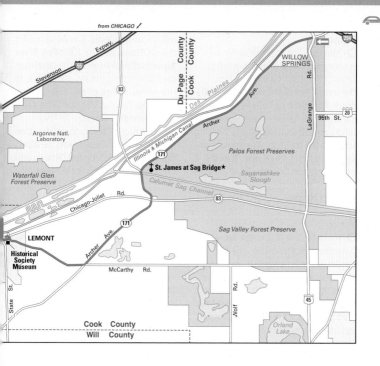 *Continue south on State St. (Rte. 171) into Joliet. Turn right on Cass St. (Rte. 6).*

Joliet★

The entrance to Joliet is marked by the **Old Illinois State Penitentiary** (1857, William W. Boyington) resembling the architect's Chicago Water Tower with its castlelike limestone walls and towers. Cass Street leads into downtown Joliet and toward the riverboat casinos that boosted its economy in the early 1990s. Historic highlights include the restored **Union Station** *(50 E. Jefferson St.)* from 1907, and **Rialto Square Theatre★** *(102 N. Chicago St.)*, erected in 1926 by Rapp & Rapp. An opulent mirror-lined lobby leads into the rotunda dominated by an enormous, hand-cut crystal chandelier, claimed to be the largest in the US *(performances Sept–May, for tickets call ℘815-726-7171; 1hr guided tours available year-round Tue 1.30pm; call to confirm; ◯closed major holidays; ⛄$5; www.rialtosquare.com).* Also of interest is **Bicentennial Park** *(201 W. Jefferson St.)* with its waterside walk, mosaic mural and boulders commemorating impor-

tant events in a city defined in the 19C by limestone quarrying and the steel industry *(♿ 🅿 ℘815-724-3760; www. bicentennialpark.org).*

 Return to Chicago via Rte. 30 and I-55 (about 40mi).

Southern Section— Channahon to LaSalle/Peru

The following sights are not part of a driving tour. You may choose to spend an entire day at one of the state parks, hike or bike along the 61mi canal trail, or rent a canoe and paddle down the canal. Access to each sight has been given from I-80. If you wish to drive through the various towns, follow Rte. 6 West to Ottawa, then continue on Dee Bennett Road to Utica, returning to Rte. 6 for LaSalle. Though industrialized, the southern section of the Heritage Corridor boasts numerous recreational opportunities in the wide Illinois River Valley. Fishing aficionados will find a wealth of choice spots, while hiking and biking enthusiasts can follow the canal for miles along the rambling trails.

Channahon

▶ *From I-55 (Exit 248), follow Rte. 6 for 2mi through the town and turn left at Canal St. onto I&M Canal State Trail.*

The scenic 61mi **I&M Canal State Trail**★ (from Rockdale to LaSalle) provides a historic route for hiking, bicycling, canoeing and snowmobiling. Offering access to the trail, a lovely park at Channahon includes **Lock nos. 6 and 7**, a weir where the Du Page River crosses the canal, and an original 1840s **Locktender's House**.

Morris

▶ *From I-80 (Exit 112), follow Rte. 47.*

Downtown Morris retains the feel of a canal town and county seat. Just outside town the **Aux Sable Aqueduct**, near the Locktender's House and Lock no. 8, carries the canal over a creek. **Gebhard Woods State Park**★ *(401 Ottawa St.)* includes a visitor center and the Nettle Creek Aqueduct. Picnic tables scattered under oak and maple trees make this a pleasant lunchtime spot *(visitor center* ○ *open year-round daily 10am–4pm;* △ &⃞ P⃞ *℘815-942-0796).*

Farther west along Route 6 lie the old canal towns of Seneca and Marseilles, as well as Lock nos. 9 and 10. In **Seneca**, note the 65ft-tall, 70,000-bushel capacity **grain elevator** erected in 1861; a rare survivor from the canal's heyday, it towers over the canal, today it is nothing more than an overgrown ditch. **Marseilles** comprises a quaint downtown of pubs and antique shops.

Ottawa★

▶ *From I-80 (Exit 90), follow Rte. 23.*

Here you will find a wealth of history, including **Washington Square Park**, where **Abraham Lincoln** and **Stephen A. Douglas** held the first of their famous 1858 debates, an event that is reenacted each August. The park is surrounded by historic buildings, most notably the large Italianate **Reddick Mansion**★ built in 1856 *(100 W. Lafayette St.;* ↝ *visit by guided tour only, Mon & Wed–Sat 11am–2pm; Sun noon–2pm;* ○ *closed major holidays;* ⊜ *$5 donation suggested;* &⃞ P⃞ *℘815-433-6100; www.*

reddickmansion.com). The canal itself is dry in Ottawa, but the 100ft **Fox River Aqueduct**, which carried the canal over the intersecting stream, still stands at the eastern edge of the community, while the famous Ottawa silica sand quarries lie to the west.

Several historic sites are located on Dee Bennett Road *(access off Rte. 23)* along the Illinois River between Ottawa and Utica. At **Buffalo Rock State Park**★ take the River Bluff Trail down to two overlooks affording fine **vistas**★ of the Illinois River *(1300 N. 27th Rd.;* ○ *open year-round daily 8am–dusk; water turned off Nov–Mar;* &⃞ P⃞ *℘815-433-2220; www. dnr.state.il.us).*

At the western end of the parking lot, a wooden platform provides views of the **Effigy Tumuli**, giant earth sculptures in the form of indigenous aquatic animals completed as part of a strip-mine reclamation by artist Michael Heizer in 1985 *(trail access from platform).*

Farther west is the modern **Illinois Waterway Visitor Center**★ erected by the US Army Corps of Engineers *(Rte. 1 Dee Bennett Rd.;* ○ *open year-round daily 9am–5pm;* *℘815-667-4054; http:// dnr.state.il.us/lands/landmgt/parks/i&m/ east/WATERWAY/Home.htm;* &⃞ P⃞ *℘815-667-4054).* Exhibits describe the workings of the modern waterway connection between the Great Lakes and the Mississippi River that superseded the I&M Canal in 1933. From the observation deck, you can watch the lock in operation as barges enter the lock chamber and are slowly raised or lowered. Near Utica, the four-story sandstone **Sulphur Springs Hotel** (1852) marks the halfway point on the old stagecoach trail between Chicago and Peoria. West of the hotel is the Grand Village of the Illinois, an archaeological site where 10,000 Illinois Indians and members of related tribes lived in the late 17C.

Utica

▶ *From I-80 (Exit 81), follow Rte. 178.*

The **LaSalle County Historical Society Museum** *(101 E. Canal St.)*, located in an 1838 canal warehouse, features an eclectic collection of artifacts related to the county's history, including furnishings, clothing, tools and even a carriage used by **Abraham Lincoln** in 1858 (open Apr–Nov Wed–Fri 10am–4pm, Sat–Sun noon–4pm; Dec–Mar Fri–Sun noon–4pm; www.lasallecountymuseum. org; P 815-667-4861).

The canal can be canoed from Utica to LaSalle, and bicycles can be rented here to visit Split Rock, a dramatic limestone outcrop through which the canal was carved. Utica is also the gateway to the popular **Starved Rock State Park**★, 2,600 acres of forested bluffs. Some 13mi of trails lead down canyons to lovely waterfalls and pools along the Illinois River (open year-round daily 5am–9pm; P 815-667-4726; www.starvedrockstatepark.org). The rustic **lodge** was built by the Civilian

Conservation Corps in the 1930s. Step inside to view the massive fireplace dominating the Great Room.

LaSalle

From I-80 (Exit 77), follow Rte. 351.
The twin towns of LaSalle and Peru mark the end of the canal and the Heritage Corridor. Located in downtown LaSalle, **Lock no. 14**★ is the only restored lock on the canal. The 15-lock system allowed barges to conquer the 160ft difference in water level between Chicago and the Illinois River.

Adjacent Peru contains the remnants of a historic waterfront district along **Water Street**.

Return to Chicago via Rte. 351 and I-80 (about 100mi).

ADDRESSES

STAY / EAT

Hotels and restaurants can be found in the major commercial hubs of Joliet, Morris, Ottawa and LaSalle. Here are a couple of places to start.

$$$ Starved Rock Lodge and Conference Center – Rte. 178 & 71 Utica. 815-667-4211 or 800-868-7625. www.starvedrocklodge.com. Built in the 1930s by the Civilian Conservation Corps, this historic landmark at Starved Rock State Park offers 70 well-appointed lodge rooms and 13 comfortable cabins secluded in the woods. The Great Hall, made from recycled pine logs, warms guests in winter by its double-sided fireplace. Amenities include breakfast, lunch and dinner served in the spacious main dining room, and an indoor pool with a hot tub and sauna.

$$$ Tallgrass – 1006 S. State St., Lockport. 815-838-5566. www.tallgrass restaurant.com. Dinner only. Closed Mon and Tue. Wed–Sun. Reservations required. Choose from among a generous list of menu items—featuring organic produce and sustainable fish, meat and poultry—to fashion your own three-, four-, or five-course, fixed-price meal.

RECREATION

Camping – Class A Campsites are available at Starved Rock and Illini state parks. These sites furnish showers, electricity and vehicular access. The Starved Rock campground also has a children's playground and picnic facilities. Permits should be obtained from the park staff upon arrival. Fees for both parks are $8 plus a $3 utility fee per night. Other, more primitive tent campsites are located at designated sites along the I&M Canal State Trail.

Hiking – I&M Canal State Trail follows the old towpath 61mi from Rockdale to LaSalle. Other trails can be found in state parks and forest preserves throughout the corridor. **Cross-country** skiing is permitted on most hiking trails.

Biking – The paved I&M Canal Bicycle Trail (open sunrise-sunset; helmets required for riders 14 years and younger) offers 8.9mi of riding fun in two 3.3mi loops and another 2.3mi section that connects them.

Canoe Trails – Paddlers can navigate the Des Plaines River from Lyons to Lockport (23mi); or canoe along the I&M Canal between Channahon and Morris (15mi); or between between Utica and Peru (4.6mi).

North Shore★★

Each with its own personality, Chicago's northern suburbs collectively conjure up a vision of elegant living called the North Shore. The lovely—and unusual—geography of ravines, bluffs, beaches and woodlands, and the area's architecture and history combine to make a drive up the shore a pleasant excursion.

A BIT OF HISTORY

All of the North Shore communities described here were established in the mid- to late-19C. Prosperous city folk, drawn by the beauty of the lakeshore and tired of life in an increasingly crowded, industrial Chicago, moved north with the help of the railroad (operating here by 1855) and the development of Sheridan Road. The Chicago Fire in 1871 and the Haymarket Riot in 1886 hastened the exodus; the sylvan glades to the north seemed far removed from such urban cataclysms. As a result, an array of building styles crafted largely by prominent architects spread from Evanston to Lake Forest. Today Sheridan Road twists, turns and dips up the lakeshore, revealing grand vistas of homes and landscape. You will have ample opportunities to stop and admire architecture and nature on foot, shop and dine, or pick up picnic supplies for lunch in a lakefront park.

DRIVING TOUR

Evanston★

A cosmopolitan community, Evanston makes a good segue from city to suburbs. First settled in the 1830s, Evanston blossomed in the 1850s around a new Methodist university later to be known as Northwestern. Four bursts of growth characterized the town's development, and many of its homes date from the 1870s, 1890s, 1920s (marked by a flurry of apartment building) and 1950s.

At the city line, Sheridan Road (which briefly turns into Burnham Pl. and then

- ⓖ **Michelin Map:** p249.
- ⓘ **Info:** Chicago North Shore Convention & Visitors Bureau, 8001 Lincoln Ave., Suite 715, Skokie, IL 60077. ℘847-763-0011. www.cnscvb.com.
- ⓟ **Parking:** Parking can sometimes be found on neighborhood streets.
- ⓐ **Don't Miss:** An evening at the Ravinia Music Festival.
- ⓣ **Timing:** This makes a nice day trip.

Forest Ave.) enters the **Evanston Lakeshore Historic District**★, listed on the National Register since 1980. Explore this compact district on foot, beginning at Dawes House (225 Greenwood St.). The **Charles Gates Dawes House**★ serves as the home of the Evanston Historical Society (⬤visit by 1hr guided tour only, ⓣyear-round Thu–Sun 1pm, 2pm and 3pm; ⓞclosed major holidays; ⬤$10; ⓖ ℘847-475-3410; www.evanston historycenter.org). One of the few area houses open to the public, it offers a rare glimpse into opulent 19C North Shore life. Perhaps the finest example of the Châteauesque style in the region, the mansion was designed in 1894 by **Henry Edwards-Ficken** for Northwestern University treasurer Robert Sheppard. The house has been beautifully restored to the residency of **Charles Gates Dawes**, who purchased it in 1909. Dawes won the Nobel Prize for his part in developing an economic recovery plan for Europe following World War I. He also served as vice president under Calvin Coolidge, and composed popular music in his spare time. The home comprises 28 rooms and 14 fireplaces; among the restored and furnished rooms on display are the elegantly wood-paneled library and second-floor nursery.

ⓞ Walk south on Forest Ave.

Houses in the surrounding blocks span years of development and many

PRACTICAL INFORMATION

Access – By car: The excursion up the North Shore is 62mi round-trip. From Chicago, drive north on Lake Shore Drive, which turns into Sheridan Road and continue through Rogers Park toward Evanston. To return to Chicago, take **Rte. 41** to **I-94**. The **cta Purple** line reaches **Evanston**; the Metra North line (schedules and fares: ☎312-836-7000) accesses each suburb's downtown and is particularly convenient for visiting **Ravinia Park** and **Market Square** in **Lake Forest**. **Union Pacific North Line Trains** leave Chicago from **Ogilvie Transportation Center** at West Madison and Canal Streets.

styles, from the post-Chicago Fire cottages planned by **Luther Greenleaf** in the 1870s—**1218** and **1244 Forest Avenue**—to the imposing Tudor structures of **Ernest Mayo** dating from the 1910s, as seen at **nos. 1210** and **1203 Forest Avenue**, and the Prairie school work of Tallmadge and Watson. Note the lovely windows at **1315 Forest Avenue**, built in 1907. Now subdivided, the block bounded by Burnham Place, Forest Avenue, Dempster Street and Lake Michigan was once the estate of renowned city planner and architect **Daniel Burnham**, who moved there in 1887. The circuitous course of Sheridan Road (actually Burnham Place to Forest Avenue) undoubtedly reflects the influence of Burnham and his neighbors.

⊙ Drive north on Forest Ave., which merges with Sheridan Rd. To tour Northwestern University on foot, park along Sheridan Rd. at Centennial Park just south of campus.

Northwestern University★

The campus extends east of Sheridan Rd. to Lake Michigan, between Lincoln and Clark Sts. ☎847-491-3741. www.northwestern.edu. ▢Parking permits are required for all university lots; visitor permits are available at the Parking Office (1819 Hinman Ave.; open 8am–4pm; ☎847-491-3319).
This prestigious Big Ten university originated as the dream of a group of devout Methodists in 1850, who selected a swampy parcel of land along Lake Michigan about 14mi from downtown Chicago as the place to plant their college. By 1855, with one building (since demolished) and 10 students, the school already formed the nucleus of a growing town. Responsible for the platting of Evanston (named for Dr. John Evans, a founder of Northwestern), the university fathers also set the temperate moral tone that would come to influence the sweep of the North Shore. The university's charter established a "4mi limit" that prohibited the sale of alcohol within that radius of the campus.

Architecturally, Northwestern never developed along a master plan and seems today a random collection of buildings that bridge two centuries. Past **Fisk Hall (A)** (1899, Daniel Burnham & Co.), which fronts Sheridan Road and houses the renowned Medill School of Journalism, lies the Arts Circle, a cluster of buildings devoted to the fine and performing arts.

The **Mary and Leigh Block Museum of Art (B)** (40 Arts Circle Dr.; ◷open July–Aug Tue–Sun 10am–5pm; rest of year Tue and Fri–Sun 10am–5pm, Wed–Thu 10am–8pm; ◷closed major holidays; ☎847-491-4000; www.blockmuseum.northwestern.edu) expanded to 6,000sq ft in 2000. The space allows the museum to display its permanent collection of some 5,000 works on paper.

An **outdoor sculpture garden**★ **(C)** surrounding the museum includes works by Jean Arp, Jacques Lipchitz, Joan Miró and Henry Moore. For an extended walk providing fine views, take the path around the human-made lagoon behind the Arts Circle. The tower of **Garrett-Evangelical Theological Seminary (D)** (not affiliated with the university) rises above the monochromatic assembly of lecture halls, laboratories and offices that form the core of the campus and date mostly to the early 1970s. At the heart of the old campus west of the Arts Circle stands its most venerable building, the Gothic-style **University Hall (E)** (1869, Gordon P. Randall), surrounded by lush greenery. **Annie May Swift Hall (F)** (1895, Charles Robert Ayars) contrasts with its warm red decorative brickwork and Arts and Crafts styling. The classically collegiate **Deering Library (G)** (1932, James Gamble Rogers) was augmented in 1971 with three connecting pavilions (Skidmore, Owings & Merrill). From the corner of the campus at Sheridan Road and Chicago Avenue, it is a short walk to **Rest Cottage** *(1730 Chicago Ave.)*, the home of Frances E. Willard, well-known educator, suffragist and national president of the Women's Christian Temperance Union (WCTU) from 1879 until her death in 1898. Run as a museum by the WCTU, the home is furnished with period pieces and Willard's personal belongings. It was built in 1865, a lovely example of residential Gothic style *(visit by guided tour only, 1st & 3rd Sun of every month 1pm–4pm; contribution requested; ℘847-328-7500; www.franciswillardhouse.org)*.

▷ *Drive north on Sheridan Rd. Turn left on Central St. and continue to Central Park Ave.*

Mitchell Museum of the American Indian

3001 Central St. ○*Open year-round Tue–Sat 10am–5pm, Thu till 8pm, Sun noon–4pm.* ○*Closed major holidays.* ⊜*$5.* 🅿️♿℘*847-475-1030. www.mitchell museum.org.*

Founded in 1977, the museum presents the history, culture and arts of Native Americans via a collection of 10,000 objects dating from the Paleo-Indian period to the present day. Permanent exhibits explore the native cultures of the Woodlands, Plains, Southwest, Northwest Coast and Arctic regions. "Touching tables"👥 give you the opportunity to handle native pottery, baskets, clothing and stone tools.

▷ *Return to Sheridan Rd.*

Evanston Art Center★

2603 Sheridan Rd. ○*Open year-round Mon–Thu 10am–10pm, Fri & Sat 10am–4pm, Sun 1pm–4pm.* ⊜*$3 suggested donation.* ♿🅿️℘*847-475-5300. www.evanstonartcenter.org.*

Beautifully situated at the edge of the lake, the art center occupies a one-time private home built in 1926 by Richard Powers and presents changing exhibits of contemporary Midwestern artists. Outside, the naturalistic landscaping of **Jens Jensen** makes a lovely buffer between house and beach. Jensen, who designed several Chicago parks, was a leading proponent of Prairie school principles as they applied to landscape architecture. He advocated a return to natural prairie where possible and used native plants extensively. His influence pervades the parks of the North Shore. The beach has been restored as a small **dune ecosystem** to give a sense of the primordial Lake Michigan shoreline.

Built in 1873, the adjacent **Grosse Point Lighthouse**★ *(2601 Sheridan Rd.;* 🔦*visit by 1hr guided tour only,* ○*Jun–Sept weekends 2pm, 3pm, 4pm;* ⊜*$6;* 🅿️ ℘*847-328-6961; www.grossepoint lighthouse.net)* comprises a 90ft tower, two 1880 structures used to house steam-powered fog sirens (removed in 1922) and a lightkeeper's cottage. On summer weekends, you can climb 141 stairs to the top of the tower for a wonderful view. The lighthouse is a stunning reminder of the time when thousands of ships plied the hazardous waters of Lake Michigan. The collision of the paddlewheeler *Lady Elgin* with a lumber schooner off Wilmette's shores in 1860, resulting in the loss of nearly 300 lives, provided considerable impetus for a landmark at this location. The lighthouse structure was restored in 1980.

▷ *Continue north on Sheridan Rd. to Wilmette.*

Wilmette

Early developers envisioned Wilmette (so named for its first settler, fur trader

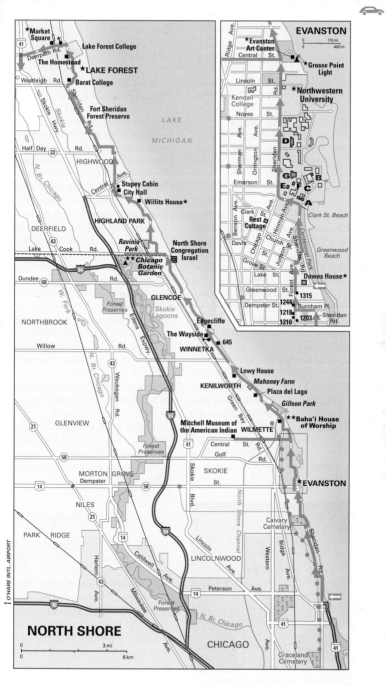

NORTH SHORE

0 ———— 3 mi
0 ———— 6 km

Antoine Ouilmette) as a true railroad suburb and successfully lobbied for a train stop there by 1871. One year later, Wilmette's population swelled to 300 and the village incorporated. In contrast to booming Evanston, however, Wilmette remained a sleepy rural community until well into the 1880s when suburban amenities—sewers, library, schools, telephone service— became available. The question of consolidation with Evanston hindered Wilmette's independence until voters finally rejected the possibility in 1897.

Baha'i House of Worship★★

100 Linden Ave. ◑*Open year-round daily. Visitor Center open Mon–Fri 10am –5pm, Sat 11am–7pm.* ◔*Guided tour available.* ♿🅿 *✆847-853-2300. www.bahai.us.*

The lacy, opalescent dome of the Baha'i temple startles motorists on Sheridan Road passing from Evanston into Wilmette. The mammoth, nine-sided structure, rising 191ft to its pinnacle and set about with beautifully landscaped gardens, cuts an exotic profile against the low suburban skyline. This is the North American seat of the Baha'i faith, which maintains six other equally monumental houses of worship around the world. Its presence in the Chicago area dates to the religion's introduction here at the World's Columbian Exposition in 1893. Baha'is, who follow the teachings of the 19C Persian prophet Baha'u'llah, believe in the "oneness" of religion and of humankind, and hopefully anticipate complete equality among people and the evolution of a global civilization. They draw inspiration from all of the world's great faiths and consider Buddha, Christ, Mohammed and the other major prophets to have been messengers from a single God.

Although the origins of the Baha'i faith are Persian, and the temple itself bears a distinctly Eastern look, in fact its design elements are eclectic and intended to represent unity in their blend. A close inspection of the intricate interlocking patterns that inscribe most surfaces of the building reveals the influence of the organic ornamentation of Louis Sullivan. Icons of the world's great religions decorate the outside columns. Other aspects of the temple carry symbolic significance for the Baha'i, such as the circular plan and the nine entryways, each surmounted by an inscription.

The temple is the work of French-Canadian architect **Louis Bourgeois**, who began its planning in 1909. Construction did not start until 1920, however, and proceeded slowly until completion in 1953, beset by funding and technical problems. The elaborate lacework on the dome posed the biggest challenge; crafted of quartz and white cement, the panels were shipped by rail from Earley Studio in Rosslyn, Virginia and hung on the temple's steel framework.

The interior space, infused with natural light, soars elegantly to the apex of the dome where the invocation "O Thou the Glory of the Most Glorious" appears in Arabic calligraphy. The auditorium seats 1,191 people.

▷ *Continue north on Sheridan Rd.*

Just around the bend from the temple is the 59-acre lakefront **Gillson Park**, a nice spot for a picnic lunch. Farther along, **Plaza del Lago** outdoor shopping mall offers several restaurants as well as **Convito Cafe and Market** (✆847-251-3654), a trendy food shop and bistro, where you can sit down to lunch or purchase fixings for a gourmet picnic.

Built in 1928, the stores and apartments along the north side of the plaza comprised one of the nation's first shopping centers. Located in a no-man's-land outside Wilmette proper, the complex

Bahà'i House of Worship

Chicago's North Shore CVB

included a speakeasy that was popular among Chicago's Prohibition-era drinking crowd. When the notorious roadhouse caught fire in 1932, adjacent villages refused to send fire fighters and cut off the water supply, ensuring its destruction. Wilmette annexed the area in 1942, and the shopping center filled with hot-dog and ice-cream stands befitting its lakefront location.

In 1968, after high-rise apartments blocked the beach, Plaza del Lago opened in its present form. Its bell tower is original to the 1920s.

Continue a short distance north on Sheridan Rd. to Kenilworth.

Kenilworth

Incorporated in 1896, the town of Kenilworth is named after Sir Walter Scott's romantic novel. Inspired by the English countryside, businessman **Joseph Sears** envisioned a genteel village that would attract a certain caliber of residents. In 1889 he purchased the land and developed amenities to entice property buyers, platting the village with such care as to ensure that its houses would enjoy so many hours of daily sunlight. He spared nothing on public works and even laid the first stretch of macadam road on the North Shore.

Contemporary of Frank Lloyd Wright, renowned Midwestern architect **George W. Maher** designed more than 40 buildings in the community, his work chronicling the transition in architectural styles from late-Victorian to Prairie. Today Kenilworth retains an air of exclusivity.

Just north of the southern gates of Kenilworth lies **Mahoney Farm Preserve**, which originally straddled Sheridan Road. This land was deeded to Kenilworth for use as a park, and in 1933 the village asked **Jens Jensen** to design a sanctuary for birds and flowers there. In addition to native plantings, Jensen included seven **"council rings"**—stone seating areas meant for quiet contemplation that grace many of his landscapes. The park was restored and added to the National Register in 1985.

To visit this sanctuary, park in the neighborhood across Sheridan Rd.

East of the intersection of Sheridan Road and Kenilworth Avenue, note the two adjacent houses closest to the lake. Both built in the early 1890s, they typify the elegance that characterized the village's early homes.

Continue north on Sheridan Rd. to Winnetka.

Winnetka

Although it grew slowly, Winnetka (from an Indian word meaning "beautiful land") developed a political and cultural milieu apart from its neighbors, largely due to the influence of **Henry Demarest Lloyd**, who made his home there in 1878. Lloyd, an essayist and social reformer with a strong belief in direct democracy, viewed family and community as the linchpins of society and eschewed the power of corporations and monopolies. As a leading citizen of Winnetka, he succeeded in applying his theories of government on a practical level, striving to involve the people in municipal decision making.

Around Lloyd grew something of a cultural and political salon; he often entertained the likes of social worker **Jane Addams** and railroad union founder **Eugene Debs**.

At 140 Sheridan Road, the **Felix Lowy House** (1925, Mayo & Mayo) is a fine example of the Tudor style popular in the 1920s. The lakefront home at **no. 645** was built in 1902, and the grounds and lovely cemetery at **Christ Church** (784 Sheridan Rd.) date to 1876. At no. 830 stands Henry Lloyd's home, **The Wayside**, some parts of which date to the 1850s. It was listed on the National Register in 1966. At no. 915 the twin gatehouses of **Edgecliffe**, designed in 1930 by **Samuel Marx** for businessman **Max Epstein**, signal the elegant formality of the mansion beyond.

Continue north on Sheridan Rd. to Glencoe.

Glencoe

After a poorly planned scheme to develop Glencoe fell apart in the 1870s, the village lagged behind its growing neighbors. Its lovely ravines and woods continued to attract excursionists and picnickers and the village gradually blossomed. Poet **Archibald MacLeish** was born here in 1892.

At 1185 Sheridan Road stands **North Shore Congregation Israel**. The curvilinear, organic lines of the temple to the north (1963, Minoru Yamasaki) contrast sharply with the geometric post-Modern cylinder of the smaller sanctuary created by Hammond, Beeby & Babka in 1983.

> ◐ *Continue north on Sheridan Rd. until it turns westward as Lake Cook Rd. (a half mile farther on, Sheridan Rd. continues north). Follow Lake Cook Rd. straight ahead 1mi to the Chicago Botanic Garden.*

Chicago Botanic Garden★★

1000 Lake Cook Rd. ◐*Open year-round daily 8am–sunset.* ✕⚖.🄿 *($20/car)* ℘*847 -835-5440. www.chicago-botanic.org.* This 385-acre preserve makes a lovely stop any time of year. With 23 garden areas, over a million individual plants of nearly 9,500 different varieties and a plethora of bird life, the site attracts three-quarters of a million people annually. Established in 1965 under the auspices of the venerable Chicago Horticultural Society, the garden considers itself a "Noah's Ark for plants" devoted to colle-

ction, education, research, plant testing and conservation. The **Grand Tram Tour**, which provides a general overview of the grounds, is a good way to see the far-flung 15-acre **prairie** *(end of Apr–Oct daily 10am–4pm every 30min; round-trip 35min; commentary;* ⊜*$5;* ⚖*).* Changing exhibits in the Education Center explore botanical topics, while greenhouses feature exotics, succulents and topiary. The heart of the garden occupies the largest of nine islands in the 60-acre human-made lagoon. Each garden setting rivals the next. In the formal **Rose Garden**★, 5,000 plants include 100 varieties of the fragrant blossoms. The **English Walled Garden**★ encompasses a charming collection of six "rooms" representing various English gardening styles. The tactile and fragrant plantings of the **Sensory Garden** encourage you to use every sense to enjoy them. Across the lagoon note the carillon, whose 48 bells chime on the hour and play evening concerts in the summer. The **Regenstein Fruit and Vegetable Garden** demonstrates the variety of ways local gardeners can succeed in small balcony planters or extensive backyard plots. The **Japanese Garden**★, Sansho-En ("The Garden of Three Islands"), offers a peaceful and contemplative refuge. A bridge connects two of the islands; the third is to be observed from afar. In Japanese style, shape and form create serene spaces, a concept that works beautifully in the quiet "dry garden" of sand, rocks and carefully placed vegetation.

Chicago Botanic Garden

▷ *Return to Sheridan Rd. and continue north to Highland Park. Follow the signs carefully as the route takes some unexpected turns.*

Highland Park

One of the larger North Shore communities, Highland Park was incorporated in 1869 and grew through several annexations, including that of Ravinia in 1899. The Highland Park Building Co. shaped its early development, selling lots and building houses from pattern books. The natural beauty of the ravines and the extensive hardwood forests of the area attracted year-round and summer residents alike, and made the perfect setting for the work of **Jens Jensen** (who lived in Ravinia) and other naturalistic landscape architects.

Highlighting this town is 36-acre **Ravinia Park**, home to the world-renowned **Ravinia Music Festival** from June to September *(418 Sheridan Rd.; ℘847-266-5100; www.ravinia.org)*. Originally intended as an amusement park to attract riders on the adjacent interurban railroad, the grounds were converted in 1911 to a venue for opera and symphony performances. Wildly successful over the years, Ravinia has hosted Arthur Rubinstein, George Gershwin, Ella Fitzgerald, Placido Domingo and hundreds of other internationally acclaimed performers. The summer home of the Chicago Symphony Orchestra since 1936, Ravinia today also offers everything from jazz, popular and chamber music to folk, dance and children's programs. The complex includes restaurants, covered seating in the pavilion, and two indoor theaters. Most fun, however, is to enjoy performances with a picnic dinner on the expansive lawn.

At 1445 Sheridan Road stands Frank Lloyd Wright's masterpiece, the **Ward W. Willits House**★, familiar as an archetype of the Prairie school. This 1902 commission—six years before Wright's Robie House—gave the architect his first full-blown opportunity to apply his theories of "organic simplicity." The house exhibits the hallmarks of Prairie school design: strong horizontal lines, a symbiosis with its natural surroundings and the influence of Japanese domestic architecture. Beyond the Willits House, Sheridan Road winds through Highland Park's business district as St. John's Avenue. Note the stately **City Hall** *(1707 St. John's Ave.)*, built in 1930, and the adjacent **Stupey Cabin**, which dates from 1847, the oldest building in town.

▷ *Continue north on Sheridan Rd. Follow signs to a short detour on Central Ave. and then Oak St. before returning to Sheridan Rd.*

Fort Sheridan was established in 1887 following the Haymarket Riot and deactivated in 1993, a victim of cuts in defense spending. The military base is unusual in that most of it was designed by the private architectural firm of **Holabird & Roche**. Today the **Fort Sheridan Forest Preserve** *(enter off Sheridan Rd. just north of Elm Rd.* ○*open year-round daily 6.30am–sunset;* 🅿🚹 *℘847-367-6640; www.lcfpd.org)* shares the base's 274 acres with a residential community featuring both historic and contemporary homes.

▷ *Continue north on Sheridan Rd. through Highwood to Lake Forest.*

Lake Forest★

Lake Forest has long cultivated a reputation as Chicago's most elite suburb, though its creation was inspired by a group of Presbyterians who chose that locale to build a college in the 1850s. They hired a St. Louis landscape architect named Almerin Hotchkiss to lay out the town in 1857, and he designed picturesque streets to curve along the natural contours of the hills and wind through the forest with calculated leisure. The spacious lots offered privacy for the most gracious homes. Lake Forest's high society flourished as wealthy summer visitors took up residence year-round, bringing with them the trappings of Chicago's aristocracy. F. Scott Fitzgerald equated Lake Forest with Newport and South Hampton, and that sense lingers today.

As Sheridan Road passes into Lake Forest, note **Barat College**, founded in 1858. The middle campus of **Lake Forest College**, established by Presbyterians as Lind University in 1857, occupies the intersection of Sheridan and College roads. Immediately on the right, handsome **Reid Hall** (1899, Frost & Granger), the original college library, blends Gothic, Norman and English-abbey elements into a collegiate whole. Farther ahead, one of the earlier buildings, **Young Hall** (1878), comprises three stories of yellow brick topped with a mansard roof. Hidden in the trees to the east, stout **Hotchkiss Hall** (once the gymnasium; 1890, Henry Ives Cobb) is noteworthy for its solid Romanesque lines and massive redstone construction. On a small rise immediately across from campus sits **The Homestead** *(570 N. Sheridan Rd.)* built in 1860 for **Devillo R. Holt**, a Chicago lumberman and a founder of Lake Forest. The house's exterior remains unaltered today.

▷ *Continue north on Sheridan Rd. to Deerpath Rd.*

The massive Shingle-style **First Presbyterian Church** (1887, Charles Frost) at the corner of Sheridan and Deerpath roads is testament to the Presbyterians who founded Lake Forest. This Shingle church exudes the summer-resort ambience that once characterized the town. Across the street, on the north campus of Lake Forest College, note the Richardsonian Romanesque **Durand Art Institute** (1891, Henry Ives Cobb).

▷ *Turn left on Deerpath Rd.*

Just west of the train tracks at 700 North Western Avenue, **Market Square**★ has defined the character of downtown Lake Forest since 1916. Designed by **Howard Van Doren Shaw** to resemble an English town market, the square includes elements derived from several European traditions. Among America's earliest planned suburban shopping centers, it today houses boutiques and restaurants.

▷ *To return to Chicago, drive west on Deerpath Rd. to Rte. 41 South, which merges with the Edens Expwy. (I-94). Head south on I-94 toward Chicago.*

Indiana Dunes National Lakeshore★

A sliver of pristine land lining the southern edge of Lake Michigan, the Indiana Dunes National Lakeshore encompasses 14,000 acres of windswept beaches, dunes, marshes and forests containing a great diversity of species. Over the years, much of the area around the dunes was industrialized, and today parklands are interrupted by steel and power plants. Yet this industrialization has not thwarted the mass of urban dwellers who crowd the trails and beaches in their ubiquitous search for unspoiled land.

◔ **Michelin Map:** Map of principal sights.

▤ **Info:** National Park Service. ✆219-926-7561. www.nps.gov/indu.

▷ **Location:** The expansive National Lakeshore actually surrounds the Indiana Dunes State Park.

▣ **Parking:** Abundant lot parking provided.

◉ **Don't Miss:** The sunset from Mt. Baldy.

▲▲ **Kids:** Talk to the animals at the Chellberg Farm.

◕ **Timing:** A lot of hiking and exploring can be done in a full day.

PRACTICAL INFORMATION

Access – By car: Drive south on I-94/I-90 *(Dan Ryan Expwy.)* to **Chicago Skyway** tollroad *(I-90)*. Past Gary, Indiana, exit at **US-20/US-12** *(Dunes Hwy.)* and continue eastbound. Stay on US-12, forking left as US-20 forks right. All **Dunes** sights can be accessed from US-12. From Chicago Loop to West Beach entrance is 37mi; to Buell Visitor Center, 49mi; to Mt. Baldy, 54mi.

By train: the **South Shore Railroad** *(schedules and fares: ☏219-926-5744)* departs daily year-round from the **Millennium Park Metra** station; get off at Dune Park and walk north.

A BIT OF HISTORY

Glaciers that carved the Great Lakes sculpted the first chapter in the history of the dunes some 15,000 years ago. As the glaciers retreated to the north, they left moraines—ridges formed from glacial till—south of present-day Lake Michigan. Glacial meltwaters created further ridges as the shoreline shrank to the north by stages. As the Ice Age drew to a close about 11,000 years ago, various ecosystems developed between the ridges. Ice Age plants such as bearberry and jack pine persisted, while cacti and other southern plants began to thrive in the warmer climate.

Prevailing northwesterly winds and lake waves continue to create new sand dunes at the lakeshore, while older dunes beyond the shoreline gradually evolve from sparse grasslands and marshes into dense forests. When University of Chicago ecologist **Henry Chandler Cowles** (1869–1939) began to study the dunes in the 1890s, he was fascinated by the fact that the plant forms on each ridge continue to change over time. Cowles discovered that plants alter their environment, providing fertile ground for new species that crowd out the originals. Marram grasses establish on sand dunes, gradually collecting water and humus until a pine or cottonwood forest takes root, eventually to be succeeded by oak-hickory and then beech-maple. The effort to preserve the Indiana Dunes began in 1911 when landscape architect **Jens Jensen** and other Chicago conservationists formed the Prairie Club, leading train excursions to the then-unbroken 25mi stretch of dunes between Gary and Michigan City, Indiana. In 1913 Dr. Cowles led 10 European botanists on a trip to the dunes, which they determined to be one of the four most important natural sites in America, along with Yellowstone, Yosemite and the Grand Canyon. Chicago-based

Indiana Dunes National Lakeshore

© National Park Service

Chellberg Farm

National Park Service

efforts to preserve the dunes met great resistance in rural Indiana, but a small state park was established in 1923.

As industry grew again after World War II, Bethlehem Steel bought large tracts of the Central Dunes for a steel plant, harbor and sand mine. A new effort to save the dunes was led by Illinois senator **Paul Douglas**. Legislation passed in 1966 preserved a 6,400-acre area split in two by the Bethlehem complex, designated the **Indiana Dunes National Lakeshore**. Park expansion continued into the 1980s, even as lakefront industry mushroomed.

Today the national lakeshore, which includes **Indiana Dunes State Park**, encompasses some 1,400 plant species—from arctic wildflowers to prickly pear cacti. Vistas along the numerous trails take in dunes, lowland marshes and dense forests in the space of a few hundred yards.

VISIT
West Beach Area★
❍ *Turn left on County Line Rd. shortly after entering the park.*
◷*Open Memorial Day–Labor Day daily 9am–dusk; Mar–Oct daily 7am–dusk.* ☞*$6 fee charged summer only.* ✕*(May–Sept).* ⚊🅿. ⊘*Trails through sand dunes can be strenuous due to the rapid elevation changes.*

Known for its popular **West Beach**, this section of the park includes Long Lake and 3.5mi of hiking trails. Behind the visitor center, greatly eroded "blowout" dunes slowly evolve as water collects in the center and forms interdunal ponds, stabilizing the dune and allowing it to mutate into the next ecosystem—a cottonwood or conifer stand.

A walk along the **Dune Succession Trail**★ offers a look at the park's surprising biological diversity, constantly changing between seasons and over the years. The 1mi boardwalk trail runs from the beach to the parking lot near the visitor center, providing excellent **viewpoints**★ and one of the best views of rapid ecosystem change.

Bailly Homestead and Chellberg Farm★
❍ *Drive 6mi east of Inland Marsh, passing through an industrialized area before re-entering the park. Turn right on Mineral Springs Rd. and continue about 1mi.* ◷*Open year-round daily 7am–dusk.* ⚊🅿.

This stop provides a historic counterpoint to the natural wonders of the dunes. A 2mi **trail** burrows through a lush forest of basswood, beech and sugar maple to an 1820s settlement consisting of several log structures and the two-and-a-half-story **Bailly Homestead**, illustrating early European life in the region. The trail follows an old Native American path before reaching a cemetery, and then loops back to the preserved 1880s **farm**⚊⚊ of the Swedish immigrant Kjellberg (later Chellberg) family.

Indian Dunes National Lakeshore Visitor Center
❍ *Take Mineral Springs Rd. south to Hwy 20 and drive east to Rte. 49. Turn right.* ◷*Open Memorial Day–Labor Day daily 8am–6pm; rest of the year daily 8.30am–4.30pm.* ◷*Closed major holidays.* ⚊🅿 ☎219-926-7561. www.nps.gov/indu/planyourvisit/idnvc.htm.
Shared by the Indiana Dunes State Park and the National Lakeshore, the visitor center presents a short audio-visual

Fun for Kids 👥

Sights in this guide that are specifically geared toward children are indicated by the 👥 symbol. A selection of such sights described in this guide are listed below with their address and the entry under which they appear in the guide.

Caribbean Reef,
John G. Shedd Aquarium
© Shedd Aquarium/Brenna Hernandez

- **Willis Tower Skydeck** – Entrance on Jackson Blvd. between Wacker Dr. & Franklin St. *The Loop*

- **Niketown Chicago** – 669 N. Michigan Ave. *Magnificent Mile*

- **The Hancock Observatory** – 875 N. Michigan Ave. *Magnificent Mile*

- **American Girl Place** – 835 N. Michigan Ave. *Magnificent Mile*

- **Navy Pier**★★ – E. Grand Ave. at Lake Michigan. *Magnificent Mile*

- **Chicago Children's Museum**★ – Navy Pier. *Magnificent Mile*

- **Thorne Miniature Rooms**★★ – 111 S. Michigan Ave. *Art Institute of Chicago*

- **Field Museum of Natural History**★★★ – *Museum Campus*

- **John G. Shedd Aquarium**★★★ – *Museum Campus*

- **Adler Planetarium**★★ – 1300 S. Lake Shore Dr. *Museum Campus*

- **Lincoln Park Zoo**★★ – 2200 N. Cannon Dr. *Lincoln Park*

- **Farm-in-the-Zoo**★ – 1901 N. Stockton Dr. *Lincoln Park*

- **Notebaert Nature Museum**★ – 2340 N. Cannon Dr. *Lincoln Park*

- **Museum of Science and Industry**★★★ – 57th St. at S. Lake Shore Dr. *Hyde Park/Kenwood*

- **Brookfield Zoo**★★ – 8400 W. 31st St. *Excursions*

- **Mitchell Museum of the American Indian** – 3001 Central Ave. *Evanston; Excursions*

- **Chellberg Farm** – Mineral Springs Rd. *Indiana Dunes National Lakeshore; Excursions*

introduction to the park, its glacial formation and its continuing evolution by the forces of the wind and water. Exhibits explain the ecosystems, plant and animal life. Regular guided nature walks are listed in the activity schedule.

Indiana Dunes State Park

▶ *Go north on Rte. 49 into the park.*
🕑 *Open daily year-round 7am–11pm.*
🎫 *Entry fees vary.* ⚠♿🅿 ☎*219-926-1952. www.in.gov/dnr/parklake/properties/park_dunes.html.*

With 3mi of beachfront and 16.5mi of hiking trails, the state park offers myriad recreational opportunities. Amenities here include a bathhouse/pavilion, picnic areas and a nature center. Try scaling

Mt. Tom, the park's tallest dune at 192ft *(height varies due to shifting sands).*

Mount Baldy★

▶ *Return to US-12 east to reach Mt. Baldy.*
One of the largest *(123ft)* dunes in the park is constantly shifting by a process called saltation, in which the lake winds whip the sand inland across the surface of the dune to the forests beyond. Mt. Baldy is moving inland at a rate of 4–5ft a year, killing the trees behind its crest. The walk up and around the dune is very steep. A great bowl of sand leads down to the beach from the summit, which provides a grand **panorama** of the lake, the dunes and the Chicago skyline in the distance.

Chicago Marathon winds through the city
© Patrick L. Pyszka/City of Chicago/GRC

Where to Stay

One perquisite of Chicago's popularity as a convention town is its considerable number of hotels and motels, especially in the heart of the city. Downtown hotel rooms number over 30,000, and most of the major chains are represented. Chicago also boasts a delightful collection of boutique hotels that offer a more intimate milieu, most of them clustered along the Magnificent Mile, with several newer additions in the Loop.

The properties listed below were selected for their ambience, location and/or value for money. Prices reflect average cost for a standard double room *(two people)* in high season *(not including any applicable city or state taxes)*. Room prices may be considerably lower in off-season, and many hotels offer discounted weekend rates. The presence of a swimming pool is indicated by the ⌘ symbol.

$$$$$	over $350
$$$$	$250–$350
$$$	$175–$250
$$	$100–$175
$	less than $100

ACCOMODATION

$$$$$ Four Seasons Hotel – *120 E. Delaware Pl., Magnificent Mile.* ✕⛶🅿⌘Spa *℘312-280-8800. www.four seasons.com/chicagofs. 346 rooms.* Done in dark woods and rich colors, guest rooms wrap you in luxury with marble baths and plush terry robes. Deluxe rooms on the 30th to 46th floors offer sweeping views of Lake Michigan or the city skyline. For dinner, savor contemporary American fare in **Seasons ($$$$)** opulent dining room.

$$$$$ The Peninsula Chicago – *108 E. Superior St., Magnificent Mile.* ✕⛶🅿⌘Spa *℘312-337-2888 or 866-288-8889. www.chicago.peninsula.com. 339 rooms.* The Peninsula is indeed a luxurious stay. Quietly elegant, trim and classic, the hotel is nonetheless 21C in every appointment, including steamless TV screens in the bathrooms. Visit the lobby on Friday and Saturday nights for the decadent chocolate bar and live jazz. **Avenues** restaurant **($$$)** consistently rates among the city's best.

$$$$$ Sofitel Chicago Water Tower – *20 E. Chestnut St., Magnificent Mile.* ✕⛶🅿⌘ *℘312-324-4000. www.sofitel.com. 445 rooms.* The Sofitel's dramatic "upside-down" 32-floor glass prism exterior and slick interior are all the architectural buzz. The techno-hip lobby employs decorative lighting and artwork to distinct advantage, and the rooms carry through with contemporary European styling. The sleek brasserie, **Café des Architectes ($$)**, serves fusion dishes with a flare.

$$$$$ W Chicago Lakeshore – *644 N. Lake Shore Dr., Gold Coast.* ✕⛶🅿 Spa *℘312-943-9200. www.starwood hotels.com. 520 rooms.* Overlooking the lakefront, W's rooms afford great views of Navy Pier and the lake beyond, while those dubbed "wonderful" face the cityscape. With serenity in mind, the decor takes something of a Zen twist in its deep colors and strong lines.

$$$$ Allerton Hotel – *701 N. Michigan Ave., Magnificent Mile.* ✕⛶🅿 *℘312-440-1500 or 888-789-4399. www. theallertonhotel.com. 443 rooms.* The Allerton has served Chicago as a hotel since 1924, and a recent renovation nicely restores its original polish, inside and out. Guest rooms, outfitted with marble baths and upholstered headboards, glow with rich wall and fabric colors. Check out the view from the 25th-floor fitness center.

$$$$ Amalfi – *20 W. Kinzie St., River North.* ⛶🅿 *℘312-395-9000. www.amalfihotel chicago.com. 215 rooms.* Your room is your "sanctuary" here, complete with Egyptian cotton linens, a pillow-top mattress and multihead shower. There is no on-site restaurant, but a continental breakfast is served on each floor, and 24-hr room service is catered by Harry Caray's Italian Steakhouse.

$$$$ The Drake Hotel – *140 E. Walton Pl., Magnificent Mile.* ✕⛶🅿 *℘312-787-2200 or 800-553-7253. www.thedrake hotel.com. 530 rooms.* Since 1920, the Italian Renaissance-style limestone building at the top of the Magnificent Mile has been the address for visiting celebrities. Antique solid-brass candelabras and the original mahogany ceiling inset with hand-painted tiles set the tone in the lobby. Rooms, some overlooking Lake Michigan, combine floral fabrics with dark woods.

$$$$ The Fairmont Chicago Millennium Park – *200 N. Columbus Dr., Loop.* ✕ & P Spa *312-565-8000 or 866-540-4408. www.fairmont.com/ chicago. 682 rooms.* Rising northeast of Millennium Park, the Fairmont has long provided a home-away-from-home for the glitterati. Spacious rooms, newly redecorated by David Rockwell, shine with contemporary style and striking floral artwork. This is a great location for attending summer music festivals in the lakeside parks.

$$$$ Hotel Felix – *111 W. Huron St., River North.* ✕ & P Spa *312-447-3440 or 877-848-4040. www.hotelfelixchicago. com. 225 rooms.* As befits its Silver LEED certification, this well-located boutique hotel offers guests earth-friendly housekeeping products, organic materials and in-room motion sensors to control heat and air-conditioning. Quiet rooms mix earth tones with upscale amenities such as luxe linens, comfy bathrobes, and in-room safes.

$$$$ Hotel Monaco – *225 N. Wabash St., Loop.* ✕ & P *312-960-8500 or 866-610-0081. www.monaco-chicago.com. 192 rooms.* Two blocks from the Magnificent Mile, this boutique property features airy rooms done in apple-green striped wallpaper with bright accents. Animal-print robes, CD players and Aveda bath products are just a few of the amenities. Downstairs, **South Water Kitchen ($$)** serves up well-prepared contemporary American cuisine.

$$$$ Hotel Palomar – *505 N. State St., River North.* ✕ & P ≋ *312-755-9703 or 877-731-0505. www.hotelpalomar-chicago.com. 261 rooms.* Art in motion makes a fitting theme for this new Kimpton hotel, set as it is in the midst of the artsy River North district. Soothing colors and frette linens assure a good night's rest, while a full-size desk accommodates business travelers. Billing itself as a "gastro-lounge," **Sable Kitchen &**

Bar ($$) offers handcrafted cocktails and season-driven American dishes.

$$$$ Hotel 71 – *71 E. Wacker Dr., Loop.* ✕ & P *312-346-7100. www.hotel71.com. 307 rooms.* Billing itself as an "urban boutique hotel experience," 71 has given a tired 1950s hotel an extreme makeover. Though the facade retains a retro look, the interior public spaces and stylish rooms have been boldly redone with upbeat colors and sleek furniture; light sculptures add a chic touch. Rooms on the north side overlook the Chicago River.

$$$$ Hyatt Regency Chicago – *151 E. Wacker Dr., Loop.* ✕ & P ≋ *312-565-1234. www.chicagoregency.hyatt.com. 2,019 rooms.* Think bigger is better? Then this humongous Hyatt is for you. Besides the sheer size of the place, the hotel's **Big Bar** sports the longest freestanding bar in North America—not to mention more than 1,400 beverage choices. In the glass-enclosed lobby, huge windows peer out onto the river. The hotel's location is convenient to both sides of the river, as well as to the Millennium Park and the lakefront.

$$$$ InterContinental Chicago – *505 N. Michigan Ave., Magnificent Mile.* ✕ & P ≋ *312-944-4100 or 800-327-0200. www.chicago.intercontinental. com. 790 rooms.* This Mag Mile classic began life as a men's club in 1929 and still retains many of the club's original embellishments. Egyptian, Renaissance and Middle Eastern motifs ornament the public spaces, while lavish majolica tile sets off the junior Olympic-size swimming pool. Redecorated rooms in the historic tower are furnished in smart European style; those in the main building tower sport a modern look.

$$$$ Swissotel – *323 E. Wacker Dr., Loop.* ✕ & P ≋ Spa *312-565-0565 or 888-737-9477. www.swissotelchicago.com. 661 rooms.* Designed by prominent Chicago architect Harry Weese, the Swissotel cuts a shimmering 43-story silhouette, its crisp triangular shape wrapped entirely in glass. The property exudes a quiet elegance and in spite of high-rise buildings to the east, good views can still be had. Pamper your bod at the Penthouse Health Club and Spa.

RESERVATION SERVICES	TELEPHONE	WEBSITE
Hotels.com	800-246-8357	www.hotels.com
Hotel Discount	800-715-7666	www.180096hotel.com
Hot Rooms	800-468-3500	www.hotrooms.com
Great Hotels of the World	888-222-8859	www.ghotw.com/list/country1/home/illinois.htm
Quikbook	800-789-9887	www.quikbook.com
Central Reservation Service	800-555-7555	www.reservation-services.com
Bed and Breakfast Chicago	800-462-2632	www.bedandbreakfast.com/chicago-illinois.html
Hostelling International Chicago	312-360-0300	www.hichicago.com

$$$$ Talbott Hotel – *20 E. Delaware Pl., Magnificent Mile.* ✗ ♿ 🅿 ☎*312-944-4970 or 800-825-2688. www.talbotthotel.com. 149 rooms.* Snug, intimate and decorated in an English fox-hunting theme, the tony Talbott features antiques and two fireplaces in its wood-paneled Victorian-style lobby. Guest rooms and suites, some with full kitchens, are simply but tastefully appointed in period reproductions.

$$$$ theWit – *201 N. State St., Loop.* ✗ ♿ 🅿 Spa ☎*312-467-0200. www.thewit hotel.com. 298 rooms.* Towering 27 stories over the Chicago River, theWit appeals to business and leisure travelers alike. Some 7,000ft of meeting space and a private multimedia theater cater to the former, while two restaurants, a spa, and an indoor-outdoor rooftop lounge provide plenty of off-hours activity. Outside, the attractions of the theater district, the lakefront and Mag Mile lie within easy walking distance.

$$$ City Suites Hotel – *933 W. Belmont Ave., Lakeview.* ♿ 🅿 ☎*773-404-3400 or 800-248-9108. www.chicagocitysuites.com. 45 rooms.* City Suites inhabits a neighborhood that bustles with street life day and night, crowded as it is with restaurants, bars and nightclubs. Most of the units in this Art Deco restoration are suites furnished with hide-a-beds and refrigerators. Rates include a daily continental breakfast and access to a nearby fitness club.

$$$ Dana Hotel & Spa – *660 N. State St., River North.* ✗ ♿ 🅿 Spa ☎*312-202-6000. 216 rooms.* Tranquility awaits at the Dana, where sleek rooms come with Egyptian cotton sheets, Keurig coffeemakers and rain showerheads. Drop by the 24-hour gym to keep those muscles toned, after which a massage may be in order at the spa. Feeling social? Check out the nightly DJ at Vertigo Sky Lounge. Seasonal Asian fare is meant for sharing at **aja ($$)**.

$$$ Hotel Allegro Chicago – *171 W. Randolph St., Loop.* ✗ ♿ 🅿 ☎*312-236-0123 or 800-643-1500. www.allegro chicago.com. 483 rooms.* Bold colors and prints have transformed the North Loop theater district's 1926 Bismarck Hotel into a stylish Hollywood set. The lobby's fluted glass and oak-paneled walls are the backdrop for blue velvet chaise lounges and magenta velour sofas. Guest rooms feature geometric-patterned wallcoverings, cobalt-blue headboards and mirrored work desks.

$$$ Hotel Burnham – *1 W. Washington St., Loop.* ✗ ♿ 🅿 ☎*312-782-1111 or 877-294-9712. www.burnhamhotel.com. 122 rooms.* Designed by Daniel Burnham's architectural firm in 1895, the historic Reliance Building now houses the fanciful Hotel Burnham, where original design elements blend with bold and colorful interior stylings. Located across from Macy's, the hotel is within walking distance of theaters and the lakefront.

$$$ Majestic Hotel – *528 W. Brompton Ave., Lakeview.* ☎773-404-3499 or 800-727-5108. *www.cityinns.com/majestic. 52 rooms.* In the vicinity of Wrigley Field and steps from Lincoln Park and Belmont Harbor, this comfortable English-style inn is nicely situated for North Side activities. A continental breakfast is included with your room.

$$$ Millennium Knickerbocker Hotel –*163 E. Walton Pl., Magnificent Mile.* ☎312-751-8100 or 866-866-8086. *www.millenniumhotels.com. 306 rooms.* Transformed several times since its construction in 1927, the Knickerbocker's lit marquee still welcomes guests as it did in Prohibition-era Chicago. Rooms are small but have recently been redecorated with 40-inch flat-screen TVs, down comforters and Frette linens.

$$$ Silversmith Hotel – *10 S. Wabash Ave., Loop.* ☎312-372-7696 or 800-979-0084. *www.silversmithchicago hotel.com. 143 rooms.* Tucked into Jeweler's Row just feet from the "L" tracks, the beautifully appointed Silversmith comes as an elegant surprise. Built in 1897 as a warren for jewelry makers, the landmark hotel has been renovated in turn-of-the-century Arts and Crafts style.

$$$ The Wheeler Mansion – *2020 S. Calumet Ave., Near South Side.* ☎312-945-2020. *www.wheelermansion. 11 rooms.* A stay here will give you a glimpse of life on Chicago's once-elegant Near South Side. Built in 1870, this landmark is set in the Prairie Avenue Historic District. The house is convenient to McCormick Place and the lakefront. On-site parking and a gourmet breakfast are included.

$$$ The Whitehall Hotel – *105 E. Delaware Pl., Magnificent Mile.* ☎312-944-6300 or 866-753-4081. *www.thewhitehallhotel.com. 222 rooms.* Just off the Mag Mile, this venerable inn is among the original small hotels in the city, serving an elite clientele since 1974. Today it retains its polish, thanks to an English country manor atmosphere. The attentive staff provide efficient and personalized service.

$$$ The Willows Hotel – *555 W. Surf St., Lincoln Park.* ☎773-528-8400 or 800-727-5108. *www.cityinns.com/willows. 55 rooms.* The Willows occupies a vintage 1920s building just off busy Broadway. Decorated in 19C French country style, the lobby is warm and inviting. Though bathrooms are small, the rooms are restful, done in a soft palette.

$$ The Carleton of Oak Park – *1110 Pleasant St., Oak Park.* ☎708-848-5000 or 888-227-5386. *www.carleton hotel.com. 154 rooms.* The Carleton offers pleasant accommodations convenient to downtown Oak Park and about 20 minutes from the Loop via the nearby elevated train.

$$ The Essex Inn – *800 S. Michigan Ave., Grant Park.* ☎312-939-2800 or 800-621-6909. *www.essexinn.com. 254 rooms.* Though its rooms are basic, the Essex appeals for its good prices and convenient location. Across the street, Grant Park makes a lovely front yard.

$$ The Margarita European Inn –*1566 Oak Ave., Evanston.* ☎847-869-2273. *www.margaritainn.com. 42 rooms.* Ten miles north of the Loop, the Margarita is close to Northwestern University and the train to downtown. In addition to rooms with shared and private baths and several suites, the 1915 Georgian inn features an elegant Grand Parlor where a complimentary continental breakfast is served daily.

$$ Red Roof Inn – *162 E. Ontario St., Magnificent Mile.* ☎312-787-3580. *www.redroof.com. 195 rooms.* Comfortable and clean, this budget inn lives up to its swanky location just off Michigan Avenue without pretension. While the room decor is basic motel fare, the lobby shows off marble and chandeliers. Adjacent is **Coco Pazzo Café ($$)**, the trattoria version of its pricier namesake in River North.

$$ The Write Inn – *211 N. Oak Park Ave., Oak Park.* ☎708-383-4800. *www. writeinn.com. 66 rooms.* This suburban inn is located along a shady stretch of residential street not far from local shopping, dining and trains to the Loop. It offers a wide variety of rooms and suites decorated with 1920s antiques.

Where to Eat

Choosing a restaurant in Chicago can be an overwhelming task, given the quantity, variety and quality of local eateries. While famous for its pizzas and hot dogs, the city's culinary aptitude reaches well beyond those simple pleasures. As noted elsewhere in the text, ethnic eateries abound—from Ethiopian to Israeli—and nothing is left to be desired in the upscale restaurant department. Top-notch chefs vie for honors here, to the great delight of Chicago's enthusiastic diners. As a result, restaurants come and go at a breakneck pace. One thing is constant, however: Chicago's dining scene offers something to satisfy every appetite and please every pocketbook.

The venues listed below were selected for their ambience, location and/or value for money. Rates indicate the average cost of an appetizer, an entrée and dessert for one person *(not including tax, gratuity or beverages)*. Most restaurants are open daily—except where noted—and accept all major credit cards. Call for information regarding reservations and opening hours.

Additional restaurants are listed in Address Books throughout this guide. See Index for a complete listing of eateries described in the text.

$$$$	over $75
$$$	$50–$75
$$	$25–$50
$	less than $25

RESTAURANTS

$$$$ Alinea – *1723 N. Halstead St., Lincoln Park. Closed Mon & Tue.* ♿. &#9P; *(valet).* ☎*312-867-0110. www.alinea-restaurant.com. Dinner only. Reservations required (8 weeks in advance).* **Contemporary**. Protégé of Spanish master Ferran Adrià, culinary wünderkind Grant Achatz has redefined the American restaurant with his experiments in molecular gastronomy.

A meal in the serene space offers only two options: a 12-course tasting and a 26-course "tour." Esoteric titles like Hot Potato Cold Potato only hint at the glorious complexity of flavors, textures and temperatures in a tiny butter-poached ball of potato covered by a black truffle and skewered with a cube of parmesan—all intended to be eaten in a bowl of cold potato soup.

$$$$ Arun's – *4156 N. Kedzie Ave., Wrigleyville. Closed Mon.* ♿. ☎*773-539-1909. www.arunsthai.com. Dinner only.* **Thai**. Reputedly among the best Thai restaurants in the country, this elegantly appointed spot offers only a prix-fixe menu. Multiple family-style courses invite diners to sample a delightful array of delicacies and flavors, selected and blended with exquisite attention to detail. At meal's end, enjoy a glass of the palate-cleansing lemongrass elixir.

Lad Nar, Arun's

$$$$ Blackbird – *619 W. Randolph St., Near West Side.* ♿. &#9P; *(valet).* ☎*312-715-0708. www.blackbirdrestaurant.com. Dinner only.* **Contemporary**. In contrast to its minimalist decor, the food at this tiny Market District hot spot is a feast for the eyes, prepared in a style that Chef Paul Kahan describes as "seasonal American with French countryside influences." Hearty ingredients anchor dishes such as stuffed bobwhite quail with black cumin sausage, and roasted Colorado lamb saddle with spring pea felafel. Just as good, casual younger sister **avec ($$)** is right next door. Mediterranean-inspired small plates are avec's claim to fame.

Blackbird

Blackbird

$$$$ Charlie Trotter's – *816 W. Armitage St., Lincoln Park. Closed Sun & Mon.* ♿. ☎*773-248-6228. www.charlie trotters.com. Dinner only. Jackets required.* **Contemporary**. Tables at the restaurant run by esteemed chef Charlie Trotter get booked *(reservations required)* 12 weeks in advance. The draw? One-of-a-kind dishes prepared with naturally raised meats, organic produce and vegetable-based sauces in a late-19C brownstone. Three daily changing prix-fixe menus include a spontaneous feast created before your eyes at the kitchen table.

$$$$ Everest – *440 S. LaSalle St., Loop.* ♿🅿 ☎*312-663-8920. www.everest restaurant.com. Dinner only. Closed Sun & Mon.* **French**. Named for its lofty perch on the 40th floor of the Chicago Stock Exchange, Everest commands a sweeping view of the city. Award-winning chef Jean Joho crafts the finest seasonal ingredients into mouthwatering creations, adding accents from his native Alsace.

$$$$ Spiaggia – *980 N. Michigan Ave., 2nd floor, Magnificent Mile.* ♿🅿 ☎*312-280-2750. www.spiaggiarestaurant.com. Reservations and jackets required.* **Italian**. Overlooking the north end of Michigan Avenue and Lake Michigan beyond, Chicago's toniest Italian restaurant offers a soaring array of dishes that are well grounded in regional Italian

cookery. Ricotta gnocchi with ricotta sauce and black truffles, for instance, might precede a hearty wood-roasted veal chop. Next door, dressed-down **Café Spiaggia ($$)** serves pasta and entrées at more palatable prices.

$$$$ Tru – *676 N. St. Clair St., Magnificent Mile. Closed Sun.* ♿🅿 *(valet)* ☎*312-202-0001. www.trurestaurant.com. Reservations and jackets required.* **Contemporary**. At once lush and spare, the dining room at Tru sets the stage for the epicurean theater to follow. Original Warhols and other artworks add color to the room, and the tables are serenely minimalist. After you choose your menu, acclaimed chefs Rick Tramonto and Gail Gand send out course after jewel-like course from the prix-fixe menu of your choice, each more exquisite than the last in taste and presentation.

$$$ One sixtyblue – *1400 W. Randolph St., Near West Side. Closed Sun.* ♿🅿 *(valet)* ☎*312-850-0303. www.onesixtyblue.com. Dinner only.* **Contemporary**. Michael Jordan is a silent partner of this trendy restaurant, but celebs and locals alike are drawn to the sleek and sexy loft-like dining room. Here the mood is set for inventive fare such as cedar-roasted Loch Duart salmon and bacon-wrapped saddle of rabbit.

$$$ Topolobampo – *445 N. Clark St., River North. Closed Sun & Mon.* ♿. 🅿 *(valet)* ☎*312-661-1434. www.rickbayless.com.* **Regional Mexican**. Chef Rick Bayless has given his sophisticated cuisine a nationwide reputation by the skillful blending of traditional regional Mexican flavors. Bayless has a winning way with chilies, and his stand-out fish dishes are paired with the likes of salsa Veracruzana, mole, and sesame pipián. The same quality—at less cost—can be found at **Frontera Grill ($$)**, which shares space with Topolobampo. Seasonal menus, a sustainable seafood bar, and Bayless' incomparable personal touch set these two restaurants apart.

$$ Ai – *358 W. Ontario St., Gold Coast.* ♿. ☎*312-335-9888. www.aichicago.us.* **Japanese**. The name of this new sushi place is Japanese for "love"—fitting since locals do love the sleek dining space and signature sushi such as toro tartare, hamachi carpaccio and the soft-shell crab volcano roll. An omakase (chef's choice) menu is also available.

$$ Brasserie Jo – *59 W. Hubbard St., River North.* &.*312-595-0800. www. brasseriejo.com. Dinner only.* **French**. Chef Jean Joho (of Everest) works magic with the country fare of Alsace, offering among other hearty dishes a marvelous choucroute Alsacienne, classic *tartes flambées* and mussels steamed in Alsace Reisling. The largely Alsatian wine list, good beer and authentic Parisian brasserie atmosphere complete this delightful dining experience.

$$ Café Ba-Ba-Reeba! – *2024 N. Halsted St., Lincoln Park.* &.*773-935-5000. www.cafebabreeba.com.* **Spanish**. Chicago's original tapas bar offers seven seating areas *(accommodating 360 diners)* decked in bright Mediterranean colors. Ambience and food still sizzle, and the crowds come to enjoy hot and cold small plates, paella and a selection of sangria, sherry and Spanish wines.

$$ Club Lucky – *1824 W. Wabansia Ave., Bucktown.* *773-227-2300. www.club luckychicago.com.* **Italian**. In a neighborhood where eateries come and go, Club Lucky has endured. Potent martinis precede big portions of homestyle Italian cooking—rigatoni with veal meatballs, eggplant parmigiana, chicken oreganato. That, along with the funky 1940s supper-club decor make this place a long-lived hit.

$$ Erwin – *2925 N. Halsted St., Lakeview. Closed Mon.* &.*773-528-7200. www. erwincafe.com. Dinner only & Sun brunch.* **Contemporary**. Seasonal specialties with Midwestern flavor grace chef/owner Erwin Drechsler's simple but robust menu. Creative vegetable and fruit preparations and savory sauces embellish basics like roasted whitefish and grilled flank steak. The small, comfortable space feels like a friend's dining room.

$$ Green Zebra – *1460 W. Chicago Ave. Near West Side. Closed Mon.* &.*312-243-7100. www.greenzebrachicago.com. Dinner only & Sun brunch.* **Vegetarian**. Chicago may be known for its steaks, but Green Zebra is all about vegetables. Named for a variety of heirloom tomato,

this hot spot pulses with a hip vibe evident in its buzzing dining room and techno-modern decor . Fresh vegetables, exotic and familiar, combine in surprising and colorful ways on the tempting seasonal menus.

$$ Harry Caray's – *33 W. Kinzie Ave., River North.* &.*312-828-0966. www. harrycarays.com.* **Italian Steakhouse**. Cub fans will revel in the atmosphere here, which is chock-full of baseball memorabilia relating to the Hall of Fame career of late baseball announcer Harry Caray. The house specialty is chicken Vesuvio (chicken sautéed with garlic, then baked with crispy potatoes). You can dine for under $50 unless you go for one of the pricier cuts of prime beef.

$$ HotChocolate – *1747 N. Damen Ave., Bucktown. Closed Mon.* &.*773-489-1777. www.hotchocolatechicago.com.* **American**. Award-winning pasty chef Mindy Segal runs this urban cafe where contemporary American dishes (grilled Kobe flank steak; crispy skin Arctic char) fill the menu, and dessert is de rigueur. How could you pass up a warm chocolate soufflé tart with salted caramel ice cream, and a cup of decadent dark hot chocolate with house-made marshmallows?

$$ Paramount Room – *415 N. Milwaukee Ave., Near West.* &.*312-829-6300. www.paramountroom.com.* **Gastropub**. This stylish gastropub wins raves for its tasty cuisine, craft beers and daily budget-friendly food and drink deals. The internationally inspired fare runs from a croque monsieur to an Amish chicken breast satay. Try a black and tan float (Guinness ice cream and Abita root beer) for dessert.

$$ Terzo Piano – *159 E. Monroe St., Loop. Lunch daily; dinner Thu.* &.*312-443-8650. www.terzopianochicago.com. Museum admission not required.* **Italian**. Located in the new Modern Wing of the Art Institute, this sparkling new space brags the acclaimed cuisine of Chef Tony Mantuano, of Spiaggia fame. Products from local farms and food artisans paint masterful strokes in dishes such as roasted Great Lakes walleye pike with Nichols Farm cippollini onions and almond-herb purée.

$ Green Door Tavern – *678 N. Orleans St., River North.* &. *312-664-5496. www. greendoorchicago.com.* **American**. Constructed only one year after the Chicago Fire of 1871, the tavern is among the oldest buildings downtown and shows its age in a 10-degree list to starboard and sloping floors. It's been a tavern since 1921 and today serves good burgers, bbq ribs, pasta, and 35 different kinds of beer.

$ Half Shell – *676 W. Diversey Pkwy., Lincoln Park.* *773-549-1773. www.half shellchicago.com.* **Seafood**. This quint-essential neighborhood dive is located below street level. Though small and dark, it lures loyal locals craving wonderful fresh crab legs, shrimp, oysters and fried seafood. The curving bar takes up half the room, and eager diners can eat there rather than wait for a table.

$ Twin Anchors Restaurant and Tavern – *1655 N. Sedgwick St., Old Town.* &. (valet). *312-266-1616. www.twin anchorsribs.com. No lunch weekdays.* **Barbecue**. Beloved for its succulent ribs, Twin Anchors has been a popular neighborhood joint since its opening after Prohibition. (Frank Sinatra stopped here regularly in the 1960s.) The relaxed and modest atmosphere makes a nice escape from upscale chic.

$ Wishbone – *1001 W. Washington Blvd., Near West Side.* &. *312-850-2663. www. wishbonechicago.com. No dinner Sun & Mon.* **Southern**. Have a hearty Cajun breakfast, a heaping helping of hoppin' John or mix and match down-home sides with blackened catfish and jambalaya. Wishbone's colorful, lively dining room attracts an eclectic crowd.

$ Xoxo – *449 N. Clark St. (enter on Illinois St.), Loop. Closed Sun–Mon.* &. *312-334-3688. www.rickbayless.com.* **Mexican**. The newest restaurant by celebrity chef Rick Bayless, Xoxo (pronounced "show-co") is literally the "little sister" of Topolobampo and Fronter Grill. Mexican street food steals the show here in fried *churros*, crusty *tortas* and made-to-order *caldos*. Cacao beans from Mexico, used to make Xoco's multiple versions of hot chocolate, are ground on-site.

Entertainment

PERFORMING ARTS

Chicago provides a variety of music and entertainment year-round. Close to 120 theaters host dramas and musicals, ranging from traveling Broadway productions to performances by highly acclaimed local companies. Dance, symphony and opera productions are performed at venues throughout the city. Small clubs specializing in jazz, blues, rock and country offer first-class music in an intimate setting. Popular rock and alternative performers play in stadiums or convention centers in outlying areas. Summer brings the **Ravinia Music Festival** (see p253) in Highland Park as well as outdoor performances at parks and downtown plazas. For a detailed listing of events, call the **Mayor's Office of Special Events** (*312-744-0626*).

USEFUL NUMBERS *(pre-recorded information)*	
Mayor's Office of Special Events	*312-744-0626*
Fine Arts Hotline	*312-346-3278*
Jazz Hotline	*312-427-3300*

TICKETS

As some of the more popular events sell out months in advance, it is advisable to buy tickets early. Full-price tickets can be purchased directly from the venue's box office or from Hot Tix or Ticketmaster; major credit cards are usually accepted (*a service charge of $1–$5 may be added to the ticket price*), but not at all locations. Licensed ticket agencies sometimes have tickets available when the box office is sold out but expect to pay a substantial service fee (*up to 35 percent*). The hotel concierge may be able to help secure tickets for a performance.

CLASSICAL MUSIC

The city's vibrant classical music scene is dominated by, but hardly limited to, the Chicago Symphony Orchestra. For the full scoop, check online at www.chicagoclassicalmusic.org.

Chicago Symphony Orchestra – *Symphony Center, 220 S. Michigan Ave. (Loop).* ℘*312-294-3000. www.cso.org.* Chicago's world-class orchestra will begin its 2010/2011 season under the musical direction of renowned Italian maestro Riccardo Muti.

Chicago Philharmonic – *Northwestern University Campus, Evanston.* ℘*847-866 -6888. www.chicagophilharmonic.org.* Performing at Northwestern's Pick-Staiger Hall, the Philharmonic aims to spotlight some of the area's finest musical talent at affordable prices.

Chicago Sinfonietta – *Symphony Center, 70 E. Lake St. (Loop).* ℘*312-236-3681. www.chicagosinfonietta.org.* Founded in 1987, the racially diverse Sinfonietta boasts a wide-ranging repertoire and an excellent outreach program.

Chicago Opera Theater – *Harris Theater, 205 E. Randolph St. (Millennium Park).* ℘*312-704-8414. www.chicago operatheater.org.* The Opera Theater stages the great operatic works of the 17C, 18C and 20C.

Grant Park Orchestra – *Jay Pritzker Pavilion, 205 E Randolph Dr. (Millennium Park, mid-Jun–late Aug).* ℘*312-742-7638. www.millenniumpark.org.* Chicagoans flock to hear the orchestra play during the Grant Park Music Festival, which features free classical music concerts every summer.

Lyric Opera – *20 N. Wacker Dr. (Loop).* ℘*312-332-2244. www.lyricopera.org.* This internationally acclaimed opera company has been delighting local audiences at the Civic Opera House since 1954.

Old Town School of Folk Music – *909 W. Armitage Ave. and 4544 N. Lincoln Ave. (Lincoln Park/DePaul).* ℘*773-728-6000. www.oldtownschool.org.* In addition to offering classes in music, dance, theater and visual arts, the school stages music and dance performances in its 400-seat concert hall in Lincoln Park.

ROCK AND POP

From pop bands like The Buckinghams to alternative performers such as The Smashing Pumpkins and Liz Phair, Chicago really rocks. Here are some of the main venues to catch your favorite bands when you're in town.

Allstate Arena – *6920 N. Mannheim Rd., Rosemont.* ℘*847-635-6601. www.allstate arena.com.* Home to the Chicago Wolves hockey team, this sports arena also hosts concerts by the likes of Shakira, Fleetwood Mac, the Rolling Stones and violinist Andre Rieu.

Aragon Ballroom – *1106 W. Lawrence Ave. (Uptown).* ℘*773-561-9500. www.aragon.com.* Designed in 1926 in the style of a Spanish palace courtyard, the Aragon can seat up to 4,500 people for events ranging from wrestling matches to concerts.

Double Door – *1572 N. Milwaukee Ave. (Wicker Park).* ℘*773-489-3160. www.doubledoor.com.* Smaller than an arena, this Wicker Park club opened in the 1990s to provide a mid-size venue for talented local bands.

Metro – *3730 N. Clark St. (Lakeview/Wrigleyville).* ℘*773-549-0203. www.metrochicago.com.* Big sister to Double Door, Metro is the place to hear local, regional and national emerging bands. The venue can accommodate 1,150 between the main floor and the balcony; the back of the room is just 25ft from the stage.

First Midwest Bank Amphitheatre – *19100 S. Ridgeland, Tinley Park.* ℘*708-614-1616. www.livenation.com.* This outdoor amphitheater is located about an hour from downtown. Santana, Iron Maiden, the Jonas Brothers, and Christina Aguilera number among the performers who grace the stage here during the summer season.

Skyline Stage – *Navy Pier, 600 E. Grand Ave. (Streeterville).* ℘*312-595-7437. www.navypier.com.* The sides of Navy Pier's white-domed stage, set behind the Ferris wheel, are open to lake breezes. The season, which runs from May through September, features acts like Natalie Cole, Penn & Teller, and Cirque Shanghai.

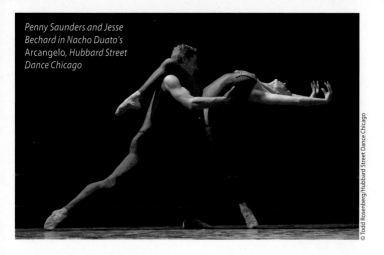

Penny Saunders and Jesse Bechard in Nacho Duato's Arcangelo, *Hubbard Street Dance Chicago*

© Todd Rosenberg/Hubbard Street Dance Chicago

Star Plaza Theatre – *8001 Delaware Pl., Merrillville, IN.* 📞*1-800-745-3000. www.starplazatheatre.com.* Plush red seats in this 3,400-seat semicircular theater provide comfortable places to listen to mainstream pop, rock and country acts.

United Center – *1901 W. Madison St. (Near West Side).* 📞*312-455-4500. www.unitedcenter.com.* When United Center isn't hosting the Stanley Cup Champions, the Chicago Blackhawks, it's staging the biggest rock acts in town. Carol King and James Taylor, Rihanna, and Tom Petty and the Heartbreakers alternate with shows such as *Disney on Ice*.

DANCE

Chicago dances to its own beat, from the *pas de deux* of the Joffrey Ballet to the tribal rhythms of Muntu Dance Theatre. Throughout the year, visiting companies stop in to add to the mix. You can find the low-down online at www.seechicagodance.com.

Ballet Chicago – *17 N. State St., (Loop).* 📞*312-251-8838. www.balletchicago.org.* Formed in 1997, the Ballet Chicago Studio Company focuses on the works of George Balanchine. Their staging of *The Nutcracker* is a Christmas classic. Performances are held at the Athenaeum Theatre in Lakeview.

Hubbard Street Dance Chicago – *Harris Theater, 205 E Randolph Dr., (Millennium Park).* 📞*312-704-8414. www.hubbardstreetdance.org.* A partnership with choreographer Twyla Tharpe in the 1990s helped expand the repertoire of this acclaimed contemporary dance company, which mixes elements of jazz, ballet and modern dance. In addition to the troupe's spring and fall season, you can often catch them at the Ravinia Festival in summer.

Joffrey Ballet of Chicago – *Auditorium Theatre of Roosevelt University, 50 East Congress Pkwy.* 📞*312-386-8905. www.joffrey.com.* Founded in New York City by Robert Joffrey and Gerald Arpino in 1956, the Joffrey Ballet took up permanent residence in Chicago in 1995. The classical company's Academy of Dance now has a new home in the sparkling Joffrey Tower in the Loop.

Muntu Dance Theatre – *Various venues.* 📞*773-241-6080. www.muntu.com.* The largest African dance company in the US got its start in 1972. Since then the Muntu Dance Theatre has blossomed; the group is renowned for its innovative interpretation of contemporary and ancient African and African-American dance, music and folklore.

THEATRES AND PERFORMANCES

The Windy City's history as a theater town dates back to the late 19C, when the first music hall rose in the Loop. By the 1920s, Randolph Street reigned at Chicago's "Great White Way." After overcoming urban blight in the 1960s and 70s, the Loop stars again today as the heart of the city's theater district. For a comprehensive list of what's playing in the city's many theaters, check online at the League of Chicago Theaters' website: www. chicagoplays.com.

Hot Tix offers half-price tickets for selected events on the day of the show. Purchases must be made in person (72 E. Randolph St.; 163 E. Pearson St. at N. Michigan Ave.; www.hottix.org; offices open Tue–Sat 10am–6pm, Sun 11am–4pm).

Ticketmaster offers full-price tickets (72 E. Randolph St.; 163 E. Pearson St. at N. Michigan Ave.; charge by phone: ☎312-902-1500; www.ticketmaster. com). Both Hot Tix and Ticketmaster are located in the Water Works Visitor Center (☎312-744-8783).

Apollo Theater – 2540 N. Lincoln Ave. (Lincoln Park/DePaul). ☎773-935-6100. www.apollochicago.com. The Apollo's glass and concrete design houses a three-quarter thrust stage and 440 seats. Recent shows here include *Million Dollar Quartet*, based on a 1956 jam session with Johnny Cash, Jerry Lee Lewis, Carl Perkins and Elvis Presley.

Athenaeum Theatre – 2936 N. Southport Ave. (Lakeview/Wrigleyville). ☎773-935-6860. www.athenaeumtheatre.com. Consisting of one large 1,000-seat theater and three smaller studios, the Athenaeum hosts a varied program of musicals, dance (i.e. Ballet Chicago) and drama.

Auditorium Theatre – 50 E. Congress Pkwy. (Loop). ☎312-922-2110. www. auditoriumtheatre.org. When it was designed by Louis Sullivan and Dankmar Adler in 1889, this 4,200-seat venue boasted electric lighting and air conditioning. Today audiences still admire its 24-karat gold-leaf ceiling arches and ornate bas-reliefs while they enjoy presentations ranging from the Bolshoi Ballet to the Ensemble Espagnol Spanish Dance Theater.

Briar Street Theatre – 3133 N. Halsted St. (Lakeview/Wrigleyville). ☎773-348-4000. www.foxtheatricals.com/briar-street.htm. With its good sight lines and fine acoustics, the Briar has been the Chicago home to the long-running Blue Man Group since 1997. The building was originally a stable for Marshall Field's horses.

Cadillac Palace Theatre – 151 W. Randolph St. (Loop). ☎312-977-1700. www.broadwayinchicago.com. Marble walls, gold leaf and crystal chandeliers, give this 2,500-seat venue—opened in 1926 as a vaudeville playhouse called The Palace Theatre—the look of a French palace. Renamed for the Cadillac division of General Motors, which bought the naming rights in the late 1990s, the Cadillac Palace now stages Broadway hits like *Mamma Mia!* and Disney's *The Lion King*.

Chicago Shakespeare Theater – Navy Pier, 600 E. Grand Ave. (Streeterville). ☎312-595-5600. www.chicagoshakes.com. The glass-box complex that houses this Tony Award-winning courtyard-style

Courtyard Theater, Chicago Shakespeare Theater

theater also contains an English-style pub. Its 48-week season encompasses some 600 performances of the Bard's finest work.

Chicago Theatre – *175 N. State St. (Loop).* ☎*312-462-6300. www.thechicago theatre.com.* The model for America's lavish movie palaces, the 1921 Chicago Theatre takes its design cues from several French venues, including the Paris Opera House. Past performers include Jackson Browne, Melissa Etheridge and Cheech and Chong.

Court Theatre – *5535 S. Ellis Ave. (University of Chicago).* ☎*773-753-4472. www.courttheatre.org.* The University of Chicago's Court Theatre knows its way around the classics, from Gershwin's *Porgy and Bess* to Shakespeare's *The Comedy of Errors.*

Drury Lane Theatre – *175 E. Chestnut St. (Magnificent Mile).* ☎*312-642-2000. www.drurylaneoakbrook.com.* Musical productions such as *Sugar* (based on the movie *Some Like It Hot*) and Monty Python's *Spamalot* entertain audiences here. You can purchase a dinner package that includes a meal in the dining room of the Drury Lane Conference Center, in which the theater is located.

Goodman Theatre – *170 N. Dearborn St. (Loop).* ☎*312-443-3800. www.goodman theatre.org.* First-rate actors and top-notch productions are what you can expect at the Goodman, whose present home is built on the site of a pair of rococo movie houses. The Goodman's annual staging of Charles Dickens' *A Christmas Carol* is a local holiday family tradition.

Greenhouse Theater Center – *2257 N Lincoln Ave. (Lincoln Park/DePaul).* ☎*773-404-7336. www.greenhousetheater.org.* Formerly owned by Victory Gardens, this complex of four performance spaces is home to several independent theater companies, including Shattered Globe, IMPAACT and Teatro Vista.

Lookingglass Theatre – *821 N. Michigan Ave., (Magnificent Mile).* ☎*312-337-0665. www.lookingglasstheatre.org.* Ideally located in the Water Tower Pumping Station, the 270-seat Lookingglass Theatre stages several

original shows each year. *Friends* star David Schwimmer was one of the theater's founders.

Mercury Theater – *3745 N. Southport Ave. (Lakeview/Wrigleyville).* ☎*773-325-1700.* A relatively new (1996) performance venue in Chicagoland, the Mercury occupies an early-20C nickleodeon. The calendar encompasses an eclectic mix of touring and local productions as well as music and dance shows.

Oriental Theater/Ford Center for the Performing Arts – *24 W. Randolph St. (Loop).* ☎*1-800-775-2000. www.broadway inchicago.com.* The ornate decor of this 1926 movie palace was inspired by the Far East. *Ragtime, Fosse,* and *Billy Elliot the Musical* represent the Broadway shows that play here.

Royal George Theatre – *1641 N. Halsted St. (Lincoln Park/DePaul).* ☎*312-988-9000. www.theroyalgeorgetheatre.com.* Four different stages here vary in capacity from 50 to 450 seats. The main stage has hosted the likes of Neil Simon's *Lost in Yonkers,* and Ken Ludwig's *Lend Me A Tenor.*

Steppenwolf Theatre Company – *1650 N. Halsted St. (Lincoln Park/DePaul).* ☎*312-335-1650. www.steppenwolf.org.* This award-winning ensemble company has launched the careers of actors such as John Malkovich and Gary Sinise. Steppenwolf's intense, dramatic performances rank among the best in the city.

Theatre Building Chicago – *1225 W Belmont Ave. (Lakeview/Wrigleyville).* ☎*773-327-5252. www.theatrebuilding chicago.org.* Developing original musical works and supporting emerging theater companies and artists is the goal of this performance space.

Victory Gardens Theater – *2433 N Lincoln Ave. (Lincoln Park/DePaul).* ☎*773-871-3000. www.victorygardens.org.* Occupying the beautifully renovated historic Biograph Theater, VCT devotes itself to the work of new playwrights. As such it has produced more world premieres than any other Chicago theater.

NIGHTLIFE

Nightlife in Chicago ranges from quiet, elegant hotel lounges to lively rock bars along Rush and Division streets or sultry blues and jazz clubs on the North and South sides. The city has also garnered a excellent reputation for its numerous comedy clubs, which have hosted the likes of John Belushi, Dan Aykroyd and Steve Carrell. Consult the arts and entertainment sections of local newspapers for a detailed listing of events. Some establishments have a cover charge for entertainment. Many bars and clubs serve food *(menu may be scaled down to light appetizers after 10pm or 11pm)*. Since alcoholic beverages are served in nightclubs *(some clubs impose a drink minimum if you are not having a meal)*, proof of age is required to enter. Following is a list of clubs organized by type.

BLUES CLUBS

Chicago has been singing its own unique version of the blues since the 1920s, when a hybrid guitar-driven style based on urban themes emerged here. In the the 1940s, local musicians experimented with amplification, and by the 1950s Chicago had surfaced as the capital of the hard-driving electric blues, with Muddy Waters as its king. That tradition continues today.

Blue Chicago – *536 N. Clark St. (River North).* 312-661-0100. *www.blue chicago.com.* Local blues bands with some of the best female vocalists in the city draw locals to this club.

B.L.U.E.S – *2519 N. Halsted St. (Lakeview/ Wrigleyville).* 773-528-1012. *www. chicagobluesbar.com.* Open seven nights a week, this intimate club entertains serious blues fans with local talent.

Buddy Guy's Legends – *700 S. Wabash Ave. (South Loop).* 312-427-1190. *www. buddyguys.com.* Legendary blues guitarist Buddy Guy's "home of the blues" moved to its new South Loop location in spring 2010.

Checkerboard Lounge – *5201 S. Harper Ct. (Hyde Park). www.checkerboardhyde park.com.* 773-684-1472. A mix of locals and University of Chicago

students hang here Friday and Saturday nights to hear live blues music.

House of Blues – *329 N. Dearborn St. (River North). www.hob.com.* 312-923-2000. Located in the Marina City complex, House of Blues hosts a mélange of music that goes well beyond the blues.

Kingston Mines – *2548 N. Halsted St. (Lincoln Park/DePaul).* 773-477-4646. *www.kingstonmines.com.* Established in 1968, Chicago's oldest and largest blues club features traditional blues musicians as well as emerging new talent.

COMEDY CLUBS

ComedySportz Theatre – *929 W. Belmont Ave. (Near West Side). www. comedysportz.com.* 773-549-8080. Let the games begin! At this family-friendly club, two improv teams are pitted against each other to vie for your laughter and applause.

iO Theater – *3541 N. Clark St. (Lakeview/ Wrigleyville). www.iochicago.net.* 773-880-0199. There's a theme for each evening's performance at ImprovOlympic; the cast then builds their skits and songs around it.

The Second City – *1616 N. Wells St. (Old Town). www.secondcity.com.* 312-337-3992. Chicago's most famous comedy venue, Second City's sketches and improvisational comedy has been tickling funny bones for over 50 years.

Zanies Comedy Night Club – *1548 N. Wells St. (Old Town).* 312-337-4027 *www.chicago.zanies.com.* Jay Leno, Jerry Seinfeld and Tim Allen all cut their teeth on Zanies stage. Famous for its stand-up comedy, the club is just down the street from Second City.

DINNER THEATRE

For interactive theater, you can't beat this genre. Tickets include dinner and a staged play or musical, and the show often involves the audience in its madcap action. Themes range from marriage to mobsters—take your pick.

Tommy Gun's Garage – *2114 S. Wabash Ave. (Near South Side).* 312-225-0273. *www.tommygunsgarage.com.* Relive the Roaring 20s with a satiric twist in this musical comedy review. Feast on lasagne or roasted prime rib in a speakeasy setting as you enjoy the fun of Chicago's longest-running dinnner show. Just don't let the cops see you drinking "hooch!"

Tony & Tina's Wedding – *230 W. North Ave. (Old Town).* ☎*312-644-8844. www. tonyntina.com.* Reopening in 2010 after a short hiatus, this raucous show includes the audience in the zany Italian-American wedding festivities of Tony and Tina. You'll experience it all, from cocktails to dinner and dancing.

JAZZ CLUBS

Jazz migrated from the South with the likes of King Oliver, Jelly Roll Morton and Louis Armstrong to Chicago, where it soon pulsed with its own hot tempo, explosive rhythm sections, and elaborate instrumental interplay. If you're a fan, plan a visit the first weekend in September for the world-renowned Chicago Jazz Festival.

Andy's Jazz Club – *11 E. Hubbard St. (River North).* ☎*312-642-6805. www. andysjazzclub.com.* Andy's packs the crowds into its casual and intimate River North digs with its full restaurant and bar, and two sets of music every night.

The Back Room – *1007 N. Rush St. (Gold Coast).* ☎*312-3751-2433. www. backroomchicago.com.* A long block off Michigan Avenue, The Back Room packs a well-dressed crowd into its small candlelit space, where jazz mixes with a host of other musical genres. No standing is allowed, so you'll be assured a seat at a table or at the bar.

The Green Mill – *4802 N. Broadway (Uptown).* ☎*773-878-5552. www.green milljazz.com.* Modeled after Clark Monroe's Uptown House in Harlem, the Green Mill recalls the jazz era of the 1920s and 30s (when Al Capone was a frequent guest; check out the booth he used to sit in). Musicians jam here until the wee hours of the morning.

Jazz Showcase – *806 S. Plymouth Ct. (South Loop).* ☎*312-360-0234. www.jazz showcase.com.* The historic Dearborn Station Building now houses this venerable club, founded in 1947. Charlie Parker, John Coltrane and Pat Metheny are among the jazz legends who have played here. Children are welcome at the Sunday matinee.

Pops for Champagne – *601 N. State St. (River North).* ☎*312-266-7677. www.pops forchampagne.com.* If it's bubbles you crave with your jazz, you'll find more than 100 bottles of Champagne and sparkling wine at Pops. Pair your choice with a selection from the menu of cheeses, charcuterie and small plates.

Underground Wonder Bar – *10 E. Walton Pl. (Magnificent Mile).* ☎*312-266-7761. www.undergroundwonderbar.com.* From rhythm and blues to reggae, you'll hear it all live at singer/songwriter Lonie Walker's jazz club, 365 nights a year. Get there early and save some dough; there's no cover charge on Sun–Thu before 9pm, and Fri–Sat before 8pm.

NIGHTCLUBS

Dick's Last Resort – *315 N. Dearborn St. (River North).* ☎*312-836-7870. www.dicks lastresort.com.* Located in Marina City Towers, Dick's is a raucous club where rock bands play every night and the waitstaff is intentionally surly.

Excalibur Entertainment Complex – *632 N. Dearborn St. (River North).* ☎*312-266-1944.* Multiple nightclubs fill this 1892 red granite building, designed by Henry Ives Cobb to house the Chicago Historical Society. Whether you want to party until 4am on the city's largest dance floor, or relax in one of the cozy lounges, the Excalibur can oblige.

Red Dog – *1958 W. North Ave. (Wicker Park).* ☎*773-278-1009.* Catering to party animals of all stripes, the Red Dog has been revived with the help of Joey Swanson (a.k.a. Just Joey). For long-time fans, it's still the place to go for house music in Wicker Park on Saturday night.

The Wild Hare – *3530 N. Clark St. (Lakeview/Wrigleyville).* ☎*773-327-4273. www.wildharemusic.com.* Bob Marley's spirit lives on at the Wild Hare in Wrigleyville, where reggae reigns supreme. A 2007 renovation fitted the place with a state-of-the-art sound and video system. No cover charge on Tuesday and Thursday.

Shopping

A world-class shopping mecca, Chicago attracts residents and tourists alike to its famous department stores, designer boutiques and trendy second-hand shops, not to mention its large flea market featuring live blues. The main shopping areas are clustered around downtown, but the various neighborhoods offer their fill of tiny stores stocked with used books, unusual crafts or ethnic fare. Most stores accept major credit cards and traveler's checks, but are reluctant to take out-of-state checks. Many shops extend their hours during the holiday season (typically starting in mid-November).

MAIN SHOPPING AREAS

Large department stores and malls in downtown are generally open Mon–Sat 10am–7pm and Sun noon–6pm; hours vary seasonally. Opening hours for smaller stores vary.

The Loop

Macy's *(111 N. State St.; 312-781-1000; www.macys.com)* anchors the main shopping area along State Street. **Jewelers Row** *(Wabash Ave. between Madison & Washington Sts.)*, the center of Chicago's jewelry business, includes the 190 vendors of the **Jewelers Center at the Mallers Building** *(5 S. Wabash Ave.; 312-853-2057; www.jewelerscenter.com)*. The **Atrium Mall** *(ground level of James R. Thompson Center, 100 W. Randolph St.; 312-346-0777; www.atriummallchicago.com)* includes 40 retail stores and restaurants in its sun-lit atrium.

River North

Best known for its art galleries and boutiques, River North also includes the **Jazz Record Mart** *(27 E. Illinois Ave.; 312-222-1467; www.jazzmart.com)*, which claims to be the world's largest jazz and blues record store. **Jay Robert's Antique Warehouse** *(149 W. Kinzie St.; 312-222-0167; www.jayroberts.com)* houses 54,000sq ft of antique furniture and housewares on three floors.

Lincoln Park/DePaul

This district offers an eclectic assortment of antique shops, funky boutiques, and a plethora of home and garden stores on Clybourn Avenue between North and Armitage avenues.

Hyde Park

This neighborhood is a bookworm's delight, offering numerous bookstores, grouped around the University of Chicago and along E. 57th and E. 55th Streets, featuring new, used and hard-to-find books. **O'Gara & Wilson Ltd.** *(1448 E. 57th St.; 773-363-0993; www.ogaraandwilson.com)* ranks as Chicago's oldest used bookstore and houses a treasure-trove of antique volumes.

Devon Avenue

Between Western and California Aves. The "Midwest capital of gold dealers" contains nearly 20 jewelers selling mostly 22- and 24-karat gold jewelry. The heart of Chicago's Indian community, Devon also features Indian restaurants, sari shops and electronics stores.

Magnificent Mile

🚌 *Bus no. 151 makes a loop from W. Harrison and S. State Sts. to Walton St. and N. Michigan Ave.* This section of North Michigan Avenue between Illinois and Oak streets is the prime shopping area of Chicago. It includes expansive malls, department stores (Macy's, Neiman Marcus, Saks Fifth Avenue, Nordstrom) and some of the world's finest designer boutiques *(located primarily on Oak St. between N. Michigan Ave. and Rush St.).*

Malls

For locations, see map (opposite page).
The Shops at Northbridge – *312-327-2300. www.theshopsatnorthbridge.com.* Upscale Seattle retailer Nordstrom —with its own spa on the third level— anchors this mall, which features four levels of shopping along with 20 eateries and restaurants. **Water Tower Place** – *312-440-3165. www.shopwatertower.com.* Some 100 shops on eight levels encompass Macy's, Sephora, Ann Taylor and American Girl Place, to name just a few. Foodlife and Mity Nice Grill number among the restaurants here.

600 North Michigan Shops – ☎312-266-5630. A multiplex movie theater marks this complex, along with stores such as Marshall's and Eddie Bauer, as well as several restaurants.

900 North Michigan Shops– ☎312-915-3916. www.shop 900.com. Bloomingdale's, Gucci, Michael Kors, Christofle and the Spa at Equinox give a taste of the more than 70 luxury retailers that reside in this mall, which connects to the Four Seasons hotel.

ART GALLERIES

In general, most commercial galleries open between 9am and 11am Tuesday through Saturday, and close at 5pm or 6pm; many close between exhibits. The *Chicago Gallery News (free, available at galleries and visitor centers)*, published quarterly, provides a comprehensive listing of exhibits and their locations.

Chicago's **main gallery districts** are located in **River North** *(between N. Wells, N. Orleans, W. Superior and W. Huron sts.;* ⓖ*see p114)* and **North Michigan Avenue** *(between E. Oak and E. Ontario Sts.)*.

Clusters of galleries can also be found on the **West Side** along North Milwaukee Avenue *(between N. Damen Ave. and N. Wood St.)*, on the **North Side** off North Lincoln Avenue *(between W. School and W. Division Sts.)*, and in **Evanston** along Sherman Avenue and Grove Street.

NEW MAXWELL STREET MARKET

S. Desplaines St. between Harrison St. and Roosevelt Ave. Open Sun 7am–3pm. ☎312-745-4676. A makeover of the historic Maxwell Street Market, this colorful, open-air flea market moved to Canal Street several years ago to accommodate the expansion of the University of Illinois. In its present—and third—location, the market features more than 500 vendors hawking a mixture of antiques, collectibles, and new and used merchandise—arrive early for the largest selection. In addition, there's a live blues band, and a host of Mexican food vendors proffering an inexpensive array of enchiladas, tacos and tamales.

North Michigan Avenue Shopping

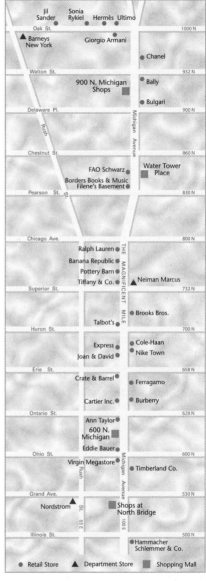

Jil Sander • Sonia Rykiel • Hermès • Ultimo • Oak St. — 1000 N
▲ Barneys New York — Giorgio Armani — Chanel •
Walton St. — 932 N
900 N. Michigan Shops ■ — Bally • — Bulgari •
Delaware Pl. — 900 N
Chestnut St. — 860 N
FAO Schwarz — Water Tower Place ■
Borders Books & Music — Filene's Basement •
Pearson St. — 830 N
Chicago Ave. — 800 N
Ralph Lauren • — THE MAGNIFICENT MILE
Banana Republic • — Neiman Marcus ▲
Pottery Barn •
Tiffany & Co. •
Superior St. — 732 N
Talbot's • — Brooks Bros. •
Huron St. — 700 N
Express • — Cole-Haan •
Joan & David • — Nike Town •
Erie St. — 658 N
Crate & Barrel • — Ferragamo •
Cartier Inc. • — Burberry •
Ontario St. — 628 N
Ann Taylor •
600 N. Michigan ■
Eddie Bauer •
Ohio St. — 600 N
Virgin Megastore • — Timberland Co. •
Grand Ave. — 530 N
Nordstrom ▲ — Shops at ■ North Bridge
Illinois St. — 500 N
Hammacher • Schlemmer & Co.

• Retail Store   ▲ Department Store   ■ Shopping Mall

Sports and Recreation

Chicago's primary recreation area is an almost continuous span of public parks along the city's 30-plus miles of lakefront, including Lincoln, Grant, Burnham and Jackson parks. The Chicago Park District maintains these parks, and well over 500 other recreational areas offering a wide range of activities including swimming, archery and bocci ball *(information and maps: 312-742-7529; www.chicagoparkdistrict.com).* The Forest Preserve District of Cook County provides information about natural areas and facilities outside the city boundaries *(800-870-3666; www.fpdcc.com).*

ON THE LAKE
SWIMMING

Over 30 public beaches are scattered along Lake Michigan. Lifeguards are on duty from Memorial Day–Labor Day *(9am–9.30pm; South Shore Beach closes at 8pm; 312-742-3224).* Many beaches have refreshment stands and changing facilities; no alcoholic beverages are allowed.

BEACHES	BLOCK
Howard St. Beach	7500N
Fargo Ave. Beach	7432N
Jarvis Ave. Beach	7432N
Jarvis Ave. Beach	7400N
Loyola Beach	7100N
Rogers Park	6700N
Berger Park	6200N
Lane Beach	5900N
Foster Ave. Beach	5200N
Montrose Beach	4400N
North Ave. Beach	1600N–2400N
Oak St. Beach	1000N–1400N
49th St. Beach	4900S
57th St. Beach	5700S
South Shore Beach	7100S

FISHING

Lake Michigan abounds with various species of fish, including coho and chinook salmon *(prime season May–Jun)*; brown, rainbow and lake trout *(prime season Jul–Aug)*; and yellow perch. Most charter boats depart from Burnham Park Harbor *(southeast of Grant Park)*. A fishing license is required; one-day nonresident licenses are available in fishing supply stores *(equipment rental may be available)*. Ice-fishing is permitted on area lakes when the ice is at least 4 inches thick; contact the **Forest Preserve District of Cook County** *(800-870-3666; www.fpdcc.com)* for more information. Onshore fishing *(prohibited May 15–Oct 15)* is allowed at Burnham and Montrose harbors and at Jackson Park.

BOATING

The lake is a great location year-round for sailing and power boating. Contact the **Harbor Division** of the Chicago Park District for temporary docking facilities *(312-742-8520; www.chicagoharbors.info)*. Sailboat rentals are available through **Chicago Sailing** *(hourly rates vary according to boat size and day of week; sailing proficiency necessary, instruction provided; 773-871-7245; www.chicagosailing.com)*. Contact **Chicagoland Canoe Base** *(4019 N. Narragansett Ave.; 773-777-1489; www.chicagolandcanoebase.com)* for rentals and information about places to canoe or kayak.

ON LAND
BIKING, HIKING AND JOGGING

Bike Way is a paved 18.5mi lakefront path extending along Chicago's shoreline. The path is also open to pedestrians and in-line skaters. In addition, 15 Chicago parks offer dedicated bicycle paths *(contact Chicago Park District for information)*. For more information and a map of bike routes in the area, contact the **Chicagoland Bicycle Federation** *(9 W. Hubbard St. Suite 402; 312-427-3325; www.activetrans.org)*. Bike and in-line skate rentals are available from

FITNESS CENTERS		
CLUB	**ADDRESS**	**TELEPHONE / WEBSITE**
Chicago Fitness Center	3131 N. Lincoln Ave.	✆773-549-8181 www.chicagofitnesscenter.com
Chicago Hilton Club	720 S. Michigan Ave.	✆312-294-6800 www.hilton.com
Lakeshore Athletic Club	1320 W. Fullerton Ave. 211 N. Stetson Ave	✆773-477-9888 ✆312-616-9000 www.lsac.com

Bike Chicago (locations at Millennium Park, Navy Pier, North Avenue Beach, Foster Beach; ✆888-245-3929; www.bikechicago.com). The **Chicago Area Runners Association** provides maps and information about local races and routes (549 West Randolph, Suite 704; ✆312-666-9836; www.cararuns.org).

EXERCISE

Clubs listed in the chart below allow non-members to use their facilities (weight rooms, aerobics classes and pools) for a daily fee. Many private fitness centers are open to guests of major hotels; check with the hotel's concierge. **YMCA** memberships are valid worldwide; call for closest recreation center and available facilities (✆312-932-1200; www.ymcachgo.org). Free equipment rental is available (when there is more than 3 inches of snow on the ground) at Northerly Island, just south of Adler Planetarium.

WINTER ACTIVITIES
CROSS-COUNTRY SKIING

Extensive trails for cross-country skiing and snowshoeing are available throughout the Chicago area for both tourists and residents (open Mon–Fri 2pm–9pm, weekends noon–5pm, weather permitting; rentals available at some facilities; Chicago Park District, ✆312-742-7529).

ICE-SKATING

Enjoy ice-skating downtown (weather permitting) among the skyscrapers at **Daley Bicentennial Plaza** (337 E. Randolph St.; Nov–Feb daily; hours vary; $6 skate rental; ✆312-742-7650); or take in superb views of the lake and city while gliding at the ice rink at **Millennium Park** (55 N. Michigan Ave.; mid-Nov–mid-Mar daily; hours vary; $10 skate rental; 312-742-5222). Many of the city's public parks also operate ice-skating rinks in winter; check with the Chicago Parks District for more information: ✆312-742-7529; www.chicagoparkdistrict.com.

SNOWMOBILING

The Forest Preserve District of Cook County (✆800-870-3666; www.fpdcc.com) maintains five snowmobiling areas. Courses are open when the snow depth reaches over 4 inches. Snowmobiles must be registered with the Forest Preserve.

Iceskating in Millennium Park

©Jim Jurica/iStockphoto.com

SPECTATOR SPORTS

Tickets can be purchased at the individual venue or through Ticketmaster (312-902-1500). (See information box below.)

Chicago's muscle-bound image is nowhere more apparent than in the fanaticism of its sports enthusiasts. The *Saturday Night Live* "Superfans" skit parodied supporters of "Da Bears" for years after the 1985 squad won Super Bowl XX, and the team's near miss at the championship in 2007 drove the town wild. In baseball both White Sox and Cubs fans are devotedly loyal, despite the fact that neither team had won a World Series since World War I until the Sox clinched it in 2005. Although the nation's professional baseball and football leagues trace their origins to Chicago, it was basketball superstar **Michael Jordan** and six nearly consecutive NBA titles (1991–93, 1996–98) that gave the city its most dominant sports team and a personality to outshine mobster Al Capone in worldwide notoriety.

BASEBALL

The **Chicago Cubs** are the oldest original franchise in professional sports, dating back to the founding of the National League by team president Walter A. Hulbert in 1876. Nicknamed the "lovable losers" of the North Side, the Cubs last won a World Series in 1908 and have not appeared in the fall classic since 1945. Cub fans have wallowed in failure for so long that in 1989, newspaper columnist **Mike Royko** (1932–1997) popularized a new baseball statistic invented by local writer Ron Berler: the ex-Cub factor. Essentially, the claim is that any baseball team with three or more former Cubs players cannot win the World Series, having been "infected" by association with the lovable losers. Each year, Royko pointed out which teams would be unable to triumph because they had too many ex-Cubs on their roster. To date, the ex-Cub factor has proved to be an accurate prognosticator. Another local legend began when Sam Sianis, owner of the Billy Goat Tavern (*see Magnificent Mile*), was denied entry into Wrigley Field with his famous pet goat and placed a curse on the team to prevent its success. Years later, Sianis' son was invited by Cub management to attend a game with his goat to remove the curse, but even this bit of ungulate hoodoo has not brought success to the North Siders.

In 1916 the team moved to its present home of Wrigley Field, which hosted several World Series in the 1920s and 30s. The 1969 season saw the first-place Cubs fade in the face of the New York "Miracle Mets," denying star slugger **Ernie Banks** a shot at the World Series. The team was purchased from the Wrigley family by the Tribune

Wrigley Field

© City of Chicago/GRC

Northwestern Wildcats

Chicago's North Shore CVB

Company in 1981, and has had some moderate success with division titles in 1984, 1989 and 2003. In the historic 1998 season, Cubs MVP **Sammy Sosa** slugged 66 home runs. In 2007, the Tribune Company put the club up for sale. The team is now owned by the billionaire Ricketts family, whose scion, Joe Ricketts, founded TD Ameritrade. His son, Tom, is currently operating the team on a daily basis. Members of the American League, the **Chicago White Sox** (founded in 1901 as the White Stockings) draw support from South Siders. In 1991 the State of Illinois built a new Comiskey Park replacing a 1910 stadium that hosted the first All-Star game and the first Negro League All-Star game. (The park has been known as US Cellular field—the "Cell"—since that company purchased the naming rights in 2003.) White Sox fans are undying in their support of a team that last went to a World Series in 1959 and last won one in 1917. In 1920 the "Black Sox" scandal revealed that eight players in the 1919 World Series had conspired to "throw" the games for gamblers. When the team advanced to the World Series in 1959, Mayor Richard Daley set off air-raid sirens. The team emerged as a contender again, winning division titles in 1983 and 1993.

White Sox fans' unflagging support paid off when the team won another World Series in a 2005 four-game sweep of the Houston Astros.

♦ **Cubs (NL)**
Apr–Oct
Wrigley Field
☎ 773-404-2827
www.chicago.cubs.mlb.com
🚇 Red Line to Addison, or bus no. 22, or no. 152 express service to night games

♦ **White Sox (AL)**
Apr–Oct
U.S. Cellular Field
☎ 312-674-1000
www.chicago.whitesox.mlb.com
🚇 Red Line to Sox-35th or bus no. 24 or 35.

FOOTBALL

The University of Chicago produced a Big Ten conference powerhouse in the early 1900s, the "Monsters of the Midway," under coach Amos Alonzo Stagg. Football was abolished there in 1939, leaving Northwestern University to carry on the Big Ten tradition at Dyche Stadium in Evanston. George S. Halas founded the **Chicago Bears** and the National Football League in 1920, pioneering the "T" formation and launching a team defined by defense and running plays. The Bears played in Wrigley Field until 1971 when the team moved to Soldier Field. Chicagoans are as proud of their harsh winters as they are of their football team—"Da Bers" in the local dialect. Fans often speak of the advantages of "Bear Weather" to their home team, which has always played outdoors and portrays a tough, "smash-mouth" image cultivated by ferocious tacklers like **Dick Butkus** and elusive runners like **Gale Sayers** and **Walter Payton**. In fact, the team is just as likely to lose as win when the weather is inclement. Weather or not, in the years after winning the Super Bowl in 1986—a dominating victory that prompted tens of thousands of fans to celebrate in the streets despite the icy cold—the Bears failed to return to the championships. Coach Mike Ditka was fired in 1992, and the team's record turned dismal. Three new coaches later in 2006, under the leadership of Lovie Smith, the team finally returned to the playoffs after an exciting season. The dream 2006 season ended in bitter disappointment, however, when the Bears lost Super Bowl XLI 29-17 to Midwestern rivals, the Indianapolis Colts, by a score of 29–17. Nonetheless, loyal sell-out crowds returned to the stands the next fall, awaiting the return of their heroes.

♦ **Bears**
Sept–Dec
Soldier Field
☎ 847-295-6600
www.chicagobears.com
🚌 Bus no. 128 express service to games.

BASKETBALL

Professional basketball was a latecomer to this sports-minded city: the **Chicago Bulls** were formed in 1966, 70 years after the University of Chicago beat the University of Iowa in the first modern college basketball game in 1896. The Bulls' first championship came in stellar fashion in 1991 as **Michael "Air" Jordan** led the team to the first of three consecutive titles. Jordan retired in 1993 and dabbled in baseball before returning to Chicago in 1995 for three more championships seasons (1996, 1997 and 1998). When Jordan retired from basketball for good in 2003, his lifetime scoring average led the

league. The Bulls have a long-standing tradition of wearing black shoes during the playoffs, no matter whether they are home or away. They broke that tradition during the 2009 playoffs by wearing white shoes and socks in game 3 against the Boston Celtics; they lost that game by 21 points. You can watch the Bulls play at the United Center on the Near West Side.

♦ **Bulls**
Oct–Apr
United Center
☎ 312-455-4000
www.nba.com/bulls
🚌 Bus no. 20 express service to games.

HOCKEY

Like many North American cities, Chicago has a devoted cadre of hardcore hockey fans who regularly fill the seats at United Center to watch the **Blackhawks**. One of the NHL's original six franchises, the Blackhawks won the coveted Stanley Cup in 1961 and earned a 1967 division title, thanks to stars **Bobby Hull** and **Stan Mikita**. In 2002 the Hawks advanced to the conference quarter-finals, only to be defeated by St. Louis. Nearly 50 years after their 1961 championship, the Blackhawks ended their long dry spell in 2010, when they beat the Philadelphia Flyers in the 4–2 playoff series by one goal in sudden-death overtime. Blackhawks' captain, **Jonathan Toews**, who scored seven goals in the playoffs, was awarded the trophy for the most valuable player. Members of the American Hockey League and the AHL affiliate of the Atlanta Thrashers, the **Chicago Wolves** have never had a losing season in their history. Their most recent championship victory was when they defeated the Wilkes-Barre/Scranton Penguins to win the Calder Cup in 2008.

♦ **Blackhawks (NHL)**
Oct–Apr
United Center

Soldier Field,
home of Chicago Bears

© City of Chicago/GRC

☎312-455-7000
www.chicagoblackhawks.com
🚌 Bus no. 19 express service.

◆ **Wolves (AHL)**
Oct–Apr
Allstate Arena
☎800-843-9658
www.chicagowolves.com

SOCCER

In 1994 Chicago hosted the first
World Cup soccer match in the US as
Germany defeated Bolivia 1–0. Three
years later, Chicago entered Major
League Soccer with the **Chicago Fire**
playing at Soldier Field. The team
ended the reign of Washington, DC's
United in October 1998, claiming a
2–0 victory in the MLS Cup match held
at the Rose Bowl. On October 30, the
Chicago Fir e became the second team
in three years to capture the American
"double" in the 21C; the team has won
the US Open Cup three times.

◆ **Chicago Fire (MLS)**
Mar–Oct
Toyota Park
☎908-594-7200
www.chicago-fire.com

BOXING

Chicago earned renown as a national
boxing center in the early 20C, when
Soldier Field was selected as the site
for the "Long Count" championship,
allowing heavyweight Gene Tunney to
beat Jack Dempsey in 1927. Ten years
later, **Joe Louis** began his string of

victories with a triumph over Jim
Braddock at Comiskey Park, while the
Chicago Stadium hosted
middleweight **Sugar Ray Robinson**'s
epic 1951 defeat of Jake LaMotta,
and **Rocky Marciano**'s win over
Jersey Joe Walcott in 1953. The city's
boxing heyday ended in the 1950s
when the Supreme Court ruled that
its International Boxing Club held an
unfair monopoly.

OTHER

In 1895 the *Chicago Times-Herald*
sponsored the first automobile
race in America, a 54mi affair
completed by only two vehicles.
Today the **Chicagoland Speedway**
in south suburban Joiiet is a popular
destination for rabid fans of NASCAR
auto racing.
The Chicago Golf Club in suburban
Wheaton, Illinois, built the first 18-hole
course in the US, and the Chicago
area hosts the third-oldest US golf
tournament, the **Western Open**.
First played in 1899, this tournament
now goes by the name of BMW
Championship (part of the four-event
FedEx playoff series).
Every summer, hundreds of graceful
sailboats ply the deep waters of Lake
Michigan in the 333mi-long **Chicago
Yacht Club Race to Mackinac**.
Known as "The Mac," this race starts
at the Chicago Lighthouse just off
Navy Pier and ends at Mackinac Island.
Despite its amateur status, the race
attracts some of the best sailors in
the US.

INDEX

INDEX

INDEX

INDEX

INDEX

STAY

EAT

MAPS AND PLANS

THEMATIC MAPS

MAPS AND PLANS

COMPANION PUBLICATIONS

MAP 583 NORTHEASTERN USA/ EASTERN CANADA

Large-format map providing detailed road systems and including driving distances, interstate rest stops, border crossings and interchanges.
 ♦ Comprehensive city and town index
 ♦ Scale 1:2,400,000 (1 inch = approx. 38 miles)

MAP 761 USA ROAD MAP

Covers the principal US road network and presents shaded relief detail of the overall physiography of the land.
 ♦ Features state flags with statistical data and state tourism office telephone numbers
 ♦ Scale 1:3,450,000

MAP LEGEND

★★★   **Highly recommended**
★★   **Recommended**
★   **Interesting**

Sight symbols

→ ▬▬▬   Walking tour with departure point and direction

Church, chapel	Building described
Synagogue	Other building
Letter locating a sight	Small building – Lighthouse
Other points of interest	Forest preserve
Statue, monument	Park described – Other
Fountain	Wooded park described – Other
Panorama – View	Cemetery described – Other

All maps are oriented north, unless otherwise indicated by a directional arrow.

Other symbols

Interstate Highway   US Highway   Other Route

Highway, interchange	Visitor information
Toll road, bridge	Hospital
Tunnel with ramp	Gift Shop
One way street	Restrooms
Pedestrian street – Steps	Elevator
Airport	Restaurant
Train station – Bus station	Parking – Post office
Metra station	Gate
Elevated station	Golf course – Stadium
Underground station	County boundary

You know
the Green Guide

...Do you really
know **MICHELIN**?

MICHELIN
A better way forward

The world No.1 in tires with 16.3% of the market

A business presence in over **170 countries**

A manufacturing footprint
at the heart of markets

In 2009 **72** industrial sites in **19** countries produced:

- **150** million tires
- **10** million maps and guides

Highly international **teams**

Over **109 200** employees* from all cultures on all continents including **6 000** people employed in R&D centers in Europe, the US and Asia.

*102 692 full-time equivalent staff

The Michelin Group
at a glance

Michelin competes

At the end of 2009

- **Le Mans 24-hour race**
  12 consecutive years of victories
- **Endurance 2009**
  - 6 victories on 6 stages in Le Mans Series
  - 12 victories on 12 stages in American Le Mans Series

- **Paris-Dakar**
  Since the beginning of the event, the Michelin group has won in all categories
- **Moto endurance**
  2009 World Champion
- **Trial**
  Every World Champion title since 1981 (except 1992)

Michelin, established close to its customers

○ **72 plants in 19 countries**
- Algeria
- Brazil
- Canada
- China
- Colombia
- France
- Germany
- Hungary
- Italy
- Japan
- Mexico
- Poland
- Romania
- Russia
- Serbia
- Spain
- Thailand
- UK
- USA

● **A Technology Center spread over 3 continents**
- Asia
- Europe
- North America

○ **Natural rubber plantations**
- Brazil

Our mission

To make a sustainable contribution to progress in the mobility of goods and people by enhancing freedom of movement, safety, efficiency and the pleasure of travelling.

Michelin committed to environmental-friendliness

Michelin, world leader in low rolling resistance tires, actively reduces fuel consumption and vehicle gas emission.

For its products, Michelin develops state-of-the-art technologies in order to:
- Reduce fuel consumption, while improving overall tire performance.
- Increase life cycle to reduce the number of tires to be processed at the end of their useful lives;
- Use raw materials which have a low impact on the environment.

Furthermore, at the end of 2008, 99.5% of tire production in volume was carried out in ISO 14001* certified plants.

Michelin is committed to implementing recycling channels for end-of-life tires.

*environmental certification

**Passenger Car
Light Truck**

Truck

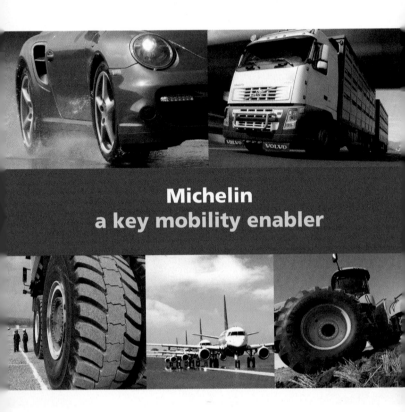

Michelin
a key mobility enabler

Earthmover

Aircraft

Agricultural

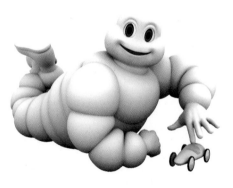

Two-wheel   **Distribution**

Partnered with vehicle manufacturers, in tune with users,
active in competition and in all the distribution channels,
Michelinis continually innovating to promote mobility today
and to invent that of tomorrow.

Maps and   **ViaMichelin,**   **Michelin**
Guides   travel   **Lifestyle,**
                    assistance   for your travel
                    services   accessories

MICHELIN
plays on balanced performance

● **Long tire life**

◐ **Fuel savings**

○ **Safety on the road**

... MICHELIN tires provide you with the best performance, without making a single sacrifice.

The MICHELIN tire pure technology

1 **Tread**
A thick layer of rubber
provides contact with the ground.
It has to channel water away
and last as long as possible.

2 **Crown plies**
This double or triple reinforced belt
has both vertical flexibility
and high lateral rigidity.
It provides the steering capacity.

3 **Sidewalls**
These cover and protect the textile casing
whose role is to attach the tire tread
to the wheel rim.

4 **Bead area for attachment to the rim**
Its internal bead wire
clamps the tire firmly
against the wheel rim.

5 **Inner liner**
This makes the tire
almost totally impermeable
and maintains the correct inflation pressure.

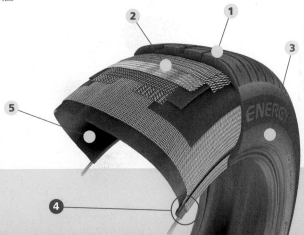

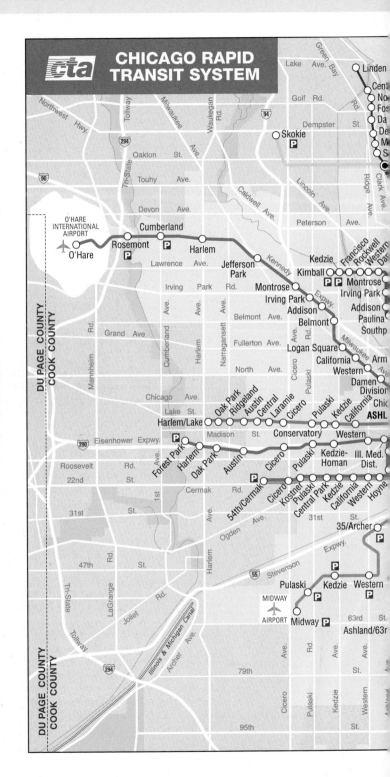

CHICAGO RAPID TRANSIT SYSTEM

cta

Heed
the MICHELIN Man's advice

To improve safety:

- I drive with the correct tire pressure
- I check the tire pressure every month
- I have my car regularly serviced
- I regularly check the appearance
  of my tires (wear, deformation)
- I am responsive behind the wheel
- I change my tires according to the season

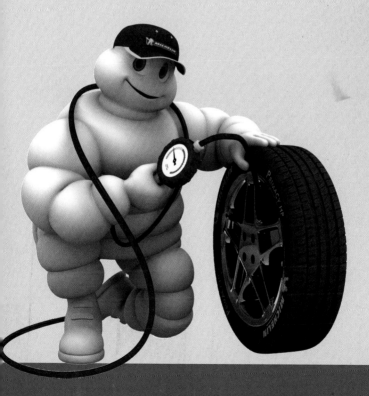

www.michelin.com
www.michelin.(your country extension – e.g. .fr for France)

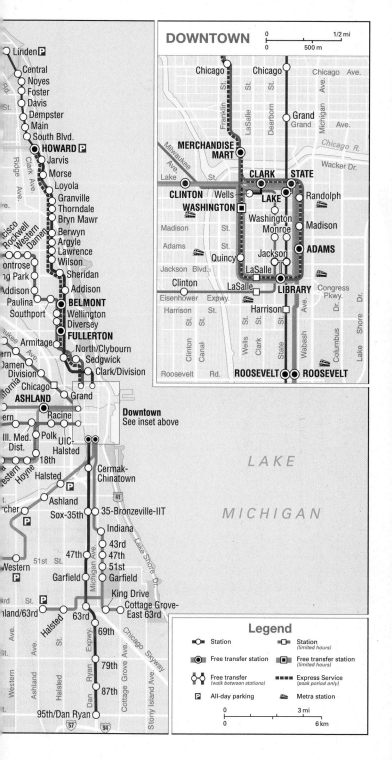

Michelin Apa Publications Ltd

A joint venture between Michelin and Langenscheidt

58 Borough High Street, London SE1 1XF, United Kingdom

No part of this publication may be reproduced in any form
without the prior permission of the publisher.

© 2011 Michelin Apa Publications Ltd
ISBN 978-1-907099-20-5
Printed: November 2010
Printed and bound in Germany